MEN

RIVERS

AND

CANOES

Ian Player
Pencil drawing by Hugh Dent, 1963

MEN, RIVERS
AND CANOES

SECOND EDITION

IAN PLAYER

Echoing Green Press

This second edition of *Men, Rivers and Canoes*
is published in 2007 by

Echoing Green Press CC
P. O. Box 12194
Empangeni
3880 South Africa

www.echoinggreenpress.com

ISBN 978-0-9802501-2-1

Typesetting and book design by Echoing Green Press
Plain text typeface: Times New Roman
Headings typeface: Herculanum
Printed in South Africa by Interpak Books, Pietermaritzburg
Dust jacket design by Kim Longhurst, Durban

DEDICATION

- ∞ -

TO MY WIFE ANN

WITHOUT WHOSE HELP AND ENCOURAGEMENT
THIS BOOK COULD NEVER HAVE BEEN WRITTEN

CONTENTS

ACKNOWLEDGEMENTS

The author expresses his gratitude to the many people who assisted him during the writing of this book and its preparation for the first edition, published by Simondium Publishers (Pty) Ltd in 1964, and to Jim Phelps of Echoing Green Press CC, and all those who assisted him, for their work in preparing this new edition.

To the late Colonel Jack Vincent, M. B. E., for his Foreword to the first edition, which, in error, was not included then and so appears here for the first time, and, with Miss Frances Eastwood, for their reading of the typescript and correcting many mistakes in the first edition.

To the late Hugh Dent, BA, for his pencil portrait of the author, and the maps, small motifs and diagrams used in the first and this edition.

To his wife, Ann, for typing and re-typing the original manuscript, and making careful editorial revisions, at his direction, for this edition.

To the early members and friends of the Natal Canoe Club whose help and encouragement made writing this book a rewarding, new challenge.

To the Editors of the *Daily News*, *Mercury* and *Witness* newspapers for permission to use their photographs in the first and this edition.

To Inkosi Zibuse Mlaba, Graeme Pope-Ellis and Willem van Riet for their generous Forewords that have embellished this edition.

To Tim Cornish for preparing the outline of key points in the Dusi's development, the entrant statistics, and the comprehensive lists of results and finishers that are included in this edition.

To Dave Macleod, and Robbie Stewart, Sheila Whitfield, Brian Moore, Tim Cornish, Derek Howe and Mark Conway who assisted him, for writing for this edition the short history on the social engagement initiatives arising out of the Dusi.

To Kim Longhurst for designing the dust jacket of this edition.

The author records that he consulted the following sources when writing this book:

A. T. Bryant. *Olden Times in Zululand and Natal.* (1939).

The Hon. Henry Drummond. *The Large Game of South and South-East Africa.* (1875).

Government Blue Book No. C6200.

D. Leslie. *Among the Zulu and AmaTonga.* (1875).

PUBLISHER'S NOTE

Canoeing played a dramatic part in my young life, so the publication of this new edition of Ian Player's classic *Men, Rivers and Canoes* is of personal significance to me. Without my knowing it at the time, Ian influenced the way I learned to live, through canoeing.

In the mid-1950s in Pietermaritzburg the early canoeing stories making news aroused my father's interest, and kindled his boyhood memories of canoeing on the River Torridge in Devonshire. When I had polio in 1952, he realised how canoeing was a sport that, even if only in a modest and non-competitive way, I would be able to enjoy. It turned out we lived near Ernie Pearce, and my father asked him for plans to build a canvas-covered canoe. He gladly helped us, and that started it. The adventure began as I helped my dad build a single PBK 13, I think it was called. When the building was done, we launched it on the Dusi in the flat water above the Commercial Road Bridge. That was an exciting day. Soon afterwards we built another canvas canoe so we could paddle together.

As I grew older our expeditions became more ambitious. We canoed mostly on the Umgeni, frequently paddling sections from Morton's Drift to Albert Falls and the Greytown Road Bridge, and down to the Bayne's Drift Bridge. We slogged our way into headwinds across what was then Peattie's Lake, now submerged by the Albert Falls Dam, and shot as many rapids as we could. Some of my boyhood friends joined us on various expeditions—Rendall Garrett in particular. Eventually we tried the Umkomaas, twice, putting in both times at the Hela Hela Bridge. Both of these expeditions ended in disasters, but we survived, luckily, and tell the tales to this day.

Canoeing with my father more than anything tied the deep bonds of friendship that have strengthened for a lifetime between us. Canoeing also taught me lessons for life—rapids epitomise the unknown coming at you fast, and I had to learn to think and act quickly while mastering fear in the face of danger, and, at the other extreme, to enjoy the quiet of nature as one finds it only on a river, paddling silently along. Talking of nature, once a snake swimming across the Umgeni mounted my canoe (as if it were a

floating log in its path), slithered over my legs, and then, out like flash, snaked with silvery esses onwards to the other bank.

It seems to me therefore that it was natural in the years ahead that I would undertake the publication of the book about the pioneering days that led also to my own canoeing adventures and friendships.

For all this, and including the historical significance of *Men, Rivers and Canoes*, what has been decisive for me as a publisher is that Ian is such an engaging writer and memorable story teller. He is more interested in other people than himself, and, as he weaves his human story into the embracing context of the natural world, he brings our inner and outer worlds together.

Turning to practical matters, a brief note on the text and the other inclusions in the new edition is appropriate.

The text appears almost exactly as it did in the first edition. Ian felt some slight modernisation of terms here and there was needed, and these minor changes have been silently effected. It was also decided to divide the book into two parts, the first dealing with the Dusi beginnings, and the second with the exploration of the Pongolo River. This helps emphasise that Ian had canoe adventure and exploration in mind when he began it all—racing grew out this.

We have kept the spelling mostly as it was in the original text. In the first edition the spellings Umsindusi and Umgeni (as used here) were given for the rivers' names. These common at that time. This edition retains these earlier versions, although recent scholarship has set new standardisations. The reason for this is to maintain the authenticity of the original, and because in particular it is from "Umsindusi" that the affectionate and widely used name, the "Dusi"—both for the river and the race—derives.

The correct modern spellings, as established in the authoritative book, *Zulu Names*, by Professor Adrian Koopman (Pietermaritzburg: University of Natal Press, 2002), are uMsunduzi and uMngeni. Professor Koopman discusses the origins of these names, and they could not have been more apt with reference to the Dusi Canoe Marathon.

We learn that uMsunduzi means "the river that pushes away," or "the river that pushes everything before it" (page 138). No doubt many paddlers would confirm its appropriateness, particularly when heavy rains have fallen the night before the race. The uMngeni gets its name from "umunga" (page 147), the name of the widespread thorn trees found in the valleys of the two rivers, though especially of the uMngeni. Certainly paddlers, and seconds too, would confirm the appropriateness of this

name—how many who have paddled, portaged and seconded remember scratches, or worse, from these thorn trees?

In the first edition the Foreword by Col. Jack Vincent was erroneously omitted, so it appears here for the first time. To reflect the way the Dusi has grown over the years three important people who have done so much to increase its fame—Graeme Pope-Ellis, Willem van Riet and Inkosi Zibuse Mlaba—were approached to write additional Forewords. Their stature as men and canoeists adds a fitting lustre to this edition. Their contributions are deeply appreciated.

There is much history that has built up around the Dusi, but, in many ways, how the relationship has evolved between the race and the people of the river valleys reflects this more importantly than anything else. It was Lylie Musgrave who pointed this out. So I approached Dave Macleod, and he, drawing on the weighty knowledge and assistance of Robbie Stewart, Sheila Whitfield, Brian Moore, Tim Cornish, Derek Howe and Mark Conway, rose admirably to the task. Together they have produced the informative supplement on this subject, which is published here. Inkosi Mlaba enriches the theme in his Foreword. Surely the Dusi in its many facets must become the focus of local history studies in the years to come, and this new material should be seen as a stimulus for this.

Ian wanted the new edition to reflect as fully as possible the community that has grown out of the Dusi. This motivated the inclusion of the authoritative lists of results and the more than ten thousand finishers, from the first race in December 1951 till last year's Dusi in 2006. Graeme Pope-Ellis introduced me to Tim Cornish, and he made this achievable. All those involved in the Dusi owe Tim a debt of gratitude. He has quietly worked away over the years to produce the magnificent record of results and finishers that we are proud to include in this edition.

Numbers of people have assisted in preparing the new *Men, Rivers and Canoes*, and especially in launching it to the canoeing community and the world—thanks especially are due to Ann Player, Charlie Mason, Cameron Mackenzie and Ray de Vries.

Jim Phelps
Echoing Green Press
Empangeni

October 2006

FOREWORD TO THE FIRST EDITION

– ∞ –

COLONEL JACK VINCENT

With a considerable degree of justification it is often nowadays said how difficult it is to find young men who display initiative, drive, determination, or, indeed, any other great quality associated with leadership.

The writer of this book is one who possesses in full measure all those attributes that appear to have become so rare, and throughout the many years that I, as Director of Wild Life Conservation in Natal was associated with him, I greatly admired his resourcefulness and high sense of responsibility.

Behind this fascinating story of Mr. Player's canoeing exploits can be seen an overmastering impulse successfully to achieve whatever he sets out to do, and a sincere determination to demonstrate by personal example those achievements which he would like to see the goal of so many others.

The reader will perceive that physical fitness too, has always been a fetish with Mr. Player, and he rightly appreciates how difficult it is without it to do full justice to a worthwhile task. He mentions the fullness and satisfaction he has found in his life as a senior wild life conservation officer, and I should like to take this opportunity to pay tribute to his organizing ability and sincerity of purpose. The standard he sets is an extremely high one, and although he asks a very great deal from all those who work with him he expects no more than he is fully prepared to accomplish on his own.

It must be most gratifying to Mr. Player to know that the journey by canoe which he started with such indomitable spirit, has now developed into the Pietermaritzburg to Durban canoe race: an annual event that attracts an ever-increasing number of entrants from all over South Africa. To win it, or even to cross its finishing line is an honour being sought by more and more young men and, as has since happened in yet other spheres,

Mr. Player, by his own example, has done much that is valuable in the development of true manhood among many others.

I hope that the book may be widely read and that more and more persons may not only appreciate from Mr. Player's entertaining narrative how much is to be gained from real endeavour, but also that they will find, as I have done, that his book is a difficult one to put down.

In conclusion I would express the hope that Mr. Player may later decide to let us have further anecdotes, culled from his many interesting and unusual experiences and accomplishments.

Morges, Switzerland

September 1963

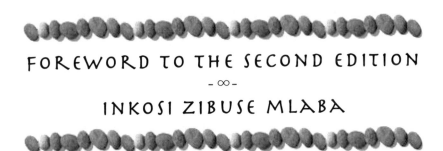

FOREWORD TO THE SECOND EDITION
– ∞ –
INKOSI ZIBUSE MLABA

I am much honoured by the invitation to write the Foreword to the second edition of Ian Player's famous book, *Men, Rivers and Canoes*.

I am most grateful too, because it gives me the opportunity to state publicly what I have learned through the great Dusi Canoe Marathon, which was started by Ian Player's adventurous spirit.

My first involvement in the race was motivated by my concern for my people. Little did I realise how much I would learn, and continue to learn, through this race. Then I entered the race myself, and that experience taught me new and different lessons.

In my early years, as I grew up beside the river, almost the only white people I would see were the canoeists who passed through the area. They were a curiosity to my friends and me. There was no effective communication between them and us, and so on both sides there was ignorance. We couldn't understand them, and we used to think of them as mad, crazy. Why did these people come from all over to race this race, with some nearly drowning, others getting injured, and all suffering and struggling in the heat? But whether we understood them or not, the race was clearly important to them, and each year it continued to grow.

In the period from 1984 to 1995 political violence escalated in the valleys, and it was inevitable that unless there was effective intervention it would spread over to the race. In 1995 I decided to engage with the race organisers. I was welcomed. From the beginning my vision was that through the race we could start to heal the violent divisions amongst my people, and help them improve their economic conditions. The major event that got the transformation started was the big meeting between the people, the amakhosi and the Dusi organisers, held at Dusi Bridge in 1995.

The changes happened as a miracle really, over the forthcoming years. Many positive things began working together. My involvement with the organisers started to open up my mind, and there was eagerness to learn on both sides.

Then through my participation in the race, people in the valleys began to see that perhaps the canoeists weren't so crazy after all. And the media gave exposure not only to the canoeists but also to the people who gathered along the riverbanks to watch. Everybody began to feel they were now part of the race. Instead of throwing stones, the youngsters wanted to help the canoeists with their portaging, till they learned this was against the rules. You can understand there were many new things for all to learn.

The activities of the Sports Trust and the work of Bruce Fordyce, amongst other famous people, boosted the young canoeists' development programme. From this many youngsters gained the opportunity to learn the sport and become competitive, and are becoming increasingly so each year.

For me the most wonderful achievement to come from involvement in the Dusi was the way it helped bring about peace in the valleys, spreading all the way to Durban. The way one good thing led to another was the most valuable lesson to learn from the race.

The valley people started to be interested in canoeing as a sport, and from this there was a real meeting across the racial divides. More importantly, for my people there was a new meeting between themselves, outside of politics. When the people saw they had a new common ground in canoeing, other sports could also grow—soccer and mountain biking, to mention just two—and around all the various sports new organisations have started, and in the new clubs and societies people have found new interests and common causes.

These positive developments began to draw the attention of provincial and national government, and even international organisations took note that through sport, and canoeing especially, peace and progress could grow. The European Union started initiatives in the valleys, attracted by the possibilities of peace. It became clear for all to see that social and economic development was far more important than divisive and violent politics.

Out of the peace that sprang from the Dusi the government used our area as a positive example. We became amongst the first to have water, electricity, and telecommunications installed. This followed with tarred roads and other improved infrastructure—the upgrade of the sports stadium, clinics, classrooms and a new sports centre and gymnasium.

With the acceptance of canoeing, and all those who come with the canoeists, the way has opened for tourism in the valleys, and with this, new jobs. Other kinds of businesses are also starting. People have new hopes and expectations, and they have an interest in seeing that peaceful conditions continue so that prosperity will grow. The challenge is to build on this. The positive energy drives along many good things, but the

indunas and amakhosi also keep a watchful eye out because they still are the foremost local authorities for maintaining peace and order. From this you will see how the race was firstly most important for me as a social force with the potential to reach out into the community.

Through canoeing, peace has prevailed, and peace has paved the way to increased prosperity.

However, this social interest led me to enter the race itself, and from this experience I entered into a whole new awareness. Firstly, I discovered the value of fitness, which I'd never thought about seriously before. This discovery has changed me, and healthy living and the discipline of training are now important elements of my daily life.

Although I grew up close to nature, canoeing helped me see it in new ways. Not only did the animals of the river—crocodiles, snakes, birds—become more familiar to me, but also I changed my attitude towards them. I learned to see them as having their own special place in nature as a whole. My new realisation is that we must respect and care for nature.

The physical challenge of the river, when you are close to the water in a canoe, is most important for your learning. I had to find courage and strength I did not know I had. Canoeing builds you emotionally, as you become more aware of yourself in relation to all that is around you. It gives you lots of excitement and you must build up athletic skills, but you must also develop perseverance and patience, because many times you are just struggling with the heat, exhaustion and pain. In my last race I badly injured my thumb, but after some years of rehabilitation, I am getting ready to race in 2007. I want to experience the special excitement and struggle again.

Dr Player, I salute you and thank you. Through canoeing, you have started a great sport for all our people.

I wish you great success with this new edition of the story of your early canoeing journeys. The present and future generations are fortunate they now can share, and learn from, this stirring account of our local and national history.

KwaXimba, Cato Ridge

September 2006

PREFACE TO THE SECOND EDITION
- ∞ -
IAN PLAYER

This new edition of *Men, Rivers and Canoes*, first published in 1964 and now long out of print, comes after much discussion with Jim Phelps of Echoing Green Press. I am most grateful to Jim for believing so strongly in it, and for insisting that a new edition was necessary—because, he said, of the way canoeing has grown so much and that new generations would be eager to learn more about the traditions and roots of this great sport and recreation—though it is now forty-two years after the first one.

Men, Rivers and Canoes arose out of a meeting with Donald Morris, the American author of *The Washing of the Spears,* the graphic and comprehensive history of the Anglo-Zulu War of 1879. We were on the slopes of the famous Isandlwana hill when he told me that the only good personal account of the Anglo-Zulu War he could find was George Mossop's book, *Running the Gauntlet*. It was he who encouraged me to write a personal account of my own canoe journeys and experiences, and his criticism of the first draft was pertinent and constructive. He was a good friend. Canoeing was one thing, but writing about it was a new adventure, and he started me on a different kind of learning by inspiring me to put the two together.

As I reflect back now on my original expeditions down the Umsindusi and Umgeni, and the explorations of the Umzimkulu, Umkomaas and Pongolo rivers, I realize how important they were for my personal development. I feel greatly honoured that those early adventures of mine have led on to many thousands of canoeists to grow in their lives too.

On the Umkomaas expedition during an intense thunder and lightning storm I had the feeling of entering another world. My partner, Fred Schmidt, and I were separated for long stretches, and during those moments of being utterly alone with the river, the krantzes, the fig trees and the wailing trumpeter hornbills, I was at one with the world. Many years later I realized that this was a wilderness experience—an encounter

with God through the wild. It became the main task of my life to propagate this experience. I saw it as being the most important way of saving wild places on our planet. Hundreds, perhaps thousands of Dusi participants will have had similar insights and become one with the earth for a few brief moments. Some canoeists have paddled and portaged the Dusi more than thirty times. They have their own insights from moments of deep emotional connection with nature. Ultimately they don't do it to win, but because, as a phenomenon of wild nature, the Dusi is there, as Mallory said of Everest.

Many people have asked me, "Why did you first do the Dusi?" As always with major undertakings, there is more than one reason. I had promised myself in the winter of 1944, in Italy, when I was with the 6th South African Armoured Division, that if I survived the war, the Pietermaritzburg to Durban canoe expedition was what I wanted to do. This might simply have been the fantasy of a seventeen year-old youth, but because it went much deeper in me, I carried it through. I think now that an important part of it came from my determination to overcome feelings of exclusion, if not rejection, following a boyhood accident. I must digress briefly here to explain.

Until the age of twelve I had been a sportsman. I played various sports and was in my school's first soccer team. Schoolmasters said I had a promising sporting career ahead, but unlike my brother Gary, for me it was not to be. In 1940 I had a fall, a stone pierced my knee joint and the wound became septic. Penicillin was scarce and sulphur drugs were inadequate to control the infection. Pus seeped out through the tubes stuck into my knee and it swelled to the size of a small pumpkin. I was in Grey's Hospital, Pietermaritzburg, in the same ward as soldiers who had been wounded in the war in the desert and overworked nurses transferred their infections to me. The pain was excruciating and the doctor wanted to amputate my leg.

My mother came down from Johannesburg and refused to let the doctors amputate. She arranged for me to go to the Sanatorium where I was looked after by a saintly nun, Sister St. Peter. Never will I forget her kindness and devotion. But my knee worsened, and more operations were necessary. With the gross swelling the bones grew at wrong angles and I was to become a partial cripple.

Conventional sport was now a forlorn hope. Neither soccer nor rugby was possible, and I loved both. Exclusion and rejection, I felt, became a way of life. In early 1944 I tried to join the armed forces, trying the air force, the navy and the army in turn, to be rejected each time. The air force was a particularly bitter blow because I cited the heroic RAF pilot Douglas Bader who flew with no legs. But each time the medical officers said no.

Nevertheless, I persisted and was eventually accepted in the Q section. A few months' later heavy casualties forced the medical officers to re-evaluate and, with some sleight of hand, I slipped through and was sent to join the Transvaal Scottish in Potchefstroom. This was the regiment that my Uncle Cedric had served in during the First World War and was killed, in the Battle of the Somme.

After six weeks basic training I was sent north. The regiment was soon disbanded and we were put into a tank regiment, the Prince Alfred Guard, Port Elizabeth based. Towards the end of the war I was riding on the back of a tank, holding a 44-gallon drum of petrol. I fell off and the drum rolled near me, striking a glancing blow to my knee. Fortunately though, this merely disfigured it further; I could still walk, although with a more pronounced limp. Later, as a game ranger, my Zulu fellow-workers were quick to nickname me Madolo—the Knee. It was a distinctive feature, and they perceived it was a key to understanding me.

I returned from the army in 1946 to a South Africa in economic depression and work was extremely difficult to find. My father got me a job as a learner miner on Crown Mines, and later I went to Robinson Deep where I worked at 6000 feet below the surface. But the experience of toiling in the bowels of the earth made me yearn for the sun, trees, rivers and birds.

When the Nationalist government won the 1948 election and General Smuts was defeated, the South Africa I knew was finished, and so I went to Rhodesia (Zimbabwe) to try to join, first the army, then the British South African Police. I was again rejected, and ended up in a factory producing oxygen. I chose the night shift to give me time to read. The Bulawayo library was superb, and I came across T. E. Lawrence's *Seven Pillars of Wisdom*, for me one of the great books of the twentieth century. It inspired me to look for a life of adventure and a cause I could devote myself to, and eventually fate was to point the way.

In time I left Rhodesia (Zimbabwe) and came to Pietermaritzburg, because that was the point of departure for my long dreamed-of canoe journey, and also because Natal was the province of my ancestors, English, Scottish and Afrikaner. I was coming home. A new life beyond my wildest expectations was soon to unfold.

I applied for and was given a job in the stores department of the Aluminium Company, close to the Umsindusi River. I talked of my plan to canoe to Durban with many men in the factory. Only one was interested, Desmond Graham, and we struck up a friendship. Desmond was a good athlete and he tolerated my inability to keep up with him when we ran to work each morning to get fit for the great adventure. He was the first of the

numerous friends I have made through canoeing, many of whom I tell about in *Men, Rivers and Canoes*.

As the time approached—Christmas 1950—to go down the rivers to Durban the newspapers grew increasingly interested and I started to make friends with reporters and editors. The friendships with the press I made have endured since then and were invaluable when I went into the conservation field to meet rejection again, this time from cattle ranchers, cane farmers and government officials, amongst others. Without the support of the press we would never have been able to win the conservation battles that lay ahead. But it was my canoeing, particularly down the Umsindusi and Umgeni rivers, that interested the press, and this turned me into a public figure. Such apparent fame can inflate your ego. It can also lead to jealousies and personal attacks, and I have had my fair share of those. At the time, it was the good friendships I made with journalists that were important, but from this grew the opportunity to get attention for the causes I became involved in.

Press interest from the beginning put the first canoe expedition and the subsequent early races on the front page. It gripped the imagination of many young men, and later of women too, I'm happy to say, and year-by-year the Dusi canoe marathon became more popular. The Dusi winners and those in the lead receive much attention—and of course this is always an incentive—but there is other racing going on between individuals and groups. This is what makes the Dusi a personal challenge for all participants, and through this, every year there are acts of magnificent bravery that are seldom recognized. The race has become a spectacle available to a worldwide audience through television, radio and print, and I would like to say again, that without the press in the 1950s, the race could never have taken off. The press interest has grown over the years to include the news media as a whole—we canoeists owe them our gratitude.

Before our first contemplated departure in 1950, Desmond Graham and I were told that we must be daft—exactly what thousands of subsequent canoeing initiates I'm sure are told. Today such taunts are still voiced, but, thankfully, are now roundly dismissed. The annual Dusi has become a rite of passage for hundreds of newcomers, and a deep, inner exploration for many veterans. Graeme Pope-Ellis, the uncontested Dusi King, has described his Dusi experiences as ultimately spiritual. Great and enduring friendships have developed through canoeing and, sadly, sometimes other friendships have fallen apart. Such is the profound challenge the Dusi presents.

I have a sense of pride in that I was able to initiate a new sport, but far more importantly for me is the pleasure I get from knowing that

canoeing opens people up to discovering their own inner selves in the encounter with wild nature. Through this they can discover what many others are less open to learning—the deep connections between the outer and inner worlds, between nature and human nature. Canoeing was vital for me as a way of learning about the power and vulnerability of the environment, and about some of the ecological problems, such as catchment damage, soil erosion and river pollution, that are signs of the environmental harm we are causing in South Africa. My hope is that canoeists will also learn these things and take up the challenge of doing something about it.

Ernie Pearce and I had rousing support when we wanted to form the Natal Canoe Club, and the motto we settled on was *Ezanzi Nemfula*— Down the Rivers. From the Dusi, particularly because of the enthusiastic organisation that grew around it, the sport spread to the Berg River Marathon, which Willem van Riet, a winner of three Dusi races, initiated. Transvaal (now Gauteng) participants started races on the Vaal and the Crocodile rivers, and the sport grew over the years so that races are now paddled on many rivers in the country, and canoeing has diversified into many forms, with the Olympics an inspiring goal for the very best. South African canoeists have participated in international events all over the world, and have won. Many people who, like me, are physically handicapped have been able to participate and prove to themselves that they were able to overcome their physical constraints through canoeing. I never dreamed all this would unfurl from what began as a personal promise to myself.

There are other aspects too. The exploration of new rivers has become popular. This pleases me greatly, because I think canoeing isn't only about racing, exciting as that is. The Umzimkulu River has been canoed and explored by girls' high school groups. Harry Fisher, a winner of the Dusi in the 1950s, led an expedition down the Zambezi River, and Willem van Riet has canoed many rivers, including the mighty Colorado River in the United States and the Cunene in Namibia and Angola. No doubt there are other canoeing expeditions that have been high points in the lives of many men and women. In these there are vivid stories to be told.

The Dusi became a rite of passage for game rangers in particular. They would train on the Black Umfolosi River where there were huge rapids and equally enormous crocodiles. My good friend Nick Steele, who was new to canoeing, asked me what would happen if he fell out in a rapid. I pointed to the crocodiles and said, "You won't." He did the Dusi with Paul Dutton and, like tall John Tinley, finished the course. Numbers of

other rangers over the years have completed the race too, and I would be delighted to find this tradition continued.

Pietermaritzburg, historically once a small, almost unknown, garrison town, now holds two of the most important, internationally recognised, sporting events in South Africa: the Comrades Marathon, and the Umsindusi-Umgeni Canoe Marathon—the Dusi.

It is for me one of the finest positive consequences of the Dusi that many people in the Valley of a Thousand Hills, including those who need it most, have benefited materially from the race. The admirable contribution of the clinics and classrooms that have been built from funds raised by canoeing associations is a mark of this. My hope is that the productive relationship between the Dusi and the people of the river valleys will grow from strength to strength in the years ahead. Especially encouraging to me is how, in more recent years, young people from the valleys have become canoeists themselves, and entered and excelled in the Dusi. This is surely an inspiration for our country, and must set transformation goals for the Dusi in the years ahead. Indeed, since 1994 and our first democratic election, it has been truly heartening to see how the Dusi has been at the forefront—we see this in the non-racial diversity of the many participants. Canoeing is such a great sport and recreation. It embraces people from all quarters of our country.

I know from long conversations with generations of canoeists and members of the public, how grateful everyone is for the generosity of spirit of the officials who have dedicated themselves to the continuation of the race. It is a tradition that officials are very proud to be part of. The spirit of the race is probably unequalled in any other sport.

To participate in the race you need a degree of physical fitness and the discipline of training is in itself worthwhile. Organizing the race takes many hours of devoted work from volunteers and, most importantly, excellent leadership. Fortunately such leadership, initially with Ernie Pearce, has always been forthcoming. All these aspects about the Dusi, and indeed canoeing as a countrywide sport, give me much satisfaction.

I want also to praise the women who have increasingly participated over the years. Many of their feats of endurance and courage are outstanding—indeed, if I were to name the book today it would have to be *Men, Women, Rivers and Canoes*.

I have repeated countless times during speeches and in print that once you have canoed the Dusi, your life cannot be the same again. Layers of your personality are peeled off and you are exposed to aspects of yourself you were not aware of, and sometimes it is the dark part that vents anger on partners, spouses or seconders. It comes as a shock to know that

there is such anger inside you. More often, I'm pleased to say, deep bonds of comradeship are forged that last a lifetime. There are also those moments when you could have a mystical revelation in the reflected rays of the dawn or sunset, and time, for a brief moment, stands still. The words of the psalmist are appropriate here: "Be still and know that I am God". It is after these and similar experiences that your world can never be the same again. So my hope is that this new edition of *Men, Rivers and Canoes* will play a part in making more clearly conscious for new readers what the Dusi and other canoeing adventures are in human terms, making them deeper and richer for canoeists themselves, and for those who paddle the rivers in their minds.

Although I did not know it at the time, on reflection I realize that the pioneering journey down the Umsindusi and Umgeni rivers in 1950 was the beginning of a long inner and outer spiritual exploration that was to lead me deep into nature and the important world of dreams. A new life was beginning. Destiny and the unconscious were guiding me to a career where my life would never be the same.

It is also one of my hopes that this new edition of *Men, Rivers and Canoes* will encourage other canoeists, women and men, to write their own personal stories, whether of the Dusi itself, or other canoe expeditions. The Dusi, and all wild water canoeing, is the source of extraordinary dramas, deep personal discoveries, and unexpected developments. Every year there is something new. Recently the Dusi inspired Andrew King, of the Mamu Loman Club, partnered by Melissa Rankin, to canoe upstream from Durban to Pietermaritzburg—a phenomenal physical achievement. Then there is the 2006 non-stop, one day, Dusi singles canoe record set by Hank McGregor of the Dragon's Canoe Club, when he beat all the doubles. The results of those who have excelled in the Dusi are in this book. I admire and salute them all. Such achievements are brilliant, splendid, and heroic—though I never forget the mainstream of canoeists, and how much the Dusi is the highest adventure of the year for them. That is why I have asked that all the names of those who have completed the race be printed in this new edition. We have all been initiated into a special community through the Dusi—a brotherhood and sisterhood. How far have we all come, and how far have we yet to go from what began in those arduous six days of the first race?

For many years now I have stood at the start of the Dusi race with stalwarts such as John Oliver, Sheila Pearce and Cameron Mackenzie, and watched the grand spectacle of paddles flashing in the morning sunlight, as batch after batch of canoeists take off on their great adventure. It is a time of rivalry between the top canoeists, where sometimes only minutes

separate participants. But the great camaraderie that develops amongst the many who are hours behind is where the great heart of the Dusi pulses— what a source of lifetime stories, jokes, laughter, and disappointments too, that flows from it all.

I had predicted in the very early days that the Dusi would become as big and as popular as the Oxford-Cambridge boat race. Overly boastful as that may have been at the time, events have proved me not altogether wrong. Mr Warmback, the Mayor of Pietermaritzburg at the time, smiled to himself when he heard me say this, but he said nothing. This was very kind of him because he could only too easily have ridiculed me. In fact, he repeated my wild prediction publicly. Little did he and I know then what a famous race the Dusi would really become.

Phuzamoya, Karkloof

August 2006

CANOE PLAN

A plan for an early fibreglass canoe. These came onto the scene from about 1956, after the canvas-covered and other kinds of canoes used in the expeditions and races described in this book.

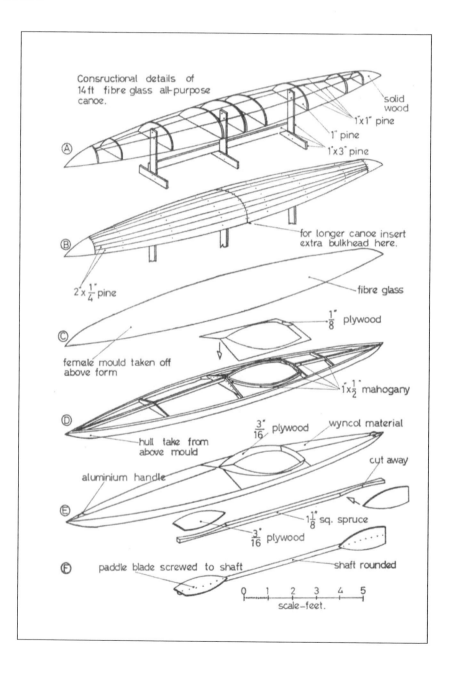

Consructional details of 14 ft fibre glass all-purpose canoe.

Ⓐ

solid wood
1"x1" pine
1" pine
1"x3" pine

Ⓑ

for longer canoe insert extra bulkhead here.

2"x¼" pine

Ⓒ

fibre glass

⅛" plywood

female mould taken off above form

1"x1½" mahogany

Ⓓ

hull take from above mould

3/16" plywood

wyncol material

aluminium handle

cut away

Ⓔ

1⅛" sq. spruce

3/16" plywood

Ⓕ

paddle blade screwed to shaft

shaft rounded

0 1 2 3 4 5
scale–feet.

PART ONE

BEING AN ACCOUNT OF THE
ESTABLISHMENT OF THE
PIETERMARITZBURG TO DURBAN
UMSINDUSI AND UMGENI RIVERS
CANOE MARATHON
AND OF EARLY EXPEDITIONS ON THE
UMZIMKULU AND
UMKOMAAS RIVERS

FOREWORD TO PART ONE

_- ∞ -_

REFLECTIONS ON THE DUSI

_- ∞ -_

GRAEME POPE-ELLIS

Sports events involving endurance and the excitement of adventure have always appealed to me. There are no doubt many reasons for this but certainly it is this appeal that has made canoeing, *par excellence*, play such an important role in my life. The challenges of endurance and adventure are not unique to canoeing, but in this great sport you certainly get them in full measure.

That I have had the good fortune in my life to experience much of this I undoubtedly owe to Dr. Ian Player, who, through his pioneering courage and vision, started the Dusi Canoe Marathon, and so made canoeing part of my life from the days of my boyhood. Not only the race itself took a hold on me, but also his book, *Men, Rivers and Canoes*, in telling about it, deepened my learning of its lessons. I have read it numbers of times. I am greatly privileged therefore to be able to make a small contribution to the publication of this new edition of his famous book.

The Umsindusi—which has always been affectionately called the Dusi as long as I can remember—and the Umgeni Rivers have always been a part of my life. I grew up on a farm in Ashburton, which had one of its boundaries on the Dusi. This meant my family and I had a close relationship with it. From the farming perspective, I came to respect the river for its ability to mould and change the landscape around it, slowly through time, and quickly after storms and heavy rains. As one who enjoyed being out in the natural world, I grew to respect the Dusi for the animal and bird life it supported. Though my involvement in the Dusi Canoe Marathon has made the race and its future of special importance to me, it is my deepest concern that respect for these great racing rivers will grow, and the environment around them—from their catchments to the

sea—will be protected and wisely used. Without this care, the race as we know it will not be possible.

There are three significant elements those who have competed in the Dusi Canoe Marathon will be familiar with—the encounter with nature, self-actualisation, and the awakening of a spiritual sense. I would like briefly to describe my experience of each of these to illustrate the deep impression the Umsindusi and Umgeni Rivers make upon you once you have traversed their courses between Pietermaritzburg and Durban.

After the gun has fired, signalling the start of a Dusi Canoe Marathon, and you have negotiated the Dusi's first few obstacles, the true atmosphere of the race has far from begun. It is only after the ambience of Pietermaritzburg begins to fade and you have caught a last glimpse of the city far behind that your race really begins. As you set off on the first arduous portage through sugar cane fields you begin to understand the true character of the race. Nature envelops you and your boat, and before your mind has fully realised that you are leaving civilisation, you are surrounded by African bush. Residential areas change to farm houses, and farm houses to rural and informal settlements, and finally there is nothing but you, your boat and the river.

Though the feeling of solitude may have changed somewhat with the growth of the race in recent years, it is when you find yourself moving in the currents of the river through some of the most beautiful African bush that you have the same full encounter with nature as did the race pioneers. Each turn in the river reveals a new surprise. A fish eagle takes flight as you pass under a tree, a leguan splashes into the water, or your adrenaline begins to rush as you hear the surge of water in the rapids ahead.

This brings me to the second of the three elements—the encounter with yourself. The distance you cover in the Dusi gives ample opportunity to contemplate what your mind and body are capable of, yet it is fitting that all contestants take a moment to think about the founder of the Dusi, Ian Player, as he pressed on through the valleys of the Dusi and Umgeni rivers to complete the pioneering expedition that led to establishing the Dusi Canoe Marathon. That first time he took a long six days to reach Durban. Racers today can experience again something similar to what he faced, but, thinking about what he achieved, deepens your understanding of what the race is really about—courage, determination, the danger and exhilaration of canoeing wild water. The thought alone is enough to make you hold this man in high esteem.

We have to appreciate the gift that has been given us in the human body and mind when thinking of Ian Player's first journey. By reading *Men, Rivers and Canoes*, we gain insight into the essence of determination,

and see what the reward of self-accomplishment can be. Indeed, all who take on the Dusi must at some time feel what must have been strongest for Ian Player, as he pushed through that first time, determined to make it all the way to the sea. In its purest form, the Dusi Canoe Marathon opens you up to the realisation of your undiscovered abilities and potential. This creates a sense of self worth and self-realisation—you learn what you are capable of, and, more importantly, you discover that you can act with that capacity, and through it, find out something new about yourself.

The final element is that of spirituality. Through the prolonged and intense exposure to the natural environment and the power and surprises of the rivers, and through the sheer physical struggle encompassed by the Dusi, you come to the realisation of something spiritual. That has been my experience in every Dusi I have competed in. Whether it is an almighty Creator or a sense of special guardianship, the experience you take away after completing a Dusi is one of transcendence. Emerging from the valleys at the end of the Dusi will stimulate a multitude of emotions, but salient among these must be a deep feeling of respect for the natural environment that mankind continues ever more to encroach upon, and the need to take responsibility for it. In my humble view, I think it was this that helped make Ian Player into the great conservationist he has become.

Bishopstowe

August 2006

Photo: Jack Shepherd Smith

The very first journey

Fred Schmidt and Dennis Vorster
Steel was not lighter than wood

Photo: Natal Witness

First victory

CHAPTER 1

My interest in rivers was first aroused when I was nine years old, by my grandfather, Frank Player. He gave me a graphic description of crossing the Tugela River during the Zulu war of 1879, when he was a corporal in the Natal Hussars. As I grew older, my father used to take me fishing in the Vaal, Klip, Wilge and other Transvaal and Free State rivers. The thrill of feeling a rod bending with strain as a yellowfish streaked through the water was enough to endear me to rivers forever.

Some of our holidays were spent at Umkomaas and other South Coast resorts on rivers. My father would hire a boat and take me salmon fishing at night. When I was tired I would lie on the dank-smelling floorboards of the old clinker boat and listen to the lapping of the river against the sides. The surf thundered in the background and I was filled with dreams. It was always a terrible wrench when I had to leave Natal and return to the dry Transvaal.

My father's grandfather came out as a settler from England in 1850. He settled in Pietermaritzburg and had a business in Longmarket Street above what used to be Kean's Tearoom. Both my mother and father were born in Natal. Many of my great-uncles were transport riders in their youth, before they turned to farming. They were all very old by the time I was able to appreciate the history of Natal. Some I never saw or even knew existed, until I browsed through old papers in the Archives or the Natal Society Reference Library. One of them, Tod Player, trekked into Swaziland and was one of the two witnesses to sign Theophilus Shepstone's proclamation of Swaziland as a Protectorate in 1889. Nothing was heard of him for years, until eventually it was learnt that a trusted Swazi man had reported to officials that he had died of fever in some lonely outpost. Although as a youngster I was unaware of all this, I nevertheless always experienced some deep emotion when the train crossed the border into Natal.

It was in the mountains of Italy that the first desire to canoe from Pietermaritzburg to Durban was born. A few of us were gathered round a lignite fire at the 6th Division Reserves Headquarters at Santa Barbara,

south of Florence. We were, as usual, hungry and talking about home. Someone, I think it was Alan Morton, brother of the post-war Olympic wrestler, said that what he'd like to be doing was lying on the hot sands of Durban beach. An argument about the merits of the Natal and Cape beaches started. I stared into the fire, oblivious of the argument, for at the mention of Natal a flood of memories overwhelmed me: the white mists rolling down the green hills and wooded valleys round Pietermaritzburg— mists with a smell of wattle bark, Zulu fires, burnt grass and the red wet earth of the Natal Midlands; Indian mynahs chattering and the rickshaw pullers running down the broad streets; the coast with the musty smell of dense undergrowth in the bush near the beach; the Natal robin calling, the bou-bou shrike and the lovely liquid sound of the coucal; a storm over the sea, rain clouds scudding along and white horses dancing crazily on the tops of dark green swells; the long rolling, booming, grinding roar of thunder; weird gashes of forked lightning illuminating the sky for brief seconds; the wind blowing in savage gusts, sand whipping along the beach and the waves pounding on the reef; a lone grey-headed gull flying fast and low above the boiling surf—it was "all this and heaven too!"

The days I spent watching the gannets diving far out to sea when the sardines came in their white millions during the annual migration up the coast; fishing in pools, the rocks pitted by wind and water and covered with tiny mussels, limpets, barnacles and other multi-shaped crustaceans sheltering in tiny holes; flicking the rock-bait into narrow gullies foaming with translucent green, then the sudden tug and mad fight of a blacktail on the line, the rod vibrating and the line cutting through the water, and all the time the sun burning down from a clear blue sky.

Someone shouted "Have some coffee!" and the memories faded. Somebody asked me the name of the river that flowed through Pietermaritzburg. I answered, and began thinking about the best way to see the country between Pietermaritzburg's rolling hills and the sea. I mentioned it to one of the chaps, who replied: "Why don't you go by boat?" Thus the idea was born.

Six years later I was working for the Aluminium Company in Pietermaritzburg. The Umsindusi River flowed a few hundred yards from the gate. Every day I crossed the river on my way to work and wondered about its course through the gorges and ravines until it joined the Umgeni.

I mentioned my desire to canoe from Pietermaritzburg to Durban to Desmond Graham, one of my workmates, who immediately became enthusiastic. We both knew nothing about canoes, nor had we any idea what the river country between the two cities was like. We realized, however, that it would be essential to be perfectly fit, so we used to meet

early in the morning at the top of Loop Street and run to work. Desmond played rugby regularly and was in very good physical condition. Running had never been my forte and for the first month it was agony plodding along the tarred road. Desmond had to massage me with wintergreen at the end of every run, otherwise I was too stiff to run the next day; but thanks to his help I was in good shape at the end of six weeks.

Every time the Umsindusi came down in a minor flood, we used to grab our costumes and go for a swim. People looked at us as though we were mad, but we found it much more fun to swim down or across the dirty and fast-flowing Umsindusi than in a clean swimming bath. We were also the source of much amusement to the other employees in the factory, who would laugh and comment when they passed us in cars or in the factory bus, as we were running.

As our plans became more widely known, someone told a newspaper and we were asked to give them a story. It was the beginning of some of the best friendships I had ever made. While other people were quick to scoff at our ideas, the newspaper reporters gave encouragement and advice. They told us about applying for permits to pass through Zulu reserves, whom to go and see and what reception we were likely to get. Their company was always stimulating and refreshing.

After the first report of our intended journey had appeared in the *Natal Mercury*, Derek Kain, a local correspondent for a group of papers, got in touch with us. He was enthusiastic about the idea.

Although our plans were made and the dates decided, we were still having difficulty in getting a canoe. Nothing could be found in Pietermaritzburg, and only after searching round Durban for a few days did we eventually find a two-seater canoe. We were dubious about the thin canvas skin, but our day of departure was looming up, so we bought the craft. It was a two-seater Folboat type, and we had Indian paddles specially made.

Our first trial run took place when the river was low. We started below Grey's Hospital footbridge and paddled over stones, old jam tins, bottles and pieces of barbed wire that had been washed down by previous floods. Before we had gone five hundred yards the canoe was leaking badly. We dragged it out of the water and examined the covering. It looked like a pincushion. Patching made very little difference. The canoe had been in storage so long that the canvas had perished. We took it to a local tentmaker who fitted another layer of canvas and charged us a fabulous sum. This extra canvas made the canoe weigh over 80 lb., and when wet it was considerably more. However, the craft could now slide over rocks, tree stumps and other obstacles that had been a serious threat.

We trained hard, running to and from work, and canoeing in the late afternoon in the Hat waters at Alexandra Park. We were always an attraction for the prep-school little boys, who would run along the willow-lined banks making uncomplimentary remarks about our paddling prowess. As our proposed journey got more Press attention, somebody wrote a letter challenging the newspaper statement that there was no record of the trip having been done before. The correspondent, who signed himself "P. K.", claimed that a well-known Pietermaritzburg man, W. T. M. Foley, did the journey in just under seven days. Foley was supposed to have taken five and a half days to get to Table Mountain, and just over one day to go from Table Mountain to Durban. He used a 9 ft. canoe. This correspondent said he was supposed to have accompanied Foley, but his parents had raised such objections that he had had to give up the idea. He was not sorry to have done so after hearing of all the hardships Foley had experienced.

A short while after this had appeared in the Press, I received a kind letter from Mr. E. C. Uppink of Sezela on the South Coast. He said that he and Percy Fitzsimmons had planned a similar trip just before the First World War. They got as far as building the canvas canoe, but were then forced to abandon their adventure. They both went over to Europe with the original Springbok Brigade. Percy Fitzsimmons was wounded on the Somme in 1916, and was killed at the Butte de Warlencourt later the same year. Mr. Uppink said that two other Pietermaritzburg men had taken over from where he and Mr. Fitzsimmons had left off. They were "Timber" Wood and Sonny Mitchell. Starting from the Bulwer Street boating club, they set off one afternoon. That night there was a real Pietermaritzburg storm and the Umsindusi came down in flood. This helped the men to reach Durban.

Our interest was now fully aroused, and we were keen to find out more about these "old timers" on the Umsindusi and Umgeni. Then from out of the blue a letter arrived from Mrs. D. Rathbone of Renishaw. Mr. R. R. ("Timber") Wood was her brother. Mrs. Rathbone said that Sonny Mitchell and "Timber" Wood did the trip some time between 1910-1914 and were the only people to succeed. According to Mrs. Rathbone, Mr. Foley did not complete the journey.

Wood and Mitchell had a very hazardous trip. Once, when their canoe was upset in a deep pool and they were swimming around trying to retrieve their belongings, Zulus came running down and shouted to them to get out, as a large crocodile lived in the pool.

We then received a letter from "Timber" Wood's brother, Mr. R. S. Wood, of Isipingo, who wrote: "I recollect some claim being made that the journey had been done before, at the time of Reuben's and Sonny's trip,

but the whole matter faded out, and as no proof was ever adduced, one can only conclude that it was the usual notoriety-seeker's claim. Certainly no one had heard of its being done before, and in those days such a matter would have received wide publicity."

Mr. Wood then gave a graphic description of the river. "The river beyond Bishopstowe is still as wild and isolated as I knew it first forty-five years ago. It is a very snaky place, but so long as you don't interfere with the snakes, they won't worry you. There is so much advice one could hand out that it would take pages. The young men of today, however, don't think much of old stager's advice and it is a waste of breath to hand it out."

"If Father Time would hand me back forty-five years, I wouldn't mind going too, but my days for sleeping along with the grasshoppers are over."

On the 7th December 1950, we did a trial run from the boating club to beyond the sewerage farm. We thought it would be a pleasant afternoon's experience. How wrong we were!

We launched *Umthakathi* early in the morning and paddled over the calm stretch of water above the Dorp Spruit. Our only interruption before Mussons Weir was by five schoolboys running away from a Portuguese market gardener. They all plunged into the river, fully clad, and swam rapidly over to the other bank. The gardener contented himself with hurling abuse.

We passed a few fishermen fishing for barbel at the Dorp Spruit junction, with huge yellow spiders for bait.

As we paddled into the weir pool, some hadedahs took flight from the south bank and winged their way overhead, uttering their raucous "hah-hah-haahs".

"Sounds as though they're laughing at us," Desmond said as the canoe bumped against the weir wall.

The noise of the rapids below Barbel Pool reminded me of R. S. Wood's words: "I don't think a canvas canoe is suitable, as it is too frail for the rough going over the rapids, and believe me, there are more rapids than clear water in the Umsindusi!"

We let the canoe down into Barbel Pool, climbed in and paddled across to our first rapids. The double canoe bumped and scraped its way over the rocks, for the river was low. Using the paddles as levers, we gradually made our way down to two narrow channels separated by a reed island. We dithered for a few moments, undecided which course to take. The canoe gathered speed, and before we knew what had happened we were shooting down the right hand fork. A half submerged log lay directly ahead. "Back paddle!" I yelled frantically. Too late! We hit it and the

canoe turned broadside on. Slowly and gently it keeled over, depositing us in the river. It was the first of many hundreds of spills I was going to have on canoe trips, but I had learnt a lesson: don't dither. We dragged *Umthakathi* to the bank and heaved and strained to get the water out. The timbers creaked ominously and I wondered if they would break.

Getting the craft into the water again, we hung on, edging it down the rapids until we reached the Mountain Rise low-level bridge. We climbed in and paddled off.

Two hundred yards down we heard the roar of another rapid—then came two channels. This time there was no hesitation, and we chose the one with the most water. The canoe shot forward, bobbing over the rocks: a few flicks with the paddles, and we were riding the small waves again. We had conquered a rapid, and were thrilled with the experience. Paddling past some bush, we saw a thick black pipe stretching across the river, and from the stench we soon realized we were in the sewerage farm. The river twisted and turned until we found our way blocked by fallen trees. We let the canoe come sideways on, then got out on to the logs and, balancing very carefully, lifted the canoe over.

A hundred yards further on we came to a packed and solid mass of logs piled thirty feet high. The water simply disappeared. The logs had damned the river into a pool—a trap for every conceivable type of garbage. Rotten oranges, cabbages, carrots, dead cats and other foul smelling refuse lay in a thick scum on the still water.

We floated a while, wondering what to do. The slithering of a snake down a willow tree galvanized us into action, and within minutes we were on the pile of logs. We struggled for over two hours to get the boat back into the water, and then we were dead beat. We no sooner got going again, than we turned over and had to battle once more to right the canoe. Three spills later we reached the Sobantu Zulu village at dusk, where we encountered another pile of logs. We decided to stop and carry the canoe over to Jimmy Schorn's store, although we had originally hoped to reach Foxon's farm.

The rain began to fall as we lugged the heavy canoe through the luxuriant sewerage farm vegetation. Stinging nettles burned our bare legs, our wet sandshoes chafed our heels, and thorns tore our clothes as we dragged our way along. It was two very muddy, bedraggled and tired young men who limped into Jimmy Schorn's store. Mrs. Schorn gave us coffee and bacon and eggs—ambrosia! We thankfully accepted Jimmy's offer of a lift back to Pietermaritzburg.

We had to rest for a few days before returning to training. Then as we jogged along to work each morning, I prayed the day would pass

quickly so that we could get into the canoe. The vivid memory of bobbing over the rocks and riding the waves at the bottom of the rapids had gripped my imagination: it was a thrill I had never before experienced.

The hardships of the trial run were, on reflection, not as bad as I had thought at the time. The soul of the river had lightly touched me, and it demanded more of my attention. I came to crave the peace and quiet of gliding down the slow-flowing river from the old boathouse to Mussons Weir, while guinea fowl squeaked like rusty hinges and dikkop rose with fast-beating wings to give their mournful cry in the rapidly approaching evening. It was the beginning of a new world. Life became more worthwhile and made me want to tell everyone about this magnificent sport. One Saturday afternoon, as Desmond and I were walking down to the river, we passed a long queue of youths outside a cinema. It was a beautiful afternoon—clear blue sky with the surrounding Pietermaritzburg hills showing up vividly in the bright sunlight. How could anyone who was young and fit want to sit inside a stuffy cinema on such a dazzling day? As we did our usual practice run I couldn't forget the sight of all those youngsters. Desmond and I agreed that cricket, rugby and other sports had lost their appeal because they lacked the excitement these youngsters wanted. The more I thought about it, the more convinced I grew that canoeing as a sport has much to offer the present generation. If after only a month's experience it had done so much for me, what wouldn't it do for youth after a year?

I discussed the subject with some of my friends, but the general opinion was: "If you think anyone else is going to be as crazy as you. . . ." "But this is pioneering," I argued, "you can get back into the past this way."

This brought roars of laughter. Who on earth wanted to get back into the past? As for pioneering and exploring—that was storybook stuff. I listened impatiently to their arguments and refused to believe that the pioneering spirit was dead in the heart of modern youth. If someone made them aware that this was something new and exciting, perhaps the cinemas would lose a few patrons. I realized, of course, that my ideas were ambitious and would not be fulfilled in a few months, but might take as long as twenty years before they really bore fruit.

One evening a young reporter, Ken Brokensha of the *Daily News*, came to interview me. It was the beginning of a lasting friendship. With some heat I told him of the general derision that greeted my ideas about canoeing. He listened carefully, told me where he thought I was wrong, but agreed in principle with most of my ideas.

"If you want to get those experiences of yours across, you'll have to

publicize them at every opportunity," he said. We talked late that night. My kind old landlady, Miss Massam, sent us pots of coffee, for she was wholeheartedly giving us support in our venture.

I told Ken Brokensha that I hoped our pioneering run would eventually develop into a race which would be as well known in South Africa as the Boat Race is in England. Ken reported me in the *Daily News* the following day as saying: "I should like to see this grow into something big . . . there is no reason why others shouldn't follow suit, and so it might one day develop into a race."

This gave many of my friends and acquaintances lots to laugh about. "A race?" they asked incredulously. "You're going from bad to worse. No one in his right senses would think of people chasing one another down two boulder-strewn rivers."

"Time will tell," was my stock defensive reply.

I took to meeting Ken Brokensha at night after training. We would drink coffee and eat anchovy toast at Perks's Tearoom, while we discussed the possibilities of canoeing developing into a recognized sport.

"The newspapers are the ones to tell," Ken would say. "The more the papers print, the more chance there is of your ideas being accepted. If you express them often enough, people will become conditioned. The power of the printed word is unbelievable."

Ken introduced me to Jack Shepherd Smith of the *Natal Mercury* (he also wrote The Idler's column) and Jack ended up by accompanying me on the last half of my first trip. I met Ken's brother, Miles, also of the *Mercury* and he too became my partner, in the first canoe race. We spent some very interesting evenings together, and as we were all in our early twenties, my ideas fell on fertile ground.

"Publicity, that's what you need," Miles and Jack would say expansively. Their talk was a real tonic.

Our big day drew nearer, and Desmond and I grew more and more excited. List after list of equipment was made out, only to be pruned of all but the bare necessities—cane knife, sheath knife, matches, chocolate, biltong, bully beef, billycan, powdered milk, tea and sugar. It was useless to try to carry blankets, because we knew we should be turning over in the rapids. Waterproof containers were a big problem; after discussion and experiment, we decided that one-gallon paint tins would be the best. By the time we were finished, we had all our kit in seven extremely heavy, unwieldy tins. One morning a letter from a Kurt Engelbert of Durban arrived. Mr. Engelbert had seen one of the newspaper reports and was anxious to join us. He said he had raced regularly in the first crew of the Durban rowing club, of which he was secretary. I kept his letter, just in

case there was a chance of another person wanting to come along too.

Desmond and I stopped training a week before our departure date. Hardly a day passed without some minor crisis arising about kit or snakebite outfit, or how to get back from Durban.

Three days before we were to leave, Desmond came to me at work looking terribly depressed.

'What's wrong?" I asked.

"My father's been taken ill suddenly and I'll have to leave for the Cape today," he replied mournfully.

I agreed that his first duty lay with his family, but I didn't know what to do about our trip. There was only one alternative, and that was to go alone. The prospect didn't please me at all. There was no chance of postponing it, because we had only a limited amount of leave and the journey had to be done in the rainy season. I could hardly sleep that night for worrying: I had decided it would be better to go alone than to give up the whole idea, but how was I going to cope with the canoe, weighing over 100 lb. unloaded, plus tins of kit?

Late in the morning of the following day I remembered Kurt Engelbert's letter, and after much frantic telephoning I managed to get in touch with him. He said he'd be only too glad to join me, but wouldn't be able to leave Durban until the evening of the day I left, so we arranged that I should leave on time as planned, and meet him at a point some ten to fifteen miles downriver.

Brian Jackson, a fellow worker at the factory, offered to meet Kurt that night and take him by motor-bike or car to the lower portion of Pope-Ellis's farm. From there we would continue our journey together. It was a great relief to know that the trip would not have to be abandoned. I carefully checked over the canoe to see that there were no tears in the canvas, or broken ribs or cross members. Then I packed everything into the seven paint tins and rammed the lids home. My biggest regret was that I was not able to take a decent camera. I had to be content with a cheap miniature, which turned out to be quite useless.

It was just after 1.45 p. m. on the 23rd December 1950, a dull drizzly day, with the promise of heavy rain later, that we launched *Umthakathi* into the muddy Umsindusi. Representatives from all three of Natal's newspapers were there to see me off. Photographers took pictures; reporters shouted good luck and pulled my leg about getting washed over a waterfall, thus making a really good story. I pushed *Umthakathi* into the main current, climbed in and began paddling.

In a few minutes there was not a white man in sight. A few abafana ran along the bank, shouting in Zulu for me to give them a ride. They

quickly tired, and I had the river to myself. My fear of facing the rapids alone soon vanished as I fell under the river's spell. I drifted past high reeds and under stony outcrops, afraid to paddle and break the stillness. A gust of wind blew upstream, carrying with it the sound of rapids. The water level was low, and I knew I should have to get out and swim behind the canoe in the bad patches.

As some protection against the cold, I had smeared my body with olive oil, but I need not have bothered, because it soon washed off.

The river narrowed and flowed faster; rocks were more frequent; in some places bush grew right down to the water's edge. Thorn trees ripped my skin when I passed too close, but I felt at home on the river. It started raining, and the wind blew hard through the trees, but I was happy, for it sounded to me as though the trees were singing to the river "Msunduze, Msunduze, u-ya-hamba, u-ya-hamba."

The river rises in the great hills beyond the town of Pietermaritzburg and flows through some of the most beautiful valleys of Natal. I was not to know then that the cancer of soil erosion was eating into the earth, the river washing it down to the Umgeni and then to the sea. After a few minutes in the water my white shorts were stained dark brown; they never regained their former whiteness, but I did not understand what it meant. It was only years later that I realized what was happening to the beloved country: millions and millions of pounds of topsoil being carried down to the sea every year; mainly from the overstocking of land with animals by Africans in their reserves. Now the desert is coming; already it has laid its red-hot fingers on northern Natal, but it is ignored in the ever-loudening cry "Industrialize!" Factories are considered the key to success. What pride can there be in the truth that industrialization is merely a duplication of other countries' achievements, at the expense of our own country's irreplaceable natural beauty and resources?

Downriver the rapids thickened, so that I had to jump out and hang on to the back of the canoe, guiding it down some of the channels. The very bad rapids I manoeuvred by tying one end of a piece of rope to the back of the canoe and the other end round my waist.

The water ran faster and occasionally gushed over fifteen feet drops. In one place the canoe shot over and down; before I could do anything, the backwash pulled it under the drop; in a few seconds it was full of water. I quickly dived and got my back under the canoe; then, with my head just above water, carried it to the nearest bank. I took everything out, to find that one tin had burst and that the repairing canvas had gone. Fortunately the glue was left, so it would be possible to repair the craft with pieces of clothing soaked in glue.

One stretch of rapids was impossible to navigate, so I was forced to drag the canoe out of the water on to the bank. I cursed and swore, because it meant at least three journeys: one to carry the canoe and two to carry the kit. I surveyed the rapids again, hoping to find one small channel, but a thundering mass of foaming water, with wicked-looking rocks, was all I could see.

Reluctantly I took out all the tins, picked up the canoe and staggered for a few yards, then had to rest. Next time I managed to cover half a mile. As I swayed along a footpath, I heard screams from some herdsmen as they ran away at top speed, yelling and shouting the whole way. I couldn't understand why, until it struck me how frightful I must have appeared to them: the canoe covered my head and shoulders and my hands gripped the gunwales. A pair of grimy shorts, mud-spattered legs and sandshoes squelching water, completed the picture. It was a dull day, the sun had already set, and I was coming over the skyline. No one could blame the abafana for running. Shouting to them to stop only made them run faster, for my voice was muffled in the cockpit of the canoe. They were soon out of hearing, leaving the grazing cattle and goats. As it was still some distance to our rendezvous I jogtrotted back to fetch the tins, trying to hurry in the gathering darkness.

I paddled for only a hundred yards, and then reed islands and channels split the river. In some places there seemed to be no water. I pushed and hacked my way through the overhanging reeds, their needle sharp points drawing blood and leaving tiny, smarting wounds. It was darkening swiftly and heavy drops of rain fell from a lowering sky.

"Everything has got to end," I repeated, trying to ignore the oppressive atmosphere. "Not much further now," I thought as I lugged and heaved the canoe from one channel to another.

I slipped and the prow smashed down on rocks with a loud snap. Fortunately it was nothing very serious, only a broken rib. The relief gave me energy and I pushed on.

The river narrowed so that its water converged on the two remaining channels. The canoe moved more easily as I hung on to the bank, pushing in the shallow water and swimming in the deep pools.

On the south bank, where undulating bushy hills met the water's edge, I saw a Zulu standing on the skyline. It was a typical position—dead still, with arms folded. It was very cheering to see another human, and I waved my hat. There was no answering wave. The river turned south, and I was able to get a clearer view of my distant watcher: a solitary aloe silhouetted against the sky.

A little further, and I could lean back and paddle again. Three small

sets of rapids were easily passed, and I floated down a long calm stretch between two high sandstone banks. In the soft layer of red sand, at the very top, pied kingfishers and sand martins had made their nests. It was a joy to watch them hovering and darting above the river—they took no notice of the canoe.

As the river turned east sharply, I saw a tree lying halfway across the main stream, its lower branches touching the water. Something warned me to look up, and there—dangling in my path—was a green snake. Hastily back paddling, I tied the painter-rope to a small tree and searched amongst the tins for my small .32 revolver. I fired six shots at the snake and was extremely lucky to hit it twice. It fell and was carried away by the river. I reached our rendezvous with no time to spare: it was too dark to canoe. I dragged *Umthakathi* to the top of the flood-level bank in case the river came down, filled the billycan and set about making a fire. All the wood was sopping wet and very thorny; my hands were so quickly a spiky mess of thorns that I almost gave up the idea, but the thought of hot tea and food made me scout further down the bank, where I found some old driftwood from the previous year's floods. This was ideal.

I broke small dry twigs into a ground wigwam shape and held the match low until the twigs glowed. One burst into a tiny flame. I broke bigger pieces and placed them carefully, so that the air could fan every flicker of flame. Smoke poured out of the rotting bark and spiralled into the darkness, then came a crackling and a snapping as the flames got a firm hold and raced up the driest pieces. A few minutes more, then I rolled logs on to the flames and the fire was established.

The billy dangled above and queer shadows moved on the rough bark of the overhanging acacia trees. I cut slices of steak, skewered them on green sticks and roasted them near the fire. Flames leapt, danced and flickered and the wet wood hissed. I lay back, content, with a bellyful of grilled meat and tea. The smell of the meat, mingled with wood smoke, faded as the rain came down more heavily.

A noise in a patch of bush frightened me. Something shuffled towards the camp. I shone the torch in the direction of the noise: a jackal blinked its eyes in the bright light. It stood for an instant, turned, then trotted into the darkness. Silence—then came its screeching, wailing cry. I leapt to my feet in fear, with a cry of my own.

I had just built the fire up again when shouting in the valley told me Kurt Engelbert and Brian Jackson was near. Brian stayed for a cup of tea, and then walked up the valley, back to his car. I showed Kurt my maps and told him what the preceding stretch of river was like. It was soon obvious that Kurt knew a lot about canoeing, and I envied him his equipment. His

waterproof lumber jacket with a hood was ideal for the rainy weather we were having.

It rained all night. We took turns to stoke up the fire, but we were too wet ourselves to get much warmth from it.

Early the next morning, after a quick cup of coffee and some dry biscuits, we climbed into the canoe and set off. The river had levelled considerably after its steep drop from Foxon's farm to Pope-Ellis's farm. In view of Kurt's previous canoeing experience, he took the important, and far more comfortable, rear cockpit. For five miles we had an enjoyable cruise, jumping long sets of small rapids until we reached Scott-Riddel's farm. At a bad set of rapids we both got out, hung on to the canoe and let ourselves down the channels. My foot caught between two rocks and in an instant one of my rope-soled sandshoes was off, but my frantic plunge after the white sole in the water was too late. The thought of continuing the journey thus was most unpleasant, so we made our way to a Zulu muzi on the slopes of a nearby hill to ask its occupants whether they could sell us a pair of shoes. Zulu etiquette demanded far more from dishevelled Europeans, and we were politely told that there was a farmhouse a mile or so away.

We walked across ploughed fields and irrigation pipes to the farmhouse where Mrs. Scott-Riddel, the farmer's wife, very kindly gave us tea and a pair of her husband's leather-soled shoes. Her generosity was much appreciated.

We were shown a local footpath, which was a short cut to the river, so that we were soon on our way again. All signs of rain had disappeared and a hot sun beat down out of a clear blue sky. The river widened, making it impossible for both of us to sit in the canoe, so we took it in turns. One of us would walk in front to see what lay ahead, while the other canoed as best he could.

We made good progress for a few miles, and then it was my turn to walk. Soon I heard a muted roar. My heart sank. I reflected that this was one lot we were not going to negotiate, as from a small krantz I looked down upon a formidable set of cascades over a mile long. Water churned and foamed over boulders of every shape and size. It would have been impossible to let the canoe down with rope—our only alternative was to carry everything round. We found a footpath on the west bank, which led right to the end of the cascades. It was a strenuous double trip. First there was the heavy canoe, then the trek back to get the tins and other kit. There were times when we thought our shoulders and backs would break; it was well into the afternoon before we climbed into the canoe again.

The next three hours were the most delightful of the whole

expedition. The river flowed beneath rugged stone krantzes rising hundreds of feet, and then took a big horseshoe bend, Buffelshoek. Everywhere there were birds—red bishop birds with their brilliant red backs and black chests and faces; long-tailed widow birds or sakabula, such as I had often run after over the Chase Valley hills on misty mornings; yellow weavers, chattering, and making their nests on overhanging branches; scimitar-billed wood hoopoes, or "hlekabafzi" (laughing women), flew from the thorn trees on the slopes of the dry hills, their cackling cries full testimony to the Zulus' ability to name animals and birds. Pied wagtails hopped from stone to stone, their tails bobbing. A pied kingfisher hovered above the shallows, dived, then in one rapid movement hit the water and rose with a small fish struggling in its beak. European swallows swooped and caught insects just above the water. A brown-hooded kingfisher flashed across our path, its wings a vivid blue against the dark green river foliage. Reed warblers chirped and sang, even when we passed only a few feet from them. A pair of yellow-billed ducks floated and swam in front of the canoe for miles. The whole area was a private bird sanctuary, and a real blessing it must be to the owners.

Lower down the river we saw two scared grey duiker scamper up the bank. I had imagined we should see many antelope near the river, but these were the only wild animals we saw; it was difficult to believe that they were some of the last remaining animals which had once abounded in this great Valley of a Thousand Hills—staggering evidence of man's greatest sin in South Africa: the destruction of wild life. It was the sight of these two frightened duiker that eventually led me to my present job of game warden.

We paddled silently round the big bend, shocking many Zulu bathing parties into activity. One nthombazana, who could obviously read, got a double fright when she saw the name of our craft. "Umthakathi!" she screamed to a friend as she raced up a steep footpath. We reached the boundary of the Zulu reserve—two single strands of barbed wire strung across the river. The great Table Mountain rose abruptly ahead, its rocky southern buttress a dull red in the afternoon sun. From the tip of this great fortress the Zulu impis of old had looked out upon the clans that lived in the valley. Bryant in his magnificent book, *Olden Times in Zululand and Natal*, describes how the invincible Zulu impis chased and scattered the Njilo, Nyavu and Ndhlovini clans, the last-named clan deriving its name from the elephants that roamed the valley. Bryant's graphic description of the aftermath of Zulu plundering came to mind: "This idyllically beautiful Mgeniland, with its myriad green hills and bosky ravines, studded a year ago with numberless hamlets, resounding with the pan-pipes and merry

laughter of Nature's own children, had soon become a still and soulless solitude, strewn with ruins, harbouring but a few craven and famished vagrants lurking out of sight in the darknesses of the woods. For these helpless and defenceless fragments of obliterated clans it would be neither profitable nor safe to linger longer in their wild and lonely homelands."

In contrast to this scene of more than a hundred years ago, muzis now dotted the hills, still in their traditional shape surrounding the cattle enclosure, but the constant use of sledges, pulled by oxen and donkeys, had worn dangerous dongas, marring the whole landscape.

A little below the fence the river churned into rapids. We decided to camp and soon found a pleasant spot below a flat-topped thorn tree. Two abafana who appeared, joyously gave us a hand to lug the canoe to the top of the bank. They chatted gaily, expressing surprise at our stupidity in braving the perils of the Umsindusi in so small a boat.

"Hau! You should see the river when it is angry! See that?" and they pointed to the far bank. "The water flows over the top, and everything is washed before it. We have seen an ox float away and oxen are far stronger than your boat!"

Their bright talk was a relief from the moodiness of some parts of the river we had passed through.

CHAPTER 2

With the knowledge of ages past the abafana soon had a fire going, our billycan was filled and we waited for it to boil. A green-spotted wood dove started its mournful dirge and the abafana chanted in unison. "Ngi-yabe ngiya zalela umntanami boya nthatha ngizwa inhliziyo yami ithi do-dodo-do dodo." (They are always coming and taking my young and my heart goes do-dodo-do dodo.)

We opened some tins, ate the remainder of our bread, made tea, then settled back and listened to the abafana talking. I tried to improve my Zulu by asking them the names of the surrounding hills, the small streams and the trees and birds. Darkness fell and the abafana built up the fire. Flames flickered on their dark faces and sharpened the whites of their eyes when they got excited and tried to impress some new Zulu word on my mind. Then we all fell silent and watched the moon as it climbed higher into the evening sky. Table Mountain became a vast altar in silhouette. I felt this was the way to get nearer to God.

When the fire had died down again, the abafana got up and said "Salani kahle", and I replied "Hambani kahle" as they left for their kraals.

We unrolled our sleeping kit and soon fell asleep, but not for long: someone shouted from the high bank behind us. I asked what the trouble was. A man's voice said, "Where are my two children?" I replied that they had gone home. The man got abusive and said we must have "eaten" the two boys, because they had not come home. No explaining on my part would satisfy him, but eventually he left.

We settled down again, only to be badly frightened when several huge stones were flung in our direction, crashing through the branches of the tree above. I got hold of my revolver and swore out loud that I would not hesitate to use it if more stones were thrown. Peace prevailed at last and we slept till dawn.

We awoke stiff and sore from the previous day's paddling and carrying the heavy canoe. After a scant breakfast we changed into our wet canoeing kit and started off down river. The water level had dropped slightly, making it impossible for both of us to sit in the canoe, so we took

it in turns to paddle *Umthakathi* and scout ahead for the best channels. The river turned sharply to the right and flowed over some terrible rapids. I was paddling and had to call Kurt to give me a hand to lug the canoe over the mass of boulders. We struggled for an hour, and then decided that carrying it could not be much worse. We got on to a sledge path, and heaving and panting with the strain, we walked until we reached another path leading through a mealie field to a cattle dip. Before launching the canoe, we opened a tin of fruit to celebrate Christmas Day.

After smoking my last cigarette, we climbed into the canoe and made fairly rapid progress to the Umsindusi Bridge. It was strange seeing motorcars and buses whizzing along the tarred road that led to the Umgeni dam. I flagged a few cars, hoping to get some cigarettes; one car stopped, and the driver kindly gave me a packet. We did have hopes of being transported to the Umgeni, but no one seemed to be interested in our troubles. We were tired and sat below the bridge, resting and wondering how we were going to reach the Umgeni before nightfall. Then a well-built Zulu youth approached us, and we began talking. I asked him what the chances were of getting the canoe carried to the Umgeni. "Have you any money?" he asked in a rather ominous tone.

"A little," I replied.

He got up and strolled towards two strapping nthombazanas and began haranguing them in a loud voice. Eventually they came over and stood staring at the canoe. One laughed, then bent down and touched it. The other tightened the strip of cloth that scarcely covered her bulging breasts, and also bent down to touch the canoe. Then with a shout they lifted it on to their heads and did a little dance.

Then the haggling began, and it went on for at least half an hour before they eventually agreed to carry it for £1.

We set off again along an old track which led to the Umfula trading store, finding it difficult to keep up with the two girls, who were walking at a cracking pace. In the end I was forced to jogtrot. They danced, sang and played a mouth organ, changing the canoe from one to the other.

After a few miles we turned down a path that led to a dry watercourse. A huge mountain of bare rock came into view on our right, and we could hear the faint roar of water in the distance. We reached the river and the girls dumped the canoe on the bank.

I gave one girl a pound, which was immediately snatched up by the Zulu youth, who had been following. The girl did not remonstrate, so we said nothing. Then the youth began to argue and demand more money, until I opened a tin and casually displayed my revolver. Without another word he turned and left. The nthombazanas followed, giggling loudly. We

heard them shouting and laughing as they walked through the bush, then all became quiet except for the roar of the river.

It was getting late, but we decided to push on as far as possible before darkness. Deep channels flowed between a mass of flat and round boulders, so we were able to canoe without much trouble. The atmosphere of the Umgeni River was markedly different from that of the Umsindusi. We soon realized we could not afford to take chances, so hugged the bank, ready to leap out and have a look before jumping a rapid.

After two hours' paddling the light began to fail and the bare mountain on our right cast long shadows across the river. The bush looked sinister, and although there was some cultivation to the river's edge, we could see no human being. Suddenly, above the noise of the river, we heard a human voice shouting. We stopped paddling and looked round, but saw no one. Then a movement in some mealies caught my eye, and I saw a small umfaan gesticulating wildly. We paddled across and I asked what was wrong. He said that there were "amatshe mkulu" round the bend ahead of us, and that our canoe would get smashed to pieces if we went anywhere near. We crossed to the southern bank, left the canoe and went to have a look at the rapids the umfaan described. He had not exaggerated. Drops of four and five feet, swirling whirlpools, deep channels gouged through masses of flat rock and a precipitous krantz on either side made it obvious that we could go no further that night.

After a short search we found an ideal camping site between a group of boulders. We unpacked, made a fire and brewed some tea. We were both depressed, for it was a hard blow to meet with such difficulties after all our trials of the previous days.

When we had had something to eat, I scouted round to see if there was a footpath leading out of the gorge. Only a faint track led straight up the side of a krantz, and the thought of carrying our heavy craft was alarming. On the way back to the camp I met a kehle (old man). He gaped when he saw the canoe and asked whether we had crashed in an aeroplane. I explained that it was a boat, and he asked if we crept inside when we were going. When I told him that we had come from Maritzburg and hoped to reach Durban, he stood up, spat and said "Unamanga Nkosaan!" You lie young man). It took a lot of convincing, but after we had told him everything, including paying the nthombazanas a pound to carry the canoe from the Dusi Bridge, he calmly remarked, "It would have been better to pay ten shillings in Maritzburg and catch the pullman to Durban." Unanswerable logic.

My feet were raw and badly swollen from continually going barefoot, and my shoulders ached from sunburn and fatigue. After the

unaccustomed exposure to the savage heat of the valleys, Kurt was feeling grim too. We slept very little. I rolled onto the fire during the night, and was bitten on the leg by a spider. All in all, it was a most miserable night, and Kurt woke up with a splitting headache.

The day dawned grey and cheerless; after a hurried breakfast we set off, carrying the canoe. We climbed straight up the path I had discovered the night before. We were absolutely exhausted by the time we reached the top of the krantz, only to find that the path led back into the gorge. We rested for an hour, then wearily made our way down once more. We passed a few Zulu youths who were on their way to a beer drink. They gave us the very cheerful news that only a few miles downstream we would find the Umfula trading store. The thought of a cup of tea and a good meal gave us added strength, so we kept going until we reached the river again.

There was no chance of getting up the krantz once more, which meant we had to stick to the river. The sun now blazed down out of a cloudless sky; the early morning mists had gone and so had the coolness. Sweating and straining, we edged the canoe down the most frightful rapids. The river turned to the east again and we entered a succession of large pools. I was in the water pushing the canoe from behind in one foaming pool, when my foot kicked against something. I quickly looked down and saw a shoal of scalies swimming away. I made a mental note to return one day to fish the pool: two years later I did, and caught over twenty big fish in an hour.

The river flattened out once more, and Kurt walked on ahead to the store. Three-quarters of an hour later I reached the pipeline bridge, left the canoe and walked up to the store. I met the two owners, Mr. Clayton and Mr. Page. Mr. Clayton had just had the unpleasant experience of almost stepping on a black mamba, which made me realize how lucky we had been.

Kurt and I had then to part, as he was due back at work the following day, and there was no chance of us finishing the trip in so short a time.

After a big meal with Mr. Page, I had a good sleep in his spare room and awoke feeling very refreshed. I went down to the river and with the aid of two boys brought the canoe back. That night Bernard Page and I pored over my map and discussed the possibility of my reaching Durban alone in one day. I was obsessed by the river now, and was determined to conquer it. However, sixty miles by myself over some very rough water in the large two-seater canoe was impossible. There was nothing else to do but abandon the trip temporarily. Bernard Page put forward the best suggestion, saying I should return to Maritzburg, then come back and finish the journey over the New Year weekend.

As I lay in bed that night, I could hear the owls hooting from the store roof and the bark of a bushbuck in the kloof. The noise of the river rose and faded as the wind bore the sound of it away. These sounds were part of the old Africa. Something still remained, despite the age of motorcars, skyscrapers and macadamized roads. Outside my room the moonbeams filtered through the flat-topped acacia trees; on the hills in the background, tall aloes stood in sharp relief. The old brooding spirit of Africa was there, but you only realized it when you had battled against it. I knew that my life could never be the same again. I had tasted the waters of the real Africa, and realized I would have to spend the rest of my days learning more of its mysteries.

I awoke the next morning to the chattering of nthombazanas and the cackling of old women as they stood about waiting for the store to open. When the doors opened, the women flocked in, and the hubbub grew as they asked for tickey soap, paraffin, cooking pots and materials. A long mirror was propped up against one wall, and no woman could resist snatching a gaily-coloured bandana, draping it round her neck and admiring her reflection. Screams and giggles followed an imitation of a sophisticated European girl parading up and down before a mirror.

"That one has obviously been a house servant," Bernard Page remarked with a laugh.

Half an hour later the lorry left for Cato Ridge, and I climbed aboard. "See you next week," Bernard Page shouted as we started grinding up the steep road.

We chugged away over the rough construction road, twisting and turning round hairpin bends. Then we wound our way down to the river again, crossed a low level causeway, and passed the dry watercourse we had struggled along the previous day. An hour and a half later we reached Cato Ridge, where I climbed off and started hitchhiking to Maritzburg. My clothes were tattered, I was barefoot and had a bright red scarf, bought from the store, round my neck. Cars whizzed past, the passengers without a backward glance. I could not blame them, and started to jogtrot. I ran for fifteen miles before a lorry, pulling a racehorse trailer, stopped and gave me a lift.

A few hours later I walked into the office of the *Natal Witness* to tell my friends what had happened. Some of the typists looked at me with horror; others retreated rapidly when I strode barefoot down the passage. Stan Eldridge, the News Editor, and Derek Kain, the reporter, greeted me.

"You look almost sorry to see me," I said.

"It would have made a better story if you'd gone over a waterfall," Derek Kain said.

26

While reporters hurried up and down the passage, and telex machines hammered out the up-to-date news, I spoke to Derek Kain who quickly wrote the story.

Ten minutes later I was on my way home and went straight to bed. That night I could hardly sleep for crippling stomach cramps and violent attacks of dysentery. The "Gyppo guts" of Army days were mild in comparison.

Next morning at seven o'clock I staggered off to work. The gateman, who knew me well, demanded my clock card.

"Don't you know me?" I asked with some astonishment.

"No!" came the reply.

I looked in the mirror and saw a figure with drawn cheeks and wild eyes.

After two days of good rest, however, I felt capable of finishing the journey, and was overjoyed when Jack Shepherd Smith of the *Natal Mercury* volunteered to go with me. Jack was the ideal height and weight, and despite his slender build, he was wiry and tough. He had once ridden from Maritzburg to Durban on a donkey for a bet-no mean feat in itself.

Early on the Saturday morning we left Maritzburg with Stewart Carlyle, another *Mercury* reporter, and Ken Brokensha of the *Daily News*. We arrived at the Umfula trading store at 5.45 a. m., offloaded our kit and went to collect the canoe. When we turned it over, a huge spider ran out from underneath the wooden struts.

"A very bad omen," Ken Brokensha said. He retreated rapidly as Jack swore at him for being a sensation-mongering reporter of a yellow rag.

At 6.30 a. m. we launched the canoe, but we had to tow it for a few miles. The last words from Ken and Stewart were, "What kind of flowers do you like best?"

Our tattered Union Jack fluttered in the early morning breeze of the valley. For years it had been my lucky symbol, and now it had a place of honour on the canoe.

The river divided, then became one stream, and we were able to climb in. It was Jack's first time in a canoe since he had left school and the tin canoes he had played with as a child. We leapt away with a jerk and Jack paddled furiously.

"Take it easy," I yelled, but it was too late. We raced over a rapid, swerved towards a reed island and overturned. Spluttering and heaving we managed to right the canoe and manoeuvre it to the island, while fifty yards away another rapid roared menacingly. We sloshed water out of our craft, dried our sopping clothes, then carried the canoe round the big rapid.

Soon we were on our way and had an enjoyable stretch of a few miles.

Jack suddenly turned and yelled, "Look at this!"—Another hairy spider was crawling out from the bow of the canoe. Jack tried to twist to let it pass him, the canoe overbalanced and in a flash we were in the water again.

As I surfaced, Jack was shouting, "My shoe, my shoe!" Something white turned slowly over in the brown current, Jack made a dive, but it was out of his reach. Although it was a serious matter, I could not help laughing at Jack's sad face. For the next twenty miles he suffered every time we had to carry the canoe a few yards.

We paddled on below the hill, known to many travellers between Maritzburg and Durban as the Sleeping Beauty. A magnificent view of the whole valley can be seen from this point, krantzes and rolling green hills sweeping downwards. Mist drifted into the kloofs and wooded gullies, and smoke from Native kraals spiralled into the sky. Above the constant roar of the river we could hear the shouts of children and the barking of dogs, as they chased the cattle down to the drift to drink. We carried *Umthakathi* over the bush weir, then paddled down to Mbetche's Store. From this point, until we reached Khumalo's store, there were few rapids to worry about and we were able to look at the magnificent scenery and the variety of birds.

Many hammerheads had built their huge, ungainly nests in the fig trees lining the banks. Two Bateleur eagles circled round in the thermals, occasionally throwing back their heads and uttering their fascinating "cor cor de cor" cry. Their black, red and white colouring made a vivid splash against the blue sky. Pied wagtails jumped from rock to rock in company with the odd common sandpiper. Once I thought I heard a greenshank ahead, but when we came round the bend there was no sign of one. Bishop birds worked furiously amongst the reeds, building their beautifully shaped nests. Reed warblers whistled continuously, and swarms of doves alighted on the sand banks to drink. White egrets stalked behind the cattle grazing on the bank, their long necks darting forward whenever an insect flew off. A solitary black-headed heron stood on one leg staring into the shallows, waiting for a frog or small fish to show itself. At the foot of almost every set of rapids a pair of hammerheads would be feeding on the small fish trying to leap upstream. If we came upon them suddenly, they would take off with a peculiar squeaking cry. There were sacred and hadedah ibis on the odd, marshy spots near the river.

After twelve hours of continuous paddling we reached Khumalo's store. While I rearranged the kit, Jack went to see if he could arrange some place for us to sleep. A horde of inquisitive umfaans plied me with

questions—where had we come from and where were we going? They wanted to finger and touch everything until I told them it was bewitched, and to prove my point, I dragged tin after tin from the prow and stem of the boat. They all retreated to a safe distance and stood whispering. Jack came back from the store looking very puzzled.

"What's the matter?" I asked.

"A Zulu woman asked me in pure English with an Oxford accent where I had sprung from," he muttered.

Khumalo, the storekeeper, let us put our canoe in an outhouse and we caught a bus to the Inanda police station where we spent the night. It poured with rain and we congratulated ourselves on being under a roof instead of in the bush.

Early the next morning we walked back the five miles to Khumalo's in pouring rain, and without coats or shoes. Our morale was at a low ebb when we reached the store. We dragged the canoe down to the river, slipping and sliding on the muddy path. As we launched the craft we both fell into the river, which made us wet and miserable for the rest of the day.

We travelled only six miles that day, the rapids being impossible to jump because of the low water. We had to line the canoe down every rapid. This meant tying a rope to the stem of the canoe and letting it go down the rapids alone, while one of us jumped from rock to rock alongside or behind. Sometimes we had to swim and guide it down. In some places the krantzes dropped in a sheer mass to the water, so we had to cross the river continually. At one stage it took us three hours to cover a mile. I learnt a good lesson: a canoe and kit weighing over 150 lb. were not suitable for Natal rivers.

By 5 p. m. we were in the heart of the Krantzkloof gorge, and a gloomy place it looked under the lowering skies. Everything we had was soaking wet, for we had fallen into the brown river more times than we cared to count. Even our matches were sodden, which meant a night without fire—this was the most depressing aspect of all. We stopped to discuss our plight, which was soon made worse by a burst of thunder and more pouring rain. At that moment an umfaan herding goats suddenly appeared from the bush.

He told us that a white man lived at the top of the gorge, so Jack volunteered to go with the umfaan to see if he could arrange a place to sleep. It was almost dark when the boy returned with a note from Jack saying that a farmer had agreed to put us up for the night. I cursed Jack for not taking one of the three haversacks, for it meant that I had to carry two.

The umfaan and I set off when it was nearly dark. We stumbled over a black mamba, which reared, then turned and slid away into the bush. The

umfaan paled. We crawled up the side of the krantz along game and locals' footpaths, the haversacks bumping and catching onto every low, hanging branch. The only thoughts I had were of snakes. Twice we stepped over night adders. The umfaan said that this particular gorge was renowned for its reptiles, and goats and cattle were always being bitten. It was after 8 p. m. when we reached the farmhouse.

Mr. and Mrs. Bohmer treated us with great kindness. They offered me brandy, but I drank twelve cups of tea instead, and after a meal we went to bed.

At 4.30 the next morning we were on our way back to the river, bare-footed, but marvelling at the magnificent sunrise. We could see the Indian Ocean and the mouth of the Umgeni River—so near and yet so far. The sun climbed slowly up behind the towering, bush-covered krantzes and gorges; we climbed painfully down the grim paths of the previous night's hell until we saw the brown thread of the Umgeni river way down in the gorge below us.

We reached the canoe at six o'clock and set off again. Until noon we battled with rapids and weirs that were unmarked on the map. The unexpected sight of the river suddenly dropping ten feet to jagged rocks below was terrifying, particularly as we had come so far without serious mishap. For the two miles before we reached the Natal Estates' pumphouse we had to line the canoe the whole way. Jumping from rock to rock, and using the paddles when the canoe jammed between boulders, we gradually made our way down. Once the line was wrenched out of my hand, and the canoe shot forward on its own way downstream. Jack was ahead and I shouted and pointed. Without hesitation he dived into the fast-flowing stream and thrashed after the boat, catching it just before it went over another set of nasty rapids. He hung on grimly until I managed to get close and grab the line. His action prevented our trip ending in failure.

It was just after midday when we reached the Natal Estates' pumphouse. The river level had dropped considerably, and we now struggled over the sands. Crossing and recrossing the river whenever a suitable channel presented itself, slowly we made progress. An easterly breeze from the sea forced us back and brought with it the foul smell of factories and other refinements of civilization. It seemed unbelievable that as short a way back as 1906 there were still hippo in the Sea Cow Lake adjoining the Umgeni River.

I was suddenly filled with an overwhelming loathing at the thought of going to the stinks and massed houses of the city. I had come to hate every aspect of town life: bare plane trees and piles of dry brown leaves on the squared pavements, the smell of pines and the association of local

respectability, the acrid stench from urinals and public lavatories, the overpowering foulness of alcohol from public bars and cheap hotels. I was filled with the primeval urge to return to the veld—atavistic and overpowering. Unreasoning fear clutched madly at my mind as the ghastly transition from wilderness back to urban life began. I was filled with an insatiable mental hunger for the sight of dry, twigged acacias and the green grass underneath, the smell of a raw Zulu kraal and nthombothi wood smoke, and to see birds wheeling in a sky that was not hazy with smog.

At 4.30 p. m. we climbed out of our canoe at the Blue Lagoon tearoom. Strains of the latest popular record echoed over the river, while white-suited Indian waiters rushed from car to car with piles of hot food, pots of tea and steaming cups of coffee. Our journey was over. I felt flat, stale and altogether uninterested in life—a terrible anti-climax.

The following day I was posting requisitions into stores ledger cards. My leisure hours were spent reading, or trying to write a story of the canoe trip. My effort was a hopeless failure. It lacked any form or style, and the manuscript was returned with the Editor's compliments with monotonous regularity. I was, however, convinced about the future of canoeing and was ambitious for achievement, not for recognition.

After a month at work I was desperate to get out into the country again; thus plans began to formulate in my mind for a trip down the Umzimkulu River. *Umthakathi* had been badly damaged on the Umgeni trip, and I had little hope of actually finishing the journey of 130 miles from Umzimkulu village to Port Shepstone, but I reasoned that it might just as well be smashed on a bad set of rapids as rot in a garage.

Interest had been aroused in canoeing, and I wanted to sustain it. I tried to find someone to do the trip with me, but no one seemed particularly keen. Then a letter arrived from Raymond Cruickshank of Durban. He and some friends had arranged to go down the Vaal, and at the last moment his friends had decided not to go. Raymond was anxious that we do the trip together. I replied that I had only a week's leave and suggested that he join me on the Umzimkulu venture.

He wrote back: "Very interested to hear about the Umzimkulu trip. I have never been down that way and am keen to try. I can get hold of a canoe, but it isn't very suitable, being a homemade one and not in the best condition. It weighs around 100 lb. I don't think I would be able to carry it very far by myself. Actually, before I wrote to you, I had intended to make the Vaal trip by myself on a surf-ski. There seemed to be many disadvantages to a lone journey, but I was too stubborn to consider them, although everyone warned me."

In the evening of 17th February 1951, my uncle, Mr. H. G. Ferguson,

took Raymond and me to Umzimkulu where we spent the night at the local hotel. Early next morning we launched the canoe into the swift-flowing Umzimkulu River and set off on our journey.

Umthakathi looked and felt very wonky. We shot the first rapid without any trouble, and that gave us confidence. We sped down three more sets of rapids, then paddled along a pleasant, flat stretch. It was a magnificent relief to be away from the city and crowds again.

About ten miles from the village of Umzimkulu we heard a hoarse thunderous roar ahead. As we approached Raymond shouted, "Let's get out!" I looked ahead and thought I saw a suitable channel down the rapids. I shook my head and replied, "Let's give it a go!"

A fatal decision: halfway down there was a two-foot ledge. *Umthakathi* went over, then turned broadside on to the full force of the river. We nearly drowned as we struggled to smash the struts that were trapping us in the canoe. Exerting superhuman strength, Raymond succeeded in smashing the cross-member pinning him inside the cockpit. He then broke mine and we swam ashore, clambered onto the bank and lay gasping and puking water. After a short rest, we dragged the canoe from the foaming and gushing brown Hood and rescued what kit we could.

Then, having made a fire and boiled a billy of tea, we discussed our plans. It was a great relief to hear Raymond voice my thoughts, "If we can't canoe down, we'll walk there!"

I wrote a note to a nearby farmer, Mr. J. B. Hulley, asking him to put the remains of the canoe and some of our kit in his garage.

Half an hour later we left. We spent the first night at Mr. Chipps's farm, then walked to the river the following day.

We slept one night at a mission where we had a most enjoyable time talking to the priest in charge. While drinking good wine and eating excellent food, we heard of the mission's struggles for recognition. It made me realize the foolishness of disregarding the wonderful work done by these people in out-of-the-way places of South Africa. By teaching Christian principles to the African they have saved the European from innumerable dangers.

We left early the following day, got a lift in a Native bus for a few miles, then walked down into the valley and followed the river once more. A day and a half later we were in Port Shepstone. As we had lost nearly everything when the canoe overturned, our funds were low, so we started walking back towards Durban along the beach. We spent the night on the sands near the little village of Southport, which had many memories for me, as it was a favourite holiday place of my family. The fishing there had always been magnificent, and I remembered one night in particular when

my father had caught a beautiful 56 lb. kingfish.

Raymond and I got the camp organized, then lay listening to the roar of the surf and the swishing of the waves as they swept up the beach. Terns with swept-back wings dived out at sea, and gannets flew above the swells behind the breakers. Our solitude was shattered by some hobos who asked us for matches, milk, tea and any other food we could give them. We hadn't the heart to refuse. Some of them volunteered their stories, and we sat around the fire, listening late into the night. Some, who had reached the depths of degradation and then come to their senses, found they still preferred the life of the open road.

At dawn we bathed in the calm sea, packed our haversacks and set off for Durban. It was enjoyable walking along the sands until the heat of the day made us thirsty; I felt I understood what the shipwrecked people must have experienced on their long treks up the coast to Lourenco Marques.

Late that afternoon we left the beach and made for the main road from where we hitchhiked to Durban. Then I said good-bye to Raymond and made my way to Maritzburg.

The Umzimkulu trip, although it had ended in failure, had kept the interest in canoeing alive, and a bundle of letters awaited me from young men from all over the country. They wanted to know which rivers were suitable for canoeing, what were the best types of canoe, what kit to take and so on.

Raymond Cruickshank made plans for a lone trip down the Umzimkulu in July to test his surf-ski on rapids. We had made arrangements to partner each other in the first canoe race we could organize. Then Raymond had the chance of getting aboard Tom Steele's yacht, the Adios. He left his job, dropped everything else he was doing, and a short while later was away on his big adventure. Between Durban and Cape Town the yacht ran into stormy weather, and for days there was no news. Aircraft were chartered to look for the missing boat. A few days later the Adios limped into Durban harbour, dismasted and in serious trouble.

Raymond has been at sea ever since; he recently acquired his own craft and set off on a solitary world cruise. He will, I am sure, eventually find his name in the annals of the sea.

CHAPTER 3

By October 1951, no one had come forward to compete in a race from Maritzburg to Durban, so I decided to try my luck down the Umkomaas River and, as nobody was keen to accompany me, I determined to go alone. Two first-class canoes on the style of P. B. K. 10 were built for me, and I slowly got the rest of my kit together.

Then in November 1951, Ernie Pearce and John Naude said they intended canoeing to Durban over Christmas, as they wanted to better my time. It was a challenge to a race that was eagerly accepted.

I met Ernie Pearce, and the outcome of our first meeting was the plans to form a Canoe Club. On the night of 10th December Ernie Pearce, Fred Schmidt, Denis Vorster, Basil Halford, Jack Shepherd Smith, Derek Kain and I met in my room to draw up the constitution and a badge for the club. I also produced a list of rules for the first canoe race, and we decided that the race should start from Alexandra Park on 22nd December 1951.

I sent a copy of the rules to the Mayor of Maritzburg, and asked him to become our patron. Mr. Warmback gave us his full support and wrote messages of greetings for the canoeists to give to the Mayor of Durban. Our club emblem consisted of crossed assegais, flanked by two snakes surmounted by a leopard's head, with a canoe and "Enzanzi nemfula" written below. It created much interest and several young men joined the club.

Ernie Pearce's help in the early days of the club's existence was invaluable. Before he became interested in canoeing, Ernie was a champion cyclist. Wiry and extremely tough, with a most pleasing personality, he was the ideal chairman for the new club. As an ex-serviceman, Ernie was in full agreement with me about making the conditions of the race as hard as possible. He had served in the Royal Natal Carbineers during the war in the northern frontier district of Kenya, and in the desert where he was taken prisoner while escaping from Tobruk. He escaped from a P. O. W. camp in Italy and walked to Switzerland.

I was fortunate to find Miles Brokensha, brother of my old friend Ken Brokensha, willing to be my partner on this first canoe race. Miles and

I were the only two contestants who were not employed by the Railways. One newspaper carried a report about Denis Vorster and Fred Schmidt being "hot favourites" and heavily backed to win by their colleagues.

Amongst the contestants there was great rivalry. Everyone was determined to win, and spent many hours during the night and weekends building their craft. I had a strong suspicion that some of the canoes were not going to be suitable.

A few days before the race the rules were printed in the Press. Some contestants said they were far too harsh, but Ernie Pearce, Fred Schmidt and I were adamant, and nothing would make us change our minds.

I had a few arguments with Miles Brokensha, because I knew he was not training. Miles simply could not believe how hard the race was going to be. I had to laugh when one day I asked him what training he was doing and he replied, "Well, I walk up the stairs to the office instead of catching the lift!"

Our canoes were completed only four days before the race, and Miles and I went down to the Umsindusi to try them out. One canoe was ten feet long and weighed 50 lb. unladen; with provisions it weighed 70 lb. The other weighed 40 lb. unladen and 60 lb. laden. I took the heavier canoe, which I considered light in comparison with the first *Umthakathi*. The draught of each was about ten inches, which was more than I had originally reckoned on, but I was very satisfied with their performance.

All the other canoeists had double canoes, which, although lighter than our canoes' combined weight, were not, I thought, suitable.

Every competitor claimed to have a secret weapon; we did too. Ours was the simple device of making a bag of American oilcloth. All our clothes and food were stuffed in it, so despite constant submerging remained quite dry. During previous canoe trips everything had been saturated whenever the canoe had turned over. There is nothing more demoralizing than sleeping in wet kit, and riverbanks can be freezing even in midsummer. Sleeping well was important from the point of view of morale.

Interest continued to mount in Maritzburg as the race drew nearer. The newspapers played their part nobly—interesting young reporters in the project had paid dividends. There were times when I was terrified that the whole thing would be a flop—even the more conservative papers came out with headlines.

The day of the race dawned fine and clear, but it was with much trepidation that I made my way down to the river to meet Miles. Some three hundred people were gathered on the banks of the Umsindusi in Alexandra Park. Although there were only eight of us we made quite a

colourful scene: bright shirts and shorts and multicoloured canoes. All contestants wore the leopard-skin hatband, the insignia of the Natal Canoe Club.

Ernie Pearce and I laughed loudly at Fred Schmidt and Denis Vorster who appeared carrying a basket of homing pigeons.

"You'll end up eating them!" Ernie exclaimed.

The Mayor inspected us, made a short speech prophesying that the race would become as popular as the Oxford-Cambridge boat race, whereupon there were howls of derision from the crowd.

At 8 a. m. Ernie Pearce and John Naude set off, followed at four-minute intervals by Miles and me, Basil Halford and William Potgieter, then Fred Schmidt and Denis Vorster.

With weighted packs banging against the back of the canoe, Miles and I made our way down the first flat stretch to the Victoria road bridge weir, by which time Miles was already almost at his last gasp. Then he saw the crowd, who yelled encouragement, and someone waved a bottle of brandy. I don't know whether Miles saw it or not, but he leapt out into the water neck deep and splashed to the right-hand bank, dragged his canoe out and carried it for a hundred yards to the rapid below the willow trees. I followed close behind then, balancing with one foot, we jumped in and paddled off down the long, winding, placid reaches of the Umsindusi until the Dorp Spruit joins it.

After what seemed an interminable time we heard the water pounding on the rocks below Mussons Weir. Half dragging and half carrying, we ran to Barbel Pool, paddled a little way, got out again and lined the canoes down the rapids until just before the low-level bridge. Getting in again, we paddled hard and caught up with Ernie and John as they were passing under the sewage pipe. A few seconds later we got entangled with a pile of logs, but after struggling, we disengaged the canoes and paddled on, in time to see Ernie and John heaving their heavy plywood craft, "Kontiki", up the slippery bank. This was the last time we saw any of the other competitors.

Foolishly we tried to clamber up the slippery path left by "Kontiki", but almost at once found ourselves floundering in the water. Eventually Miles crawled up the bank; I threw him a rope, pulled myself out, then together we tugged and strained to lift the canoes up. It was a full fifteen minutes before we were on our way across the morass of reeds and bog adjoining the sewage farm. Swearing and cursing, we hurried through the stinging nettles and spiky reeds to the road running to Schorn's store.

There was no sign of anyone as we jogged down the road with the canoes bouncing on our heads. I realized that mine was too heavy and was

going to be the cause of much suffering. It was a relief to reach the river and paddle down the gushing rapids near Foxon's farm. This time I knew better, and we carried the canoes over the neck, instead of taking the long, winding course I had followed on my first canoe trip. In the river again we were soon lost in a maze of small channels and high reeds. It was misting up and a little while later a steady rain began to fall. We needed it badly for the river was low, enabling us to ride over only a few rapids.

Before we emerged from the reeds and small channels, I heard a shout and turned to my left to see a man on horseback. We splashed over to him and gratefully accepted a cigarette.

"How far do you think you'll get today?" he asked.

"Beyond the cascades, I hope!" I replied.

He looked up into the sky and remarked that it would soon stop raining. We quickly smoked another cigarette, then pushed off, fearful that Ernie would catch up with us.

An hour later we passed my first camp of the year before. Miles was handling his canoe like a veteran, and by the expression on his face it was obvious he was enjoying himself.

At 5 p. m. we reached the cascades and decided to camp. By now it was drizzling, so we took cover in a donga leading into the Umsindusi, which was dangerous, for had there been a thunderstorm during the night we would have been swept into the river. We found a few pieces of driftwood and soon had a fire blazing. The billy boiled and we grilled some potatoes on the coals. We had a cigarette, then put on all our clothes, dug holes for our hips and tried to sleep.

I lay awake for some time, worrying as to whether we had established a good enough lead, not knowing that we were already the only two left in the race! By midday four of the canoeists had retired.

Potgieter and Basil Halford capsized in a rough stretch of the river, and their craft was forced up against a fallen tree. Branches on the tree holed the boat in four places. After a long struggle they managed to free it, and used up all their pitch repairing the holes. They later found that rocks had also damaged the craft, so they decided it would not be worth continuing. William Potgieter told a reporter that he did not think youngsters would be able to do the race.

"It is damned tough," he said, "a real obstacle race; every 150 yards a big tree straddles the river, and it is difficult to get your canoe out. I am so stiff I can hardly walk. I cannot even hold the telephone receiver, my arms are aching so much!"

Ernie Pearce and John Naude carried their heavy craft to the river below Schorn's store, overturned a little further on and were badly bruised

as they were washed over the rocks. They tried to carry on, but their boat immediately sank in six feet of water. They salvaged what they could, walked to Campbell's farm (where they got a lift to Sobantu village) and then walked the rest of the way home.

Fred Schmidt and Denis Vorster were holed nine times by 3.30 p. m. The last stretch of rapids they tried to jump was too much, and their canoe was smashed.

Miles woke at dawn, and without even waiting for a cup of tea, we packed the canoes and pushed on. A handful of dried fruit served as our breakfast. We kept glancing back, expecting to see a canoe. By midday we were extremely tired, so we stopped for ten minutes' rest.

We were soon on our way again, dragging our canoes through the shallow water. The river level had dropped to a few inches, making it impossible to canoe at all. We were both too tired to carry the canoes, so there was no alternative but to plod along through the sand, dragging them behind us. It was exhausting work.

At 3 p. m. a terrific storm was building up in the south: within an hour it was upon us. We were almost completely exhausted, having struggled for hours through the sand, our shoes filled with the painful grit. Miles was behind me when the storm struck us. He caught up with me and above the roar I heard him shout, "Let's take shelter, I'm almost all in". I, however, knew that in a few minutes the river would be rising, and then every stream and donga would be raging full. We should get soaked travelling in the storm, but at least we should be able to sit and paddle the rest of the way to the bridge.

There were flashes of lightning and savage roars of thunder, the noise reverberating in the valley as each burst echoed from krantz to krantz. I was afraid—we were so exposed and I had always heard how water attracted lightning. It seemed hours before the river began to rise, though it could not have been more than an hour. At last the water started to move faster, and patches of foam floated past—a sure indication that the level was rising. I felt the water reach my ankles, then my calves. I put my foot into the canoe and pushed off. When I sat down the relief was so great, I wept.

By the time we reached the big U-bend before the Umsindusi Bridge, it was dusk. I spoke to Miles and told him to leave his canoe with me, then walk to the bridge and collect firewood before it was too dark. I watched him shoulder his pack and walk into the reeds along the bank.

"Try to make coffee!" I screamed as he faded into the gloom. He didn't answer or wave.

For a while I paddled, towing the other canoe, then I came to a rapid;

Photo: Natal Daily News

The battle for the lead in Alexandra Park, Pietermaritzburg

Over the rocks

Photo: Natal Daily News

Photo: Natal Witness

Nick Steele and Paul Dutton, dismayed but not disheartened game rangers

Photo: Natal Mercury

Wrapped around a rock

The end in sight

Photo: Natal Mercury

Photo: Natal Mercury

One canoe saved

Tom Howcroft having a rest

Photo: Natal Mercury

the water was not high enough for me to risk jumping it, so I lined one canoe down then returned for the other. Ten minutes later it was pitch dark. For two hours I struggled, paddling down the easy stretches and feeling my way down the rapids. It was terrifying. When I reached the bridge I was so exhausted that I could only drag the prows of the canoes out of the water. I knew it wasn't safe, but hadn't the strength to do more.

I shouted. After a silence Miles answered. I crawled up the bank and found him huddled under his waterproof, protected by a big acacia tree.

"God, man, where's the fire?" I moaned.

"There's not a piece of wood to be found anywhere—the bloody storm has washed everything away," Miles replied wearily.

At that moment an African walked past. I was about to ask him to collect some firewood, and put my hand to my belt where I had tied the waterproof bag containing all our money, my watch and the Mayor's letter. It was gone!

'I've lost everything!" I said to Miles. He didn't reply.

"Let's get the torch out and I'll go up the road and see what I can find," I said, feeling that under the circumstances it was the only consolation I could offer.

With numb fingers I opened the pack and searched the waterproof inside for the torch. It was not there. I had forgotten it in my haste. Miles lay back and groaned.

Then I remembered the canoes.

"Quick! The river will have risen and taken the canoes!" I yelled as I scrambled down the bank, sick with anxiety and all fatigue forgotten.

We stumbled around in the dark, but without light it was impossible to do anything. Miles remembered putting an old candle in his bag as an afterthought. We went back, lit it and, cupping the flame, crept on hands and knees down to the river. When we reached the place where I had left the canoes there was nothing to be seen. I thought it was the end of our effort. We turned back, but something prompted me to look for tracks, and when we couldn't find any I realized that the canoes were lower down. Twenty yards further on we found them. I said a quiet prayer when we at last got them to the top of the bank.

Finding the canoes gave us new strength. We tore branches off the thorn trees. Most of them were almost green, but I knew that once the fire got going they would burn. The candle saved our lives again. We built a small wigwam of dry twigs and put the candle inside. In a few minutes they were burning; gradually we piled on more and more wood until we had a blazing fire. Too tired to eat we stripped, put on dry clothes, crept as near to the fire as possible and slept.

The next morning stamping feet and a loud bellowing awakened us. I sat up to see about a hundred oxen running straight towards us. Leaping up in a panic—we were petrified that the cattle would trample the canoes to smithereens on their way to the water—we swore and yelled at the herdsmen to turn the herd, but the cattle came on. They stopped abruptly a few feet away and milled round undecidedly. Grabbing our opportunity, Miles and I screamed and lashed out at the leaders until they turned and led the rest of the herd away.

"A series of misfortunes, old boy," Miles muttered wearily.

We walked to a small, white rondavel that served as a dispensary when the District Surgeon came to the area once a week. We found the caretaker to be a very pleasant old African who insisted upon giving us tea and magnificent fruitcake. It must have surprised him to see how we gobbled the cake without leaving even one small crumb, but his kind black face remained impassive.

We asked whether he had heard anything of the other fellows in the race, hoping that the bush telegraph had reached him, but he knew nothing and was amazed when we told him what we were doing. He followed us with concern to the river and helped us to stow the kit. A few minutes later we were off downstream and moving fast on the river, which was swollen after the previous nights' rain.

For the first time since our rough awakening I was able to appreciate the lovely morning. The air was clear and fresh after the rain; Table Mountain and the surrounding green hills looked close enough to touch. Wisps of mist clung to the high peaks, and water, glinting in the sun, cascaded down the rocky slopes. Reed warblers sang continuously and the green-spotted wood dove droned on and on. By nine it was very hot and the cicada beetles had set up their deafening singing. After three miles of paddling we reached the path leading up the hill to the three huts that have served as a landmark to so many canoeists in later years.

As we climbed out and dragged the canoes onto the bank, I asked Miles whether he would mind taking the heavy canoe for a while to give me a rest. He assented without a murmur, so I took the light boat and went quickly ahead—the difference in weight was incredible. At the top of the hill I climbed over a thorn bush boma that guarded the mealie fields. A whistle stopped me in my tracks, then a bou-bou shrike called again and I laughed at being caught.

I turned round to look for Miles, but the only object in sight was a tortoise-like shape crawling up the hill—Miles under the canoe, creeping uphill on all fours. Some girls working in the fields had been watching our progress, and they now burst into screams of laughter and clutched one

another for support. I dropped my canoe, cursing the women, and ran down to help Miles, but when I reached him we looked at each other and began laughing uproariously. For some time we lay there, unable to move; anything either of us said, no matter how stupid, was enough to send us into fits of renewed laughter—our first laughter since leaving Maritzburg. Eventually we struggled weakly to our feet and carried the canoe to the top of the hill.

The girls waved gaily as we moved over the brow down the short cut that saved us fifteen miles of twisting, boulder-strewn Umsindusi. Before we had covered half a mile of the maze of footpaths that led to the Umgeni, we were panting with exhaustion. The bush, shimmering in the fierce heat, resounded with the shrill cries of insects. We disturbed a pair of drongos attacking a lizard buzzard as the canoes scraped the low overhanging bushes shading the dry river course; otherwise there was no sign of life.

We had to rest four more times before we reached the main dry watercourse that led to the Umgeni River. Once we both collapsed, and slept for half an hour before we could summon up the energy to pick up the canoes again. Walking in the soft sand made our calves ache, while the continual ripping of thorns on the canoe hulls added to our fatigue and irritability, and we snarled at each other for the most trivial reasons. Thirst, too, was driving us crazy; all we could think about was water.

About a quarter of a mile from the junction of the dry watercourse with the Umgeni is a cluster of boulders, and under these we saw small pools of clear water. Dropping the canoes we rushed forward and flung ourselves down on our bellies to drink noisily. When we stood up we had difficulty in not retching; every step of the last few hundred yards to the river was agony with water gurgling in our stomachs as we walked.

At last the Umgeni; the sight of it made my heart miss a beat. It was in flood. This meant trouble. If we went through the gorge we would never be able to line the canoes down the cataracts, which in turn would mean climbing out of the gorge over the worst imaginable country, where even mountain goats and bushbuck moved with difficulty. I had done it with Kurt and knew that it would finish Miles.

I told him what was involved, suggesting that we climb out of the valley and make for the pipeline road that led along the hills, then wound down to the Umfula trading store. It was a ghastly climb, but at least there were local footpaths to follow. I put it all to Miles, but he was tired, so tired that the sight of the river and the thought of canoeing a few miles was too strong a temptation. I fully appreciated his feelings, and were it not for having experienced what was to follow myself, I too would have had no

other thought but the river.

We pushed our canoes into the Umgeni and in a few seconds were moving fast down the main current. Miles was in front when we hit the first rapid; halfway down he slid onto a flat rock. For a few seconds he perched precariously, and then the canoe overturned broadside on and the full force of the Umgeni poured into the cockpit. My mind flashed back to the Umzimkulu trip; this, I thought, was the end of the race. Mercifully the inch-thick keel held; gradually the canoe swung round and bumped down the rapids with Miles clinging to the stern. He was badly shaken by this hammering. His shoulders were bruised and a bad cut over his eye was bleeding freely. We sat on a rocky island to rest. Blood poured from Miles's eye, colouring his shirt, dripping onto the white rock then rolling into the brown flood.

"What can we do about your eye?" I asked anxiously.

"Oh, let's leave the bloody thing. With a bit of luck I might bleed to death!" he answered.

Half an hour later a giant scab had formed on the cut, so we set off to paddle the few miles to the gorge. This stretch was pleasant canoeing, the Umgeni divided into many deep, rocky channels that in turn narrowed into swift rushes of water sliding over flat rocks. We swept down these channels with exhilarating speed, but the roar of the pounding water in the gorge ahead soon put an end to any pleasure. I wondered frantically how we could best avoid it.

I noticed a young herder on the left bank. His posture reminded me of the Dinkas at Malakal who stood like storks with one foot resting against the other knee; I had seen them many years before when returning from the war.

I hailed Miles and together we beached the canoes near the umfaan.

"Sakubona umfaan," I said.

"Yebo," he answered my greeting politely.

I asked him whether he knew of any path leading down the left bank to the Umfula store.

"There are many," he said portentously.

I pointed to the canoes and asked, "Do you think we could carry those along a path without much difficulty?"

He grinned, shrugging his shoulders.

"Why don't you go on the water?" he asked.

I gestured to the tumbling mass of water that poured over the jagged rocks.

"But those are boats!" he exclaimed.

It was obviously useless talking to him. He was probably bored with

watching the multi-coloured cattle and was hoping for conversation. Leaving the canoes, we walked a little way down to look for a decent path. Only a short distance away we found what looked like a well-beaten track, so we returned for the canoes.

Following the track for half a mile was easy going; I began to rejoice despite the heavy load. I thought we had found the key to the gorge, but my jubilation was short lived, for as we rounded a bend the path disappeared into a low, overhanging tunnel of bush. We had to crawl along on hands and knees, but after another hundred yards the path came to a dead stop. We turned, retraced our steps to the umfaan, and then walked upstream to put a little distance between us and the lip of the gorge. This would give us time to paddle across the swift Umgeni. We climbed into the canoes, a few quick strokes took us to the middle of the river, then by paddling and using the current we reached the opposite bank. As both canoes were now leaking we had to help each other tip all the water out before carrying them. Then we helped each other to get the canoes up. We portaged our way round the first thundering waterfall down a goat path that twisted among huge boulders until we passed the campsite where Kurt and I had camped the year before. For some inexplicable reason I searched, in vain of course, for traces of our campfire.

The day grew hotter and the sun beat down mercilessly. The white rocks threw back a glare that made our eyes smart and ache painfully. We were now in a bad way physically and had to stop every hundred yards for a rest and a drink of water. Since it was lukewarm, we were never satisfied. Miles groaned and I turned round to see that he had tripped and fallen. The cut over his eye had opened up again, but it was when I saw his feet that I realized he could not go much further; they were swollen to twice their normal size, while both heels were raw and festering.

A wave of compassion swept over me.

"Hell, I'm sorry I got you into this, Miles," I said.

"And I'm sorry I won't be able to go much further," he answered.

"Have another rest," I said. It was becoming my stock phrase.

While we were lying baking in the sun an old Zulu came singing up the path.

He stopped when he saw us and asked if we were fishing. I explained where we were going. He nodded his head gravely.

"What you need is beer," he said firmly. "Come! My muzi is not far and we will drink umquomboti."

We staggered upright and grabbed the canoes. He led the way, laughing and singing while he pointed out plants and trees.

"You see that one?" he would say. "A tiny drop of its sap in your eye

and you will be blind. Now that one the young women like, for they crush it and rub it on their bodies to make themselves smell nice. Ha-ha! This one is for people you don't like; boil the leaves and put the juice in the beer and everyone dies!"

He kept up an incessant commentary while we stumbled along the stony path. We both dropped into a short but deep sleep when we reached the muzi.

When we woke up he came over to me and asked where we were going. I explained once more in detail. His face set in a scowl as he unexpectedly said, "Umanga Nkosaan! Umanga abalungu!"

Anyway he brought the beer, so I had a long drink, which combined, with my exhausted state to make me very unsteady. Miles wisely abstained, whether from natural inclination or because he remembered the poisoned beer story, I do not know. The old man was annoyed.

"Drink!" he said imperiously.

Miles wearily shook his head.

"Never thought I'd see the day that you refused a drink, Miles, " I joked, feebly.

Eventually the old man promised to show us a footpath leading out of the gorge. Gathering up the canoes we plodded after him for a cruel hour under the pitiless sun, our heads buzzing with the singing of insects, only to end up in a worse predicament; the old man led us on a roundabout route back to the worst of the gorge rapids. We slumped down with our heads in the shade of the canoes.

"Let's go and have more beer," the old man muttered to me.

"Only if you carry the canoes to the Umfula store," I replied.

He shook his head indignantly, got up and stalked away, shouting abuse at ungrateful white men.

When he had disappeared Miles quietly remarked that he could carry the canoes no further.

It was no use urging him on; he was physically in a bad state, so bad in fact that it was amazing that he could have carried on for as long as he had done with his feet in such a horrible condition. He had shown great courage and endurance.

When we had rested again we hid the canoes in a dense patch of euphorbias, then started off for the Umfula trading store which we reached at sunset after three hours of strenuous hiking.

Mr. Bernard Page and his father gave us a warm welcome and fed us royally. I asked for news of the other canoeists and was shocked to hear that we were the only two left in the race. Long after we had gone to bed I lay awake wondering what to do. At last I made up my mind to carry on

44

alone; I was desperately afraid that the whole race would become a fiasco if someone didn't go right through this time, though the thought of those fifty long, lonely and tough miles was frightening. But this race was my idea and I had to establish it; this was the real test.

We awoke early the next morning and after a good breakfast began our trek back to fetch the canoes. Miles was still limping painfully as every step was pure agony for him, and it took us the whole day to get the canoes back.

Miles got a lift to Cato Ridge that evening then caught the Pullman home. I was sorry to see him go; we had been through a lot together and had established a firm friendship, but it was impossible to expect him to go any further.

I worked on my canoe late into the night, repairing the broken ribs and patching the canvas where it had worn through after constant rubbing on the rocks. Bernard Page brought me tea and encouraged my idea of going on alone.

In the early morning I heard the river come down; I wondered if I would reach Durban alive.

Later I went down the pipeline bridge to have a look at the river. It was a frightening sight; the rapids below the bridge were invisible except for an occasional yellow wave that began at the corner and rolled viciously up river, foaming and hissing until it broke. The noise from the gorge was terrifying, a thunderous, continuous roar, rising and falling in volume with the wind.

"Give it a miss!" I thought. "You'll never get out of this lot alive—you're crazy! Just look at the river, look at those waves—and the logs! If one hit you, it would be the end."

I walked quickly up the hill, straight into Bernard Page's lounge. I had made up my mind that I couldn't face the journey alone.

Bernard was drinking coffee. He must have sensed my feelings, for he rose immediately, saying, "Have a strong cup of coffee, it will put you right." As he poured the dark liquid into the cup he spoke quietly and earnestly.

"You've come a hell of a long way," he said. "Now, to cap it all, the river is in a raging flood. Don't let it put you off. This canoe race is going to be something great. You've started something and a lot of people believe in you—including me! Don't let them down: Get into that canoe and go!"

I drank the coffee and he led me to the kitchen where the intombi had prepared an enormous breakfast. Bernard's encouragement and the bellyful of food, which he knew I needed badly, made all the difference to my

outlook.

I examined the canoe again, made the final minor repairs, then with Bernard's help carried it to the river. Once again I was almost overcome with fear of the dark brown water; I desperately wanted to stay at the store, secure, but it was too late. In a daze I shook hands with Bernard and then climbed into the canoe. One gentle paddle—the boat shot forward into midstream. It was impossible to turn round to wave, so I held my paddles aloft when Bernard shouted, "Go to it, boy! You'll make it!"

After a few yards all my confidence surged back and I cursed myself for the display of cowardice at the store.

"You dirty yellow bastard!" I repeated aloud with increasing intensity. "Haven't got the guts of a white mouse! Why didn't you break down and blub like a schoolboy."

I cursed myself in this childish way—it was a relief, so I kept it up until the first big rapid, when I had to concentrate with every nerve. The canoe was sucked forward into the lip of the rapid; I held the paddles at the ready. Water flew from the blades into the river as the craft rushed forward with gathering speed. Two rocks appeared in front, awash at one moment, submerged the next; digging the left paddle blade in hard I guided the nose past the first rock, then using my right hand I pushed the bows away from the second rock. The canoe lifted dangerously, then righted itself as the current swept me on again.

Thirty feet away the main current swung sharply to the left, flowing over a flat boulder with a narrow channel on either side. I glanced quickly to the right—nothing but churning water and a mass of jutting rocks; only one way to go, so I paddled to the left, straight for the flat boulder. As I reached it the prow of the canoe slid gracefully along until the weight of my body forced the centre onto the rock, where it stuck. The stern began to turn dangerously. I struggled to lever myself over the boulder with the paddles, but as I turned the canoe in the right direction, a log swept into the channel and crashed into the side, so that I lost my balance. The canoe filled with water and I battled to right myself, but the relentless pressure of the river, forcing the log forward, pushed the craft right over. I fell out, then I was swept beyond the canoe, but hung onto the paddles and pulled myself back, hand over hand up the rope attaching the paddles to the canoe. Then I swam downstream, guiding the canoe through the channels to a small island in the centre of the rapid.

It was an exhausting job, pulling the waterlogged canoe out, then lifting it up and getting rid of the water. Eventually it was ready and I got in—one leg in the middle of the floorboards, the paddles inside, hands gripping both gunwales and the other leg outside to give a good shove off.

The rest of the rapid was comparatively easy and I was soon moving down a calm but swift-flowing section. I paddled with deep racing strokes and the canoe whipped along. Rounding a corner I heard a shout and saw a very well built Zulu man gesticulating with a bowl in his hands.

"Puza! Puza!" he shouted laughingly.

"Cha! Cha! Yebonga!" I yelled in reply, as I swept past.

The bush weir, covered by the floodwater, gave me no trouble. I paddled past the old store down a few minor rapids, soon reaching the long flat stretches on the way to Khumalo's store. With the river as high as it was, the going was easy, until the familiar thunder of rapids drew nearer. Ahead was a great pile of driftwood and enormous logs which had formed a rapid, so broad that I had to carry the canoe round it. It was now near midday; the sun was burning hot and in spite of being well tanned, my insteps and calves were painfully sunburnt. A herd of drinking oxen gave me inspiration; scooping up parts of their wet dung I plastered it on the tender, sunburnt areas, knowing it would harden and give protection from the sun, as indeed it did.

After an hour's uninterrupted canoeing I once more heard rapids ahead—an almost welcome sound as it meant, for a change, less paddling. As I approached the rapid it was obvious that it would be foolhardy to try to negotiate it without looking for a channel, so I beached the canoe, then walked along the bank, searching for a suitable passage.

To the left was a likely looking patch of marshy ground; I had barely taken two paces when something moved under my right foot. I looked down to see, with a shock of horror, a night adder, striking. I leapt back, hardly aware of the sharp, stinging sensation in my leg, I ran flat out to the canoe. There I washed the dung off—this had undoubtedly saved me from the full bite. One fang had penetrated the skin while the other had left a scratch. This was bad enough; in rising panic I delved into my rucksack and with shaking fingers withdrew a phial of permanganate of potash and a small blade, then slashed at the fang marks. The pain increased sharply as I rubbed the crystals into the raw flesh, and I felt nauseous and very frightened; night adders, I knew, were dangerous. My panic mounted with the increasing pain—had the snake managed to inject a lethal dose? What on earth could I do, I wondered dazedly.

At last I remembered there was a bus that ran between the Black reserve and Inanda; the road could not be more than a few miles away; so, lifting the canoe, I set off. Only a mile later pain forced me to leave the canoe and struggle on alone, staggering with a blinding headache that shattered my head at every step. I reached the road on the point of exhaustion, to lie spewing and coughing in the shade of a scraggy acacia,

hoping that a bus would pass some time during the day.

A group of singing Africans appeared; they glanced at me casually in response to my query about the bus, then walked on, singing and laughing. I was by then on the verge of tears in my pain and despair, but realized my appearance was far from imposing: long, matted hair, several days growth of beard, tattered shorts, a blood-spattered red scarf (Miles's blood), one leg plastered in dung and, to cap it all, the remains of a partly digested breakfast lying near me.

I was violently ill again, then fell asleep. It must have been over an hour later when a headache, which defies description, woke me; my leg looked as thought it had begun to swell, but it was difficult to see through the pain. Another bout of sickness followed, then faintly came the sound of a vehicle. I stood up groggily, feebly waving my red scarf at the oncoming vehicle. It stopped and the Indian driver climbed down to speak to me. I will never forget his kindness and understanding; he listened to my garbled story, dispatched some Africans to fetch my canoe, then helped me onto the bus. I collapsed, sleeping, on a back seat—short-lived oblivion, for a stunted, drunken African sat a few inches away from me, playing a mouth organ. On and on he played until I screamed at him to stop; he took no notice, so in my state of enraged agony I tried to hit him—he moved a few inches away, yelled with laughter, and began playing again. Even my being sick did not deter him.

I had reached the end of my tether when the bus stopped and the driver came to help me get off.

"This is the Inanda Police Station," he said. "The sergeant here will help you."

With no second bidding I grabbed my haversack and staggered to the door, climbed down and tottered to the police station. An African sergeant who was in charge took me to a room and let me lie down. Soon a vehicle drew up and I heard a European speaking.

"Is this another inquest?" he asked. Then he came into the room and introduced himself—Sergeant Smuts. The relief of speaking to someone who understood was almost too much for me.

Sergeant Smuts left the room to fetch a snakebite outfit.

"Never given an injection before," he muttered, "but you've got to have one now!"

He filled a syringe and jabbed the thick needle into my buttocks, arms and back. Five hours later the relief from pain and nausea enabled me to drink and eat a little.

Only then did I notice that something was wrong with my shoulder, so I asked Sergeant Smuts to have a look at it. He examined me and said that it was dislocated; after moving my arm about and rubbing in various places he pronounced it better than before.

I was very grateful for all his help.

The following day I tried everywhere to find someone to help me get the canoe to the river; in the end an Indian storekeeper came to my rescue. I have always liked the Indian community of Natal; polite and courteous, they are frequently most helpful and, I think, one of the most law-abiding peoples in South Africa. It was a rough road leading to the river, and the car was battered when we reached the Umgeni, but the storekeeper was very kind about it all; he refused all offers of payment.

The final seventeen miles to Durban were most unpleasant; I was violently ill several times before reaching the pumphouse where I was able to coast the rest of the way without fear of further rapids.

The smell of the sea gave me fresh heart. I paddled on to the mouth—the end of the trip. A small group of holidaymakers stared at me as though at a freak—I didn't blame them.

I was taken to Miles Brokensha's house, given some clothes and tea, then caught the Pullman back to Maritzburg that evening. Once again severe attacks of dysentery and cramp followed; I spent a restless night.

On Monday morning I reported for work, knowing that there was going to be trouble: I was two days overdue from my leave, and factories do not take kindly to that sort of thing. It was hardly possible for me to feel contrite at that stage, and besides I was still suffering from the effects of the snakebite and the exhaustion of the whole journey.

I was called to the secretary's office. He was very rude and immediately began to castigate me for coming late. I was in no mood to argue, so replied that if he didn't like it he knew exactly what he could do. He at once changed his attitude—he had no doubt expected me to crawl, but this is something I've never been in the habit of doing.

"Come, come!" he said. "You are sorry you have come back to work late, aren't you?"

His approach was too late: his initial rudeness had made me extremely angry, so that it was without hesitation that I replied, "No!"

He was taken aback and tried to smooth things over, but he must have known he was wasting his time.

"I have no option but -" he began.

"Yes I know all about that," I said, abruptly. "All I want is a month's pay in lieu of notice."

I got it.

I have never been sorry for losing that job. Some time before I had applied for work as a game ranger.

CHAPTER 4

I was struck with Fred Schmidt's personality and particularly with his sense of humour. We usually went home together after Canoe Club meetings, and we discovered a common and fanatical interest in fishing. Fred's family were famous fishermen on the Natal coast and his brother, Lefty Schmidt, held many records. As we became more friendly, I asked Fred if he would like to have a go at the next canoe race; but in order that we should get to know each other well, I suggested that we do a trip down the Umkomaas river first. Fred was agreeable, so we started making arrangements and getting all the necessary kit together. I had a light, but very strong, canoe of canvas and Philippine mahogany, which proved to be one of the best I ever owned. Fred was keen to experiment with a light and narrow canoe; the journey turned out to be a nightmare for him because his canoe was so unstable.

During a week-end towards the end of March, 1952, we went to Josephine's Bridge on the Maritzburg-Ixopo road, left the car under some trees and walked twenty miles down river, having a good look at the rapids and anything else of interest.

We camped above a bend and began fishing. The water was alive with barbel and eel, and for two hours we pulled out fish after fish. Some people might scorn dirty barbel and eel as sporting fish, but to fanatical fishermen like us it was a taste of paradise. As darkness fell, we realized how hungry we were, so Fred set to cooking barbel and eels. His knowledge was expert, and in half an hour he had produced a first-class meal. Never had fish tasted so good!

After dinner we baited up again and threw in, then left the rods with the ratchets on while we lay near the fire and tried to sleep. An umfaan walked past on the footpath above and asked whether we were not afraid of the mambas that lived on the ridge overhead. This gave us quite a start. We had been so busy fishing that we had not worried to look for a good camping spot. It was too dark to move, so we built up a smoky fire and lay down again.

I had barely fallen asleep, when a ratchet screamed. We both made a

grab at our rods and almost knocked each other into the river in our excitement. With muttered curses, we grabbed our respective rods and struck hard. The fish was on Fred's line and I watched his rod bending at an acute angle in the starlight. A few minutes later he hauled in a 15 lb. eel. We baited up and threw in again, and crept back to the fire to sleep. Five minutes had hardly passed when the ratchets screamed. We dived for the rods and struck.

"I'm on!" yelled Fred.

"Me too!" I shouted excitedly.

The fish cut across-river and we battled in the dark to sense which way they were going. Gradually it became obvious that our lines had crossed. Bad language flowed like the river, and we reached a point of almost pushing each other into the water. Knowing that I would come off second best. I was prepared to hang on desperately and pull Fred in with me. Eventually reason prevailed, and we managed to lift two huge eels on to the stony ledge, then spent an hour untangling our lines. I had reached saturation point and wanted nothing but sleep, but Fred's blood lust was up and he wanted to go on fishing. All night long his ratchet screamed, as he pulled out eel and barbel galore; by dawn the next day he had caught well over twenty-five fish. It had been an exhausting night for him, but never had I seen a more smug and satisfied expression on anyone's face. He was in his element. If he had ever had any misgivings about going down the Umkomaas, they were forgotten now, and wild horses could not have stopped him.

On our way back to the car we noticed a well-kept muzi on the slopes of a green hill; we made our way towards it, hoping to get a khamba of Zulu beer. On a hot day, with a long walk ahead, there is nothing to beat tshwala. A Zulu kehla came out and greeted us politely. At our request he brought a pannikin of cold beer and we drank noisily; he smiled at our thirst and jokingly said that it was fortunate that the valley was not populated with people like ourselves, otherwise the river would always be dry.

As he grew more expansive, I asked him about the lore of the valley. He said that wild animals had ceased to be of any significance many years before. In his youth he and his father had hunted leopard that used to live in the krantz overlooking the river, and he pointed to a precipitous slab of rock overhanging a ravine. When he was an umfaan he remembered white men coming from Richmond and Ixopo to shoot the crocodile that once inhabited the pool where we had been fishing the night before.

Baboons had plagued the valley dwellers by swooping on the ripening crops and destroying many weeks of toil in a few hours. The

baboons seemed to know that the women were powerless to act, and only when the men came storming home from a beer drink would they beat a hasty retreat. The tribesmen persuaded a group of white farmers to help, and within a year the baboons had been reduced to one troop. Late one afternoon this troop was surrounded and wiped out with rifle fire.

The old man seemed a little sad when he spoke of the animals, and I wondered if he was sorry they had gone. He must have read my thoughts, because he smiled wistfully and said, "We were sorely troubled by the wild animals, but they gave us much sport and kept us fit when we hunted them. Now there is nothing left to hunt, and we all grow fat and lazy sitting in the shade of our huts while the women till the fields."

On reflection, I only wish that more Africans had the same sentiments as this kehle. There would be more wild animals left and Africa would not be losing its age-old character so rapidly.

For the next week we bought supplies and made preparations for our journey; then on Saturday, 5th April 1952, we motored to Josephine's Bridge again with our two canoes balanced on the hood of my old Nash.

In the cold, grey dawn mist we pushed our canoes into the muddy racing waters of the Umkomaas and paddled down the first stretch towards the sea. Our excitement was subdued, because this was a journey that no one had ever before attempted. As the first rays of the sun flashed on our paddles I thought how strange it was that in this twentieth century there was still so much adventure, so much to conquer.

As we rounded the bend I heard Jack Shepherd Smith, my companion of the first canoe trip, shout out, "Take it easy, you silly bastards!" The term was one of endearment.

"Enzanzi nemfula!" we roared in reply, hoping that our voices would at least sound brave. Then we were round the first bend in the river and Jack was lost to sight. For the next seven days we should be out of communication with the outside world, for there was hardly a chance of seeing a white man until we reached the river mouth at Umkomaas village.

As we approached the first line of rapids, I noticed that my fifty-pound pack was a little too big to fit into the prow of the canoe; I could see that Fred was also having difficulty with his. We were fully laden with sheath knives, groundsheets, cane knives, biltong, beans, coffee, sugar, snakebite outfit and a small camera. We had divided everything, in case one of us came to grief; this would mean half rations only, but at least there would be something to eat.

The roar of the rapids grew louder. Then my canoe shot forward and bobbed about in the frothing maelstrom; by paddling and back-paddling I managed to ease my way past a dangerous-looking outcrop; then I raced

off at a frightening speed. I breathed with relief at getting past this hazard, when suddenly my canoe grounded on a flat, submerged rock—a canoeist's nightmare; slowly the canoe turned round and faced upstream. I saw Fred come racing towards me, stroking madly in an effort to avoid hitting my canoe. Then I turned over and was swept downstream by the current. I hung on grimly and prayed that nothing had fallen out. Half a mile further down, the river deposited me in a pool, where I struggled out on to a sandy beach. As I dragged the canoe up, I saw Fred's hat come bobbing down. He too had turned over. I gave him a hand to retrieve his belongings as he spat out a stream of brown, muddy water.

"Curse and blast this canoe!" he said. "It's going to give me a lot of trouble." His words were prophetic.

We took stock of our position and were alarmed to see that half my foodstuffs were ruined because of a leaking American oilcloth bag. Within an hour of starting, we knew that we should have to be on half-rations for the rest of the trip. Our morale suffered a serious blow, but a few minutes later we safely got over another set of bad rapids and started singing as we made our way down a silent, calm stretch.

"What the hell are we going to do about grub?" I asked.

"Ah, moenie worry nie!" Fred laughed. "Have you forgotten how many fish there are in this river?"

"Seven days of fried barbel doesn't sound so good to me I" I said.

"We can always buy mealies from the locals. Cooked in the coals they taste pretty good at any time," Fred replied.

We started to go faster, then we heard the familiar roar of more rapids. I paddled ahead to recce the position and Fred followed. This lot was worse than the first; I battled to keep my balance as the canoe ploughed through waves that were over three feet high, then turned round to warn Fred; but he had already turned over, and I saw him trailing behind his torpedo-shaped canoe. I could not suppress a grin at his anxious expression; but there was no time to laugh, as my canoe crashed against boulders and rolled from side to side, shipping water at every wave. Eventually the water was over my knees, and every muscle strained as I tried to paddle and guide the canoe between the rocks. Gradually these rocks got less, and the river calmer; then I was in a smooth stretch again. I grabbed some overhanging foliage and waited for Fred, who soon came up cursing.

"The trouble with this bloody death-trap is that there are no splash boards," he said. "Every time I hit a wave the water pours straight into the cockpit, and I start to sink; by the time I hit the fourth wave I am travelling below water."

We pressed on and I kept about two hundred yards ahead. At the start of every rapid I could hear Fred cursing loudly, both at his canoe and at me for not waiting. We hit one set of rapids that were rougher than most; I managed to jump them without turning, then waited in the pool below for Fred to arrive.

The first wave he hit half filled his canoe, the second swung him sideways on and only by superhuman effort did he turn in the right direction, only to be submerged by a third wave. He was up to his neck in water but went on paddling, and above the roar of the rapids floated some obscene oaths. Finally, all I could see was a pair of paddles held out of the water like a periscope, and a hat bobbing down the waves. Once he surfaced and spat water in all directions. I nearly turned my own canoe over I laughed so much.

Fred was really irritable, and who could blame him; from first light to sunset he was wet and miserable and missing the glorious thrill of jumping rapids. He had more than courage to keep on going.

The river was already in the shadows and we were chilled by the east wind, so we paddled on until we found a sloping bank where we could tie up our canoes. Stiff and weary, we climbed out and dragged the canoes a safe distance, then set about looking for firewood.

Running around soon made us warm, but our appetites increased proportionately, and with Fred's six-foot-three frame to fill, food was going to be short. Two black duck flew up the river and we threw stones at them in desperation. A vain hope! Then Fred disappeared for an hour. I made the fire and got the billy boiling, then baited a couple of hooks with a piece of moulding biltong.

It was almost dark before Fred returned, and I shouted with delight when I saw that he was carrying an armful of mealies. We built the fire into a blaze that the forewarners of the Spanish Armada would have envied, then cooked the mealies and drank coffee. The fish were biting and Fred caught two enormous eels. He cut them into slices and we toasted them over the coals.

We put on every spare stitch of clothing—I must say I had more than Fred—and crept as near to the fire as possible.

One of the purposes of this canoe trip, for me, was to find out whether Fred would be a good partner on the next race. Before the morning was finished, I had had my answer: his guts, determination and sense of humour made him an ideal companion.

For Fred the night was uncomfortable in the extreme, and I woke up twice to find him sleeping on top of the remains of the fire. In spite of his sleeveless jersey smouldering, he had not been aware of the fire, and had

even expressed annoyance at being wakened from his first decent sleep.

At first light in the morning we were off without even a cup of coffee to warm our aching bodies, for we knew that if we delayed our departure it would be midday before we got away. Breakfast in the veld always seems to take twice as long as any other meal.

We had two good hours' canoeing, then stopped, made a fire and boiled the billy for a cup of coffee. I know of no other smell, with the exception of nthombothi wood, that can recall the atmosphere of the bush as coffee can. Blending with the wood smoke and coming at a time when the body is crying for relief, it tastes like the nectar of the Gods. For hundreds of years it has been part of every explorer's grub box, and we in our humble way were emulating the old giants.

The scenery was breathtaking, and far more overpowering than the Valley of a Thousand Hills, which I had once thought supreme. Gigantic krantzes loomed up round every bend, and ravines with bushy banks spilled clear, cold water into the main stream. In the geological past fantastic soil erosion must have taken place and left this magnificent relic for twentieth century man.

White fleecy clouds drifted lazily over the blue mountains in the distance, and flat-topped acacia trees perched on the skyline. Kingfishers flitted across our path, their brilliance mirrored for a few seconds in the silent pools on the edge of the river. The riverine vegetation was thick, with phoenix palms and monkey vines predominating. Tall ficus trees grew along the flatter portions of the river's meandering course. An occasional monkey chattered in the trees as we glided by, but the sound was drowned by the noise of the next rapids.

Our luck had held and we had shot rapid after rapid with no danger of falling in. This was canoeing at its best: to be alone under the wide blue sky after weeks in a smog-ridden city was an exhilarating experience. For the first time I think I understood why Christ had gone out into the desert to spend his forty days and forty nights under the stars and the burning sun.

I looked behind the saw that Fred was deep in thought as he paddled along with his easy stroke, his tall, lithe body glistening with sweat in the bright noonday sun. I put a little more effort into my paddling, and felt my chest and arm muscles stretch as the paddles bit into the water. We had been moving for well over three hours and neither of us had spoken; the sound of a human voice would have shattered the wonderful peace that was spread around us. It was good to know that we were within calling distance, but other than that we were content to leave each other alone.

Every time the river took a bend there was a set of rapids to negotiate and some were over a mile long. We were fortunate that they were mild;

indeed it was a pleasant thrill to feel the canoe leap forward like a racehorse, as the swift water caught the frail wood and canvas; for two or three anxious minutes there would be a chance that the canoe would overturn, so every sinew and muscle would be used to keep the craft on an even course. We covered mile after mile in this way, and although I knew how easy it was to fall into the trap of believing that the river was benevolent, I began to wonder if there was anything really dangerous about the journey. The fear of what might be lying round the next comer is part and parcel of the joy of canoeing: it keeps the mind alert and makes one savour every second of the placid waters and easy rapids.

In the early hours of the afternoon we heard the dull booming of a very bad set of rapids, so we kept close together and, paddling near the bank, cautiously made our way towards the next bend and the rapids. As we rounded the comer, I saw that they were impossible to shoot, so I shouted to Fred to make for the bank. We clambered out and walked a few yards downstream to see how far we would have to carry. The din was fantastic and we had to shout to make ourselves heard.

Just as we were about to start lugging the canoes over the boulder-strewn flood plain, a long line of ntombis came walking down a local footpath. They looked at us with astonishment, then walked shyly forward and stared at the canoes. Fred did a few jive steps and sang, "Don't roll those bloodshot eyes at me!"

The ntombis thought Fred was screamingly funny and they crowded round, begging us to let them carry the canoes. They didn't meet with much opposition. Before we knew what had happened two abafana had appeared from nowhere, picked up my canoe and run off ahead. Three girls grabbed Fred's canoe and in no time had passed the abafana and were racing like hares to the end of the rapids. Fred galloped after them in a panic in case they fell and damaged the precious canoe. I cried with laughter as he tried to keep up with the fleet-footed girls. Every now and then he would stub his toes, and curse and scream at the girls for going too fast. They thought he was singing and acting, and shouted with laughter at his antics. Fred was not amused. Panting, and almost exhausted, he managed to catch them up and cling to his canoe before they gaily pushed it into the river.

"These bloody women wanted to shove the canoe into the river!" Fred snarled.

The girls stood around giggling, then shouted and waved as we pushed off into the muddy stream.

The rest of the afternoon was a nightmare. Gone was the peacefulness of the morning and the rapids we had jumped so easily. The

river narrowed and the water bubbled and foamed over dangerous rocks. Fred fell in over and over again, as he battled to keep his frail, narrow canoe from smashing against jagged rocks and boulders. I turned over twice; all our clothes were saturated and the remnants of our food were a soggy mess. We stopped once to smoke our last two cigarettes. Fred was shivering uncontrollably as he struggled to strike the wet matches. Neither of us spoke, because each knew the other's thoughts. Fred was worse off than I, and I didn't want him to remind me, because I felt terrible and didn't want to imagine how he was feeling.

We decided to keep going until sunset for, according to our small-scale map, we still had many miles to go before we reached our second day's target. The bends in the river were now death traps because of the whirlpools they set up. No matter how hard one paddled, one felt as though the paddles were passing through air.

After two hours of the hardest going, we started to look for a camping site. The river was running swiftly through deep, narrow gorges. At the end of one gorge two huge arches stretched across, almost meeting. I felt my canoe gathering momentum as we passed beneath and raced round a corner. Eventually the river flowed between two clumps of rocks that were not more than thirty feet from each other. I shot between them, then shouted a warning to Fred as I saw the enormous waves at the foot of a nasty-looking rapid. More by good luck than good judgment I managed to keep the canoe on an even keel and bounced my way over the rapids, through the waves and into the safety of a pool.

I turned to see how Fred was faring. He got over the rapids but his cockpit was too full of water to get him through the waves. In slow motion he sank lower and lower until the canoe was out of sight and only his torso was visible, then his submerged craft struck a rock and he disappeared.

It was the end of a ghastly afternoon: a few yards downstream we dragged the canoes into a gulley and set about making camp. It was agony trying to walk and warm up our frozen limbs after having sat in one position for hours on end, but there was little time to lose, for darkness was falling fast and firewood was scattered. I returned with a pile of wood to find that Fred had discovered another mealie field from which he had collected a large bundle of mealies.

"We eat again," he said with a smile.

"Did you see anyone near the fields?" I asked, anxious to try to check our position.

"Not a soul," Fred replied. "These mealies have been unattended for ages."

We looked about in the gathering gloom, thinking that at least one

curious local must have seen us arrive. I had the feeling we were being watched, but no one came forward. An owl screeched from the bush above us, and nightjars flitted about, chasing insects. Two bats swooped low over our heads and frogs set up a quiet chorus. A myriad of stars appeared in the dark sky, as Venus began to drop on the western horizon. Our fire was burning fiercely, and we crawled nearer to get the full measure of warmth. Fred hugged his long legs then got up and slipped his jersey on like a pair of slacks. The fire spluttered and showered us with sparks when the billy boiled over. Oblivious to heat, for our hands had become hardened with hours of canoeing, we grabbed the billy and made coffee.

With torn, wet clothes, unshaven chins and unruly hair, we looked a pair of desperadoes, and I didn't blame the locals for not coming near. There is no doubt that one's physical appearance can affect one's mental attitude profoundly, for we felt like animals and acted with animal cunning in our efforts to stay alive and conquer the river. I found that imagination played a very small part as I battled against the river and the elements. Time became a different factor and I realized how puny man really is. It was also easier to understand the mind of primitive people; they had been battling against the elements since time began. It was understandable, too, how they became such easy prey to superstitions and other primitive fancies. The darkness of the night, the owls, bats, frogs and the screams of the bush babies, all this was the right setting for those who had no strong will and listened instead to the twisted mind of the witchdoctors.

A light easterly wind blew up which moaned and sighed in the tall trees, drowning the sound of the chattering rapids at the foot of the next krantz.

"I wish to hell I had a cigarette," Fred said, breaking the spell. "It's going to be miserably cold tonight and if these clothes don't get dry, I'll freeze."

He placed the steaming clothes nearer the fire.

"One of these days I'm going to invent some sort of light, waterproof blanket that poor canoeists like ourselves can carry in a small canoe. This freezing at night is going to be the death of me," he said as he pushed more wood onto the fire.

It was a great pity we were unable to carry blankets or a sleeping bag, but as everything got soaking wet every time the canoe turned over, it was pointless taking them. I eyed my torn and wet jerseys and wondered how much longer they would last.

When all our clothes were more or less dry we put them on and lay down next to the fire to sleep.

I woke early next morning to hear Fred's teeth chattering in the

darkness.

"God! I'm cold!" he moaned.

I was stiff and sore myself so I knew how he felt.

We were on the river by the time the sun's rays pierced the blanket of white clouds on the horizon. The riverine forest was alive with birdcalls to which I listened with delight, forgetting for a few minutes the aches and pains of a disturbed night. The river almost doubled back on itself at places. The scenery was magnificent, with light mist rolling down the valleys and lingering on the table-topped hills, making an unforgettable impression.

At midday we reached a long calm stretch and Fred took the lead. For the next hour he maintained a cracking pace, and I had to work extremely hard to keep up with him. Then we had an experience that is best told in Fred's own words.

"I was about thirty yards in front of you and out of the corner of my eye I saw two black flashes shoot into the water. They were heading straight across my path and I was going into fast water. I was in two minds whether to back paddle or go like hell because I realized that the flashes were mating mambas. They swam to about ten feet in front of me then coiled round each other and balanced on their tails. They playfully struck at each other then fell with a plop into the water. As their heads turned away I put every bit of strength I had into the paddles, and literally made the canoe skim along the top of the water. I took the rapid as if it had been a mere riffle, then made for the opposite bank to wait for you."

I had been watching two pied kingfishers diving on a shoal of small fish and had missed the drama in front of me.

We pulled our canoes out of the water and sat down to rest. Fred was chalk-white after his experience. An umfaan herding a flock of black and white goats came towards us. After he greeted us, we asked casually how far the nearest store was.

"Dusa," (near) he replied, pointing to the top of a hill.

"Let's go and replenish our supplies," Fred said.

The thought of fresh bread and cigarettes was too much for us both, so we told the umfaan to lead on and show us the way.

For two solid hours we climbed out of the valley and up a steep mountain path. Fred was barefooted, having lost his shoes on the first day. The umfaan walked over a patch of pronged devil thorns without even stopping for a second to pull them out. Fred followed, then let out a yell that echoed down the valley. The umfaan whipped round as though he had been struck, and I was ready to run, thinking it was at least another pair of mating mambas.

When we did reach the store the storekeeper was on the point of closing up and refused to serve us. I was carrying a single-barrelled .410 shotgun and Fred swears I threatened to shoot the man if he would not co-operate. All I know is that I was dead tired after walking up that terrible mountain and we were not going to go back empty-handed. We could hardly blame the man, though, for we looked a wild pair.

We bought a tin of jam and three loaves of bread, and at once sat down to a wonderful meal.

The return journey to the river was broken at a kraal where the headman gave us a khamba (gourd) of beer, which we drank willingly. It certainly helped us on our way and made the walk seem shorter. We arrived at the canoes to find they had been ransacked and the last bit of sugar we had hoarded so carefully had been stolen. It was a hard blow. Without sugar our suffering was going to be increased a hundred fold, for it was sugar that gave us energy. We ranted and raved, but it was no good. Cursing ourselves for being stupid enough to believe an umfaan when he said a place was "Dusa", we climbed into the canoes and paddled on downstream.

Late in the afternoon we met a large group of Africans taking their cattle down to drink. Above the lowing and bellowing, one old man told us of a store a mile or two further on. Fred and I looked at each other when the old chap said the store was near the river.

"I've heard that story once today, and that's enough for me!" Fred said.

I echoed his sentiments and we thanked the kehla and paddled on. Fifteen minutes later we rounded a curve in the river and saw a small wattle and daub store perched on the bank. It was almost too good to be true. We hastily tied up the canoes and made our way towards the building. A short, stocky African came out to greet us, introducing himself as "Frans", the storeowner.

Frans treated us as though we were royalty. Calling his wife, he told her to get a hut ready for us while he made a cup of tea. He poured thick, sweet condensed milk into the tea, which we gulped down hot. Then we were led to a spacious rondavel and given a wonderful meal of currie and rice. After this beds with white sheets were made up, and in a few minutes we were sound asleep.

When we awoke the next morning, Frans's wife gave us coffee and rusks. While we were waiting for breakfast, Frans showed us round his store and told us the difficulties he had in making a living so far from the main road. Using donkeys and a small cart, he had to collect his stores from more than fifteen miles away, and as he had only a little capital it

meant frequent journeys. I admired his courage in setting up a store so far from the main bulk of population where he would have stood a better chance of making a living, but this was where he had been born and he had come back to serve his people. He deserved success. We will never forget his hospitality.

It was late before we got away from kindly Frans and paddled on down the river. The going was hard and for the first time on the trip we spent most of the day lining the canoes down rapids. It was exhausting work and we blessed Frans and his wonderful meals.

Frequently we would slip and come down hard on the jagged boulders. It was imperative to keep the canoes moving in the main stream and to do this we had to run alongside, jumping from rock to rock. At times we had to get into the water and follow the canoes down a bad set of rapids. Holding on grimly, we would edge our way down inch by inch, then hang on to the back and float the craft into the calm water, get in for a few minutes, then climb out at another set of bad rapids.

By four o'clock in the afternoon we had only covered about seven miles and a severe thunderstorm was building up in the south. Dark, black clouds were racing overhead and sheets of white lightning lit up the southern horizon. Thunder rolled and echoed about the valley. Nothing can be more frightening than a thunderstorm sweeping over the hills and into deep, ironstone kloofs. I saw Fred looking apprehensively up at the skies, and I wondered where we were going to find shelter. We had just come through a frightful set of rapids, quite the worst I had ever experienced, and our nerves were on edge. I stumbled and fell into the water as another whiplash of thunder cracked viciously overhead.

Half carrying and half dragging the canoes, we ploughed our way through some shallows, then leapt in to paddle down a flat stretch. On the right hand bank I saw some African children to whom I shouted, asking if there was a store nearby. They pointed to the top of a hill—"A school is there!" they shouted.

Leaving Fred with the canoes, I made my way up to look for the African schoolmaster, and found him in his office, marking a pile of essays. Speaking in English I asked whether he could give us shelter for the night; this he very kindly agreed to do; then he took me to the schoolroom where he said we could make ourselves comfortable.

It was dark when I got back to the river, to find Fred surrounded by a crowd of screaming children and a half crazed old man who looked like the local witch doctor. The old man was dancing around, yelling at the top of his voice. The din was terrible. Fred had his hands over his ears and was pleading with them to keep quiet. After such an exhausting day, I knew

that Fred's nerves were in a bad way, and to be subjected to this onslaught was enough to turn anyone's mind. My sudden arrival seemed to quieten the mob a little, so I took advantage of the lull and, swearing at the witchdoctor, told him to beat it. Then I turned and asked the children to help us carry the canoes to the schoolroom.

"Thank God you came!" said Fred, with feeling. "If they'd gone on much longer I would have had to kill someone. My head felt as if it was splitting. I pleaded and begged them to keep quiet, but the old swine of a witchdoctor kept starting them off again. I don't know what got into them."

When we reached the schoolroom we were greeted by a fat old Zulu who told us in perfect English that he had worked for a lawyer in Maritzburg. This had certainly left its mark, for at the end of every sentence he would declaim, "I tell you, my Lords, it is null and void." The old character kept us in fits of laughter with his legal jargon and we were sorry to see him go off to his homestead.

A schoolgirl brought us a basin of warm water, soap and a clean towel, and told us that the schoolmaster was expecting us to dinner. By scrubbing hard we managed to get some of the grime and muck of the river off our hands and arms, but the pungent smell of muddy water lingered on our ragged clothes.

We had just reached the schoolmaster's hut when the storm broke and a deluge poured from the black skies.

"Thank God we're not out in that lot!" Fred muttered.

Water cascaded past the hut in torrents and the wind lashed enormous raindrops against the windows, with a sound like hail. We could not make ourselves heard above the storm so we ate with great relish the plates of rice and goat meat. Our extreme hunger made the schoolmaster and his two women assistants stare at us in wonder. When we had finished eating, thick black coffee and cigarettes were provided. It was a wonderful meal and we had done more than justice to the food.

The noise of the storm dropped, and for a while we talked. I asked the schoolmaster to tell us about his occupation; although badly paid he enjoyed the work he was doing and got great intellectual satisfaction from teaching.

"It is a great adventure," he said, "to take small children from the kraals and start teaching them from scratch. The sum total of their knowledge is how to look after the cattle and goats, or how to trap birds and animals. But from the moment they enter the schoolroom they become devoted to learning and I almost have to force them to go home in the afternoons. It might interest you to hear," he continued, "how, when some

little abafana come to school for the first time and peer at a slate, their eyes water profusely, yet they can go home in the afternoon and squat round a smoky wood fire without even so much as a tear forming in their eyes."

After about an hour, someone brought out an old gramophone and one record. For the next two hours I listened, ad nauseam, to "Please don't roll those Bloodshot Eyes at Me."

Fred captivated everybody by jiving energetically to the music. He fell a few times, owing to the stiffness of his knees, but this only added to the general merriment at his antics. When he got really warmed up he had the audience gasping and cheering as he executed some very tricky steps. We left when the rain had died down to a gentle patter on the thatched roof. Stars winked in the inky blackness, and the earth smelt cool and fresh after the storm. Frogs called from every direction and we could hear that the river had risen.

Our night was peaceful and we awoke to hear the young children arriving for school at dawn. There were muttered exclamations when they saw us lying on their workbenches, but they soon overcame their shyness and surged forward to ask us questions.

While we were dragging the canoes out I heard the children chanting the first prayers of the day, then they sang a hymn. I don't think singing has ever moved me as it did that morning. Their young, rich and melodious voices rang out in a harmony I have never heard equalled. I had tears in my eyes as we said good-bye to our very pleasant host and made our way to the river. As we floated away the children broke into "Glory, Glory Hallelujah", and it echoed down the river until we reached the rapids where the sound was drowned.

The river was flowing swiftly after the rain and the foliage lining the banks looked green and luxuriant. Crickets still chirruped and frogs croaked their thankfulness. A pair of trumpeter hornbills flew out from the bush and flapped across our path, uttering their weird and mournful cries. Gradually the sun rose higher in the bright blue sky and warmed our stiff limbs. We paddled quietly, afraid to speak for fear of breaking the wild peace that is only Africa's. From the top of one of the green hills an African broke the silence with a plaintive tune, a woman took up the refrain and together they harmonized. The music was beautiful and I stopped to listen. This was the music of old Africa, undisturbed by rowdy modern motorcars and aeroplanes. The canoe floated on and I strained my ears to catch the last refrain.

All was still until a monkey chattered excitedly when we passed under his lookout post. A coucal bubbled down the scale and again I felt glad to be alive and experiencing the Africa I loved.

I signalled to Fred to come up close and we shared one of our last cigarettes. I lit mine and watched the blue smoke float lazily into the still morning air. It was good to taste the tobacco and get the feeling of contentment as I inhaled the smoke—a bad habit perhaps, but very pleasant in times of stress and after any exertion. I lay back in the canoe and let the current carry the craft forward. When the prow bumped against the bank I gave a slight shove with my paddle and floated out into midstream again. Fred followed and we spoke of the huge meals we were going to eat when we reached civilization.

Suddenly my ear vibrated slightly and in an instant all my senses were alert.

"Did you hear that, Fred?" I asked.

Fred sat up and listened carefully.

"Yes," he said. "There is a booming sound," and he pointed to the east. The wind blew a little harder and we strained our ears to hear. When the wind died down the sound grew stronger and I knew that it was the famed waterfall we had heard so much about; "The place of the pythons" the locals called it.

"This must be what that old man was speaking about," Fred said. "Do you remember how he appeared at the camp one night and we gave him some tobacco—he used it like snuff—and then he warned us of the terrible hole in the river where the monster pythons lived. He described it all so clearly I hardly slept all night for thinking that we might end up in this hole."

I remembered only too well and, like Fred, had had a very uneasy night.

By the time we reached the next bend there was no mistaking the sound of the waterfall and although it was still a long way away we kept close to the bank and looked anxiously ahead. A full hour passed and we seemed no closer.

Fred paddled up and pointed to a low, sloping hill on our right.

"It's obvious that the fall must be on the other side," he said.

The river made a deep U-bend and had we wanted to we could have carried our canoes over the hill and cut off miles of canoeing.

We passed some locals who were watering their cattle, and they hailed us. We paddled over to them and were given a lengthy warning about the waterfall. For the next half hour we were hailed by every man we saw and given severe warnings of the peril ahead of us.

When we reached the falls themselves a vast crowd of gesticulating locals waved and shouted at us. By keeping close to the bank we knew we would be out of danger, and we pretended we didn't understand what they

were trying to say. They grew frantic and some of the women put their hands over their eyes as we drew closer and closer to the brink of the falls. The men were jumping up and down, waving their hats and yelling at the tops of their voices. I repeatedly cupped my hands to my ears, then shrugged my shoulders as though I could not follow. Fred played it to the full too, and lay back nonchalantly in his canoe, singing "Don't roll those Bloodshot Eyes at Me."

By the time we were thirty feet away, everyone was frenzied and some were holding on to each other. Then with a great show we bluffed we had seen the danger and reacted with all the pomp we could muster. The crowd was delighted and roared its approval.

Getting out of the canoes, we tied them up and walked to the edge of the falls. Still mindful of our audience, we mimed great shock and staggered back at the sight of the pool below. The crowd screamed and yelled as though to say," We told you so!"

A closer look at the pool showed me how the python legend must have come about; the water struck an outcrop of rock that made it spin and from a distance it looked like a coiled snake.

We sweated for a full hour to get the canoes down the gorge and what was left of our clothes was badly torn when we had to bash our way through a forest of thorn bushes near the foot of the falls. It was far too dangerous to get into the river at that point, so leaving Fred with the canoes I scouted ahead downstream. I had to walk over a mile before I saw a point where we would be able to launch the canoes. My thirty-pound boat felt like a ton weight, and we cursed as we barked our shins on boulders and stood on devil thorns.

We were deeply tanned by the sun and I saw an umfaan who was fishing, look at us in surprise as we passed him. I asked him what was wrong and he replied that he thought we were Indians. This made Fred roar with laughter, much to the umfaan's astonishment, and he backed away as though we were two wild madmen.

Manhandling the canoes had drenched us with sweat, but we were afraid to stop in case the terrible stiffness would overcome us before we could sit once more. After two hours of backbreaking labour we were ready to go, and the canoes slid into the water.

We drifted down the flat water to rest our aching arms, after lugging the kit and boats from the waterfall. Our rest did not last long—the familiar sound of cascading water greeted us when we had done no more than a mile. The rapid was a bad one and we had to line the canoes down. Fred led the way and I envied him, with his long legs, being able to hop from boulder to boulder with such ease. Where he could leap across with one

bound I had to take two steps or get into the water and swim behind the canoe. Still, I had the better canoe and the going had been much easier for me when we were able to jump rapids. Pushing and shoving, heaving and grunting, we made our way down the rapid, leapt into the canoes then rode the waves at the bottom.

What blessed relief to sit, after our arms had been almost torn out of their sockets and our knees and shins bashed against submerged boulders! It was our sixth day out and our stamina was being tested to the utmost. I was glad of all the running to work and the press-ups and skipping that I had done, for it was standing me in good stead now.

By midday we had covered five miles, and I gave a loud cheer when I noticed that the vegetation was beginning to change—we were obviously nearing the coast. The atmosphere was different too; warm and muggy with a low haze lying on the eastern horizon.

The river had been rising steadily all morning and in the last ten minutes it had come up at least two inches. This was very much to our advantage, as it helped us to ride the rapids. For the next hour we took them in grand style. Following the deep channels, we guided the canoe prows with quick paddling then raced down, over the rocks and into the pool below. With almost unerring accuracy, we found the right channels.

We began to eat up the miles, although a slip in the middle of a big cascade could mean death if the canoe was not righted quickly enough. Once in the rapid there was no time to change your mind, you had to keep on going right to the end. If the canoe turned over it meant hanging on and letting the water take you to the bottom of the fall.

Once I stuck halfway down, and Fred came careering towards me. I tried to move out of his way and he dug his paddles in an effort to avoid me, but he hit me mid on. We came up grasping for air, then swam desperately after the canoes as they floated downstream. They disappeared into a deep pool, and we had to dive to get them out. First one then the other was dragged to the bank and emptied of water. All that was left of our already meagre food supplies was half a pound of Holsum: everything else was completely ruined.

Fred's canoe had been badly damaged and he spent half an hour making essential repairs with bits of stick and Pliobond. This modern adhesive had saved our lives on more than one occasion. Fred's ability as a carpenter was tested to the full, but he came out on top every time—I am sure that if only a piece of wood had been left he would have made a canoe out of it.

We pressed on hoping to reach the end of the rapids, but by five in the afternoon it was obvious that we should have to spend another night

out in the open. Choosing a clump of bushes as a camping spot, Fred left me to get the canoes out while he went to look for an African kraal to get some matches. I had just arranged the canoes as a shelter from a slight drizzle that was falling when Fred returned with a full box of matches and an armful of mealies.

"Thank God for the man who brought mealies to this country!" he said.

We soon had a big fire going and while the remains of our clothes were drying out, we roasted mealies on the coals and spread them with Holsum. We ate four each before stopping to say how good they tasted, but later that night we both paid dearly for eating so fast and for drinking water straight afterwards; we had severe stomach cramps and diarrhoea, which kept us awake and groaning for the rest of the night.

As soon as we could see where we were going we climbed into the canoes and set off on the last stretch. After some vigorous paddling, the pains eased off and we could breath without suffering the agonies of hell.

As the sun climbed over the eastern horizon I saw a long plume of white smoke in the distance.

"It must be the sugar mill!" I shouted excitedly to Fred.

"It's still a long way off," he replied laconically.

But it gave us heart and we paddled with extra energy towards the first sign of civilization we had seen for nearly seven days.

Two hours of hard paddling, then I saw a ferryboat on a long flat stretch of water. This was the end of the rapids and we whooped for joy. We pulled the canoes out at the ferry and while we stood talking to the ferryman a European farmer arrived. He very kindly offered us tea, which we accepted with alacrity. We sat back in easy chairs and looked at the distant range of coastal dunes; I calculated that in two hours we should be at the sea.

When we reached the river again, I stripped and had a swim, much to Fred's disgust.

"Here we have been killing ourselves to reach the sea, and now we're almost there you go for a swim!" he groused.

I found it difficult to explain that it was my way of getting rid of the tension that had been with us on the last two days. I knew we were safe now and I wanted to linger and taste the fruits of success. We were, after all, the first people ever to have tackled and conquered this big river, and although our coming and going had left no trace on the surface of the water, in our minds we had achieved something big.

I dressed slowly and tried to make my wild mop of hair look a little more respectable, and then we climbed into our battered craft and made

our way towards the sea.

Two hours later we heard the put-put-put of a pleasure boat coming to meet us. Friendly Indian market gardeners waved at us from the banks and Fred cracked jokes with them.

A few minutes later the boat drew up near us and someone shouted, "Well done!"

The pleasure craft turned round and headed for Umkomaas, and we followed in its broad white wake. Fortunately for us the tide was coming in, otherwise we should have had to push and pull over the last stretch.

As we neared the boathouse where many years before, as a small boy, I had set out with my father to catch salmon, five canoes manned by schoolboys came out to meet us. We were touched by their spate of questions and tried hard to answer intelligently.

One canoe came a little too close to us and we both nearly turned over.

"Hell, that was close," Fred whispered to me, as we struggled to balance the rocking canoes.

A group of holidaymakers set up a ragged cheer as we clambered out onto the boathouse jetty. We waved our hats adorned with the leopard skin band of the Natal Canoe Club, and were proud that our small club had given the lead to the rest of South Africa.

The proprietor of the South Barrow Hotel met us and very kindly offered to put us up for the night. We were dead beat and his invitation was gratefully accepted.

Next morning we made our way back to Maritzburg, and six days later I began my new career as a Game Ranger.

CHAPTER 5

When I left Maritzburg for Zululand, Ernie Pearce took over the running of the Natal Canoe Club and the organizing of the Maritzburg to Durban race. Under his tactful handling the club membership grew and Maritzburg became canoe conscious.

Towards the end of 1952 I was transferred to Richards Bay where I had to catch bait for fishermen—a thankless task, but one which gave me a chance to get fit. My camp was only fifty yards from the beach, so I was able to go for a run or a swim whenever there was a spare moment.

At night I would go out with a gang of Africans to the top end of the Bay and we would drag the nets for miles. When one man tired I would jump in and take hold of the net. Trudging along in water four feet deep with a heavy net in tow soon developed my back and leg muscles, but no matter how hard I tried I could never keep up with the AmaTonga and Shangaans who made up the gang. Their endurance was amazing, particularly when one considered their frugal diet. They laughed at my efforts and asked why I was so stupid as to get into the water when I could sit in the warm boat instead.

Often someone would tramp on a skate and there would be a panic as they dropped the nets and grabbed the side of the boat. One poor devil got a skate's barb right into his shin and spent over a month in hospital recovering from severe blood poisoning.

Occasionally young crocodiles would get caught up in the net and consternation would reign as we tried to get them out of the boat. Their eyes reflected like red coals as they crawled up the side of the net, and when really annoyed they would hiss and roar in a manner that soon put anyone off the idea of grabbing hold of them. When I asked the men whether there was any chance of bumping into larger crocs, they laughed and said that we made far too much noise—the crocodiles would go as soon as they heard us coming. Despite their reassurances I was quick to let go the nets if my feet touched anything under the water.

Sometimes we would work for five or six hours and get only a handful of prawns. It was heartbreaking work and all one ever received

Photo: Natal Mercury

Bob Templeton, Ernie Pearce, Fred Schmidt and Ian Player
Smiles of victory after a night of fear

The finish, Blue Lagoon, Durban

Photo: Natal Mercury

Photo: Ian Player

The rhinos came to wallow

A croc's jaws snapped

Photo: Paul Dutton

from the fishermen was a stream of abuse about the size or the scarcity of the bait. Often, after a fruitless night, we would chug across the Bay and reach the jetty as the sun rose. There would always be a group of men to meet us and I grew to loathe their sullen faces when they heard we had had a bad haul. Frequently they would get violent and threaten to throw us into the water. I swore to myself that the day that happened, at least one of them would come with me!

After breakfast I would sleep for a few hours then take out a fresh gang and net for mullet. This was really good fun, and the men would scream with delight when they cornered a shoal on the edge of a sandbank.

The net would be loaded onto the back of the boat, one man would row and the other would pay the net out. The rest of us would go four or five hundred yards away with sticks, then walk towards the net, beating the water as we moved. Shoals of mullet would panic and rush to get away. The men with the net would be waiting and as soon as the mullet were trapped, they would haul in. The water was churned into a white froth as the fish swam this way, then that, to escape. Some would leap right over the net and the men would scream and yell at the unfortunate that particular end. Once I saw a shark chasing a shoal in the shallows. Quickly rowing over, the men laid the net in a semicircle and netted the whole shoal with the aid of the shark.

Terns and gulls would follow us, screaming and diving for titbits when the men had broken the necks of the mullet. Day after day, and night after night, the bait catching continued, and I became fitter than I had ever been before. A friend lent me an old surf ski and paddles, and I used to paddle up to the islands in the middle of the Bay. This strengthened my arms and at the same time allowed me to indulge in bird watching. By paddling quietly or drifting with the current, I was able to get within a few feet of feeding flamingo and pelican. Sometimes a flock of pelicans would corner a shoal, and all hell would be let loose as they dived and caught the fleeing fish. Some birds would grab a fish that was far too big to swallow, and their pouches would be ripped open. Other birds tackled smaller ones who had fish and a most amusing tug of war would follow. In the heat of the moment the birds would forget all about me, and I got close enough to touch them.

Some days, when the sun was warm, and there was not much wind, I would float up to the waders and watch them darting about on the mud banks: avocets in their striking black and white, and greenshanks with their lovely haunting whistle. Occasionally a curlew or a whimbrel would arrive and stay for a few days and I had much delight in listening to their calls. Goliath herons would watch me suspiciously when I came too close to

71

their feeding grounds, then gracefully stalk away when they realized I was an accursed human being. I always kept a few pieces of stinking fish on the back of the ski, so that the gulls were my constant companions, following and hoping for a morsel.

These few hours spent away from my duties as a bait-catcher always renewed my batteries, as it were, and I was able to face the next day's work, without too much hate for the fishing fraternity.

Towards the end of the year I was transferred to the Umfolozi Game Reserve, where my main exercise was walking.

As the day of the canoe race drew near, Ernie Pearce wrote to me and said that this year's race would be recognized as the South African Championship, the first ever to be held in the Union of South Africa.

Fred also wrote a long letter, giving details of the canoe he was building. I wrote back and urged him to make mine strong, because I imagined I knew what the boulder-strewn Umsindusi and Umgeni rivers could do to any craft. Fred took me at my word and made something that was as strong as a battleship, not knowing what a liability it was going to turn out and how he would be forced to carry it.

I got a few days' leave before the race, which started on 9th January 1953; during this time Fred and I practised on the boathouse section of the Umsindusi. As usual we had left everything to the last minute and there was a mad rush trying to get the right food and clothing for the race. All this, plus trying to test the canoes, left us almost exhausted the day before the race. Still, we were by no means as badly off as Ernie Pearce, who did most of the organizing and had to prepare for the race as well.

The day before the race was scheduled to start, Fred told me about the first race when he had Denis Vorster as a partner.

"Vorster and I are big mates at the Railway workshops," he began. "One day Denis comes along and says that we are going to enter for the canoe race. I was all for it, because many years ago we used to live next to the Dusi, and I spent a lot of my time playing and fishing down near the river. I once built a tin canoe and had dreams of sailing off all by myself until my father found me and gave me a belting and kicked holes in the canoe; it was the depression and we had to struggle for a living, and I was supposed to be carrying gum poles and not fooling around in the river. But this didn't stop me, and many days I used to dream of sailing into Durban.

"When I started work as an apprentice carpenter I had forgotten all about it until Denis came along. Before I knew what had happened we had agreed to be partners, and I was taken down to your place. A little while after that we all formed the Natal Canoe Club. Then the game was on, and everybody was full of secrets about the canoe they were going to make.

"Denis came to me in great excitement one morning and said that he had weighed a piece of timber one inch square and a foot long, and a piece of reinforcing steel of the same dimensions, and the steel was lighter! I wish to hell he would try to tell me that now," he added thoughtfully. "Anyway, old Denis could sell an Eskimo two fridges, because one by itself would be too small. He set about making the frame of our secret canoe and as he was doing all the hard work, I didn't have much to say.

"Then one day he said, 'Come along and have a look at the completed frame and give me your opinion.' Me, the authority on tin canoes, being asked for an opinion! I tried to look intelligent and told him that everything looked dead right to me. He had everything welded, then put on a piece of very strong canvas and painted it.

"We took it down to the river, after a bit of a struggle, and to my astonishment it balanced very well. I got enthusiastic and visualized us winning the race by miles. Denis fed my imagination with all the tales of glory he could think of, and we were both sure that the race was a cinch for us.

"Then Ernie came round one afternoon: he had a scale in his pocket and was weighing everybody's canoes. We got a hell of a fright when we saw the weight: one hundred and five pounds, unloaded! It didn't seem right to me, but Denis calmed my fears by saying that the steel canoe would outlast everything on the river.

"We took the canoe down to your place so you could see it, and I remember being suspicious when you were so surprised at our ingenuity in using steel. Still, Denis was so confident, I thought you were just trying to be nice, but I could have sworn blind that I saw you and Ernie clinging to each other as we rode away with our damned Queen Mary on top of Denis's car.

"Denis was full of schemes; he spread a rumour that we had flown over the course and had found half-a-dozen short cuts you didn't know about. We laughed when we heard how worried you and Ernie were. Denis thought up something different each day, so we were winning in the psychological war.

"Then Denis came along one morning very jubilant because old man Backhouse had offered to lend him some prize homing pigeons. We could write messages and tell everyone how far ahead we were. I didn't like the idea of taking prize pigeons, but Denis was in charge and nothing would put him off; but he got me really worried when he said that the pigeons were valued at forty pounds. 'If we start to sink,' he said, 'for goodness sake make sure that you save one of the pigeons.'

"Well, as you know, we left at five minute intervals. When we got to

the first weir and picked up the canoe I knew for sure that timber was lighter than steel. My legs buckled and the Army boots we had on made us slip on every rock we touched. I knew we had made a big mistake. We only just managed to get up the river before we collapsed. Denis was petrified that the crowd would see us fall, and someone would tell you.

"Once we were in the river again, it was on with the race. We thought we were going very well until we reached the boathouse stretch where we saw a little boy paddling along in a tin canoe. No matter how hard we tried to pass him, he still managed to stay in front. It struck me forcibly that we were in a bloody barge and it was a very slow one too.

"'Hey, Denis!' I shouted. 'We can't pass this damn kid, man!'

"'Paddle, man, paddle. We are gaining on the little guy!' Denis puffed.

"There was a tree across the river and this stopped the kid's winning streak. We carried our canoe around the stump and started off again.

"Suddenly I heard the child crying and we turned round to see that he had been swept under the log. I had to dive in and haul the poor little blighter out.

"We kept on going until we reached Mussons Weir, then we had a battle to get the canoe into Barbel Pool. By the time we reached the sewage farm we were really clapped. As you know, the sewage farm stretch is nothing but a mass of trees. I had expected something like this and was prepared to battle. At one tree we nearly sank, and I made a grab for the pigeon cage. I nearly drowned trying to swim with the thing too—forty pounds' worth dragging me down. Denis saved the canoe and we rested on the bank under the willows.

"Then Denis said, 'We had better let these pigeons go, otherwise we are going to get ourselves in a lot of debt.'

"Four pigeons went off all right, but the ten pound bird was too wet to fly. It flapped away into the bush.

"'Chase it, Fred!' Denis said. 'Otherwise the thing will fall into the river and drown.'

"I raced after it through bush and stinging nettles, caught it then sat like a fool, holding it out in the sun to dry. We were in a race. That pigeon lost us a lot of time. If it had been mine, it would have been pigeon soup the first night.

"Eventually we managed to get going again, and caught up with Basil and Pottie. They had taken the canoe over a tree trunk. Basil was in the front half and Pottie in the back end. They were paddling for life but making no progress at all. At last they forced it off the trunk and got a big hole. Denis and I laughed until we cried.

"Pottie said, 'Basil, we have got a hole.'

"Meanwhile, the canoe was sinking fast. They saved it in the nick of time.

"Basil: 'We'll have to patch this damned hole.'

"Pottie: 'I can't go any further.'

"Basil; 'Why?'

"Pottie: 'Well, it's one o'clock already and we will never get to Durban by this evening.'

"Basil; 'What has this evening got to do with the race?'

"Pottie: 'I thought we would get to Durban by four o'clock so I bought bioscope tickets.'

"Denis and I left them arguing about the tickets and we carried on down the river. We met some Africans near Sobantu Village and they told us that you were three hours ahead of us. We were very disappointed and couldn't understand why we weren't leading, but I had more than a shrewd suspicion that our canoe was going to be our downfall.

"We reached the neck late that afternoon and decided to camp.

"Of all places in Africa, we had to choose an outcrop of shale. It was drizzling and damn' cold, and we couldn't get anywhere near the fire because the shale was exploding like a machine gun. We spent most of the night trying to repair the fourteen holes in the canoe.

"It was a cheerless dawn that greeted us as we tramped over the neck, lugging the ruddy Queen Mary. How we ever reached the cascades I will never know. After every few yards we automatically collapsed, and I kept on muttering to myself that steel is lighter than wood. It took us nearly two hours of dragging and carrying to reach the river again.

"We started off in grand style for the first rapid.

"'Paddle left, Fred,' Denis said. 'No, right, Denis,' I said.

"There was an almighty crash and reinforcing rods stuck out at all angles. We sat looking at the battered wreck, then Denis stood up and cut his name well and good on the prow—that was all that was left of it!"

I was weak from laughter when Fred had finished his story.

CHAPTER 6

Fred and I walked down to the Victoria Bridge in the evening to have a look at the Dusi. It was flowing very slowly and we knew it was going to be a carrying race.

That night we had a meeting in the Royal Hotel with the rest of the competitors; it was a unique occasion and we were making history. I looked around at the eager group and reflected how well worth had been the early struggles to get the sport going. I knew now that nothing would hold it back, and long after all of us, that night discussing the first National Championships, were dead, youngsters from all over the South Africa and Zimbabwe would be competing in what would become one of the premier sporting events of the country.

Ernie Pearce, who is one of the greatest veterans the race has produced, must have read my thoughts because he said, "In a few years' time this race will become famous."

Time has proved him right, and today more contestants than the Clubs and Race Committee can cope with want to race to Durban. Practically all the organization that has gone into the race has been due to Ernie Pearce's untiring efforts. A former cycle sprint champion, he learnt his club management the hard way; it was a fortunate day for Natal when he decided to give up cycling for canoeing.

I woke early the next morning with the usual butterflies in my stomach. The thought of food was nauseating, but I knew that if I didn't eat I would suffer badly after the first ten minutes; in fact we could quite easily lose the race because of it, so I ate a half-raw steak and two eggs, and felt much better.

I arrived at the staring point to find an enormous crowd had gathered. This increased my nervousness and I shuddered inwardly at the thought of falling into the river.

Fred appeared looking very worried and announced, "My guts are killing me."

We didn't know it then, but he had appendicitis. I put it down to nerves and said I wasn't feeling too good myself.

Ernie Pearce and Johnny Wright arrived with two beautiful canoes, which increased our discomfort.

Among the other canoeists were Calvin Donly and Harry Fisher, two youngsters from Johannesburg. It was their first trip and they were full of excitement. In later years they were to make history by being members of the first group of men ever to canoe down the great Zambesi from Balovale to the sea. Harry Fisher was also to break all the existing records in 1959 and win the canoe race by a large margin. Through perseverance and courage, they were to become some of the "greats" of the race.

A few minutes later Stan Dean and Dave Greenland arrived. Stan was a physical culturist, 45 years old, but without an ounce of fat on his hardy frame. Greenland, a South African Police constable, was 49, a veteran Marathon runner and as tough as they come. These two men set a great example to the youth of the country.

At ten to eight we were all ready and the Mayor of Maritzburg, Mr. D. R. Warmback, walked down the line of canoeists and shook each one by the hand.

At eight o'clock he fired the starting pistol, and we were off.

Someone shouted, "How's the water, Sarge?" as Dave Greenland paddled past. In the excitement of leaving, Dave had forgotten his watch. He tossed it to a friend on the bank and shouted, "Take it to the Scottsville Police station." The crowd roared.

Ten yards further down Dave and Stan were manhandling their double canoe over the Victoria weir when Stan stepped into a pothole and disappeared. The crowd yelled, as Dave came up and spat.

A few minutes later they laughed at me as I slid into the water while trying to get into the canoe. In an attempt to gather my self-esteem, I grabbed Fred Schmidt's canoe and said, "I'll hold it while you climb in."

Fred howled with laughter and replied, "Do you think I am paralysed, you silly bastard?"

Out of the corner of my eye I saw Ernie Pearce having near-hysterics as he overheard us.

After a battle to get up the slippery bank, made more difficult by eighteen canoeists having gone before me, I managed to climb into my canoe and paddled frantically to catch up with Fred.

I tried to shoot the small rapid in Alexandra Park too fast, bumped into a rock and holed my canoe. I yelled to Fred to come and give me a hand, and together we hastily repaired the tear. Fortunately it was a small one, and with our Umkomaas experience of repairing holes we soon made it fairly watertight.

A faint cheer rose from the few remaining people on Victoria

Bridge as we swept beneath, towards the weir.

We leapt out onto the bank, ran past the bad set of rapids and got into the river at the clump of willow trees. Paddling hard, we took the Braid Street bend in great style, clanked over the submerged stumps below the Sports Ground, and nearly overturned at the old boathouse when my hat caught an overhanging willow. We passed three teams on the flat boathouse stretch, and then came upon Sid Bauer who had an eighteen-inch tear in his canoe.

Fred led the way with his easy though deceptive stroke; I saw the muscles on his back bunching and relaxing as he leant forward and dug the paddles deep into the brown water. Sweat dripped into my eyes and my lungs felt at bursting point. My arms ached and my mind refused to function with any speed. All I could think of was how I hated this flat stretch of water. Going hard, we passed young Peter Marriot and Barry Anderson. In later years Marriot was to become one of the best younger competitors the game produced, and was to miss winning the 1954 race by a bit of bad luck.

At Mussons Weir we jumped out of the canoes and lugged them into Barbel Pool; it was too shallow to canoe, so we swam behind and pushed the canoes down the rapids over the old broken weir and into the stream behind the reed island. Clambering in again, we shot forward and bumped through the next set of rapids, reached the low level Mountain Rise bridge, let the canoes go underneath and grabbed them as they came out the other side. Eight hundred yards further down we pulled ourselves out at the sewage farm and started running through the high reeds and dense undergrowth.

We got to the fence near Schorn's store in time to see Ernie Pearce and Johnny Wright belting it along the road. We caught them up at Campbell's tearoom, and then foolishly stopped to drink a cup of tea. Fred smoked a cigarette, much to my annoyance—I told him it would tire him. He quickly set about disproving this by running up the steep hill that led to Fletcher-Campbell's farm. I soon lagged behind, cursing my shorter legs. I saw Fred waltzing past Ernie and Johnny, whistling as though he was on an afternoon ramble in the country. I shouted for him to wait for me, but he kept going and I only caught him up again at the first checkpoint. He was closely followed by Pearce, Wright, Els and Poulsen.

It was not 1.30 p. m. when we entered the river again and set off downstream. Two miles further on, while wading behind the canoes, Fred came up to me and said Johnny Wright was tiring. Using every bit of reserve energy, we put on a spurt and set as fast a pace as possible. We got to Doornhoek at three o'clock—an outstanding record in those days, but

later to be dwarfed by Ernie Pearce, Bob Templeton, Harry Fisher and Gordon Rowe. Johnny Wright couldn't stand the pace any more and I didn't blame him for not wanting to go any further. While he and Ernie were talking about it, we pushed on as hard as we could go.

By six o'clock that night we had had it, so we camped near the fence dividing the Zulu reserve from European farms. It was a cheerless night and we awoke stiff and sore the next morning. Hastily eating a handful of dried fruit and a few pieces of biltong, washed down with a mug of wonderful hot tea, we paddled off.

When we got to Dusi Bridge at the foot of Eddie Hagan Drive, we were told that Pearce had joined Els and Poulsen, so we knew that there was some formidable opposition behind us. Staying for only a few minutes to drink a cup of tea and eat a few sandwiches, we got back into the river and made for the Umfula trading store.

The low water was making the trip agony, and we had to walk down the riverbed with sand grinding in our hockey boots. We turned right at the African huts, and hurried down the dry watercourse leading to the wide Umgeni. The heat was overpowering and we were exhausted by the time we reached the river. Dropping the canoes, we stumbled to the water and drank until our bellies were swollen.

"Hell, who would have thought that dirty brown water could taste so good!" Fred panted.

We washed our sunburnt faces and wetted our cracked lips every few minutes in an effort to ease the pain. The sun was already setting; we had originally planned to keep going all that night until we reached the Umfula trading store, but this short stop and the surfeit of water soon changed our minds and we wandered down the bank, looking for a camping spot. We found some overhanging boulders under which we crept for shelter from the drizzle that started later that night.

It got so cold that in the early morning we both woke and built up the fire for a cup of coffee. We swallowed four cups before we felt warm, and were relieved of our dehydration. It was always like this after any great exhaustion—the body didn't seem to want food, but craved liquid insatiably. We sat and watched the stars until dawn, then packed and set off down the river, paddling with caution in the enormous Umgeni, its size exaggerated after the shallow Umsindusi.

Half an hour later we reached the entrance to the gorge that had been the downfall of two of my companions on previous trips. The temptation to go on downstream was great; it was with reluctance that we stopped at the head of the gorge and pulled the canoes out in preparation for the long and arduous walk along the Durban Corporation pipeline.

Humping our haversacks on our shoulders and the canoes on our heads, we started on the long climb to the road. Fred carried my canoe, which was the heavier, for the first half of the climb, then we left his canoe and carried mine to the top together. Our hockey boots chafed our heels raw, so we threw these encumbrances away, and walked on barefoot.

It was long past nine before we had both canoes and all the kit on the road. Walking at a good speed, we made our way round the hairpin bends that led to the Umfula store. At one point we took a short cut over a concrete pipeline, then had to back slowly when a herd of goats came across at the same time. It was a tricky business because a drop of several hundred feet fell away, on either side of us, but the goats were not to be deterred and we had to give way. With infinite care we backed along the pipe and heaved a sigh of relief—and a few rocks at the goats—when we were safe.

After an hour's hard going, I was almost all in, and sat on the side of the road for a rest. Fred walked on and said he would wait for me. I must have dozed, for the next thing I knew was being narrowly missed by a donkey cart as it came careering round the corner. Looking at my watch, I was horrified to see that half an hour had passed. Picking up the canoe I hurried on to catch up with Fred. I found him at the foot of the pass, fast asleep.

"What the hell happened to you? Go to a night-club or something?" he demanded.

"Carry the heavy canoe, you made the lump of iron," I said.

Fred picked it up and we set off again, walking for half an hour and resting for five minutes. I felt as though my neck had been shoved into my buttocks and my feet were bits of raw steak.

We collapsed at the Umfula store bridge and only moved when Mr. Marriot, father of young Peter, drove up and gave us a cold drink. He said some of the other competitors were right on our heels. This galvanized us into action, so we scrambled down the bank and into the Umgeni River. Paddling with all our strength, we raced ahead until we reached the foot of the Sleeping Beauty Mountain where we stopped to take a drink of water from a tiny, clear-running stream. The water was delicious—the best thirst quencher we had had on the whole race.

Soon after five we reached the bush weir and the road that led to Khumalo's store. We started carrying again and did not stop until we had reached the trading station. At eight o'clock that night we were still stumbling along the track, so fatigued that we could hardly keep our eyes open. When we did reach the store, we both slumped down outside and slept where we lay.

I awoke in the early morning, stiff and weary, to hear thunder in the east. Fred woke a little later and we watched the storm sweep in with the dawn. It was a unique sight, and for a few minutes our aches and pains were forgotten. When there seemed no doubt that we were in for a severe drenching, the wind changed and the storm sped on down the coast. Little did we know that the next night we would feel the full force of another storm and have to make our way downriver with only jagged lightning to light our way.

When it was light enough to move, we packed our kit, killed the embers of the fire, lifted our canoes and launched them into the dark brown water of the Umgeni. This section through the Krantzkloof gorges was extremely dangerous and only when we reached the Natal Estates pumphouse, some miles away, would the rapids end. In one part, the river dropped fifty feet in one mile over a series of cascades.

Steep gorges rose on either side—haunts of the hawks, swallows and swifts. It was not without misgiving that we set out on the last lap. We knew we were leading, but by how far was the burning question; if we knew the answer we could travel accordingly. I had a feeling that someone was close behind and I wanted to take chances in the rapids. Fred wisely said that while we were in the lead we should not fall into the trap of taking too many chances, so it was with caution that we approached the long, thunderous line of rapids. Working our way along the banks and lining the canoes down, we gradually made way. Once or twice we took a chance and shot a rapid with nearly fatal results, as we landed in a turbulent pool with the canoes floating upside down.

It was frightening when the canoe hit a rock and slowly overturned, depositing one in the churning brown mass. With gathering speed, water dragged the canoe, and I held on grimly, ducking and pushing in bad patches. The roar was deafening and the spray blinding, but as long as I held on to the canoe I knew all would be well. It was when by some quirk of fate you hit a rock, and the canoe slipped from your grasp, that the real trouble came. With nothing to hold on to, the water would sweep you relentlessly forward, banging and bashing you against boulders and jagged rocks. Twice this happened, but we were fortunate not to be badly injured.

The portaging was killing work, and after five miles of it we were sorely tempted to jump more rapids. Slogging and plodding along, we made our way painfully down the deep valley. It was very humid; sweat poured off our bodies, leaving a rank stench in the air.

Small streams entering the Umgeni grew more numerous, some with ferns of every kind growing on their banks. Thick, luscious grass grew down to the water's edge, where kingfishers hovered above the

mirror-clear pools, then dived accurately on to their prey. Two young Zulus and their girls came jogging down a winding path to a drift in the river. Their bodies glistened with sweat as they swayed and ran to the quick strumming of a guitar. As they went up the hillside, all I could see was the bright red and green of their scarves, then they disappeared into the dense green foliage. Higher up the mountain I saw the white mists sweeping down, slowly enveloping the granite krantzes dropping steep and straight into the river.

At three o'clock we had to rest; we flopped on to the ground and slept for ten minutes, until the damp soaked into our clothes. The distant bark of a mongrel dog woke me up, followed by Africans shouting in one of the ravines where some unfortunate wild animal was being hunted.

An hour later the wind changed and Fred, with his great fishing knowledge, said it was the rain wind. Ten minutes later a lowering and stormy sky loomed over the southern horizon—frogs croaked and crickets began to chirrup. Suddenly the coucal trilled out its low, bubbling call, and the love of the open came over me in a flood; gone for a few moments were the aches and pains and the fatigue of three days' hard going. I had always looked upon the coucal as my bird, and his call in the midst of depression was a good omen, so I pushed on with fire in my heart.

"Bacon and eggs at Blue Lagoon!" I shouted to Fred.

He responded with a thumbs-up sign, and we increased our pace. A light drizzle began to fall and I heard a guineafowl calling up the valley. Other birds joined in; sunbirds were flitting through the branches of a huge fig tree as we paddled beneath. My morale dropped again when I saw the next line of rapids, and heard the ominous roar of water threshing over rocks.

The opposite bank rose steeply from the river for three hundred feet or more; mist with dark clouds behind it made the way ahead dark and gloomy. I knew from a previous trip that a mile of broken, tumbling water stretched before us. Then Fred cracked a small joke about a fishing trip he had once been on, and sombreness of the valley lightened—at least there were two of us pitting our tiny craft against the formidable forces of Nature. This was a challenge and we were going to accept it. As we lined our bouncing canoes down the surging maelstrom, I reflected how wonderful it was that while undergoing severe hardship, a humorous word could soon turn what appeared to be an insurmountable obstacle into something easily beaten.

The mist lifted for a few seconds, and high up on the green plateau I saw a cluster of banana trees. I shouted and pointed them out to Fred.

"We've made it! We've made it!" he yelled, delighted.

82

I grinned back, not knowing that the next few hours would rank as some of the worst in my life.

The knowledge that the Natal Estates pumphouse and a cup of hot tea was not more than a few hours ahead gave us new energy and we plunged down rapid after rapid; as dusk came we reached the pumphouse. An Indian was on duty, the man in charge having just gone home for his dinner. We decided to go up and see him and ask him for news, besides hoping we would get a cup of tea.

The welcome from the man and his family was overwhelming; we were ordered inside and sat down to a feast and all the cups of tea we could drink.

They had no news, for their wireless had gone bung the day before, so we still did not know how far we were ahead—if indeed we were ahead. One never knew with this race! We were aware that Peter Marriot and his partner knew this section of the river like the backs of their hands and could quite easily have given us the slip. However, with a warm glow spreading throughout our bodies, we could relax for a while and hope that we were winning.

We smoked cigarettes, talked and rested our weary limbs. The engineer and his wife insisted that we stay the night and we were tempted to accept their offer, but the knowledge that Durban was only twelve miles away and that other canoeists were on our tail forced us to our feet. We thanked them, inadequately, for what they had done, then we opened the door and stepped out into the night.

A flash of lightning, followed by a crash of thunder, drowned our last words and we cautiously made our way down the long iron ladder. It took over a quarter of an hour to reach the river again, for the rain had begun to fall and we could barely see a yard in front of us. As we reached the canoes the rain was hissing down in sheets, with claps of thunder and flashes of lightning in quick succession. Bursts of bitterly cold wind lashed our faces and we were soon shivering. Water poured from the steep hillsides on either side and lightning flashes showed white, frothy bubbles on the river. This was a sure sign that the level was rising.

I shouted above the noise of the storm to Fred that at least we would be canoeing to Durban and not walking as I did the time before. The final stretch of the river had been so shallow that I had had to manhandle my canoe over the sandbanks.

We climbed in and pushed off from the banks. Keeping close to the edge we paddled downstream, almost blinded by the wind and rain. Before we had gone a mile we had to stop to help each other drain the water out— it was raining hard enough to fill up the canoes. Soon it was no longer

necessary to keep near the banks; the river had risen six inches and we could ride side by side.

"I wish this rain would stop for a few minutes so that we could get our bearings," I shouted across to Fred.

"I wish it would stop for ever!" Fred replied in anguish.

We halted again and drained the water out; this time the river was up to our calves and I could feel the strength of the flow. Every small stream we passed was a minor torrent and we knew by the noise when we were approaching one. Still the rain poured down as though the heavens had opened up and would never close. We could only see vague outlines until there was a flash of lightning when we quickly took stock of our position and acted accordingly.

We stopped once more to empty the canoes; this time we were up to our knees and I knew it was the last time we would be able to stand in the river.

"From now on we will have to use our hats," I screamed to Fred above the roar of the storm.

"You are telling me," I heard him shout. "The water will be over our necks next time if we don't."

The canoes were gathering speed without any help from us. In the next flash I saw Fred's drawn face and the muscles bulging on his forearms as he gripped his paddles. Waves were being whipped up; sticks and debris floated past. The river had become exceptionally dangerous—far worse than anything we had already gone through. I edged my canoe nearer to the bank so that the distance I might have to swim wouldn't be too great. Fred followed and we went forward with gathering momentum. A short dip of the paddle was enough to make the canoe leap as though it were controlled by an outboard.

"The wires! The wires!" I heard Fred yelling.

For a moment I was numb with fright: we had forgotten the sand dragging wires on the lower reaches of the river. They were not pulled out at night, and if we hit them with the river running at this speed, it would mean death.

"We are mad to go on!" I heard Fred shout again above the storm. Grabbing a piece of overhanging reed I slowed my canoe down and when Fred came close we gripped each other's paddles. For a few seconds we could speak, then had to let go before we were swept away.

"We have got to go on," I said to Fred. "There is no way out of this place until we get to below Sea Cow Lake."

Looking to our right, we could see nothing but a sea of blackness and reeds. Then the wind died down momentarily and we could hear the

reassuring sound of thousands of frogs croaking.

"Where the hell do we get out then?" I asked.

"We will have to try to make it at the paper factory, though God knows if we'll have the strength to pull our boats up that steep bank," he replied.

A log bumped against the canoes and we were separated again; the wind rose and the rain sheeted down. The river was now so full and flowing so fast it had begun to roar. I only put my paddles in the water to turn or slow the canoe down; we were going far too fast.

The river curved and I was swirled out into midstream. There was a flash of lightning followed by a shrill cry of warning from Fred. I looked straight into a thick wire cable. I ducked, too late, and it hit me a glancing blow on the forehead. The canoe rolled and I lost control, then paddling hard I righted the craft and made straight for the bank. My heart was pounding suffocatingly and I felt sick.

There was a deafening noise all round us and in the next flash of lightning I saw that debris of every sort had piled up against the cable on the left side of the river and the water was roaring over the waterfall it had formed. Had we come round on the left instead of the right, it would have been the end of us.

We knew we were amongst the wires now, so we bent as far forward as possible and, looking upwards, we could see the wires silhouetted on the skyline and had a moment's warning. The river had narrowed, so we were moving at a terrifying speed; all we could do was backpaddle. Logs ten and fifteen feet long rolled past, turning over and over, and once I thought I saw a dead cow.

"Sharks!" the thought hit me, and in panic I shouted it out aloud.

"Where? Where?" Fred yelled.

"There's a good chance they might come up the river at night!" I shouted back.

Above the sound of the river and wind I thought I heard a groan from Fred, as though this was just too much to bear. My own nerves were cracking and I panicked at the slightest thing. I gripped the paddles and guided the canoe as near to the bank as I could. The smell of the reeds and the nearness of the land gave me strength and helped me to overcome my fear.

Another flash showed a cable dangling a few inches above the water. I tried to paddle to the bank, but the current took me and I banged sideways against the wire. I leant over and with unexpected superhuman strength lifted it, so that we both scraped beneath.

A few yards down I saw the lights of the factory.

"Let's go for the lights!" I shouted, and heard Fred's answering "Right!"

Digging the paddles in deep, we surged across the river, ending up a hundred yards lower down than we had aimed for. There was no bank—just a mass of reeds with only their tops showing. I tested the depth with my paddle but could not touch bottom; so, gripping the reeds, we inched our way forwards, and after what seemed an eternity we felt the canoes bump solid earth.

We waited for the next flash of lightning, and saw with horror that a high bank rose sheer above us. I doubted whether I would ever have the strength to crawl to the top, let alone drag a canoe up.

We rested for well over a quarter of an hour then, untying our ropes, we slowly dragged ourselves to the top of the bank where we rested for another ten minutes. Then we pulled the canoes up one at a time, inch by inch. We were exhausted, and retched with fatigue.

Leaving the canoes where they lay, we walked towards the factory. Pools of water lay on the road, reflecting the street lamps. All thoughts of winning the race had been forgotten, until we were told by one of the shifts men that a wireless message had said that all canoeists were to stop at the first bridge on the Umgeni. We were about half a mile above it, but we knew that it would have been impossible to stop at the bridge, so we hoped our stopping place would be recognized.

A shifts man 'phoned Fred's brother and Ernie Comley, a family friend, came out to fetch us.

We were all in when we reached the house and crawled into bed and were soon fast asleep. I awoke after a few hours' dead sleep while Fred was, quite understandably, having a bad nightmare.

In later years I was often to wake sweating from dreams about cables stretched across a vast, roaring river.

PART TWO

BEING AN ACCOUNT OF CANOEING ON THE PONGOLO RIVER DURING GAME RANGING DAYS AT NDUMU GAME RESERVE

FOREWORD TO PART TWO
- ∞ -
MY PONGOLO RIVER ADVENTURE
- ∞ -
WILLEM VAN RIET

It was December 1964, and I was standing in the dusty streets of Mtubatuba. I was attempting to phone a certain Ian Player at the Umfolosi Game Reserve. A few weeks earlier I had discovered a book, named *Men, Rivers and Canoes*, in the library at the University of Cape Town, where I was studying to be an architect. Paging through the book I came across a picture of a tall thin fellow and a short, darker chap with piercing eyes—they were on a canoe trip down the Pongolo River. It was this picture that first really caught my attention and got me reading the book. It opened up my imagination.

Reading of the adventures experienced there made me obsessed with the idea of canoeing the Pongolo myself, and three weeks later I had sent my canoe by rail to Commondale, the nearest station to the river, and had hitchhiked up to Natal to get started on the trip. I wanted to phone Ian to find out more about the river.

Ian was out in the field that day, and so, to my disappointment, I had to start the journey without his firsthand advice. In those days there was no Jozini Dam, and the floodplain below the Lubombo Mountains was as unspoilt and as wild as any place in southern Africa. It was also the first time I would meet up with the bane of all canoeists in Africa, crocodiles and hippos. That trip introduced me to a life of canoeing as a way of adventure and exploration, and to a different pathway into wild nature.

I also, of course, read in this classic book about the Dusi canoe race, and that introduced me to the other part of canoeing as a way of life—racing. It excited my competitive nature and inspired me to enter the race, which, like Ian, I won three times.

But more than racing, canoeing enticed me with its spirit of adventure. Motivated by that first Pongolo trip, I went on explore many of

89

the rivers in Natal that Ian had pioneered, and to canoe quite a few of the great rivers elsewhere in Africa and of the world. To this day I pursue the life of adventure and exploration, and especially the quiet encounter with wild nature that canoeing opens up, and, when I can, travel to new countries looking for fresh canoeing experiences and unknown rivers.

Ian Player altered the course of my life through this book, which specifically led me to take the trip down the Pongolo. The exposure to Africa it gave me—its people and wildlife—ended my enthusiasm for architecture, and although I completed my degree, as soon as I could I left for the USA to study landscape architecture with Professor Ian Mcharg at the University of Pennsylvania—he was famous for his "Design with Nature" programme. Today, while I am working as Chief Executive Officer of the Peace Park Foundation, I still think back to the days on the winding, tree-lined Pongolo—the river that changed my life forever.

Cape Town

June 2006

CHAPTER 7

In 1954 I was stationed in the Ndumu Game Reserve, and in June of that year Ken Tinley joined me. He came to Ndumu as a learner ranger, but before a month was out we had established the closest friendship. Together we canoed and mapped all the pans and rivers in and near the Reserve. We knew it all, even to the maze of hippo runs interlocking the pans.

So often during those summer days in Ndumu we had seen the sun come up, a ball of flame, and spread its light over the lowveld, as we made our way up the stony track over the Lebombo on our way to Abercorn drift, loaded with kit and boat, to explore the Usutu river right down to its junction with the Pongolo. We had seen, in perfect silence, the Salene forest with its white sand, Nangri Island and Lake Polwe half-hidden in the mists.

We had made a fire and boiled coffee as the clapper larks flew high overhead, their wings slapping together. Four-coloured bush shrikes had called their "kok-ke-wiet" and Shelley's partridges had whistled their lyrical cries. Smoke from local huts had spiralled lazily into the morning air as shouts from awakening amaTonga filled the valleys.

After we had launched our boat near the old Abercorn punt, we would allow the river to carry us downstream with only an occasional paddle to guide the boat into the channels, while we absorbed the spirit of the wilderness, the heavy, dank smell of the river, the lush flowering plants, and the sight of tiger fish and barbel rising to the surface. At the end of one of these trips we had decided to paddle up to our house, overlooking the Pongolo River, by way of the old channel which joined the Usutu two miles above its present junction. This old channel had become a backwater when in one of its early floods the Pongolo had burst its banks some eight miles up river, flowed through two pans and back into the Usutu two miles below the original confluence.

At least five herds of hippo and some big crocodiles inhabited the "old course" as we called it. It was not wide and we had debated night after night how to bypass the hippo. We had always come to the same conclusion: "Ride over them." Once or twice before we had done this by

accident in other parts of the river: it had nearly proved fatal and we had gone through some anxious moments, perched on hippos' backs. Now we were going to court this danger deliberately. It was a sobering thought, but it had to be done, for this channel was the only stretch of water we had not travelled on. The main course of the Pongolo—the Usutu, Nyamiti pan, Polwe pan, Mvucheni pan, Banzi, Baga-Baga—we knew, and had conquered them all; only the "old course" remained.

The day came when, at the end of a long journey down the Usutu, we decided to press on and conquer the "old course". A violent storm was raging in the Pongolo valley late that afternoon, and the river came down in a minor flood. With the dark clouds low overhead, and the blue lightning flashing angrily in the sky, we turned the nose of our small craft into the tree-lined old course and began paddling upstream.

What a fantastic place it was; palm trees and lianas hung over the banks and cast deep shadow on the river, shutting out all the wind so that the air was hot to breathe. We paddled hard, with the sweat running off our bodies in streams, as foot by foot we moved up against the current. Logs and brushwood barred our path. It took us nearly half an hour to paddle eight hundred yards, so we were both finished when we made a sandbank and beached the boat.

After a short rest we started off again, and I saw the flick of a broad yellow tail as a crocodile floated past. Its tail moved from side to side as it swam downstream, leaving a wake of water that eddied and churned into the bushes on the side. Power lay in that tail.

A little further on we saw the first signs of hippo—telltale bubbles and lumps of flat dung. We stared ahead, gripping the paddles and digging the blades deep into the brown water; then, without warning, there was a gurgle like water running out of a giant-sized bath and a hippo snout emerged. We stopped, fascinated, but fearful of what might come next. Another nose appeared, then another and another, until we counted eight. We were surrounded by hippo. With all our strength we drove the boat forward and over the herd; seconds later we looked back to see the hippo watching us from a distance.

We passed a channel leading from Lake Baga-Baga to the old Pongolo. What a fearsome sight it was in the fading light, with the electric storm raging overhead. Further on an enormous crocodile lay on the bank and, slowly turning its head, watched us go by. It got our wind, came off the bank with a rush and a splash, then started to swim towards us. I yelled for a rifle, certain it intended to attack. Not much was needed to overturn us. Fortunately it was only a mock charge, but some time lapsed before the hairs on the back of my neck lay down. Never had I seen such a

monstrosity: even we—and we loved them—felt it should not be alive.

Shortly after this, some hadedahs flew out with squawks of alarm. We both jerked back in fright, then laughed our tension away when we saw the birds.

The force of the river grew stronger as the small stream running off the Lebombo and the Ingwavuma rose after the storm. We could not paddle any longer. Reluctantly we got out our small, three-and-a-half horsepower Seagull outboard and attached it to the boat. It always seemed sacrilege to destroy the peace of the wilderness with the put-put-put of the engine, but with the gathering gloom and the speed of the rising river, we had no alternative.

It was strange how quickly our fears subsided once the outboard noise drowned all sound. It made me realize that, in pristine surroundings, one reverts very quickly to the primitive, and noise plays a big part in causing fear.

A few weeks earlier we had made one of our periodical patrols down the river and were paddling south of the new junction, when a sleeping hippo was aroused by our scent and came careering off the high bank on our right, crashing through the reeds and landing with a mighty "galoomph" in the river. We were almost paralysed with fear. The same thing happened this day, but because the sound of the hippo's progress was drowned by the outboard, we didn't turn a hair!

Taking turns to steer the boat, we made our way slowly up the Pongolo. Twice we passed over herds of hippo, but with the water so high there was no danger, for they dived deeply and we rode safely over.

It was getting dark when we reached the old fig tree that marked our "landing stage" as we rather grandiloquently termed it. In fact, it was merely a slight indentation in the riverbank, which we had cleared with cane knives and spades. Four game guards stepped forward and old Catuane saluted us. Poor old Catuane was drowned in the Usutu River two years later, when a ferry punt overturned on the way back from Portuguese territory.

While the guards hoisted the boat out of the water, we made our way along the tiny local footpath leading through swamp. Mosquitoes were out in their thousands, and between swipes at the pests, Ken spoke of some future trip on the Pongolo.

"We have got to give this river a go: starting from Otobotini and coming right to here. And we will not use any mechanical form of power!" he added fiercely. "This river has got us and we simply must know it all. Somehow we must lay our hands on a large canoe, then we'll give it a go!" he said.

I watched his tall figure striding ahead, his feet squelching through the mud and his long mop of uncut fair hair bouncing on the back of his neck. I warmed towards him, for here was the true companion. Although he had only just left school, he was the real adventurer, yet with a difference from the man or boy who simply looks for thrills. Ken also had a questioning, scientific mind, and although completely undeveloped at that stage, he was to do great things later on.

Nobody or any circumstances stood in his way when it came to birds. He had a passion for birds. How often since Ken joined me, did we take our little green boat and paddle down the rivers and over the pans, looking for his beloved birds—waiting and listening for Heuglin's robin to sing, or Burchell's coucal to bubble down the scale, or the fish eagle shriek in triumph as it soared and floated, its white head and black wings so beautiful a contrast against the blue sky! Ken would smile with a light in his eyes and gaze rapturously about, exclaiming and pointing in delight at every sight and sound. His enthusiasm was always at fever pitch, and I was soon swept along and became as fascinated as I had never dreamed possible. We reached the stage of picking out a strange birdcall, although a hundred or more were calling at the same time. Friends would stare in suspicion or amusement as we excitedly shouted for silence when the strange bird sang.

Years later I was to forget so much that he had taught me, but Ken never lost the ability to have his mind transported whenever any bird flew past, no matter how pressing, urgent or dramatic other circumstances might be at that particular moment. How I envied him.

I well remember the look of ecstatic joy on his face as he came bursting into the house one day, with two tiny black helmet shrikes he had reluctantly collected as specimens in the Salene forest.

"It's a new record!" he had cried with unrestrained joy.

This then was the man who was to be my companion, learner ranger and friend for many years.

All the way to the house Ken talked about the canoe trip we were going to do on the Pongolo, and when we got inside he set about immediately to draw, with elaborate care, a map of the river.

CHAPTER 8

Two years later, on 14th May 1956, we left Umfolozi Game Reserve for St. Lucia Estuary to collect a 16-foot Folboat kindly given to us by Peter Yeld. Our long-awaited journey down the Pongolo River was about to begin.

As we bumped along the rough road leading out of the Umfolozi Reserve, we spoke like old-timers; and I told Ken of the experience that made me give up smoking.

It was in 1953 while I was stationed at Umfolozi. Ranger Van Schoor and I had caught a white poacher in the western Crown lands area, and a few weeks later I had been detailed to go to gather more evidence. Together with some game guards, I trekked on foot over the Mtunzini range and down into the acacia country below, past groves of nthombothi trees, over the Hlinza river and along the distinct white rhino trails to the poachers' hideout in a cave on the Hlungwana river.

I reached the cave at four in the afternoon, and after searching carefully and finding the remains of only one skin, I decided to trek back to some very old huts used by tsetse control on the Ingamazaneni River, where the water was sweet.

I picked up my haversack, called the guards and began the long walk back, I plodded along thighs aching, a peppery taste in my mouth and only the thought of water in my mind. It was dark when we reached the junction of the two rivers, but soon the new moon shone faintly and we were able to go ahead, though slowly. The last few miles up the rocky streambed of the Ingamazaneni were an agony of chafing boots and fatigued muscles, after the exhausting heat of the day.

When we reached the pools of sweet water I dropped my haversack; flopped down and drank until I was sated, then crawled a few yards to a marula tree and told the guards I would sleep there instead of walking the last hundred yards to the dilapidated hut. I dragged my sleeping bag out, put the haversack under my head and fell asleep quickly.

My dreams were wild and mixed, but one kept recurring. I dreamt that a horrible smell was invading the world, and no one could stop it. I awoke in a cold sweat and, peering into the faint light, froze to see the

sloping shoulders of a hyena a few feet away. I screamed for the game guards, and threw a handful of earth at the beast. It leapt away, padding over the leaves and through the grass.

The guards came running, horrified to hear what had happened.

"You are lucky, nkosaan," they said. "The jaws of that animal are so strong that he might have taken half your face or an arm or a leg away with him."

With shaking fingers I felt for cigarettes and matches, then was struck with the thought that smoking dulled the sense of smell. I threw the packet to the guards and did not touch a cigarette for many years.

That, I told Ken, was my introduction to the importance of smell.

We stopped on the edge of the corridor and looked back at the rolling, bush-clad hills of Umfolozi.

"That place has taught us a lot," Ken said.

There was hardly a stream or a hill that we did not know. With packs on our backs we had patrolled the length and breadth of the reserve, following game paths from the Black to the White Umfolozi Rivers, and observing the habits of white rhino and other animals.

To the west, on the Ncebe plains, a pan glinted in the sun. Only two days ago Jim Feely and I had sat silent in the bush and watched a herd of white rhino wallowing.

Jim Feely: short, thickset and brilliant; he already knew more about methods of wild life management than anyone in South Africa. Here was another man who was going to make a name for himself.

Jim carefully noted down the time each rhino arrived, the sex and the different age groups. He taught me that there was more to rhino watching than aesthetic appreciation. Nothing escaped his observant eyes. Some of the rhino drank before wallowing, others lay in the shade; a bull rolled right onto its back and calves played in the mud.

Different birds flew about, feeding on the rhino flies, and a hammerhead caught a frog that hopped away from the pan.

Other animals came to drink: warthog, nyala, grey duiker and the shyest of them all, the bushbuck. A baboon arrived, and barked.

Jim noted which animals reacted to this alarm; the bushbuck and duiker ran, while the warthog and rhino were unperturbed. Gradually a pattern formed, and I learnt the value of scientific observation.

"It's a pity Jim can't come with us," Ken said, interrupting my thoughts.

"Hugh, too," I added.

Hugh Dent: tall, with already grey hair at 27, was a trained portrait painter, an excellent Zulu linguist and an outstanding horseman.

We were leaving Jim and Hugh to look after Umfolozi, and we knew that the reserve would be in good hands.

We game rangers might be an odd lot, but we all had a common characteristic: a dedication to wild life conservation.

As we climbed into the Land Rover and drove off, I told Ken that one day I would write a book about them all; their loves, their fears, and their sacrifices for what they so earnestly believed in.

We collected the canoe at St. Lucia and left early the following morning. We passed through Mtubatuba, Myalazi River, Hluhluwe village and then on to Mkuze and Ubombo.

The whole road held innumerable memories for me, but it was at Mhlosinga and the turn-off to Nxwala Estates that so many incidents came crowding into my mind. I remembered camping beneath the lonely, boulder-strewn Nxwala hill on the Crown lands bordering Mkuze Game Reserve, watching the scorpions crawling up the tent wall as I lay on my stretcher, worrying about the following day because I had no knowledge of the law, or how to go about arresting a European poacher.

Game Guard Sigohlo had told me, in vivid detail, how poachers in lorries came down the road, crossing the southern limits of the Lebombo through the farms, then on to Nxwala Estate, shooting at every moving creature—professional biltong hunters from the Transvaal—cruel, callous men, with no feeling for wild life; local farmers too, just as inhuman, with even less reason, for they at least came into close contact with the beautiful animals of the veld. But greed overcame any finer feelings they may have had, so they came with the rest to kill and to maim.

Spent shotgun and rifle cartridges lay scattered in their hundreds in the dry red-grass veld, tell-tale evidence of poaching.

A week was to pass before anyone came, but when they did I soon saw that Sigohlo had not exaggerated. Stories of the thousands of impala to be shot on the Nxwala Estate had spread far and wide; men came hoping to emulate the local farmers who murdered the game, then took the carcases to Durban and sold them for £5 each on the market.

But our turn was to come, and we were to catch many of the cold-blooded murderers.

For four days Sigohlo and I had criss-crossed the Nxwala Estate, checking the paths and tracks, and learning the general topography. A section of the Nsumu pan with its green, lush reeds and scattered pools was on the Estate—a great attraction to the impala and wildebeest, who would trek out in thousands in the early morning and evening to feed and drink. Cattle egrets followed the wildebeest, pecking and eating the insects disturbed in the grass; red-billed oxpeckers galore hovered above the

game, alighting now and then to gorge themselves on the over-ripe ticks.

The snorting of the impala and the low "honks" of the wildebeest as they jostled each other at the muddy pools is something that brings back the romance of the old Africa, when animals had undisputed sway and man was a puny intruder, sneaking and killing the weak and sick animals. Now, after thousands of years, this had changed; the wild animals had become our charges, for us to protect and love and try to learn about their habits. But this was not to be, because some men in their insatiable greed were intent upon wiping out these remnants of the once immense herds that roamed the veld.

Cattle farmers who had grazing rights on the Estate claimed that the game was eating the grass belonging to their cattle; therefore they had the right to shoot and kill. The fact that it was out of season and shooting had been completely barred, and that a large proportion of the animals shot were females heavy in calf, was no deterrent.

One of the first poaching incidents I witnessed was a green, half-ton lorry charging at full bore along the western edge of the Nsumu pan, driving the impala out of the safety of the Mkuze Game Reserve on to the Estate and to the guns of the waiting poachers. The animals were shot down one after the other. This explained why, earlier in the week, I had come across twenty-six crippled impala, some with only three legs, others with intestines hanging out or with empty eye sockets, holes big enough to put two fists in, creeping and alive with white maggots.

I came across a hideously mutilated kudu, so badly injured that I was able to walk within fifteen feet of him. This magnificent animal's wound gave off the unmistakable stench of gangrene. The look that stately animal gave me is something I can never forget. In its eyes there was neither fear nor distress nor hate—it had simply given up. Nothing could have induced me to finish the beast off, hopeless though its chances of survival were. It turned slowly round and hobbled away.

Earlier on the day I had seen this kudu, I had chased some European poachers, but was unable to reach them in the Land Rover as we were separated by a stretch of swamp. I ran, scrambling, scrabbling and ploughing through the mud, cursing and swearing in a blind fury, in a hopeless attempt to catch these men. They escaped, but the time was to come when they would be caught red-handed. Catching them, however, was only the beginning, and in most cases, the easiest part of the operation; getting them to court was another matter entirely, when one had to deal with a bunch of prejudiced officials. One case in particular caused a train of repercussions lasting for many years.

It was on an early July morning that Ranger David Ransom and I

were lying hidden in the reeds on the edge of the Nsumu pan. Our Land Rover, filled with petrol and ready for instant action, was camouflaged in a patch of dense bush.

As the sun rose and the thousands of tiny cobwebs sparkled with dew, we heard the drone of a truck near the foot of Nxwala hill. Sound carries enormous distances over the veld on windless winter mornings, and we clearly heard the grating of gears and the spin of wheels as the vehicle crossed the Umsindusi river drift.

"Those bastards are up to no good!" David said excitedly.

I knew he was right, and that we were going to have trouble. I was afraid, for I had had enough experience of Nxwala already to know that some of these poachers were fanatics, and would not hesitate to open fire if they thought there was no chance of being found out.

The truck came nearer, then abruptly stopped, and everything was still for a few seconds. We braced ourselves and waited for what we knew was coming: Two loud reports of a .303 rifle followed each other in quick succession, the sound echoing and re-echoing. In a flash the whole veld came alive as animals raced in all directions. Monkeys dropped out of trees and fled into the long grass, some of them pausing to stand on their legs and peer in the direction of the shooting. Birds rose with cries of alarm, flying in circles above the scattered pools of the pan. Wildebeest ran wildly towards the reserve, leaving a long trail of red dust in their wake. Then the impala came out from beneath the low, stunted acacia trees. The sight of them galloping a long, single file back to the game reserve and safety was awe-inspiring. With incredible agility they sprang over the dongas and fallen acacia trees, the early morning sun glinting on their horns and red backs.

We watched, fascinated, the parade of nature, until another shot shattered the air.

Sprinting for the Rover, we jumped in and drove off at high speed in the direction of the firing. David hung on grimly as I changed down, and with my foot flat on the accelerator, raced through the tall reeds, bouncing and jolting over the hard baked mud. A reedbuck rose ahead of us and I swerved to avoid hitting it; with a shrill whistle of alarm it leapt into the reeds and vanished.

"Give it hell!" David shouted over the scream of the Rover engine. His face was set as he hung on to the safety bar.

David was a Londoner who had recently joined us. Within a few months he had become an excellent Zulu linguist and a first class naturalist. I liked him very much.

We roared out of the reeds and on to the high ground on the south,

then, twisting and turning to avoid the trees, we sped along a rough track. Red dust rose in clouds, choking and blinding us. After only a mile David was unrecognizable under the thick layer of dust on his face.

We topped a slight rise, and saw a green one-ton lorry parked in a glade. As I stopped, David leapt out of the vehicle and ran to the lorry. In a few seconds he had searched the back and produced a .303 rifle.

The occupants of the lorry sat dumbstruck, until I walked over, when they became most voluble and demanded to know "what we were up to?" We informed them without preamble that they were under arrest. Then the trouble started. As bad luck would have it, they had killed nothing, and I knew it would be a matter of opinion in court as to whether they had done the shooting or not.

David searched everywhere, hoping to find a carcass, but came back bitterly disappointed. We had to be content with confiscating the firearms and taking their names and addresses. Some months later we succeeded in getting them before court, but they got off scot-free.

Those were still the early days of game ranging for me, and there was little time to study wild animals. Man—man the poacher—was the animal to be studied.

We were seriously understaffed and had a big area to look after, so we resorted to every possible device to make our work effective. We built up a network of informers, and information began to filter in. We put fear into the hearts of would-be poachers by speaking loudly in the Mtubatuba cafe about non-existent patrols in areas we had not time to visit. We used the party-line telephone in the same way, secure in the knowledge that every gossiper in Zululand would be listening. As these stories passed from person to person, they became so distorted that it was often amusing to hear them after they had been added to and changed by at least fifty people in the poaching fraternity.

On one occasion I was in the Umfolozi Game Reserve and phoned David Ransome to tell him I was going to Mkuze Game Reserve that weekend. We talked for long enough to make sure someone had listened, then I went to Mtubatuba and let it be known to the local gossips that I was on my way to Mkuze.

When night fell I returned to Umfolozi, and without lights drove to a vantage point in the corridor—a strip of unoccupied Crown lands linking the Umfolozi and Hluhluwe Reserves. Soon I saw car lights coming along the main road. A game guard sitting near me exclaimed that someone in the back of the truck was flashing a torch. It was impossible for me to see the separate lights from that distance: the guards, with their superior eyesight, often put me to shame.

Slowly the vehicle approached, until I could see the unmistakable flash of a torch. The vehicle stopped, then started again. Half an hour passed before it appeared below us. In the reflected light of the headlamp I saw a black policeman standing on the back, shining a torch into the veld. For a few moments I was paralysed.

"No, God! Not again!" I thought.

But there was no doubt about it; a local policeman was at it. I ran down a path that was a short cut to the main road and stood, panting and breathless, waving the vehicle to a stop.

There was an icy silence as I challenged the driver. Then a policeman got out.

"What the hell do you think you're doing?" I asked.

He flew into a rage and we plunged into a bitter scene. The game guards looked in the back of the truck, but signalled to me that there was nothing there. The policeman saw them and began to abuse them; as he turned away I had a look in the cab and saw a .303 service rifle propped up against the seat. But there was no sign of any game.

There was nothing to be done. I knew exactly what he would say, and it wasn't long before he came out with, "I'm just on a routine patrol and what do you mean by stopping me?"

He said I would hear more of the matter, and we parted on the worst of terms.

A few months later he was transferred; we all breathed sighs of relief. He had been poaching for a long time, as a pile of wildebeest and reedbuck horns near his house mutely testified.

Needless to say, one man like this could give the whole Police Force a bad name. The majority of policemen in Zululand were decent, hard-working men, who took just as serious a view of poaching as we did. They realized, too, that we were serious in our efforts to put an end to European poaching, and that we did not care who was offended in the process. In later years, as the staff increased and more rangers were able to patrol the remote areas, poaching by Europeans became negligible; more and severer penalties became a strong deterrent to any would-be poacher.

CHAPTER 9

We reached Ubombo village in the afternoon.

Ubombo: it was an historic place. Many ghosts haunted it, some in hazy antiquity and some in bright sunshine.

David Leslie had rested here on his way to the flats below, to shoot the herds of wild game, which existed in thousands in the bush-covered plains. He had stalked and shot the white rhino, wildebeest, zebra, and almost massacred a herd of buffalo trapped in the Pongolo River. Then, his wagons loaded with cured and dried skins, he had returned to Natal. In the short evenings, after the day's hunt, he had written up his diary in the firelight, as hyenas and lions prowled nearby. He wrote speculatively about the future of Tongaland, and envisaged railways and farms and other forms of human invasion, yet had he known what fate would befall the game in this twentieth century, I am sure he would have been horrified.

The Hon. Henry Drummond, a friend of David Leslie, also passed here in 1860 on hunting trips, and he had the foresight to see that the slaughter of game could not last. In an impassioned appeal in his book "Hunting Adventures in South East Africa", he asked that the destruction of elephants be controlled, otherwise the following generation would never know what they looked like.

It was Drummond who related the story of a rogue black rhino, living on the Tongaland flats, which had killed at least seven people and continued to rampage until 1871, when one of Mpande's sons died and there was a big ihlambo hunt. This is the period when members of the tribe have to cleanse themselves with blood through killing. The Tulwana regiment (which was later to distinguish itself at the battle of Isandlwana) was hunting in this black rhino's area. The rhino bravely charged the entire regiment and killed fourteen men before it sank, dying, with over a thousand spears in it.

Drummond was an outstanding hunter, and his exploits became legends in the lowveld. During the Zulu War of 1879 he became closely associated with John Dunn, but it was Sir Charles Saunders who really put Tongaland on the map. In September 1887, the Secretary for Native

Down the Pongolo

Photo: J. Feely

Ken Tinley,
the good companion

Photo: Natal Witness

Photo: Ian Player

A mouthfull

Lying in wait

Photo: Dr. H. B. Cott

Affairs in Natal ordered Mr. C. R. Saunders (as he was then) to travel to the country of the amaTonga.

Saunders left Maritzburg accompanied by Mr. Giles and twenty-three Zulus. They travelled to Rorkes Drift via Greytown and Umsinga, commenting that there was no grass in the Mooi and Tugela river valleys, which necessitated buying forage for the cattle. From Rorkes Drift they made for Vryheid through the Hlubi district. Leaving Vryheid, they travelled for 30 miles and reached Ngome forest after two weeks.

Trekking on from Ngome, Saunders made for the Mkuzi River, through the area where the final battle between Mpande and Dingane was fought, then on to Marcus' road that led to Swaziland. They followed Marcus' road to the Pongolo and beyond, then east along some tracks of Boer wagons. Crossing the Pongolo, they reached the foothills of the Lebombo, passing only three Zulu homesteads belonging to the people of Usibepu, who had fled there after the battle of Tshaneni.

This area of some sixty square miles was unoccupied, but the country from the Mkuzi river to the Lebombo abounded in game; lions were particularly numerous.

They left the wagonette at a pass north of the Pongolo poort and climbed the mountain on foot up a steep path leading to the muzi of Chief Sambane. It was by Sambane's people that Dingane was killed, and Saunders was the first white man to see Dingane's grave in the Hlatikulu forest.

Chief Sambane's district was both healthy and fertile. The people resembled the Zulus, to whom they had paid tribute until the Zulu War in 1879. Sambane told Saunders that he now considered himself a British subject, and for the last three years had been paying tribute to a man named Ferreira, who claimed taxes on behalf of the British government!

For the rest of the journey into Tongaland, Saunders and his party travelled on foot and on horseback.

In later years Sambane was the focal point of a dispute between the Transvaal Republic and the British government. He tried (and succeeded) for a number of years to play one off against the other. Much acrimonious correspondence flowed between the two governments.

After leaving Sambane's kraal on the 7th October 1887, (the journey having taken twenty-six days so far) the party pressed on to the amaTonga country to the east, entering it on the 11th October.

They then trekked seventy miles, following the course of the Pongolo on its eastern bank to where it joined the Usutu. With the exception of the Pongolo, there was little water, and the amaTonga had to dig along the edge of marshes and swamps, but it was so bad they preferred travelling

ten miles to the Pongolo to get drinking water.

The soil was sandy, except near the mass of pans adjoining the river. The staple food was maize, millet and groundnuts, which Saunders found a bilious fruit.

He described in detail the wealth of animal and bird life on the pans, and at the junction of the Pongolo and Usutu he said there were elephants, buffalo, rhino, waterbuck and nyala.

The amaTonga resembled the Zulu in certain respects, but were not as powerful physically. The huts, instead of being built in a circle round the cattle kraal like the Zulus', were built in clusters. It was the custom to bury the head of any homestead, whether man or woman, in the hut in which they died. The entrance was then built up; the hut abandoned and allowed to fall.

In some deserted muzis through which they passed, there were as many as nine or ten huts closed in this manner. It was common to see three or four huts closed in a muzi.

With the exception of an old man and an old woman, they saw no one over the age of forty-five. Saunders concluded that the death rate must have been high every year during the hot season.

The amaTonga, during the minority of their young king, Umgwanasi, were ruled by Queen Zambile, a Swazi by birth and daughter of the late Swazi king, Umswazi. It was the custom of the Queen to marry late in life for fear that the heir to the throne would grow up in his father's lifetime and usurp his power.

Queen Zambile was a tall, handsome and intelligent woman some thirty-five years old. She was popular with her people, having their affairs at heart, and she kept them under superb control. Only when someone had committed a very grave offence did she have him killed.

She had an army of some 20,000 men, divided into nine regiments of different age groups. The General of the army was Umjigajiga.

Many of the people were armed with guns, an unlimited supply being obtainable from the Portuguese. Saunders said they appeared to be good shots, judging by the amount of game they killed, which was fast disappearing because of the number of firearms.

The amaTonga were not a warlike nation, and only had minor engagements with neighbouring tribes during the reign of their late king. Few of the men alive during Saunders' visit had taken part in these battles. The people said, however, that when the young king grew up, it would be his wish and that of the nation, to "wet his spears"; Chief Sambane would likely be the first object of attack because of a feud based on the alleged encroachment of amaTonga territory by Sambane's people.

Saunders met a Mr. Bruheim, a German who had been living with the AmaTonga for the past ten or twelve years, and from him got much useful information.

Saunders noticed that the people were industrious, making grain baskets and various vessels. They also carved in ivory, horn and wood. Formerly they had also made their own clothing from the bark of fig trees; this was pounded between stones, washed well and a fibrous garment produced. Two or three would be as warm as an ordinary blanket. They also used to weave garments from wild cotton found in the thorn country on the western slopes of the Lebombo, and they made canoes out of the trunks of trees, which were chiefly used for crossing the Pongolo in flood.

Half the young men were always away, working in Natal and the gold mines, and some had just returned from the Delagoa Bay railway line, where many had died of fever. On his return each man had to pay a tribute of £1 to the Queen.

The men and women married at an absurdly young age. The whole time Saunders was there he did not see an unmarried female over the age of fifteen years. Even at the royal kraals, where one would expect to see young girls, there were none. The fathers said that they thought it better for people who had to live together for life to become acquainted at an early age, but Saunders pertinently remarked that it was for the sake of obtaining money that the girls were allowed to marry so young.

Saunders noted that the people consumed large quantities of palm wine, which they extracted from the trunks of the wild date palm (*Phoenix reclinata*) and vegetable ivory (*Hyphanae crinita*).

In his book "Amongst the Zulus and amaTongas", David Leslie was far more caustic in his comments on the drinking habits of the amaTonga. He wrote: "All that a man hath will he give for his life but to such an extent is the love of drink carried amongst the amaTonga, they will give even that for rum, since they care not though they die—if they only die drunk."

Saunders, Giles and their attendants started their return journey on the 14th October. The fever season was fast approaching; they were unable to escape it and all but eight of the party got it. They had tried to keep it away by taking half a teaspoon of quinine five times a day and "keeping their bowels open".

They collected their wagonette and made their way through Usibepu's country, to Somekele's district, crossing the Umfolozi below the junction of the Black and the White. They were met by Mr. Arthur Shepstone, the Magistrate stationed at Imbabe, and stayed with him for a few days to recuperate.

They reached Maritzburg after being away for three months.

As a result of Saunders's visit and his lengthy and brilliant report, negotiations were opened with Queen Zambile, and Tongaland was annexed.

Two years later the Colonial Office requested the Admiralty to send a survey ship to Sordwana Bay, Tongaland, to investigate the possibilities of establishing a harbour.

Commander Pullen, Lieutenant Howard and the ship's doctor, Trevor Roper, went ashore to see the country. They found a few local people in the neighbourhood. Fish was plentiful in both the sea and the river, but game was scarce.

Dr. Roper took notes, which were transcribed and enclosed with Commander Pullen's detailed report. He also took samples of the stream and described the surrounding vegetation. He said the soil was bad and that the amaTonga were in a state of starvation, being able to grow only a little maize. No cattle were obtainable, only fowls, which the locals sold at sixpence apiece.

Edible wild birds were scarce, but Roper observed kingfishers, whitethroated warblers and guineafowl. He said that turtles were found on the shore, as well as edible oysters.

In order to support life, the amaTonga had killed and trapped most of the antelope.

Roper completed his notes by mentioning that the portion of the coast down by the sea was healthy, but only half a mile inland "had every appearance of being a typical place for the propagation of malarious fevers".

Commander Pullen, who was under pressure from the Admiralty, wrote a carefully worded report on the 21st February, 1889, which, if read between the lines, made it clear that the establishment of a harbour would be both risky and expensive.

Through the reports of Saunders and Pullen, one is able to get a clear insight into Tongaland before the white man made an impression.

CHAPTER 10

While Ken went off to buy some rations, I walked along to the Police station to look for my friend, Sergeant Botha. As I passed the courthouse, I reflected on my early days in the Ubombo district.

I remembered old Luke Erasmus, the first poacher I ever caught—and the finest—his figure hunched on a horse, with an impala slung across the saddle. He was going westward from Nxwala Estate, over the Lebombo Mountains to a valley near Biala.

That day was also the first time I had met Sigohlo Mbazine, a game guard in the Mkuze Game Reserve. It was from Sigohlo that I learnt all my early bush craft, and began to understand the ways of wild animals.

Now, as I peered through the court house window and saw the witness box in the corner. I remembered days spent in long argument, when poachers had been brought to court. So often they were found "Not guilty"; the law was sometimes difficult to understand.

I walked past the Magistrate's office, over the veranda to the low stone wall behind the building. I remembered the first time I saw this breathtaking view of Tongaland spread our below the Lebombo mountains-vast and overpowering, land stretching as far as one could see, dark patches of bush and open places, with bright glimpses of the Pongolo—a twisting, tortuous river snaking its way to the horizon.

I had come to locate a black rhino that was going to be shot and handed over to the Transvaal Museum. I had asked Sergeant de Villiers where I could find the animal. He had laughed quietly, and led me to the stone wall, then with a sweep of his hand indicated the wilderness below. How my heart had leapt! Where and how did one begin? There were only two days to look, before the rest of the party arrived.

I was away the next morning before there was a hint of light in the east. Then, for twenty hours of incredibly hard going, with thorns tearing my clothes, and obsessed with the fear that I would fail on my first job, I tracked the rhino. With two amaTonga guides, I wandered for miles over the Makatini flats, following this track, then that, meeting drunken amaTonga at dilapidated homesteads, drinking foul-smelling cane wine

because the water looked worse—I went on and on. I passed beneath huge, umbrella-shaped acacia trees, through dense bush, and finally had the unforgettable sight of the first fever trees on the banks of the Pongolo River.

Gratefully I sat down in the shade of a fever tree to rest and absorb the atmosphere of mystery and age.

I had not been there long when a kehla (old man) came out of the bush, driving a few goats towards the river. He stopped and spoke, and told a touching story: a crocodile had taken his daughter that summer when the river was in flood. I listened, horrified, to his lengthy description of the girl's struggle as the crocodile had dragged her off downstream, then sank into a pool on the bend of the river. I never dreamt that in a few years I would come to look upon the crocodile as an animal of beauty, and do everything I could to try to save the few remaining in Zululand.

I spent the night not far from the riverbank, with the indefinable atmosphere of Tongaland all about me, listening to the queer singing of the amaTonga in the distance and the screams of the bush babies in the sycamore fig trees.

The following morning, after a walk of four hours, crawling sometimes on my hands and knees, I heard the snort of a rhino. I crept within fifteen paces of the huge beast; then the mangy dogs of the tall, lean Tonga guide rushed forward, yelping, and the rhino crashed out of sight into another dense thicket. I had not failed in my first task.

The memory faded as I turned away from the courthouse, and walked to the Police quarters. I looked through a broken window, with torn curtains flapping gently in the breeze, and saw Sergeant Botha and a constable sitting at the old rickety table. Swarms of flies buzzed near the kitchen door and bees murmured in the orange trees.

I spoke Botha's name; he leapt to his feet, pulled me inside, and insisted that I have a cup of coffee. His greeting was overwhelming.

He had aged since I had last seen him; his face was set and the skin stretched taut over the bones. He had been too long on the mountain, but for reasons best known to themselves, the police had refused him a transfer, despite many requests.

We drank coffee, and before five minutes were over were recalling incidents from the past which we had shared: "Ginger", with his bushy red beard—what a character! None of us seemed to know where he had come from or how we had met him—he simply made himself known. At a party on the mountain one night, when everyone was imbibing liquor freely, Ginger accidentally shot himself with a small pistol he always carried in his pocket.

He lay writhing on the floor, shouting above the drone of alcoholic conversation, "I'm shot. I'm shot!"

Everyone laughed wildly and shouted back, "We're all shot!"

It was only when they saw blood that they sobered up enough to drag Ginger off to the annoyed doctor.

We were still laughing at some of Ginger's doings when Ken came in and reminded us of the goat Ginger used to keep. He had called it "Mr Jones". He and Ginger were inseparable.

"What happened to it?" Ken asked Botha.

"Oh, it got some obscure disease and had to be shot. Poor old Ginger wept for weeks. But do you remember how he used to scratch himself and mutter 'Holy horse feathers'?" Botha laughed.

"It was his favourite expression," Ken said.

Then Botha and I started talking about our first days in Zululand. We had arrived about the same time, and it was to him that I made my first statement concerning Luke Erasmus, the poacher.

"What's the poaching like nowadays?" I asked.

"They're keeping off Nxwala Estate so far, but there are bound to be a few who will chance their arms again," he said. "But the days of massed shooting are over."

"I sincerely hope so," I said.

Botha smiled faintly, then said quietly, "Yes, you had your hands full there for a little while, didn't you?"

"Have another cup of coffee," he said, handing my cup to an umfaan.

We talked until late in the afternoon, then, taking our leave of Botha, Ken and I climbed into the Land Rovers and drove down the Lebombo pass.

Ken echoed my sentiments when he said, "There's hope for this country when policemen like Botha are still around."

We left Ubombo as the sun dipped behind the high range and long shadows were creeping over the Makatini flats. A chill wind blew along the top of the mountain, and it was with relief that we took the turn to the right and bumped down the twisting road to the warm flats below. On the last bend a raging veld fire swept alongside. Combretum trees burnt fiercely and the tall *Hyperanae* grass fell in an instant before the flames. I stopped to watch and Ken drew up behind me. Before he spoke I knew what he was going to say.

"We're back in Tongaland," he said, pointing to the fire.

How right he was! The whole time I had known Tongaland I could not remember a day passing without seeing a fire. No matter where you looked on any type of day, a wisp of smoke betrayed a fire on the

Tongaland flats. No wonder the early Portuguese called this part of Africa "Terra del fumo". Shipwrecked survivors had trekked up the golden beaches on their way to the Portuguese settlement of Lourenco Marques, and all had remarked upon the huge pillars of smoke soaring into the sky.

We had nearly reached Otobotini drift, when I looked in the back of the Rover and noticed that our canoeing bag was missing. There was no option, one of us had to go back to fetch it; we spun a coin and Ken lost. I voiced a silent prayer of gratitude: the thought of going all the way back to St. Lucia was appalling. Ken climbed wearily into his Rover and soon vanished in a cloud of dust.

I stopped on a steep bank just above the pont landing and whistled and hooted for the pont workers, until there was a faint answering hail. Then a European strolled down to the pont tethered to the opposite side. It was an official who had given us a lot of trouble at Ndumu Game Reserve.

"Hello, Player!" he shouted insolently. "Are you looking for trouble again?"

"Are you the pont operator now?" I was inspired to ask in return. He swore a little.

Then the pont workers ambled down the sandy path, muttering about "Madolo" (my Zulu name). I had always tipped them well, for it saved a lot of delay. They knew their power and were not slow in using it.

The official climbed onto the pont too, and came across with the operators.

As the workers sweated and strained to manoeuvre the pont over the sand banks, I remembered how troublesome this official had been at Ndumu. He had a mania for politics and would start a violent argument on the slightest pretext, at the same time resenting any criticism of his political beliefs. Relations had become strained when we forbade him to enter the Reserve to fish in the Nyamiti pan.

Still, I bore him no grudge, and as the pont grounded, I stuck out my hand. To my astonishment, he shook it quite cheerfully.

I drove the Rover on to the pont, not without a twinge of fear because a minor miscalculation would mean ending up in the water. The chains rattled as the pont operators cast off and swung the pont round until it faced upstream, then poling with enviable skill they moved it up against the current.

The sun had disappeared, leaving colours of the greatest glory above the gap in the Lebombo range where the Pongolo pours its waters through the hills. The last light of the day was superb. Deep purples in the gorges, crimson and gold on the mountaintops and fleecy, speckled clouds stretching low until they touched the distant horizon.

The official broke the stillness and the peace. It was definite, he said, that all the land from the gorge to the Ndumu Game Reserve would be turned into an agricultural settlement.

"If that is a fact, then the whole nation will have lost something!" I retorted.

"Why?" he asked.

"Because the Afrikaner's great strength as a nation stemmed from the fact that their forefathers experienced the wilderness in its every form, and from it developed strength that tempered their characters—like this wilderness." I paused to look about me. "This wilderness which our generation, encouraged by people like you, is seeking to destroy and turn into an agricultural settlement. You as an Afrikaner should be bitterly ashamed, instead of proud, that you are going to do away with all this beauty, to say nothing of game reserves, and replace it with agricultural settlements."

My forcefulness disturbed him and he was quiet. But I was angry, and a thousand violent thoughts came flashing through my head. I thought of the day when I had first heard talk of the Pongolo dam and plans for doing away with Ndumu and Mkuze Game Reserves.

I had walked to the top of Ndumu hill and sat near the old hut that Tom Elphick had used, and looked at the reserve spread below. The Mahemane (I don't know where I am) bush stretched like a green carpet from the foothills of the Lebombo; to the north a thin glistening line marked the path of the mighty Usutu River from where it left the gorge and rocky krantzes, then stretched along the flats to its junction with the Pongolo. Above me, long black clouds had scudded along, casting finger-like shadows over the bush. Below me a Bateleur eagle soared, majestically and gracefully, uttering its "cor-cor-de-cor" foghorn cry, then crashing its wings together over its head. The Zulus call the bird "nqunqulu", for the sound of the wings is like the cracking of a knobkerrie against a shield. The bush below me was brooding and silent, whereas years before it had been alive with animals of every description—elephant, buffalo, rhino and thousands of antelope. Today there was only the impala and the shy red bush duiker. Occasionally a lone hippo left the pans and swamps and tramped along a forgotten trail, now only haunted by its ancestors.

To the south of the green scar of the fence line a large emerald circle stood out vividly, like an island in the sea, such was the contrast to the black-shadowed bush. This was Balamhlanga. It was through here that countless migrations of game had passed. Their beaten footpaths are still running in ridges towards the river. It was part of the highway to the

111

perennial Usutu where, when the veld became arid and drought stricken, the game trekked. They were harassed by lion, hyena, leopard, jackal, hunting dog and the vulture, but driven by their maddening thirst, they came inexorably onwards to the river and the lush green grass of the pans.

Here still remained part of the glory of the old Africa. We were trying to protect the little that was left, and were making progress. In a few years the 25,000 acres that comprised Ndumu Game Reserve would have got back some of its former grandeur, for the game was losing its fear and gradually recolonizing the vacant areas, giving life and colour to the veld.

Now suddenly all this was placed in jeopardy-threatened by the insatiable greed of man. I had just heard that "they" were drilling on the Pongolo banks near KwaMbuzi for stone for the quarry to supply the future dam.

What happens when the dam comes? How green was my valley? Will all this, spread out below me, be destroyed? And the hippo? My crocodiles and Ken's birds? Will they be shot and killed? Obliterated forever? And in their place, sugar cane and mealies. God forbid that with the stroke of a dictatorial pen this might happen. This time it will be man's inhumanity to nature. Would this peaceful scene be transformed into a sprawling mass of Government-built, stereotyped farmhouses, with barefooted children running and shouting in the future twilight? How charming? No! How grim.

How important this little, fractional piece of country is: it will give so much pleasure to the city dwellers, living such humdrum lives.

The game reserves must be inviolate, but who will make them so?

I voiced the last words aloud, and the Government official asked what I had been thinking about. I told him.

"Ah, the dam has got to come!" he said again.

"You will be wiping out all the good work our forefathers did. Things like this were the cause of the Great Trek, and my great-grandmother was in it," I said.

"There is nothing I can personally do to stop this area from being turned into farms!" he muttered.

I disagreed, and cited examples of individuals who had changed the world.

"From the day you turn the last wilderness into farms, so our nation will lose its particular stamp of individuality and sturdiness," I said.

"You can't stop progress," he replied.

"Too much is destroyed in the name of progress. Animals, and by animals I mean birds, mammals, fish, insects and every other form of wild life, have just as much right to a place in this country as you or I. In fact

they have even more right at the moment because there are so few left," I answered angrily.

My words made no impression, and I realized that he represented progress. He was twentieth-century man who wanted to wipe out all trace of the wilderness.

Everything would have to give way to this Frankenstein called progress. Whenever money was involved, wild animals and forests had to give way to farms and man-made, straight-lined, desperately dull, exotic plantations. Slowly and insidiously, progress would throttle all the life-giving qualities of the wilderness in Zululand, until only a few small game reserves would be left, and so many tourists would visit these that their whole original identity would be completely smothered. Nowhere in Zululand would the true primeval remain, because its natural protector, the tsetse fly and malaria, had been conquered by man.

Then Heuglin's robin burst into song, and instantly I forgot the official, and heard no more of what he had said. A water dikkop flew low above the river and landed on the opposite bank, its head jerking characteristically up and down. It took off, and gave its long wailing whistle. The noises of night began—crickets and the occasional frog. The river gurgled and swirled past the creaking pont. A tiger fish jumped and skittered along the surface of the water. I rejoiced in the fact that I had been fortunate enough to see, hear and smell all this before man ruined it completely.

The pont grounded, sliding over the sand and banging against the rocks. I started the Rover, waved to the official, then drove to the Otobotini store, where I dumped the canoe.

I left for Ndumu as swarms of bats poured from the eaves of the wood- and-iron store. A long and lonely road to cover in the open Rover lay before me.

After an hour's driving there was a faint glimmer of moonbeams through the nthombothi trees, and an eagle owl hooted above the steady hum of the engine. A snake slithered across the tracks, its slender form caught briefly in the headlights. A turn, and Mfongoso drift sprang out of the darkness. Frogs and crickets vied to break the stillness. The water splashed on the mudguards and the wheels slipped on the smooth stones. Memories once more—of rains and floods, days of breathless heat and the undercurrent of the mystery of Tongaland.

CHAPTER 11

Ken came back with the canoe bag at three in the morning, had a few hours' sleep and woke ready for our journey.

We left one Rover at Ndumu and drove the other to Otobotini; arriving at the store just after midday, we piled the sixteen-foot canoe in the back and took it down to the pont landing stage. Ken went back to the store to park the Rover while I stowed the kit carefully, managing to get everything aboard. Then I relaxed and watched our craft floating gently on the ripples of a side current. Ken's bird-collecting material and his shotgun .22 combination were perched in the cockpit.

If we turned over we should have to battle to save everything, but my past experiences in canoeing had at last come in handy, and I was glad that it had all been learnt the hard way, for it lessened the chance of mistakes. My trips down the Umgeni, Umkomaas and Umsindusi had been hard and exacting, but the knowledge gained had stood me in good stead since I had become a ranger.

The river was low for the time of the year, and flowed silently, with tiny feathers shed by a flock of cattle egrets, floating on the surface. A barbel cruised past in the shadows of the green water, then with a flick of its tail moved into the fast current. Heuglin's robin sang "Don't you do it! Don't you do it!" then broke into lyrical song. Cattle lowed in the distance and a well-built pont operator strummed his guitar. It was peaceful. This was so good after the last hectic days at St. Lucia, with masses of fishermen and their demands for bait.

Three brilliant butterflies and a wasp carrying a spider landed on the prow of "Ukudhlangwenya", the name we had given our craft, meaning "Crocodile food". The canoe swung round, and the butterflies turned to face the wind—a flutter of shimmering wings and they were away downstream. The wasp moved in quick circles round its victim, then it too flew away.

In the polished blue sky a lone Bateleur eagle, rich in its black and red, came swooping down the valley, a twist of its wings and it glided rapidly up into the thermals, there to give itself to the currents. It is the

symbol of the bushveld. How often had I delightedly watched the Bateleurs gliding near the krantzes at Mpila in the Umfolozi Game Reserve, or floating over the Mtunzini range, or hurtling down to the White Umfolozi river to land and bathe in company with the vultures at Esiwa-amanqe—and at Ndumu, when they came over the Lebombo and swept ceaselessly up and down the western part of the game reserve.

The bird above me turned and came towards me again, its black head moving backwards and forwards, its pale beak gleaming in the afternoon sun. Suddenly, with legs and talons outstretched and with crested head thrown back, it uttered its call, "cor-cor-de-cor", rising in pitch on the last notes. It turned again and swept southwards, looking for all the world like a huge bat. Three hawks came into view, circling the reeds nearby, waiting for a mouse or rat to break from cover. I was grateful for Ken's friendship, for it was he who had really made me aware of the world of birds. I would always be in his debt.

I could not completely escape into it as he could, but there were times when my entire attention could be riveted upon a single bird. When I had been miserable in towns, this had helped me and I had been able to forget the grinding traffic as a swallow swooped above the high buildings.

Ken came back from the store and we did a trial paddle upstream. The canoe seemed steady enough, so we turned, and with only a quick farewell glance at the poort, we dipped our paddles and shot downstream: our long-awaited journey was about to begin. This was going to be the culmination of all our canoeing experiences in Tongaland.

After ten minutes of hard paddling we were away from the sounds of Otobotini and civilization. Ken guided the canoe and I scribbled in my notebook. The canoe glided down the centre of the current with Ken paddling occasionally to keep it steady.

"Talk about bliss!" Ken said.

A crocodile raised itself from a sandbank and lumbered into a wide pool ahead. For us this was a glorious sight, for we knew the crocodile: it is the symbol of the river. Its nose broke surface, then its head, followed by its serrated back, and finally its tail showed above the water as it swam slowly and purposefully to the opposite bank. For a moment there was an unmistakable smell of crocodile.

Ken dug a paddle in and swung the canoe into a side current. We floated past the crocodile, its eyes and nostrils just above the water, then glided round a bend below a rocky krantz with jutting slabs of rock, and aloes standing like sentries silhouetted against the brilliant sky line. The river was deep and quiet until it narrowed between two rocks, then it murmured in soft undertones as it brushed against the uneven stones.

The silence was shattered by the sharp chatter of monkeys, and a scream of victorious freedom from a black and white fish eagle. This bird symbolizes freedom and its hauntingly beautiful cry often dissipated our worries and put new fire into us for the cause of conservation. No one could ever forget that call. We listened, tense and expectant. The bird called again and the echoes reverberated down the river; again and again he screamed out his triumphant call. Then all was silent.

Ken cursed softly. The nose of the canoe was too heavy, so it went the opposite direction we wanted it to go. We eased the kit backwards and the nose lifted a little. Ken dipped his paddle and thrust hard; "Ukudhlangwenya" rocketed forward, leaving a long line of ripples in its wake. We drifted again. Long gnarled roots hung into the water, marked with drying clusters of driftwood from the summer floods, nature's way of warning the unwary of her power in the summer months.

A chill gust of wind blew, and brittle leaves fell from the sycamore figs, crackling as they dropped onto the canvas canoe. They floated for a few yards, blown crazily here and there by every puff of wind. A water tortoise, perched insecurely on a semi-submerged log, flopped into the water as we approached. They heard the canoe before did any other form of life on the river.

Ken stopped paddling and pointed ahead to a long dark shape lying in the shadows of a high promontory. A squeak from the woodwork and the shape slid leisurely into the river. Its head surfaced; green eyes turned towards us, then it streaked across the water, the scutes on its back shining in the reflected light. Another crocodile recorded in our notebook.

There was a quick movement on our left; we turned in time to see another crocodile swim swiftly below a submerged log and catch a tigerfish. We paddled closer to try to see whether the crocodile would swallow the fish while under the water. It surfaced, the tigerfish gleaming in its jaws. It snapped its massive head, pulverizing the fish, sank, then surfaced again and swam towards us. The fish feebly flapped its tail, then lay still. The crocodile glared at us malevolently; we edged nearer, then there was a swirl and the reptile disappeared. Spreading ripples broke on the opposite bank. The river flowed on, unperturbed by the drama we had witnessed.

We paddled a few yards, floating past a dense patch of riverine forest, until the river turned, and without warning we found ourselves opposite a long sandbank. Two crocodiles lying in the shade got our wind and did the high walk towards us. Seen from river level it was a fascinating but frightening sight—the waddle and slow leaning from side to side, teeth shining and the green eyes in a fixed stare. As they neared the water, their

bellies flopped; then with a quick run they propelled themselves into the river and skimmed across only a few feet from the boat. I noted them down in the book. We were determined to count every crocodile we saw during the journey.

Ken took his binoculars out and scanned the river ahead as I paddled.

"Another Dad," he said crisply—our Ndumu slang for a crocodile.

I took the binoculars and looked at the crocodile. Its tail was submerged while the rest of the body was on the sandbank. A very interesting fact, and probably a method of cooling, for contrary to general opinion, crocodile cannot stand the rays of the sun for long; a sure way to kill a young one is to tie its jaws up and leave it exposed.

The river swung westward and we canoed into the dazzling afternoon sun. The Lebombo range came into view and I checked our bearings. The mountain was a long sharp ridge of blackness, but green forest patches showed up clearly in the afternoon light. We floated, with the river plunging into a small gorge so that our view of the outside world was blanketed, and all we could see was the deep muddy cut of the riverbank with roots and grass hanging pathetically on the crumbling slopes.

Suddenly and inexplicably we were aware that we were in another world, that of the river and its inhabitants. The world we had come from had ceased to exist and we were amongst the river dwellers—reptiles, birds and animals. The king of this kingdom is the crocodile; often unseen and seldom heard, he is nevertheless ubiquitous.

Among men and women of the other world—the one we had left—the talk is of pleasure, work, food and entertainment. On the river all conversation turns to the crocodile: on every mudbank he leaves his mark in some form, and the fear he spreads is pervasive.

We paddled quietly on, afraid to talk and disturb the stillness that had settled upon us. It was the stillness of the wilderness. We were away from the killing mechanization of that other world. There was so much to see, to hear and to smell here. The pungent odour of rotting leaves, of wood smoke from amaTonga huts, of old figs lying in the mud, of mud itself and the river, crushed insects and the big black ant that can smell as badly as a dead wildebeest, all these smells invaded our nostrils.

The river narrowed and the water flowed faster, we paddled hard then relaxed and let the canoe glide downstream. Ken lay back, enjoying the peace, until some vervet monkeys saw us and set up their loud, insistent chattering.

"Funny thing. I could have sworn I smelt those monkeys before I saw them," Ken remarked.

"It wouldn't surprise me in the least," I answered.

Ken was silent as he dug a paddle in and guided the canoe towards a strongly flowing current. Then he remarked how rapidly civilized man was losing his old senses. It was only people like the amaTonga, who really lived close to nature, and experienced daily what it took us years to achieve, who had not lost the age old instincts.

The river turned northwards again; a light wind behind us made the canoe drift faster. A group of monkeys on the opposite bank stood on their hind legs and stared inquisitively at us. One chirruped, and in an instant they all gambolled in single file towards the tall green and yellow sycamore fig trees. One bull rapidly climbed into the branches, trying to hide himself behind some leaves while he watched us suspiciously. Ken shouted with laughter as another monkey touched the bull, and almost made him lose his balance.

A loud splash and a sharp chattering from the monkeys betrayed another crocodile. We watched it swim across the top of the water: a long, inverted V, then it sank out of sight. An alarm as we saw a hidden log— quick paddling left and right, but worse followed and we ran aground.

"It always happens when we're near a damned croc," Ken muttered.

I got out to push. One heave and we were off the sandbank. Balancing with one foot, I carefully eased myself back into the seat, sat down and took out my notebook.

"Where's my pencil?" I asked Ken.

He laughed cynically.

"You're always losing your pencils!" he said. "When I was your learner ranger at Ndumu I used to buy some specially; you were for ever cursing and asking where I had put your pencils."

This set us off again talking about our period at Ndumu and what it had done for us. I told Ken about the time we had invited the local Portuguese Chef-de-Poste to dinner.

The Sergeant of Police and I had been trying for ages to get this gentleman to visit us, as we had always enjoyed his hospitality whenever we went to Catuane village. Eventually he agreed to come one May evening and stay to dinner. I battled in the kitchen most of the afternoon, preparing the food. It was, for us, an impressive menu of as many courses as I could contrive.

We were to meet on the Usutu River, and right on time his truck drew up on the opposite bank and his Askari hailed the one-eyed pont operator who was on my side.

"Hurry," I said, "otherwise the Portuguese will take you!"

The pont fairly rocketed across the wide Usutu. The Africans were petrified by the Portuguese, and not without reason. They stand no

nonsense and their laws are hard.

The Chef-de-Poste crossed in grand style, and we saluted each other. The journey to the police station in my truck was difficult, as neither of us understood the other's language, but when we arrived things improved, for I spoke in Zulu to my cook who spoke Portuguese and translated to the Chef-de-Poste.

The Police Sergeant arrived and we trooped in to dinner. We drank Nederburg Riesling from purposely small glasses to make it seem more. Alpheus Ntuli, my general factotum, played the part of waiter very creditably on the whole, disgracing himself only when he knocked over my wine glass.

We then started the interminable meal, course after course. Halfway through the menu the Chef-de-Poste felt for his cigarettes. We stopped him and indicated that more was to come. By the time the dessert arrived he had really reached his limit and grabbed desperately for his cigarettes; when we stopped him again, he shot us a pathetic look which said plainly, "'No more, for heaven's sake!"

Still—he managed the dessert and a cup of coffee with a dash of brandy. He made another move towards his cigarettes, but we stopped him once more. He gave a positive groan of relief when we proffered a cigar. Staggering to a chair he sank back, sucking his cigar.

We were discussing the merits of our countries' respective laws, and he told us there was no capital punishment in Portuguese East Africa.

"But what do you do with murderers?" I asked.

"Well, if they are found guilty, they are taken out to a tidal island off Lourenco Marques, tied up in a sack and left there."

"Surely that's capital punishment?" I remarked.

"Oh no," he replied. "There's always a chance they will be able to get out of the sack and swim the odd twenty miles through shark-infested waters to the mainland."

My cook was noticeably pale about the gills as he translated.

The Chef-de-Poste turned to the Sergeant, and asked whether it was true that murderers only paid £3 admission of guilt in our country.

The Sergeant was horrified.

It was late at night when I took the Chef-de-Poste back to the pont on the Usutu. In the dense Mahemane bush I glimpsed a dog in the headlights. I jammed on brakes and grabbed my .22, working the bolt feverishly. The Chef looked very alarmed, and in a strained voice rapidly asked his Askari what was wrong. I managed to explain that we shot all dogs in the game reserve, and he looked vastly relieved. He probably wondered what on earth he was going to be subjected to next!

At the pont he got out of the truck rather hurriedly and walked into the darkness. I followed as he weaved about in the reeds, and tried to shake his hand to say goodbye, forgetting that his bladder must have been near bursting point; my last view was of a short, slim figure balancing on the deck of the pont hastily undoing his fly.

CHAPTER 12

By the time I had finished the story, the sun had sunk behind the Lebombo Mountains and the sounds of night had started. There was an amaTonga homestead near by and we could hear them singing and thumping their drums. It was queer—almost unearthly—certainly unlike any other African music I knew: rising and falling, gaining in pitch, then fading to a drawn out wail.

We paddled on, and passed a bright green and yellow fever tree hanging at a precipitous angle over the river. No one who has seen this tree could ever forget it. The name alone is gripping and reminds one of Kipling's description. We stopped paddling, and drifted. The canoe swung round and faced upstream. The peace was unbelievable. I broke it to ask Ken whether he would like to be a bank clerk again. His reply was a spluttering invective.

It was almost dark when we heard the roar of broken water ahead. The river divided and I chose the left-hand stream. The canoe gathered speed as we flashed past high red sandstone cliffs, over a small patch of rapids and into the main stream and quiet water again. I turned round to see some small rapids on the other course, and wondered whether they were those that had given Carel Birkby's party trouble. If so, lucky they never tried the Umkomaas!

It was after five—time to camp. Five hundred yards downstream a long flat sandbank offered an easy offloading of kit. With swift and deep racing strokes we paddled hard, reaching it in a few minutes. Although we had not travelled far, my back was sore from sitting in a cramped position; it was a relief to stand up and stretch the muscles as we dragged the heavy canoe onto the sand. Ken went into the bush to look for firewood; I unloaded the kit, then examined the hull to see if there were any tears in the canvas. There was not a mark, which was surprising considering the amount of sandbanks we had dragged it over and the submerged rocks it had brushed against.

I pulled the bivvy tent out of its bag and was dismayed to find we had brought the wrong poles. We had left St. Lucia in too much of a hurry,

without checking the equipment. Ken came back with a load of firewood and swore violently when he heard the news. We laid the tent out, saw what was needed, then went into the bush and cut suitable sticks to replace the ones we had forgotten. It was pitch dark when we had the tent up, kit tidily stowed in a comer and the sleeping bags laid out on the sand. We dug holes for our hips, then lay to relax and listen to the sounds of the night before making the fire and preparing the food.

Hippo grunted in the Mayezela pan and the roar of the rapids faded and rose with the wind. An hour later Ken made the fire while I got the food out. Food supplies were a problem when I started canoeing, but in the last five years more concentrated foods had been made available. Packets of soup were a real boon.

The early morning of the 17th May, the second day of our journey, was bitterly cold, and we crawled from our sleeping bags stiff and sore. Ken took his .22-410 combination and went off after a Cape robin. I heard shot after shot coming from the riverine forest, then some guinea fowl called, and I hoped Ken thought about our stomachs as well as science. Our meals were going to be meagre, as there was not much space in the canoe even for dehydrated foods.

Although it was light enough to write up my notebook, it was some time before the sun appeared above the fig and fever trees. Then long shafts of light splashed over the shadows of the golden sandbanks. Vervet monkeys galore came down to drink and hundreds of birds were calling. Two puff-back shrikes held a shrill duet in a nearby tree and a hippo's snort reverberated up the river. Then the billy can rocked—the water was on the boil. A whiff of woodsmoke spiralled over. Strange what an exhilarating effect it has. It stirs something deep and primitive, and a prehistoric mood is pushed to the surface.

Two things had struck me since I had worked in game reserves: one was the effect of woodsmoke on people and the other was the peculiar fascination of watching wild animals drink at a waterhole. Atavistic, I supposed.

Heuglin's robin whistled his song of delight—almost deliriously so—but the mournful wailing of the trumpeter hornbill drowned his music. Then there was quiet, broken by an odd clanking noise. Coming down river was a Tonga umfaan poling a flat-bottomed punt. He seemed afraid of the canoe, and very obviously looked the other way when I tried to attract his attention. The bow of the punt swung slowly round until it felt the main force of the current, then, quickly shifting position, the umfaan leant hard on the driving pole and with one hard shove manoeuvred the punt so that it faced upstream. Two more shoves and he had reached the

other side. He splashed through the water and tethered the punt with a long piece of bark. He still refused to look my way; it was so quiet I could hear him humming to himself as he climbed the bank and disappeared into a fringe of bush—a black shadow moving away into time!

The amaTonga people: what had happened to them in the last hundred years? Man's invasion of Tongaland has only brought about its destruction. He has wiped out the game and planted exotic pine trees on the magnificent coastal plains.

Two pied crows croaked harshly from a dry stump. Their weird, rattling noise brought my mind back to life on the river, and the fact that I was hungry.

Ken appeared with two tiny Cisticola. Stomachs would have to suffer for science. He started skinning them—a long and finicky job—while I pre pared our meagre breakfast of mealie meal and condensed milk, washed down with strong tea. The sun climbed higher and the dew dried on our bivvy tent. The sand got hot and flies streamed out of the bush to settle on hippo dung and the Cisticola entrails. Some got mixed up with our food, but we were too hungry to care. Half and hour later we had finished breakfast, packed all the kit and were on our way down river once more. We paddled hard for a few minutes to loosen up, then let the canoe drift as we absorbed the atmosphere. Slowly but surely it was beginning to weave its spell. Everything else but this river world was fading.

At midday we passed crocodiles lying open-mouthed on the sands sunning themselves. We rode over the back of one. I could feel the hard scutes along its spine, rubbing on the canvas, vibrating on my calves. The fear was not immediate. Seconds later I laughed at the frantic beating of my heart.

Fish eagles shrieked wildly and a giant kingfisher flew ahead of us for miles. Hadedah ibis rose in alarm as we surprised them on the riverbank, and a crocodile crunched a barbel in a quiet backwater.

"Frightening sound, isn't it?" Ken whispered as we floated beneath a canopy of fig trees. I nodded my head, and all at once was very frightened. All this was so impersonal and we could so easily end the same way as that barbel. I lifted my paddle and used it to get beyond the crunching of the crocodile's jaws. I was afraid to speak, for voices resounded stridently across the water.

The river narrowed and the banks loomed up ten feet on either side. The sun began its descent, and as it reached the top of the Lebombo we came upon four crocodiles. As usual we ran aground. We got out, fifty feet from their lying place, to push ourselves clear; our unexpected movements panicked them, and they splashed into the water. My previous fears faded,

overwhelmed by the grace of these creatures, remnants of the prehistoric. How fortunate we were to be able to study them at such close quarters! One climbed onto a bank lower down, and it needed little imagination to visualize how their ancestors had once walked on their hind legs.

The current grew swift enough to carry the canoe forward at a good speed, so that little paddling was necessary, except to dip a paddle to stop the nose swinging too violently. The river widened again, as we passed out of the shadows into bright sunlight. It was glorious to sit back and watch as the canoe glided on and on. The wind roared through the reeds, and riffles on the water flashed in the sun.

A shout broke the stillness. We looked down river and saw a group of amaTonga women, abafana and children—in their usual dirty red cloth cloaks. They all stopped cutting sugar cane to turn and stare at the canoe. Anything new on the river is of interest. Piles of sugar cane three feet high lay on the bank. From this they would make their brew—moba.

This cane wine is the stuff that makes the drums throb in the night, as amaTonga in a drunken stupor beat until they are exhausted. They had often disturbed our nights at Ndumu with their screaming and high-pitched singing; when we had investigated we had been horrified to see women with their tiny babies on their backs, swaying and wheeling round the fires. Moba had ruined the people: it made food a secondary consideration. Liquor controlled their lives—without it life would have no meaning. These people were once a noble race; they were now drinking themselves to death.

Even worse than this is the way they ruin the earth, the only legacy they could pass to their children. Their agricultural methods are primitive to an extreme, and virgin forests are burnt, cut and stumped for a few more yards of miserable soil. Giant figs, beautiful mkuhlu and fever trees lie rotting along the bank, testimony to indifference.

Magistrates, whose task it is to teach better agricultural methods, are losing heart in the struggle against ignorance and stubbornness; the population explosion accentuates the difficulties.

These patches of ruined forest were jarring notes in the wilderness symphony. We soon saw and understood that the Pongolo River is the lifeblood of the amaTonga people. When it ceases to flow, the people will die, and the present course degenerate into a stagnant, stinking bywater.

There was so much life in the river and the pans—all interdependent and a fascinating study for ecologists. We were in the last true wilderness of Zululand—why did it too have to be destroyed by man? By floating quietly on this river we had come into the closest contact with all its inhabitants, human, animal and reptile. The wonderful silences became

intensified rather than relieved by the quiet songs of the birds and the whispering breezes. It was a stillness that was to leave an imprint on our consciousness.

We paddled on and rounded a bend to see the river stretched out ahead of us, the straightest section we had seen. Ken lifted his binoculars and scanned the bank ahead. "There's Mfungoso River," he said.

Soon we reached the clear-running and sweet-tasting stream, and offloaded our billy to make a quick cup of tea.

While we were waiting for it to boil I told Ken what I had once seen on the upper reaches of this stream. AmaTonga women were netting. Stark naked, young and old together moved upstream, chanting and splashing the water, driving the fish before them—bream, tigerfish and barbel, swirling and twisting to escape the women and the long pointed baskets they carried.

I saw a crocodile charge straight for them; the line opened for a moment and the crocodile shot through. When the fish were well and truly trapped, the excitement intensified; baskets were plunged into the shoals and the clear water was churned into a brown muddy mess. The women screamed and dragged the full baskets to the side, tipped the fish out, then plunged back to refill their baskets.

Twenty minutes later they were gone, and the stream was running clear.

We climbed into the canoe and paddled past the long, eroded paths leading to the Mfongoso dip tank. This was a dismal area. A flock of cattle egrets, four raucous crows and a lone Tonga man with two mangy dogs watched us go by.

For a while the sight of the dipping tank and surrounding wooden barricades had taken us back to the outside world, but soon we were at grips with the river again. The atmosphere of the fig trees and the thick matted bush settled on us and we were aware of the frailty of our canoe, our bodies and our minds.

A big crocodile high-walked from an opposite sandbank and fear of the primitive overwhelmed me; the small .22 rifle on the side of the canoe was not much comfort.

Then the river turned sharply, widening until there was only one mudbank reaching into the main stream. A crocodile and a hadedah ibis were side by side on the dark mud, and in the afternoon sun the iridescent green feathers on the bird's wings shone like burnished copper. The crocodile slid away (and once more we went aground) but the hadedah let us approach. For the first time I saw the full beauty of this bird and marvelled at my stupidity in not noticing the colours before. The grey head

and lighter brown feathers on the rest of its body showed it was not the dull bird I had often taken it to be.

The river narrowed and flowed more swiftly: as the afternoon shadows lengthened it seemed gloomy, and different from the lovely river we had set out on two days before.

We saw no one until mid-afternoon, when we heard voices and came upon a Tonga umfaan talking to an attractive nthombazana, washing with her back to us. He noticed us first and must have had a sense of humour, for he loudly said, "Look out! There's a crocodile!" She gave a little cry and spun round—double surprise when she saw us. We all laughed and the canoe drifted on.

Then we paddled again, digging in deep, pulling hard, and making little whirlpools swirl behind us in tiny zigzag lines. The main current flowed from bank to bank and we continued to follow it. This was hard work, but better than getting out every few minutes to push the canoe off sandbanks.

The sun dropped behind the trees and we began looking for a camping site. There was the stillness of the late afternoon in the air: the final songs of the birds had not begun, but darkness comes suddenly, so we paddled energetically.

We were moving at a good speed when I idly glanced at a fallen log on the right hand bank and saw the dark outline of a long crocodile—then another and another. We were going straight for them and it was too late to change course.

"Lift the paddles and drift past without disturbing them," I whispered to Ken.

Water dripped from the paddle tips and circles widened in the river. We were almost past when my leg jerked involuntarily and in a flash three crocodiles rushed for the water and us. We were below them as they leapt off the log. One shot past within touching distance, and the other two bumped the back of the canoe, rocking it from side to side. My thoughts seemed suspended. I waited for the canoe to roll over, but it somehow righted itself and we paddled on.

Ten minutes later Ken remarked, "Those crocs of yours gave me a fright!"

I laughed nervously. I still couldn't understand how we had escaped—one gunwale had actually sunk below water for a few seconds.

The adrenalin in our bodies gave us extra energy and we moved swiftly; soon the tigerfish began jumping, a sure sign that night was not far.

We had decided earlier that sandbanks were unsuitable camping

places, but with darkness approaching fast and dense undergrowth on either side, a sandbank would have been very welcome.

We paddled until it was light enough to see only a hundred yards ahead, when the gloominess of the river and its surroundings were overpowering. Eventually, in desperation, we stopped below a small rocky ledge, stepped warily into the water and rapidly dragged the prow of the canoe far enough out to remove the kit.

Although we were both stiff and tired, we worked quickly for it was already dark, and the danger of a crocodile swirling up and grabbing us was strong. Article after article landed with a thud on the bank until only the billycan was left up in front. Ken slid along the floor of the canoe and pulled the kit out. Billycan, potatoes, cane knife, mugs, plates and spoons came hurtling out behind him. We pulled the canoe on to a ledge then lugged all the kit to the top of the bank.

While Ken scraped the ground and put the tent up, I took the cane knife and went to collect firewood. I gathered rotting, fallen limbs of fig trees to start the fire and heavier pieces of timber from floods to keep it going.

When I got back to Ken the tent was up and he was staring across the river intently, like a pointer. I knew him well enough to say nothing. Presently he shrugged his shoulders and said, "I could have sworn blind I heard the Natal broadbill," and he imitated the call.

It was dark before we got the fire going and put the billy on to boil. There was very little to eat, but neither of us was hungry—liquid was what we wanted. We broke open one of the packets of soup, poured it into the billy and added a few potatoes, skins and all. Ken dusted some salt into the boiling mixture, rubbed his hands on his rugger pants and said, "That's all tonight."

We crawled into the tent and dug hollows for our hips, then laid our sleeping kit out. I lay down and felt the delicious waves of sleep steal over me. Ken grabbed my leg and pulled me roughly.

"None of that," he said. "You've got to have some chow. Ndumu is still a long way ahead."

I groaned and wearily dragged myself to the fire to lie soaking up the warmth as Ken stirred the boiling soup. The night was so still I could hear the barking of a Tonga dog and the cries of a child in a distant kraal. The river gurgled past the roots of giant sycamore figs and two owls began a duet.

"Grub's up," Ken said loudly as he grabbed the tin plates and banged them against his thighs to get the sand off. He sloshed the mixture into the plates and opened a packet of Pro-vita biscuits. After the first mouthful

hunger surged back and I enjoyed every morsel. We filled the plates again, and emptied them too. Ken lifted the billy and asked, "More?" I shook my head so he poured the remainder out, ate noisily and finally licked his plate.

"Now for char," he said as he picked up the billy and went to the river. He was away a very short time and came back at a trot.

"Strewth! You should see the crocs," he muttered. "It gives me the willies to be near the water alone—I've never filled a billy so quickly. I don't mind crocs in the daytime, but at night they're no joke."

We made tea and drank two mugs each. Refreshed, we lay watching the fire and inhaling the wisps of woodsmoke.

"Life can be good," Ken said.

I remembered telling Miss Eriksen at the Ndumu dispensary that I was interested in crocodiles. She said that many amaTonga had been treated for crocodile injuries; she looked up her cards and gave me the name of one, Salina Bameli. I made a mental note of the name and later asked Game Guard Mavela if he knew the woman.

He said he did not know her but that many years ago there was an umfaan who had been bitten—would I like to see him? I cursed under my breath; I don't know how many times I had told the guards that anything to do with crocodiles must be reported. Anyway, Alpheus (my personal servant), Mavela and I climbed into the Land Rover and made our way through the bush to the Nkonjane dip. We left the Rover and walked towards the Usutu along a well-beaten footpath.

A big beer drink was in progress on the Portuguese side of the river—shouts, singing and clashing of sticks echoed across the water. Mavela led us to a small muzi where two degenerate-looking amaTonga women lay outside a small reed hut. A huge pot of cane wine was on the boil. Mavela greeted them, then asked where the umfaan was. They pulled themselves upright, and pointed to a marula tree two hundred yards away.

We found the umfaan sitting under the marula with his back to us. He started visibly when we appeared and my heart went out to him—disheartened that the sight of a uniform should have such an effect.

I said, "Sakubona indoda."

He grunted a reply and stared stonily towards a small field of bananas. He was suspicious, so we sat for a full five minutes, talking among ourselves, before Alpheus spoke to him.

"We are interested to hear your story about the crocodile," he said.

The boy's expression softened immediately and he looked at each of us in turn. Then he spoke, haltingly at first, but getting more and more voluble, until words poured out and he began gesticulating freely.

Alpheus told him to calm down because I wanted to write his story. He looked at me, smiled sadly and said I must forgive him because it brought back a flood of memories. He pointed to his leg and I took a quick glance. It was badly scarred and shockingly deformed.

"What is your name?" I said.

"Nondhlongo Matenjwa," he replied.

I asked his age: he had no idea and could not remember his parents telling him of any unusual occurrence at his birth, so I had to guess. It was difficult. His body looked young, but his face was lined with suffering. Even his eyes had a haunted look. I put his age at twenty-one.

I asked him to speak slowly and try to explain in detail what had happened to him when he had been attacked.

He said that about eight years before he and an adult friend went to a marula beer drink in the Abercorn pont area. When they crossed the Ntigangwani River (a small stream which joins the Usutu and which is dry for most of the year) it was just running. In the afternoon it rained heavily, and when they returned late that night he remembered hearing the sound of rushing water.

They were both drunk; the beer had been stronger than usual and he was probably only twelve years old, so they kept walking into what they thought was the small Ntigangwani stream. It was only when the water reached his waist that he realized it was in flood, but he was still too befuddled to think coherently. The water got even deeper, but he continued to ford, and was almost out on the other side when he stumbled over what he thought was a log.

"The log moved and I knew it was an isilwane (animal), but not what kind," he said slowly.

His foot was in the middle of the animal's back when it whipped round and grabbed him just above the ankle. He pointed to the old wounds. It looked to me as though the eyeteeth had been responsible for most of the damage.

He put his hand down to feel what had caught hold of him, for he still did not realize that it was a crocodile. Then he felt the cold bulging eyes, and he screamed out, "Ngwenya!" (crocodile). At that moment the reptile moved and threw him into the middle of the stream.

He grimaced, and said, "Then I heard my bone break with a noise like"—and he pointed to my rifle.

His whole body was now in the water and he lay face downwards. The crocodile swung round so that its tail and midriff lay across the umfaan's back; the weight pushed him under the water. Nondhlongo put his hands behind his back, grasped one of the crocodile's legs and pulled

129

his head above water.

He smiled grimly and said, "I was sober now."

With his head above water, he began swimming downstream, dragging the crocodile, which followed without resistance. This was understandable: it was downstream to the Usutu where the crocodile would have taken its victim in any case.

Nondhlongo was delirious with fear and waves of pain racked his body. He screamed continuously, crying out for help.

"Nkosi, it was so dark," he said.

In the meantime his adult companion, Umlobela, had sobered up sufficiently to realize what was happening. He was armed with a heavy stabbing assegai. Floundering through the bush and falling over boulders, he followed the screams of the youth. The crocodile had still made no effort to move and the stream had widened and become shallower. Nondhlongo managed to grab onto some overhanging branches. Umlobela found him, waded in and stabbed the reptile between the shoulders. Then he dragged the boy to safety.

"That is my story, nkosi," Nondhlongo said, and leant back against the tree. I thanked him and gave him all the money I had in my pockets. He took it and smiled shyly.

We walked away to the top of the hill, then turned to have a last look at the boy. He sat as we had left him, his elbows on his knees and his face cupped in his hands. It needed no imagination to see that he was thinking about that night, years ago.

Some abafana ran past us, leaping and shouting with pure enjoyment of life. We saw Nondhlongo look up and stare at them, then he got up and limped towards the banana fields on the Usutu banks.

I asked Mavela how Nondhlongo lived. Mavela shrugged his shoulders and said he didn't know.

"Well, what does he do all day?" I enquired.

"He looks at the river," Mavela said.

The fire had died down to glowing embers.

"Yes," Ken said thoughtfully. "Crocodiles can be grim, but at least they play an important part in the life of the pans and the rivers. Nondhlongo's story is a sad one, but think how many people are maimed each year by cars."

Ken was right; without the crocodiles, thousands of amaTonga would starve. The amaTonga people depended on fish as a source of protein. The Tilapia or bream was the mainstay of their diet, and through the actions of the crocodiles, bream remained plentiful.

Young crocodiles feed on water beetles which in turn feed on the

eggs of bream, and large crocodiles feed on barbel which in turn feed on small Tilapia; so if the crocodile is removed, the Tilapia would decrease and the amaTonga go hungry. Those people who advocate the elimination of the crocodile are really doing humanity a disservice.

"We have got to know more about crocs," Ken said. "If more facts aren't presented to the world, crocs will become extinct. You have got to write and tell everyone how important they are to Tongaland," he added fiercely, his mop of fair hair gleaming in the firelight.

"How often have I heard people say 'Ugh! What horrible creatures— kill them all!'" he went on. "But, man, we have got to face facts, they are vitally necessary in places like Tongaland—you've proved that, and Dr. Cott has proved they are vital in Lake Nyasa and Northern Rhodesia; more people must know about this."

I watched him as he spoke and thought back to the day he had arrived in Zululand to be my learner ranger. In two years he had become a man advanced far beyond his age, and an ornithologist of undoubted brilliance.

He stopped speaking and laughed.

"Don't stare at me like that, Hamlet, and don't write down everything I say!"

A dikkop wailed mournfully downstream and we stopped talking to listen. Another bird answered, then a hadedah squawked in alarm and a gust of wind burst through the trees. A bush-baby was disturbed and set up its raucous cry.

"Oh, this river, the lovely beautiful river," Ken said softly. "Can you describe what it means to us; is it possible to put into words how it has become part of us—how it can frighten us, yet charm us. I wish we could live on it for ever."

His profile reminded me of Rupert Brooke and I had a premonition that here was someone who was going to become a world famous figure; some day in the future a lot of people were going to listen to what he had to say.

One small piece of burning wood remained when we crawled into the tent to sleep.

Ken woke me the following morning by pushing a steaming mug of coffee into my hand. I crept out of the bivvy and went down to the river for a quick wash. A lone fish eagle came soaring down-river, stretched out his talons and feathered tarsus and landed with a slow wing-beat on a dry sycamore fig. He turned his head and wiped his beak with a talon, then screamed out his lyrical thrilling call. Another bird answered upstream and for a glorious minute the river echoed to their duet. Wisps of mist rose

from the river and the muddy smell of the banks was like a powerful aphrodisiac.

Ken had our meagre breakfast ready when I got back. We ate quickly then set about breaking camp—always a sorrowful business for it is like leaving a part of oneself behind.

We stowed the tent and the American cloth bags and pushed the canoe into the river. The first few digs of the paddle were painful—unaccustomed exercise had left its mark. We paddled briskly for the usual quarter of an hour, then relaxed to take in all that was going on around us. I took out my notebook while Ken guided the canoe.

In some places along the banks, the force of the river in flood had washed all the soil from the fig trees and their roots hung in grotesque positions. On the left hand bank there was a rocky outcrop and we paddled over to inspect it. It was a prehistoric treasure house with hundreds of fossils, probably cretaceous period.

After two hours' going the impersonal atmosphere of the river had us in its grip; we were filled with the realization that nothing cares here; every living thing just exists.

Soon after two o'clock the river swung west, and for an instant we saw the Lebombo range and the gap where the Ingwavuma River flows. For a few seconds we were normal human beings, intent on a canoe journey, then once more we were back in the powerful grip of the wild river kingdom.

Ken lifted one shoulder, cocked his head and burbled crazily. I felt the urge too, and wanted to cackle.

This was Ndumu-itis—bush fever, Zululand tap—they are one and the same thing: a mild disease, which we knew and understood. In our early days at Ndumu Game Reserve we had had it violently—chasing fowls, stark naked, with assegais, and once I had returned from leave to find Ken, on his hands and knees, following a big buzzing fly and trying to kill it with his thumb.

The old Tongalanders used to say that six months east of the Lebombo range qualified a man to have his lunatic moments. There were hosts of stories about bush fever: an early Natal policeman found fishing in the water tank, another flapping his arms and crowing like a cock on the charge office desk. One man used to call his amaTonga servants by firing a .303 through their corrugated iron huts. In our time we had seen men blast away at spiders on the wall with .38 revolvers. Once we attended a party with the parlour game of waiting until some one went to the lavatory, then shooting wildly through the roof. Everyone collapsed with laughter when the victim came crawling out, panic stricken and minus his trousers.

One of the strange facets of bush fever was the aversion one developed for meeting unwelcome human beings. Ken and I got to the stage where we hated the sight of some people who came down the road to spoil our wilderness. Most of them came for a free drink and a chat, so we concocted a brew that was calculated to get rid of even a dipsomaniac.

We crossed to Portuguese territory and bought an enormous demijohn of cheap vino rosso, poured half of it away and filled it up with vinegar, Worcestershire sauce and anything else we could think of. It was guaranteed to cause a stomach upset in half an hour.

Unwelcome guests would come and eagerly accept the offer of a drink, and gaze with wondering appreciation at the huge tumbler full that was pushed into their hands. The first gulp was the only long one, then their expressions ranged from horror and amazement to open disgust. Politeness would force them to finish and as they got up to go we would rush forward, insisting they have another. Protestations were useless, and the glass was inexorably refilled.

When it took effect we would guide them solicitously to the lavatory—known to us as the hippo trap. It was a rickety structure and one had to step very carefully along a latticework of thin sticks. We would then stand a little distance away and audibly discuss the 15 foot black mamba that had been seen in there the week before, to say nothing of the mfezi (spitting cobra) that lived under the seat. All this had the desired effect and unwelcome visitors learned to stay well clear of our domain. The number of people who used to bother us with requests for permission to shoot "one little buck" in the Game Reserve was soon drastically reduced.

If anyone survived this treatment—and there were some really thick-skinned individuals—we had another method too: a trip on the pans with our little unstable green boat, riding over hippo and along the channels where crocodiles used to lie high up, sunning themselves. A discreet cough or a tapping on the boat at the right moment would send a dozen crocodiles plunging off the bank to land with almighty splashes in the river. No one ever came back for more of this treatment.

CHAPTER 13

At three o'clock the sun was dropping in the west when we came to a fork in the Pongolo. We had to make the unpleasant decision of which one to take. The old channel looked very gloomy. A thick mass of phragmites reeds barred the entrance and fallen trees lay everywhere. Ken imitated a hippo's grunt and we laughed. Then Ken said, "It isn't funny," and he pointed to the sandbanks on either side, where hardly an inch was not covered with fresh crocodile tracks. We paddled round and round in indecision.

The new channel was narrow and flowing very swiftly; if we took it and overturned, that would be that. We consulted the map. The distances were about equal, but we had had a lot of experience with old courses. Then we heard hippo calling—by the sound of it a big herd—from the direction of the old course.

We hesitated no longer and pushed the canoe into the lip of the channel. Our craft shot forward and I could feel my heart thumping.

"God, this looks grim!" Ken muttered.

At that moment a huge crocodile came out of the reeds, doing a ponderous high walk. We both stared at it, frozen with fear. It slid into the water.

"Did you see that?" Ken asked dazedly.

"What the hell! Something the size of a mountain moves into the water and you ask me if I saw it!" I exploded.

The channel widened a little, with steep, inaccessible banks on either side. A hippo blew nearby. We almost upset the canoe as we turned in the direction of the sound, but the frightening silence had been broken and we both laughed wildly with relief. We drifted for what seemed an age, neither of us daring to speak. Then a cow lowed in the distance, breaking the spell; civilization and people were not far off. For a few seconds we were happy, then we wanted to relive the taut experience, but it was gone, perhaps forever.

The channel continued to widen and entered a shallow pan. Groves of fever trees were dotted around and small reed islands were havens for

Photo: Dr. H. B. Cott

Crocodiles and hippos live happily together

The crocodiles came to feed

Photo: Ian Player

Dead hippo

Food for some

hundreds of cattle egrets, squacco herons, green-backed herons, sacred ibis, wood ibis, hadedahs, pied wagtails and kingfishers.

Ken stared hungrily at this ornithological paradise.

"Look at that and that," he gesticulated. "Birds, everywhere. Look at those green-backed herons and the night herons," he said. He had his notebook out and was scribbling excitedly, when a fish eagle screamed to cap his unlimited happiness.

For half an hour we drifted amongst the incredible number of different birds. I had never seen so many greenshanks, and when they took off, shrilling out their lovely calls, Ken waved his hat in the air and shouted, "Oh, you beauty you!"

A lone Tonga, fishing on the opposite shore, stared at us with his jaws agape. I knew that if he had ever doubted it before, he was now convinced that white men were mad. We waved and called a greeting. He lifted his hand as though dubious whether to recognize the madmen or not.

We drifted on, caught up again in this brilliant spectacle. The birds were not afraid of the canoe until we were almost upon them, then they would only fly a few yards and settle again. One big Goliath heron allowed us to get within touching distance before taking off with slow wing beats. An old cow hippo rose a hundred yards ahead with a piece of black weed hanging from her eyes like a *pince-nez* string. We burst into laughter and she disappeared with a splash.

A pied kingfisher dived next to the canoe and came up with a fish in its beak. It flew to a nearby branch and we watched it, silhouetted against the setting sun, as it tried to swallow the fish. Another solitary hippo swam through the reeds, leaving a long, rippling wake that worked itself out in small waves on the shore. Reeds swayed and bowed in the evening wind, moving in unison to the calls of the green-spotted wood pigeon. Fish jumped and splashed and two lone white-faced duck flew high overhead, their quaint whistles borne on the wind.

More birds appeared until even Ken was speechless. Spurwinged geese honked from an island and two white pelican fished in the shallows. Redbilled teal, stilts, and common sandpipers—one after another they paraded before us. All we could do was sit and stare at this concentration of avifauna. Reed cormorants and darters swam in front of our tiny craft, and blacksmith plovers rose from the shore with their tink-tink-tink calls of alarm. Then Ken half turned, gripped my arm and pointed; a flock of the beautiful, rare white-winged plovers flew just above our heads. This completed our day of intense joy.

As the sun sank lower the colours in the sky changed from grey, black and white to light pink that turned blood red against the open patches

of deep blue. Clouds drifted overhead, leaving wispy fragments that gradually disintegrated. Two black moths took off from a dull yellow fever tree and flew upwards towards the sun, hovered until a sharp breeze forced them sideways and out of sight.

Ken broke my reverie with, "We'll have to paddle, jong, and make camp at the first bit of solid ground."

He was right; we only had minutes left of daylight and already the mosquitoes were descending upon us in hordes. Paddling hard, we heard a roar ahead and saw the river had divided again, leaving an island about a foot out of water. A dangerous place to camp, but we had no option. We stumbled in the dark with our kit, both of us tired and aching. Mosquitoes forced us to put the tent up which was just as well, for it rained in the night.

It wasn't safe to go looking for firewood, so we ate dried fruit, prunes and apples and a few pieces of Pro-vita, then crawled into bed and were asleep in seconds.

I awoke in the early morning with water dripping on me. I tried to move to the side but touched the tent and more water poured in. Ken woke and swore because he too was getting wet.

We rummaged around for our long-sleeved pullovers to keep us warm, but sleep was impossible.

Suddenly I realized that it was the 19th of May and Ken's birthday. I solemnly shook his hand in the dark and wished him all the best.

We lay talking and listening to the sounds of the night. Once, above the clatter of the rapids, we heard a crocodile cough. This got us on to the subject of crocodiles again, and I told Ken of a day soon after I had arrived at Ndumu, when I saw crocodiles tearing a donkey to pieces.

One of the guards had reported that "Yellow Face", an enormous old crocodile, had grabbed a donkey at the eastern end of Nyamiti pan. I rushed down in the Chev truck and disturbed about ten crocodiles on the carcass. They drifted away, leaving the donkey bobbing in the ripples.

I quickly made a small hide, got comfortable and waited. It was half past eight. Two hours went by without a sign of life, until a turtle came swimming towards the dead animal. It submerged and did not appear for a while. Another turtle joined it, and then a barbel splashed and I saw its head and whiskers just below the surface. More barbel approached, and the splashing increased. Then a small crocodile moved right up to the donkey and touched it with its nose. The crocodile stayed in that position for a good ten minutes without moving. More barbel arrived, and the noise was now so loud I could hear it echoing over the pan. This seemed to attract other crocodiles, for as I scanned the water with my binoculars I saw them

136

sliding off the sandbank at Dhlozi point.

The game guard nudged me and I turned to see that as if by magic a much larger crocodile had appeared and was resting its head against the donkey's flanks. The small crocodile submerged and re-appeared near the donkey's anus, while the large crocodile swam slowly round the carcass. More arrived. One swam up with its head just above water, his big yellow pouch glittering in the morning sun.

The guard touched my arm again and pointed down the pan.

"The inkulu (big one) is coming," he whispered.

Yellow Face cruised up with slow sweeps of his tail. He too bumped the carcass with his nose and stayed stationary for a few minutes. Then he submerged and the water erupted into a boiling mass. Barbel leapt in every direction and the turtles vanished. Yellow Face had gripped onto the stomach of the donkey and was spinning round and round, his white belly showing clearly above the surface. Again he spun, then moved back and the entrails of the donkey popped out. A crocodile moved in, tore at the intestines, swam a few yards away and ate with its bottom jaw partially submerged. One after another crocodiles moved in, tore mouthfuls off and swam away to feed. At times they would submerge slightly to swallow water.

It was now late in the afternoon, and more than sixteen crocodiles were feeding. All hell had been let loose with crocodiles of all sizes grabbing and spinning, then, their heads above water, swimming to the bank and champing their jaws in the shallows.

A tegwan (hamerkop—*Scopus umbretta*) landed and strutted up and down the bank, trying to snatch a few pieces of offal.

Barbel had returned en masse and were swimming and leaping over the carcass. Some were inside the belly and I could hear a dull thumping noise; it was almost ridiculous to see the belly heaving out of the water.

Yellow Face returned, ripping into one of the back legs. When the skin was broken, the others tore off great hunks of red meat, leaving thin trails of blood on the water.

The tegwan flew a feet towards the donkey, thought better of it and returned to the bank. It was obvious that he was frightened of the reptiles. A fish eagle and a buzzard landed, which upset the tegwan, and he flew off as the fish eagle dropped next to him.

It was getting dark and the crocodiles had not finished eating, but the mosquitoes were making life unbearable, so I had to leave.

Ken reminded me of the time we decided to shoot a crocodile on the Portuguese side of the Usutu River so that we could cut it up and examine it.

Ken, Alpheus, Game Guard Sigohlo, Lancer (my dog) and I walked from the bridge over the Nyamiti pan channel through the groves of tall fever trees and past the nyala horns that had become part of a tree—in the early days of the Reserve some hunter had shot an impala and slung the horns on a branch. Pink impala lilies were blooming everywhere and the day was warm and still.

We took the track running along the edge of Uhotwe and Sabatina pans with their groups of dwarf geese; across the swamp, past Catuane's muzi and then into the dense fig forest with its fascinating bird life. We had to wait once while Ken gazed at a narina trogon, and again while Lancer chased a cane rat. He came back looking sorry for himself, knowing he had done wrong. A few months later he chased a troop of big forest baboons and came off second best.

We reached the first junction of the Pongolo and Usutu and stopped to examine the mass of tracks on the hot sand: samango monkeys, baboon, vervet monkeys and a crocodile spoor, which measured nine and a half inches. We crossed the old course by way of my tree bridge.

Hippo paths meandered over the island and we took the most direct one to the Usutu. As we came out of the forest I saw a fair-sized crocodile lying on a broad white sandbank about a hundred yards down river. Even at that distance it sensed our presence and moved towards the water.

I took aim, waited until a front leg moved, then fired. The crocodile jerked once, then lay still. I called Ken, who was watching some flycatchers, and disregarding caution we took off our boots and waded chest deep through the Usutu to the crocodile. It wasn't dead so I had to plunk another bullet into it. Even after the second shot it could still open its jaws. Ken pushed a stick towards it and in a flash the stick was in two pieces. We fired another shot, then it lay still.

I shouted to Alpheus and Sigohlo to come and help pull the crocodile to the bank. Sogohlo came without hesitation, but Alpheus refused. We had to swear at him before he took off from the bank and came dashing through the water. When he was halfway through the deep part and threshing the water, Lancer jumped into the river. There was consternation as we all yelled at him to voertsêk (go away). He turned, swam back to the bank, waited till Alpheus had reached us, then leapt in again. I called him to come but this time he got a fright and swam round in circles. In the meantime the crocodile was oozing blood, and I was petrified that this would attract others. Lancer finally swam towards us and Ken rushed in and pulled him onto the sandbank.

The crocodile was extremely heavy and we struggled to get it across the channel. Twice Ken had to dive under the reptile to stop it from pulling

us all down. We kept glancing anxiously round, expecting a crocodile attack at any moment. Lancer was the only one who was unperturbed.

We dragged the crocodile through the reed fringe and at last got it up onto the bank. We then measured every part of the body: length from tip to tail, head length, tail length, size of feet and anything else we thought would be of scientific value. Then we started to cut it up, taking the belly skin off first. In the stomach we found a partially decomposed leguan and part of an animal's foot—probably a duiker. Finding the leguan was most interesting, as this is the reptile responsible for feeding on crocodile eggs and young crocodiles. Whenever the female crocodile leaves her nest the leguan is there to dig out the eggs and eat them before she returns.

We also found hundreds of small stones which had a beautiful gloss on them. Our strangest find was the heart, which was still beating faintly even though the crocodile had been dismembered.

This was the only crocodile we ever shot at Ndumu; we became attached to the reptiles as we learnt more about them and their very important part in the ecology of the rivers.

I started corresponding with Dr. Hugh Cott of Cambridge University in England, who was doing a monograph on the reptiles. He was very anxious to learn what we knew about the so-called crocodile bird, this mythical creature that was supposed to pick the teeth of basking crocodiles. We knew from observations on the pans that the water dikkop (*Burhinus vermiculatus*) was closely associated with the crocodile and acted as a warning system. The bird also laid its eggs near crocodile nests, but we had never seen any bird picking a crocodile's teeth. We asked amaTonga about this and many of them described the white-winged plover, but that was as far as we got. We were ever on the lookout, and our long search was rewarded.

We were fishing for tiger fish one afternoon when I saw a turtle come out of the water and crawl onto the bank. It lay still and I idly focussed the binoculars on it. A tiny common sandpiper (*Acititis hypoleucos*) came into view, walked up to the turtle and pecked at something. I whispered urgently to Ken and told him to look. He took the binoculars and shook with excitement when he saw what was happening. I looked again and was amazed to see that the sandpiper was picking small leeches off the turtle's neck.

We watched for a full five minutes before the sandpiper resumed its customary behaviour of feeding along the pan edge. We were so excited we could hardly speak. Eventually I voiced what was uppermost in our minds: "If the sandpiper picked leeches off the turtle, why couldn't he do it to the crocodiles?" But did crocodiles have leeches? I could not remember

139

seeing any.

The following day we got up early, hoping we would see the sandpiper pick leeches off a crocodile.

We went to the most popular crocodile spot. When we arrived two crocodiles were lying on the sandbank. One rushed into the water, the other stayed but was uneasy, shifting its position until its head faced the pan. I was watching it carefully with the binoculars when a sandpiper strutted and bobbed nearby. It moved past the crocodile's tail and picked at something on the ground. We held our breath as it went round the sleeping crocodile, but nothing happened. Then the door of the truck creaked and the crocodile shot into the water.

We had to wait a quarter of an hour before a small one popped its head out amongst some submerged reeds and stayed in a fixed position, before moving forward onto the bank. It lay down out of sight behind an acacia tree and a clump of reeds. Five minutes later a larger one surfaced, saw the smaller one and was reassured; it swam in, clambered out with the usual slow, jerky movements, flopped onto the strip of sand, opened and closed its mouth, then left it open. Next it stretched out its hind legs until they reached almost to the middle of its back in a most peculiar and amusing way. Its eyes stayed open for a while, and it seemed suspicious.

Another ten minutes passed, and the crocodile kept opening and closing one eye. Then the little sandpiper came along and began feeding. We watched every action; in the most tantalizing way it would dash with quick little steps right up to the crocodile, only to pick up something on the ground.

Another crocodile came towards the bank, its head out of the water, its tail gently moving. It crawled out, doing the high walk, and flopped down. On the bag of loose skin hanging from the lower jaw there was a black spot. Could this be a leech? We had been there since early morning and it was now rapidly getting dark.

Two more crocodiles high-walked out, one a very big one with blotches on the tail; there were now nine on the sandbank. A water dikkop landed near the group then took off with a wail of alarm as I stretched a cramped leg. In an instant all the crocodiles, bar one, slid into the water. The one remaining had the black spot on its neck. I was watching it, when the spot dropped off. We leapt out of the truck with a shout and ran to the water's edge—the crocodile nearly did a back somersault in its fright. Ken picked up the bloated black object: it was a leech!

At six o'clock the following morning we were back at the point. It was a cold, dull, drizzly day, and hours passed before the sun came shining through a gap in the black bank of clouds.

Three crocodiles were lying under the fever trees. On the opposite side of the lake a fish eagle sat on a dead, scarred fever tree, waiting for a barbel or bream to surface. A water dikkop winged its way over the water and landed with a quick run of short steps, then it stood motionless staring ahead.

The little sandpiper came scuttling along beside the water, bobbing up and down, forever pecking. It turned away from the crocodiles and went to the end of the point. It was peaceful until, with a spurt of spray, an old black hippo rose to the surface. He eyed us blearily and moved off.

Half an hour passed and the dikkop was still standing in the same position, staring ahead. A crocodile surfaced, floating with the usual rocking motion. The clouds began breaking up and the sun shone brightly, but the wind still soughed through the fever trees, forcing the water into wavelets that broke softly on the sandbank. Another crocodile surfaced and faced us. It took half an hour to come out, then lay ten feet from us. One more bobbed up and kept its head poised like a snake ready to strike.

When eleven crocodiles were lying on the point, the sandpiper came scuttling back, but to our anger and frustration moved around behind the tails of the reptiles.

It was dark when we got home, tired and hungry, to face Alpheus's Vienna sausages and potato chips, but the day had not been wasted.

The following day a telegram ordered us to the Umfolozi Game Reserve for new duties. It was almost two years later before I actually saw a sandpiper pick a leech off a crocodile's throat, and this was on the Mkuze River where it enters Lake St. Lucia.

CHAPTER 14

The first rays of the morning sun were flooding through the tent door as we stopped talking about crocodiles. We lay on our groundsheets, soaking up the warmth and watching the sunrise spreading over the horizon.

Ken broke the stillness with, "Kom! Opstaan, koffie drink, inspan en trek!" (Come on! Get up, drink coffee, inspan the oxen and trek).

The first movements in the morning were always painful and I groaned as violent twinges shot through my back.

"Well, what shall we have on my birthday?" Ken asked sarcastically. "Porridge? Bacon and eggs? Sausages? Haddock? Hot buttered toast and marmalade?"

He ducked in time to avoid a wet sandshoe and ran away, laughing and shouting, "No, sir! It is coffee, Pro-vita and that rare and ancient dish—dried prunes!"

"Don't do anything yet, I said. "I'm going to catch a fish for breakfast."

Ken gave an Ndumu-itis horselaugh in reply.

I took my river rod and a small shad spoon, fixed up a wire trace then walked to the bank overlooking the rapids. Mist rose from the river and malachite kingfishers, their brilliant plumage glittering in the sun, flitted from bank to bank.

I cast the spoon and trailed it slowly up the rapids, wound in and cast again. The casting became automatic, for with the fixed spool reel it was so easy. Ken came and stood beside me, and pointed out a puff-back shrike on the opposite bank.

"Now look at that," he said. "Isn't it more beautiful, more magnificent than fishing for non-existent tigers?"

The bird puffed up the white feathers on its back and gave its rattling-whistling cry. The two calls were so different I could have sworn it was two birds.

To me it appeared that the rattle preceding the whistle is made by knocking the upper and lower beak together: after this the whistle follows, with the puffing out of the white feathers on the back. We became so intent

on watching the bird that I forgot to cast.

Ken laughed. "We'll make an ornithologist out of you yet," he said.

"And you'll be fishing before the year's out," I replied, flicking the spoon into the boiling rapid.

Ken walked away to a thicket where he had seen a Burchell's coucal.

I flicked the spoon overhead, watched it splash into the dun-coloured water and reeled in. Then it occurred to me that if I changed my position to the top of the rapid I could cast the spoon in, hold the line taught and keep the lure bouncing in the small waves. I did this and two minutes passed without anything happening. Just as I was about to reel in and try casting again, there was an almighty swirl and the reel screamed. A big tigerfish was on. It skittered downstream, leaping into the air, trying to throw the treble hooks out of its jaws.

I yelled for Ken to come and look; he strolled nonchalantly over but was soon caught up in the excitement of seeing the rod bend, hearing the reel whine and the sight of the tigerfish diving under the opposite bank in its efforts to get away.

"Hold it, play it, that's our breakfast," Ken shouted. The fish leapt up again and I saw the shake of its head, but the hooks were firmly embedded.

I played the fish back into the middle of the rapid and held it there so that it had to fight the current too. Then, inch-by-inch, I started to reel in. I had taken in about five feet when the fish realized what was happening and shot off downstream. The line went slack—I thought it was off. A feeling of bitter disappointment surged through me.

"It's off," I muttered gloomily.

Then the rod dipped; it was still on. Playing it more carefully than ever, I brought it into the rapid, and saw it float slowly to the surface: a real beauty of at least five pounds. It gave a few perfunctory shakes of its tail, then turned white belly up. The fight was over. Gently reeling in, I brought the fish to the bank, kept the line tight and hauled it up. The tiny rod nearly broke with the strain, but the fish was there—well and truly landed. What a thrilling fight. It lay on the bank, bright silver scales and red lines glinting in the sunlight.

"Basa umlilo" (make fire), I said to Ken. "We eat fresh fish today."

While Ken gathered wood for the fire from piles of old driftwood nearby, I gutted and scaled the fish. Then I took an old newspaper, went to the river and carefully soaked it, wrapped the fish in about five sheets then built the fire on top of it.

We built another fire for the billycan, then went off for a quick wash.

"One can't blame the amaTonga for not washing too often," Ken said as he lathered his neck. "This constant fear of being attacked by crocodiles

is enough to put me off too!"

We went back to the aromatic-smelling fires. Ken stopped near the tent and called me. "Look at this," he said.

I walked over and saw the fresh imprints of a hippo not ten feet from the back of the tent.

"We were talking too much last night!" Ken laughed.

We sat near the fires, writing and comparing notes of our journey so far. Today was the third day and already our notebooks were crammed with information.

"We need Jim Feely here to correlate all this stuff," Ken muttered. "The Brain (Jim's nickname) would soon get it into order and write an ecological report that everybody in this country should read. I wish I had just one tenth of that bloke's ability to put the right things down on paper," Ken went on.

I swore to Ken that one day we would get Jim down the Pongolo River before its life was destroyed by the powers who were going to build the dam.

Two long years were to pass before Jim Feely and I embarked at Otobotini for a similar trip down the river. By this time Ken was engaged on a vast ecological survey of Tongaland that was to make him famous in scientific circles—but all this was in the future.

"Another ten minutes and that fish will be done," Ken said, laying his notebooks aside.

I took my pencil and said to Ken, "Let's summarise what we have learnt so far."

We discussed and wrote down the broad details.

Every hippo run leading into the river was snared in some way. Snares varied from loops of thick mine cable to pointed sticks, or planks with six-inch nails pointing upwards. Only two things allowed the hippo to survive: their sagacity and their comparatively rapid breeding rate.

It was obvious that the hippo went into the adjoining pans, marshy areas and deep pools where they could successfully hide from their human predators. Only in protected areas like the Ndumu Game Reserve would they dare to stay in the river all the year round. We had seen the marked difference in behaviour between hippo in the game reserve and those outside. Inside they would come to the surface to stare inquisitively at any one who came near; in the areas that we were in now, all that we would see was a pair of flared nostrils come up to breathe, then a splash as they disappeared.

We did not blame the amaTonga for killing hippo; they were both struggling for a place in the sun.

At this time of the year the amaTonga reaped their last crops of mealies in the flood plain, and they used everything from snares to log fences and thumping paraffin tins at night to keep the hippo out. It was a never-ending war. Hippo were shot with old muzzle loaders or shotguns with solid lead plugs; sometimes they were surrounded in a small pan and the calves hacked to death, but all this was part of the balance. It was only now that it was getting out of control. In the last few years the medical skill of the white man had invaded Tongaland and the formerly high infant mortality rate from malaria had been checked, so that the population was now increasing by leaps and bounds. This could only have one result: invasion of the last wild areas and the deterioration of the whole of Tongaland.

We were witnessing the beginning of the decline, which would be accelerated when the dam wall in the Lebombo Mountains was completed.

At the moment, the amaTonga were inhabitants of a paradise, a veritable Garden of Eden, and, what was more important, they were part of the ecological complex; their whole life followed a set pattern.

In the winter they netted for fish and drove their cattle and goats on to the flood plain to graze on the thick green grass, and in the old mealie lands. All the hippo snares were removed to safeguard the domestic stock. At this time of the year the amaTonga fed on monkey apples and the bulbs of water lilies. This is also a period when crocodiles catch many, as they dive for the bulbs.

In the early summer months they planted their mealies and collected the many wild fruits—the mkwane (sycamore figs) which are dried then pounded into a powder and mixed with cooked porridge; fallen mganu (marula berries) were collected, boiled and made into a drink which can be refreshing before it ferments, but very potent once it has been left. The seeds were crushed and the kernel used for eating. Mbungwa (*Landolphia sp.*) were gathered and eaten by the children. The mdoni berries—small, black, and bitter until you get used to them—all these and many more were there for the picking.

The hippo played its part in helping the amaTonga by keeping the channels between the river and the pans open, allowing the fish access. The crocodile helped to maintain the balance with the fish. Life could be vicious and hard in Tongaland, but the balance was maintained and the people survived. All this was changing now—changing fast.

We continued to write and discuss what we had seen: the fact that the turtle had the best sense of hearing, then the water monitor and finally the crocodile. Earlier experiments had seemed to indicate otherwise, but after these days of concentrated observation, there was no doubt that the turtle

had uncanny hearing.

We had also noticed that crocodiles seemed loath to leave the warm sandbanks.

We had seen only seven crocodiles that were over eight feet long; this was a bad sign, for it was only when a crocodile grew to eight feet that it was capable of breeding. We also noticed that they frequented the fast-running water as well as the slow-moving backwaters.

We had seen numerous troops of samango monkeys, but they were shy and did not call out like the vervet until we had passed. Despite this, the amaTonga were able to kill them more easily, far more so than the vervet monkeys, who did a lot of damage to crops.

Crocodiles must have accounted for many vervet; we had frequently seen three or four crocodile hanging around where the vervet came down to drink. The vervets' choice of drinking places was never very wise either.

We had not seen one antelope: snaring was too widespread for many to survive in the riverine forests.

CHAPTER 15

We put our notebooks aside when the top sheets of the newspaper covering the fish began to burn. Ken jumped up and kicked the burning embers away, pulled the newspaper off, and we divided the fish. We added a little pepper and salt and ate with relish. Tiger fish have been described as "cotton wool stuffed with needles", but we were too hungry and starved for protein to worry about the mass of tiny bones, and we devoured everything. When the last morsel had been eaten, we made coffee and finished off with a few pieces of Pro-vita and some prunes.

We struck the tent, stowed the kit in the canoe and were ready to push off. Ken oiled his big .45 and I wiped the rust off my .22 Colt.

Ken lifted the canoe and dragged it down to the water. His back muscles bulged in the sunlight and I marvelled at his strength; over six-foot-two in his stockinged feet and weighing 195 lbs, he was a modern Apollo.

We argued about whether we should take the main course leading down the rapids, which would be the dangerous and more exciting one, but I elected for caution and wanted to stay in the pan. My council prevailed and we left, pulling the canoe through the Ulusundu pan. It took us nearly an hour to reach the main stream; by then we were both cursing my prudence, for there were moments when we were up to our waists in mud.

After we got going in the deep water, we drifted for an hour. The river had narrowed considerably and nowhere could we touch bottom. Big masses of sunken logs were dotted the whole way along, and the branches of the green sycamore figs met across the river. We saw many samango monkeys peering at us through the dense foliage and, much to our amusement, a troop of vervet ran along the edge of the pan, almost falling in their haste to get away.

The reflections of the fig and fever trees in the sluggish river were breath-takingly clear. Hundreds of birds were calling and giant kingfisher kept us company, flying just ahead.

The air was heavy with the smell of burning brushwood: the amaTonga were destroying more sycamore figs to try to increase the size

of their lands.

By half past two it was overcast. We had some bad moments when we struck a stumpy patch and a crocodile swirled past, and adrenalin flooded my system as we rounded a sharp bend and disturbed four more crocodiles. They panicked, making for the deep water and us—my heart was still pounding minutes later. Neither of us spoke; close shaves had become part of the journey. Ken merely held up four fingers and I noted the number of crocodiles in my notebook.

We paddled on into the increasing silence of the riverine forest. The only noise was the mournful wailing of trumpeter hornbills and the hissing of the river as it passed beneath gnarled roots.

We started paddling hard just before three o'clock—the river had become ominous, and in the small canoe and so close to the water, we were on equal terms with everything in the wild.

An hour passed with neither of us saying a word; voices were too harsh and strident in this primeval silence. A hadedah would fly out with loud squawks, so that we jumped with alarm. Words started, then choked and died. No one who had not experienced this could understand; Tongaland weaved a strange spell, inexplicable and awesome.

After a year in constant contact with civilization, we had forgotten what this was like. It was good, though frightening, to experience it again. The complete change in our state of mind was astounding. We were back, at grips with reality: an overturned boat and the swirl of a crocodile—a muffled scream, that would be all. The birds would chirp, the fish eagles cry and the river flow on.

Shortly before four o'clock we heard a clanking of chains downstream. We had reached Shemla's drift.

We tied the canoe to some roots, took the kit out and made camp under an old fig tree with root buttresses reaching twenty feet along the ground. An abandoned pont served us as a table. It was like camping in civilization, but we were both tired after the long hours of paddling, and the dried fruit was playing havoc with my stomach.

It was dark when we had the tent pitched and a fire going. The Tonga in charge of the pont came and sat on his haunches near the fire to warm his hands. He spoke of the hippo and vervet monkeys raiding his crops. He said that elephant were chasing people out of the Sihangwana bush, and they were now taking up the little remaining land on the Pongolo flood plain.

"This means the destruction of more sycamore figs," Ken said wearily.

Then we heard two Africans coming from the direction of Kangazini

pan. One was shouting in an angry, high-pitched voice, and the other answered back sullenly. As they approached, the argument became fiercer, and we thought they would come to blows at any moment. Then one moved into the firelight and greeted us normally.

"Sanibona amadoda," he said.

We returned the greeting and waited for the other fellow to appear, but no one stepped forward. Ken and I glanced at each other, wondering what had happened: had he been stabbed and pushed into the river? An owl whooped and a hippo grunted in the Kangazini. We all sat silent, staring into the fire.

Ken could contain himself no longer. "Where is your companion?" he asked in Zulu.

The man turned and looked behind him. "No one was with me," he said, mystified.

Ken and I looked at each other—he shrugged his shoulders; it was no concern of ours. This was Tongaland.

After some casual conversation, the man got up and walked into the night; seconds later we heard two voices arguing furiously. Bitter oaths were uttered and the noise echoed across the river. We glanced at the pont man, but he said nothing.

Ken shook his head. "Ndumu-itis in a big way!" he muttered.

We offered the pont man coffee, but he refused, saying he had to return to his homestead.

"Salani kahle" (stay well), he said as he got up and walked to his flat-bottomed boat.

"Hamba kahle" (go well), we replied.

We used to have strange experiences like this at Ndumu; it was like old times again.

At Ndumu and at Umfolozi Game Reserve we had come across Africans who had gone wild. We once found a salukazi (old woman) at Umfolozi near the Mhluzi stream. She was stark naked and appeared as mad as a hatter. When we asked her what she had been living on, she pointed to the roots of trees.

But the most amazing story was told to me by Boy Hancock, the ranger who took over Ndumu Game Reserve after we left. It was reported to him by the game guards, and Sigohlo was one of them—a trusty and reliable man.

The guards were on patrol in the Reserve on the Pongolo where the new channel cuts through into Baga-Baga pan and past Nangri, an island, which the amaTonga swore, was haunted. Dusk was falling as they made their way through the riverine forest when Sigohlo pointed to the river and

149

they saw a man floating downstream with only his head above water. The guards shouted at him to get out quickly, for the river was alive with crocodiles. When the man was directly opposite the guards he grabbed an overhanging branch and half pulled himself out of the water. At that moment a crocodile head popped up behind him, and the guards watched in horror, expecting to see him pulled under. But the croc merely bumped its head against the man's back. He turned round, gave the crocodile a gentle push with his hand, then climbed out. He looked at the guards once, grunted, and vanished into the reeds.

An almost incredible story, but what made it ring true to me was the guard's description of the crocodile bumping its head against the man's back. This is how the crocodile behaves in the water. I had seen it on other occasions at Umfolozi when zebra had been taken in the Black Umfolozi River. There was also no earthly reason why three guards should make up a story like this. Boy Hancock questioned each one individually, but there were no discrepancies in their story.

Boy also spoke to amaTonga living on the edge of the Salene forest, and they said this man was well known to them; he had merely gone wild and was living with the crocodiles.

Our rations were running very low, so we had less to eat than usual, but after a hard day's paddling I was always too thirsty to feel like eating. We drank three mugs of coffee with a pinch of salt in each before our thirst was satisfied, then we had some soup with potatoes and onions thrown in. It sloshed around in the plates, but a few pieces of Pro-vita wiped it up.

I staggered off to the tent and crawled thankfully onto my groundsheet. Ken came in later and we were kept awake by a bush baby's guttural, cackling cries. Ken fired the .22-410 combination into the air and this frightened it off and allowed us to sleep.

The last sounds were a fiery-necked nightjar beginning his plaintive song.

"Strange how it's only on moonlight nights that the night jar calls," Ken mumbled from his corner of the tent.

"An ornithologist to the last!" I replied, then fell fast asleep.

The rattle of mugs woke me the following morning. It was half past six, and Ken said, "It's going to be hot; there's a heavy mist on the water—the tiger fish are also jumping."

I tried to leap up to get the rod, but staggered giddily. I was sick-probably due to the sun, the lack of food and the violent exercise of the previous day. I crawled out of the tent to the big fig tree, then retched violently. I lay in the shade and dozed.

Some amaTonga crossed the river, playing their concertinas, then it

was quiet until fat-bellied women went past to collect water. They stared at me and said, "Bayete!" The pont crossed and recrossed, and each time the rattle of the chains woke me.

I leant against the roots of the old fig tree. This tree had seen so much come and go; yet it was doomed, for everyone who passed slashed at the roots with a cane knife, and it was being ring-barked.

I was sick, then slept again, only to have frightening dreams; twisted fever trees dancing on a vast inland sea, queer birds and animals flying and swimming, fish with crocodile's heads devouring creatures that looked like Neolithic man.

I awoke at one o'clock and said to Ken that I could stand the place no longer. The smell of chewed up sugar cane, the noisy amaTonga and the malignant atmosphere combined intolerably. Ken kindly packed the canoe with the help of the pont man, and a quarter of an hour later we were on the river, moving downstream.

Drops of water fell from Ken's paddles, reflecting like diamonds in the sun's rays. Leaves dropped from the fig trees and the wind rustled above us. Heuglin's robin whistled, "Don't you do it", and old weaverbird nests flapped from an overhanging fever tree—yellow-green and as mysterious as its name. A small bank appeared ahead and a varanus slid into the water. A sharp bend and the river reflected the trunk of a fig— bright and scintillating. We drifted past some floating leaves, browned and yellowed by the autumn sun.

Ken whispered the names of the birds and I wrote them down. Two pied wagtails were having a glorious bath on a half submerged log and a Natal robin sang its beautiful song in a dense thicket. A kingfisher's wings flashed, a blur of colour. A bee-eater flew upwards with Spitfire-like wings; a quick turn and it caught an insect. Ripe figs plopped into the water. Flies buzzed and a spider's web glinted in the sun. A frog croaked sadly and a barbel swirled in the current.

There was a roar ahead as the river flowed swiftly past some fallen logs, which bobbed up and down in slow, rhythmic movements.

Every hippo run was a mass of sharpened sticks and steel cables. A hippo snorted from the Sivunguvungu pan on our left and at the same moment we saw another hippo cable.

"What a horrible death," Ken said.

A vervet monkey gave a staccato chatter and the whole forest came to life. Ken called back in the monkey's language. The monkey was furious and chased up and down the bank in a rage. We could still hear it swearing as we floated down and into the shadows.

When we rounded the next bend, a spreading fig shaded a white

sandbank and we decided that this was the place to camp. It was only an hour since we had left Shemla's drift, but the beauty of this place was irresistible. My sickness had gone after the last hour's peace.

In a little while the camp was pitched and I fished while Ken went after some pigeons. I hooked a fair sized tiger, which bit savagely at the copper spoon, raced upstream then, with a jump and a flash, was off the line. The speed of these fish was a joy to see—when they took the spoon the whole rod jangled.

Ken shot one small dove, came back then disappeared. I made up the fire, put the billycans on and plucked the dove. Ken returned an hour later, grinning broadly and carrying a guineafowl. We lost no time in plucking it, then carefully cut it up and made a stew with our remaining onions and one potato.

A whole flock of guineafowl landed in a dry fig tree just as it was getting dark. I shot and hit one on the topmost branches. The moon was out when Ken began to climb. It was inspiring to watch him go up the trunk for at least thirty feet before he reached any branches. I would rather have had to swim the river with all its crocodiles than climb that tree. The wind rose and the branches leaned crazily to and fro. As Ken reached the top, the guineafowl flew away. The night was disturbed by peals of maniacal laughter—Ken letting off steam.

When he got down we polished off the stew, our first really good meal since we started.

The night was punctuated by the sounds of barking dogs, amaTonga drums and the grunting of hippo; symbolic of the long drawn out, fierce and bitter struggle between the primeval and the civilized.

CHAPTER 16

The following day we stayed in camp. Ken went out to collect birds and I wandered through the fig forest. I stumbled upon a snare that had obviously caught a hippo, judging by the signs of fighting. Trees had been smashed and the ground torn up when the animal tried to release itself. How I wished I could get hold of the culprit.

It reminded me of a time when a hippo had been killed on Needham's farm next to the game reserve, during a spate of hippo killings. We had had a report of a hippo destroying amaTonga mealie fields on the farm and I despatched Game Guard Mavela to find out where the animal was lying up, so that we could try to drive it back to the game reserve.

Ken and I had gone to Ingwavuma one morning and as we returned and passed the Ndumu store I heard someone blowing a police whistle. It was Mavela. He came running up, gabbling something about a hippo. I thought he was telling me that he had found its lying-up place, and gave him instructions to watch the animal.

Then he said, "But it is dead."

"Where?" Catuane, the senior guard, snapped.

"In the Umsindusi," Mavela replied.

I whipped the truck round and raced to Needham's house. We stopped to tell him the hippo was dead, then we made for the Umsindusi pools. We passed amaTonga on the flats bordering the river; they were carrying cane knives or axes.

We came to a pool covered with reeds and waterlilies. In the middle the poor old hippo floated on its back, all four legs pointing to the sky. There was a wide bloodstain on its neck; it had been shot. This was the fifth hippo in a row, all killed with a high-powered rifle.

We hadn't yet any clue who was responsible.

Two amaTonga (I took my hat off to them) volunteered to get into the pool and drag the hippo downstream to a point where we could cut it up. Gases bubbled out of the mouth and the bullet hole; the stench was foul.

I asked the two men whether they were not afraid of crocodiles, but

they said that in this river crocodiles never attacked anyone. I still thought they were taking a big chance, towing a stinking hippo that was oozing blood. Singing cheerfully, they pulled it downstream. If they jerked too violently, jets of gas would be expelled from various holes.

Game Guard Sigohlo spat, and said that anyone who stole this sort of meat was mad.

When the hippo had been pulled to a suitable spot, we tried dragging it out with the truck, but only managed to move it to the water's edge.

Our labour gang started to hack it up. Odd Africans were coming from all over the place, and our gang was amused when Ken said, "The vultures have arrived."

Alpheus sprang onto the belly and started to hack through the hide. He grinned vainly when I took his photograph. Then he put his knife in too far, and the carcass exploded. Rotten intestines came pouring out like a sausage machine. Alpheus leapt into the river with a cry of alarm, and the gang shouted with laughter as they paused to watch.

First the legs were hacked off, then the head—it took six men to carry it. Every now and then a labourer working in the water would leap out with a squeal, as a leech fastened onto his leg.

More locals came, to squat and watch the proceedings.

Gradually old Sambane, the Induna (headman), chopped through all the large bones until the ribs were left. We loaded up the truck and took all the meat to the camp.

I told Mavela that it was his area, and he must find out who had killed the animal. There was little hope, for no evidence had come forth from the other four killings, but this time we had the bullet—it looked like a Mauser 9 mm.

The Police lent us a good African constable, and the following day we roped in a suspect named "Bingalela". The constable and the game guards questioned Bingalela for an hour under a marula tree. I watched the man's face while questions were being fired at him; his expression saddened progressively, and his long jaw dropped. He seemed to know something.

The guards and the police constable said we must go to another muzi near the Usutu. We drove as far as we could, then walked down a goat path and came into a clearing where a few huts were being erected. A mob of amaTonga men, hair plastered white and done in Swazi style, sat drinking cane wine. One tall man with a cigarette dangling from his lips stood over a huge clay pot, dishing out the liquor with an enamel mug. They barely glanced at us, but there was no mistaking the tension in the air.

The constable chose a man, called him aside and spoke to him for a

few moments. Then he left him and called another, who threw a stick at a mangy dog as he walked towards us.

The second man was garrulous, and quite an actor, and it was amusing to watch his face as it registered surprise, amazement and innocence. Then he said that Bingalela had seen the hippo dead on Monday.

The African constable's eyes narrowed. He said nothing, but sucked in air through his teeth and, hunching his shoulders, sat like a snake ready to strike. Then he spat out a string of questions. The man recoiled, realizing he had said too much. The constable asked a few more questions, smiled, stood up, and dusted himself.

Then he stalked towards the drinking mob. His helmet was slung over his hips, with the strap attached to his handcuffs. Slowly he moved towards the gathering, his gait like a cowboy who has just got off his horse. Conversation faded as he approached the crowd, then bubbled like a stream as he passed and went to a woman suckling a child beside a gaudy bicycle. Her breasts were full, with swollen nipples, and the child left the breast to gape at the constable. He spoke to the woman, his voice rising in anger until she answered him shrilly. Then he walked back to me.

"We have learnt a little," he said, with a smile.

The following day, Bingalela was questioned again. He said that Mavela's old mother had said that the hippo was dragging its leg.

According to the constable, this had great bearing on the case, so we drove to the Ndumu store to find the salukazi (old woman). We had to wait while Mavela looked for her.

I watched the assortment of people at the store. One man in a pork pie hat, a string of bright beads, and a multi-coloured loincloth, strutted up and down the verandah, a child's school case in his hand, showing off to some newly married girls, whose once firm breasts were beginning to droop. Some small children with swollen bellies, their hair plastered white with Sunlight soap, sat on the edge of the veranda, playing Jewish harps.

Mavela returned with his aged mother and we drove back to the police camp.

When the old woman was asked, in front of Bingalela, whether she had said the hippo was dragging its leg, she denied it vehemently. Then she turned on Bingalela and gave him a tongue lashing that he would never forget.

The following day, the guards stationed on Nangri Island reported that yet another hippo had been killed. We received information that it was someone living in the Salene forest. As there might have been a tie-up, we left investigating the first case and went to the Salene area the next day.

155

We walked along the path that meandered across the flood plain, then crossed the Pongolo on a flat-bottomed punt, expertly poled by an umfaan no more than nine years old. Once over the river we ploughed through the sugarcane and reeds, then took the path that led along the fig trees to Lake Polwe. We waded a channel on the northern side, and Alpheus complained when two leeches affixed themselves to his legs. Once out of the pan area, we struck heavy white sand and trudged along through the dry forest country. It was hot, and every step was agony. The sand burnt through my boots and our khakis were saturated with sweat.

We reached the kraal of Chief Mzimba, and went in to pay our respects, but he was away at Ingwavuma. A pleasant, one-eyed Induna showed us round the muzi. The white sand contrasted vividly with the green bush and dull brown thatched huts.

We pressed on, and after another two-hour's walk reached the Sihangwana area. The trees were much bigger and the atmosphere was oppressive. Signs of elephant were everywhere; their spoor made those of a hippo look puny in comparison.

While we were passing one homestead, an old, withered woman pulled us in and said that the elephants had stolen all her mealies. She showed us the wrecked ngolobane (grain hut). The marauding elephant had put its trunk inside and neatly flipped off the roof. We took the old girl's name and promised to try to get compensation for her. She was overwhelmed with gratitude and wanted to give us a fowl, which I forbade Alpheus to accept, much to his disgust.

Another half hour's good walk brought us to a homestead where our informer said we would get further information. We left him on the outskirts, walked in, and began questioning the suspect. He was so surprised by our sudden appearance that it did not take long to get the truth. The guards and I were also weary and irritable from the heat, and in no mood to listen to a lot of drivel.

The suspect gave us the name of the man who had killed the last hippo, and he said that he lived just on our side of the border. There was nothing else to do but to walk all the way to the border to arrest the man.

The trek was lengthy, and when we reached the hut, the bird had flown only minutes before, leaving a trail of his belongings leading to the Usutu. Bitterly disappointed and furiously angry, we made our way back to camp.

We were never successful in getting the culprit, or in determining what part Bingalela had played in the affair, but as the spate of hippo killings ceased after our near-arrest, we were glad to let sleeping dogs lie.

I was awakened from my reverie by the banging of a billy and Ken

shouting. I walked back to the sandbank and was delighted to find that he had another guineafowl. The second good meal in two days renewed our energy, and we looked forward to the final part of the journey the next day.

CHAPTER 17

We were up early and were on our way by six o'clock. A heavy mist lay on the river and the canoe floated in a ghostlike manner; only our heads were above the mist. Two amaTonga women hoeing in a field saw us, and ran away screaming.

After an hour's paddling the sun broke the mist, and the glare from the river nearly blinded us.

Giant kingfishers were common; their recurrent screeching cries echoing about the river and through the forest. A Pel's fishing owl flew from some dense foliage; Ken was justifiably excited.

It was silent, except for the swishing of the paddles, then vervet and samango monkeys began calling. Their cries shattered the peace. A longcrested eagle flew over, alighted on a dead tree, flapped its wings and glanced around. Its crest flopped in the faint breeze. Instantly the monkeys were still.

"It is fear, little brother—it is fear," I quoted.

We paddled on, past a colony of old weaverbird nests and into the shade of fig trees; the different shades of green contributed so much to the atmosphere of the forest and river.

A small channel entered the river on the left bank. Some dead, dark lianas trailed in the water and two fallen fig trees, with smooth brown trunks and long roots, guarded the entrance; a gloomy looking spot, A trumpeter hornbill wailed out its childlike cry, startling some monkeys so that they leapt from the branches of a squat tree and stared at us through the leaves. A little one chattered and was immediately given a cuff by its mother.

The morning sun shone through the forest, the light catching the trunks of the larger trees and casting delicate shadows on the small glades. A narina trogon flitted past, a picture of grace and beauty. Drongos, bulbuls and robins all competed with one another in song, and the air was heavy with the smell of rotting figs and the dank smell of the river.

Five crocodiles lay on a white sandbank ahead; one of them was almost black. They got wind of us and plunged into the river. There was a

massive swirl and a crocodile appeared, with its head out of water. It had a barbel in its jaws and was crushing it into small pieces; presently it lowered its head into the water and seemed to be washing the barbel down.

We reached Makane's pont at half past eight. Nkunzi-Mbomvu, the famous pont man known to all Tongaland travellers, was not there. It was said that he poled the pont better after a heavy session of moba (cane wine).

A few amaTonga women, with drooling babies on their backs, stood listlessly under the big fig tree, waiting for the pont. One of them clucked and muttered about Nkunzi-Mbomvu keeping them waiting. A gust of wind blew their scent towards us—a mixture of sweat and moba.

We paddled on, reaching the Ingwavuma River two hours later. There were many more fields on the banks; the fig forests were being burnt out. We played a joke on some women hoeing their field above us. Keeping close to the bank and out of sight, we called out in deep voices, then paddled fast round the next bend. The women stopped hoeing, ran to the edge and looked over, but saw nothing. We waited until they resumed their hoeing, then repeated the performance. They grew excited and alarmed, calling out, "Myeh! Myeh! The tokoloshes (mythical spirits) are in the river!"

When we showed ourselves they stood dumb, with their hands to their mouths. We greeted them pleasantly and paddled on. After a few minutes they came running along the bank, giggling and shouting that the crocodiles would get us.

By two o'clock our journey was rapidly drawing to a close. We were sad; it had been a wonderful rest after the past year of constantly dealing with people. We had also learnt a good deal about the Pongolo, and realized a dream of many years.

Half an hour later we entered the Ndumu Game Reserve, and paddled to a landing stage below the camp.

That night we had one of the best baths of our lives, and a three-course meal—absolute luxury. Sleeping in beds was too much for us, and after tossing and turning for hours, we put our groundsheets on the floor and slept fitfully until morning.

The next day we lazed around before getting more supplies for our journey up the Usutu River to the gorge. We still had a few days leave, and we were interested to see how far the hippo went up the gorge.

Later that afternoon Ken drove to the store to buy rations, and I went down to Nyamiti pan. It was a sentimental journey and I was haunted by memories; every yard of the track had a story.

Sambane's muzi, a little way down the road, was falling to pieces. A

young Tonga man had stabbed poor old Sambane to death, just before we had left Ndumu. The fight had been over a woman. In amaTonga tradition he had been buried in front of his hut, and the supporting poles of the hut cut down. The grave had almost disappeared under a mass of weeds, and all that was left of the hut was a few poles and a pile of thatch.

I drove on down the sandy track over a dry stream, where we had once had a frightening experience when an immense black mamba had reared and struck at our open Land Rover.

I stopped at Emloyeni, the witchdoctor's homestead. He came running out and greeted me effusively. He took me to his young wife, to show me how well she was walking on crutches. She had been the victim of a crocodile attack the first night I arrived at Ndumu. Emloyeni and his brother had rushed into Nyamiti and grappled with the crocodile until it had released the woman. Then they had called me, and I had taken her to Miss Eriksen at the dispensary, and later up the long road to Dr. Morril at Ingwavuma hospital.

I left Emloyeni and took the twisting track that led through the nthombothi forests along the southern bank of Nyamiti pan. Two stately nyala bulls stalked through a glade of fever trees, and a fish eagle flapped from an old nest. It was at this nest that I had watched a pair of the birds feeding their young with barbel and tilapia.

I stopped at a high place overlooking Dhlozi point. Twelve crocodiles lay in a semicircle along the wide sandbank, and in a sheltered bay a big herd of hippo sunned themselves, their backs and heads above the water. Turtles lay on the hippos' backs, taking advantage of a sunny perch.

I scanned the pan with binoculars, and saw about eight crocodiles swimming up the eastern channel. They stopped, and milled around, while another two large ones floated quietly through the reeds bordering the bank in front of the main group. Then I saw the water boiling as a school of fish jumped out of the water. The crocodiles came silently from all directions and formed a ring about the fish; gradually the ring narrowed, then as if by a given signal the crocodiles began to catch and eat the fish. The noise attracted an osprey, which came hurtling over the fever trees, and hovered on the outskirts. Twice it dived, but came up with nothing then it swooped a third time and took off with a small barbel. A fish eagle appeared from nowhere and harried the osprey, which dived and wheeled to try to escape the oppressor.

Five minutes later the crocodiles, fish, osprey and fish eagle had vanished, and the lake was as calm as a millpond.

I drove on, crossed over the old wooden bridge and took the track

following the pan on the northern side. A more beautiful drive does not exist in Tongaland; green reeds and open glades pass in an enchanting kaleidoscope. Crested guineafowl with their kettledrum calls, bush partridges with rollicking, sailor-like runs, crossed and recrossed the track. Shy bushbuck leapt from pools in the reeds, and a small red bush duiker stood staring at me for an instant.

I passed the pan we called "Little Paradise", where the air was heavy with the scent of blue water lilies, and jacana flew with rapidly beating wings from one lily to another.

I crossed the channel leading out of Banzi pan and the big fever tree forest, then went through ploughed lands where the amaTonga were still trying to burn the heart out of a gigantic sycamore fig. Angrily I went faster, to get away from man's inhumanity to nature.

I reached the bank of the broad Usutu and thought of David Leslie, who in his book "Amongst the Zulus and amaTongas", said: "Again, curious mistakes are often made regarding the names of places. It is well that these should be corrected; otherwise original native names will be corrupted into something without sense. For instance, the custom is to speak of the Maputo River. Now the name of the river is Usutu and that has a meaning. It is taken from the word Suta meaning to be full of food and is applied because they say 'Usutu minia manzi'. The Usutu, which swallows all the water".

I stopped my truck on the edge of the fig forest and walked into the cool, leafy tunnel following the banks of the river. How many memories this place had for me.

The first time I had come, Catuane the game guard had shown me a tree with a bare patch at the base. He said that this was the playground of the samango monkeys, and swore that he had seen them holding paws and dancing round the tree. I examined the ground carefully, and saw the tracks of the little monkeys. Whenever I entered the forest after this I used to tread quietly, hoping to see them. I never did, but I was rewarded by seeing a group of samango running along a branch overhanging the river, jumping into the water with flailing arms, swimming to the side, then repeating the performance. Nature unfolds her secrets only to the patient and persevering.

A little further along the path marked the spot where Ken, my dog, Lancer, and I had heard a baboon bark in the forest.

Lancer pricked up his ears, and before we could stop him he sprinted down a hippo path with an intent expression on his face that I still remembered vividly. Before we had walked ten yards there was a shrill scream from the undergrowth and an excited bark from Lancer. Another

scream and a snarl of rage reverberated through the forest. I was afraid; Lancer would stand no chance against these monsters.

Squeals, howls, grunts and bellows followed in quick succession, but above it all savage growls of wrath came from Lancer. Ken and I could stand it no longer, and we dashed headlong into the mass of thorns and spiky plants, but Lancer had vanished. It was quiet for a while, then in the distance another cacophony of cries startled the forest. From the noise we knew that Lancer had hold of one of the baboons and was doing his utmost to kill it.

We ran in the direction of the sound and picked up Lancer's tracks that led straight to the first confluence of the Pongolo. His spoor and that of a colossal baboon lay side by side on the nearby sandbank—both had crossed the river, which was in full flood, and crocodiles were everywhere.

Ken started to strip, but I forbade him to swim over to the island; the baboons were protecting their young and Lancer was in the wrong.

There was a short silence, broken by more deep "bogoms" from the baboons and barks from Lancer. Then came a piteous howl of terror from the dog. I knew that a baboon must have got hold of him. I fired my .22 rifle towards the sounds, hoping that it would frighten the baboons off. It became ominously silent again; I was sure he could not have got away from a mob like that.

A little later we heard more "bogoms" of an old baboon. It sounded like a victory call.

We could stand the suspense no longer and were about to cross the river, when Ken spotted Lancer lying on the opposite bank. Only his head showed above a mass of lianas. He stared at us, obviously afraid to cross, knowing that he was in the wrong. I whistled, called and coaxed him to come. He hesitated, then plunged in and started swimming. Before he had gone five yards something caught hold of him. We thought it was a crocodile, and the end of Lancer, but it was a bunch of brambles trailing below the water. He turned on his back, bit savagely at the thorns then the river washed him free; but he was so weak that he began floating downstream to the swift-flowing Usutu.

Ken could bear it no longer, and jumped into the water. With a few quick strokes he reached the dog and dragged him to the bank.

I pulled Lancer out and saw a gaping wound below his right shoulder. Ken pointed out another wound; Lancer's belly had been ripped open from his sternum to his testicles and the abdomen was punctured, so that the intestines were visible.

We carried him to the Land Rover and took him to Miss Eriksen at the dispensary. She sewed him up and filled him with antibiotics. A month

later he was running around as though nothing had happened; he is still alive, but very cautious of baboons.

I sat in the forest for hours, listening to the sounds and watching the wide Usutu flow past, and brooding on our battles to preserve this last vestige of the Tongaland wilderness. Even the atmosphere was worth preserving, but how did you explain its value to people? It had no utilitarian purpose that was obvious to the masses—few would appreciate its loss, but those of us who had come into contact with it could not let it be destroyed.

Reluctantly I walked back to the truck and drove to the camp, but during the night I woke up with the moon shining on my face.

I got up and went outside, wondering what it was about the moonlight that lulls the violent senses of man and brings out the best in him. I looked at the hills, faint in the distance, with light wisps of mist above the dark valleys; I became aware of something greater and infinite. Thoughts, desires and sensations came crowding into my mind as though trying to drive out this intruder, but the sighing of the wind as it wound about the tall trees made me conscious of this infinite being and the indefinable feeling of peace: a consolidation of mind and soul: a ghost of a voice, a glimmer of light and the dawning knowledge that God is.

"God is," the wind whispered as it floated down the white sandy bed of the river; "God is," it cried in the steamy forest of clinging lianas and mighty fig trees. "God is all."

PART THREE

CONTAINING A SHORT HISTORY OF
EVOLVING RELATIONS BETWEEN THE
DUSI AND THE PEOPLE
OF THE VALLEYS,
KEY POINTS IN THE DUSI'S
DEVELOPMENT, ENTRANT STATISTICS,
AND LISTS OF THE RESULTS AND
FINISHERS FROM 1951 TO 2006

THE DUSI AND THE MEETING
WITH THE PEOPLE OF THE VALLEYS
- ∞ -

DAVE MACLEOD,
WITH CONTRIBUTIONS FROM
ROBBIE STEWART, SHEILA WHITFIELD,
BRIAN MOORE, TIM CORNISH,
DEREK HOWE AND MARK CONWAY

The unique allure of the Dusi has in more recent times attracted large numbers of paddlers into the Umsindusi and Umgeni valleys. This is not only on the race days, because during the early summer months in the build-up to the Dusi there is a programme of races designed to give Dusi participants a chance to recce the entire 120 kilometre course. These preliminary races culminate in the annual 50 Miler, which embraces roughly two-thirds of the Dusi course over two days.

On any given summer weekend therefore, many vehicles will arrive in the valleys from Durban, Pietermaritzburg, and further afield, either to race, or trip the rivers in preparation for the Dusi, immersing the paddlers, their seconds and supporters in the picturesque scenery and traditional culture of the valley communities.

It is an unusual, dramatic, and potentially problematic meeting of two communities. One is city-based, usually wealthy, and accustomed to a fast-paced existence, while the valley community lives a rural lifestyle, with far fewer luxuries and significantly less disposable wealth.

The relationship of Ian Player with the Zulu people he met on his first expedition, as he recounts it in *Men, Rivers and Canoes*, reveals his sympathetic and friendly interaction with them. This genuine interest in and feeling for those he met set the foundation for what has taken years of learning, on both sides, to develop into the positive relationship achieved in the present period.

From the earliest days when canoeists became visitors to these valleys, the relationship between the paddlers and the residents was mostly

a distant one, mainly because of the fleeting nature of the paddlers' visits. There was often curiosity amongst the local people, but it was only on rare occasions, and mainly as a result of misfortunes suffered on the river, that the paddlers and the people spent any real time together and developed a better understanding of each other's interests in the valleys. Understandably, many of the residents of the valleys saw the short visits by speeding convoys of vehicles laden with canoeing accessories as intrusive invasions. This situation was accentuated by the animosity that underpinned the ongoing resistance to apartheid rule.

With very few exceptions, all the canoeing visitors to the valleys were obviously white and apparently wealthy. They were primarily interested in accessing the river, and it was clear to the residents they had very little regard for the welfare of the communities they passed through en route to the popular put-in and take-out points on the rivers.

In its early days, beginning in 1951, the Dusi did not attract a massive entry. It was seen as an extreme challenge for a few brave, or foolhardy, young men, rather than a popular sporting event. Eight paddlers started the 1951 Dusi. A decade later that number had grown to 64, and it topped 100 entrants for the first time only in 1967. So the number of paddlers, and their intrusive vehicles entering and leaving the valley was relatively small in the early years. In those days the Dusi entered what was demarcated as a "Native Reserve", and the participants, who were generally ignorant of the Zulu culture and traditional structures, were urged not to involve themselves with the residents of the valleys.

The race rules for the 1956 Dusi warned paddlers that they had to have a permit to enter the "Native Reserve", without which the paddlers were "liable to be arrested or prosecuted if [they broke] their laws".

Considering the broader political context, and the nature of the canoeists' brief comings and goings, it was only a matter of time before paddlers became targets. They intruded as if blindly from their separated worlds, and for some members of the valley communities their presence understandably provoked opposition. Paddlers reported occasional incidents of stoning on casual trips, and in races. Assessing the stoning incidents was difficult—many were simply pranks, though others were more determined expressions of opposition. 1958 Dusi winner, Rob Gouldie, recalls a bombardment from the towering cliffs below the Pumphouse station on the lower Umgeni during the 1960 Dusi, which indicated intentional hostility.

Resulting from the inspiration of the Dusi, by the 1970s, there began a sharp growth in the number of entrants in the Dusi itself, and in the popularity of canoeing countrywide. Access to new and more suitable

river kayaks opened up at this time, and there was a great increase in the awareness of canoeing as an enjoyable and exciting recreation, and a competitive sport. By the mid-1970s Dusi entry numbers reached 500.

The Natal Canoe Union (NCU) was well organised and ran an ever increasing programme of races in the build-up to the Dusi, using the Umsindusi and Umgeni rivers. The number of private trips into the valley as part of individual paddler's training for the Dusi increased as well. This triggered an increase in hostility and protests aimed at the canoeists. Partly this was due to the insensitive imposition of the canoeists on the local communities as well as the worsening political climate in the country. As will be recalled, the 1970s and 1980s saw an ever building and more widely organised opposition to apartheid so that every activity in South Africa increasingly acquired a political dimension. The Dusi was inevitably part of this broad historical process, and racial tensions between the valley residents and the visiting canoeists increased. Some major races were held under police or military escort, as the still exclusively white canoeing community feared for its safety away from the security of insulated suburbs.

Nevertheless, there continued to be good relations with the people of the valley mixed in with the bad. Whereas in some cases positions hardened, moderation also eased the way, and more experienced canoeists and officials recognised the difference between intentional hostility and innocent pranks and youthful mischief. The innocent and mischievous confrontations were often the flip side of the friendly engagements with canoeists, who brought unusual luxuries and treats into the valleys. Gifts were given, and sometimes there were unintentional bonuses, when, after accidents the cheap soccer balls, packed into canoes for buoyancy, floated off to find their ways onto rural soccer fields. So too were the occasional fortuitous gains when paddlers lost their caps in the rivers. In the eyes of many youngsters these caps were disposable luxuries for the rich white paddlers, and the interest in securing a paddler's cap escalated, and ingenious ways were devised for lifting the caps off canoeists as they ran or paddled past. For a canoeist who had lost a cap needed for protection from sunburn, this petty theft became a source of conflict and dispute, and triggered many confrontations, usually won by the fleet-footed youngsters escaping with their trophies.

With the escalation in the numbers of canoeists entering the valleys came an increasing number of vehicles. Thoughtless paddlers did neither themselves, nor the Dusi as a growing sporting event, any favours by driving across pasture lands, parking in croplands, entering tribal lands

without seeking permission, and often leaving behind a trail of damaged crops, and gates that were not closed on their departure.

The valley community is well organised and run in tribal groupings, headed by powerful amakhosi and izinduna, whose control was, and often still is, absolute, and more immediate than the State's rule of law. The traditional leaders often met to discuss the intrusion of the abelungu, and opinions differed widely on the best way for the leadership to respond. The passionate, young, struggle activists were eager to step up the level of opposition, while the more conservative amakhosi opposed the use of aggression against the canoeists.

By the early 1980s, the situation worsened even further, aggravated by the ongoing surge in the popularity of canoeing, driven as it was by the growing enthusiasm for "doing the Dusi". In response, stonings became regular occurrences. Petty theft of caps had grown to more brazen confrontations, particularly when the paddlers were portaging—theft of shoes and wristwatches, and more, started.

Des Park was a key leader of Dusi canoeing at that time. He was a broad-minded visionary, fluent in isizulu and familiar with traditional culture and structures. He saw the need for pro-active intervention to prevent the Umsindusi, Umgeni, Umkomaas and Tugela valleys from becoming "no-go" areas.

Park was the president of the South African Canoe Federation (SACF), then a body isolated from international competition by the sporting sanctions imposed on apartheid South Africa. Park found a willing ally in Robbie Stewart, the larger-than-life chair of the NCU, himself a paddler who had won the Dusi in 1979 after almost a decade of being very competitive.

Stewart carried with him great respect and authority within the paddling community, and had little trouble persuading the members of the NCU Executive, and the clubs which held the power within the regional union, that something had to be done to safeguard the future of the sport in the valleys. Park and Stewart came up with a means through which canoeists could contribute towards the improvement of the infrastructure and lives of the valley residents.

The Valley Assistance Fund (VAF) was born in 1982, and it set a one rand levy on each canoeist taking part in all Dusi qualifying races. The funds collected by the VAF were earmarked for assisting self-help schemes committed to building improved educational facilities in the valleys.

The paddling community was at first split by this bold move, with a vocal opposition using it to direct abuse at any antagonist they encountered

in the valleys. However, the pool of money soon grew, and the NCU convened a committee charged with finding the most effective ways to distribute the funds to meet their two primary goals—to soften the hardening relations, and to aid the construction of classrooms in the valleys.

During the mid-1980s the amount raised and distributed by the VAF snowballed from an annual R8000 to well over R20 000 per annum, and Stewart and Park were actively looking for partners within commerce to provide further sponsorship for the programme.

Once the programme had started, the administrators ran into difficulties in identifying, and more importantly, controlling the funds made available for these self-help building schemes in the valleys. It was after some turbulent initial months that Nigel Wood of the Urban Foundation was co-opted, and the VAF channelled its resources through his office, subject to a number of clear conditions aimed at ensuring that the funding would impact positively on relations between the paddlers and residents of the Umsindusi and Umgeni valleys.

This worked well, largely because the Urban Foundation was passionate about supporting self-help schemes that the valley communities themselves had identified, and every potential recipient, which now included clinics as well as school classrooms, was screened and approved by the NCU Executive.

Gradually the number of classrooms being built under the control of the Urban Foundation and the VAF grew. In a nine-year period over R70 000 collected by the VAF was used to construct 40 classrooms at fourteen different locations, all of them in the valleys through which the Dusi ran.

Despite these positive developments, the desired warming of relations between the valley residents and the paddlers did not materialize as fully as had been hoped. The reasons soon became obvious. One factor was the insufficient marketing and local visibility of the efforts being made on the paddlers' behalf. This partly arose from the fact that some of the VAF money was simply added to funding from a number of other sources to finance the building projects, and so got lost in the bigger pool. But, more importantly, there was not enough community support and "buy-in" from the amakhosi and their constituents. This was because there had been inadequate personal contact and involvement by the paddlers in the community-based projects.

The NCU then fell under the new leadership of Mark Conway, another successful Dusi paddler. He was a man with the breadth of mind to keep his eye on the bigger picture when others were often shortsighted.

Under his influence, it was decided that the VAF efforts should be concentrated on one single project at a time, and that efforts should be made to get the canoeing community more directly involved so as to raise the profile of the grants from the VAF.

Des Park, as a fluent isizulu speaker, had been a big asset in the earlier days. But what the VAF needed was a new champion, and as good fortune had it, onto the stage came Brian Moore, the amiable former Stella Canoe Club chairperson, and an enthusiastic social paddler. Moore was not only fluent in isizulu, but also passionate to learn more about Zulu culture.

Moore's irrepressible enthusiasm for the VAF's objectives propelled it into a new era. An administrative assistant was hired, who worked out of Moore's computer software shop in Durban, so he could devote more of his time to going into the valley to meet the community leaders, and gradually build his own credibility as an interface between the canoeists and the valley residents.

Moore's passion for the Zulu culture led to his becoming a popular figure at traditional functions in the valleys, where he would enjoy VIP status alongside the amakhosi, dressed in his ibeshu (skins), isinene and izinjhobo (loincloth and side covering), and bearing his ihawu (shield) and umkhonto (spear). He became known by his adopted Zulu name of uBhungane Hadebe. His tireless energy and frequent trips into the valley, where he mixed easily with the local people, earned him the nickname uBhungane—meaning the cricket—because he chattered so much.

One of the first projects to benefit from the VAF's more focused strategy was the clinic in the kwaNgcolosi area, on the Hillcrest side of Inanda Dam. The dearth of medical facilities in the rapidly growing community was glaring, making the need for a clinic an obvious necessity.

Moore knew firsthand which areas of the Umsindusi and Umgeni valleys were receptive to the paddlers, and where the paddlers were unwelcome. During the 1992 Dusi he was part of a group of backmarkers confronted by tsotsis just above the confluence of the two rivers, and robbed at knifepoint of his watch and shoes.

"It was a low Dusi and I was dragging my canoe towards the confluence," recalls Moore. "Five or six youngsters arrived, with knives in hand, and demanded my watch. I told them about the VAF, and pointed out to them a school up on a nearby hill, that we had sponsored and opened just two weeks earlier.

"They told me to 'shut up, and hand over the watch'. I then saw two canoeists from Johannesburg on the bank, and clambered out of my canoe and moved towards them—all the while swinging my paddle at the gang. The gang members shouted, 'Vimba, vimba!' (Stop him, Stop him!).

172

"The funniest thing that happened that day was when I got to the 2nd overnight stop only to hear that a 14 year-old girl, Lorna Oliver, had single-handedly chased away the same group of thieves, with her paddle!"

Undeterred, Moore, with canoeing friend and ally Fundani Ndlovu at his side, quickly made contact with and won the respect of several key leaders of the valley communities.

Principal amongst those was the highly respected and dignified Inkosi Bhengu, who led the Ngcolosi clan, based in the area bordering on the Inanda dam and stretching down as far as Molweni below the dam wall. Inkosi Gwala of Maphephethweni was also receptive to the work being done by the paddlers, and positively influenced attitudes in his clan on the northern side of the dam.

Amongst others with whom Moore forged solid relationships were the late Inkosi Shangase of kwaMkhizwana, whose son continues to this day the good work started by his father, and Inkosi Bamba Maphumulo of Table Mountain, who was instrumental in easing tensions between paddlers and the persistent cap-pinchers and stone-throwers active in the area between the Maze rapid and Table Mountain.

Few amakhosi however have become as passionate about the Dusi, and the relationships with the paddlers in general, as Inkosi Mlaba of emKhambathini.

Inkosi Mlaba became actively involved in addressing conflict between valley residents and paddlers in the area from Table Mountain (the Dusi's first night stop) to the portage over Nqumeni Hill. Mlaba, however, took his involvement and commitment to the race to a new level when he decided to take part in the race himself. He went on to complete the race a number of times, in the company of a various skilled and elite partners. His participation attracted crowds to the banks of the river during the Dusi, and proved to be crucial in narrowing the gap between the onlookers and the paddlers, and planted the seed for future participation in the Dusi by residents of the valleys.

This was aided by the participation of a number of celebrities, including Bafana Bafana soccer star, Doctor Khumalo, national soccer coach Clive Barker, and former Miss South Africa, Peggy Sue Khumalo.

The co-operation between the amakhosi and the VAF, driven so vigorously by Moore, resulted in numerous capital projects, ranging from the major R1,5 million clinic development at kwaNgcolosi, to the building of over 40 school classrooms and community halls.

Pollution of the Umsindusi and Umgeni rivers has been a growing problem for the Dusi, which has always been raced at the height of summer to capitalise on the rainy season and the full rivers it brings. The

rainfall, however, also washes quantities of litter and human waste into the river. With the increasing informal population of the riverbanks, the *ecoli* levels have often increased horrifically and been responsible for the gastric illnesses that have become known as "Dusi Guts".

The VAF has tackled this issue head on as part of its investment in the valley and its peoples. Central to this activity has been a programme to construct low cost "pungalutho" toilets in communities in the valleys to help reduce the wash-off of human waste.

Another former paddler then entered the frame in the form of Derek Howe. A fluent isizulu speaker, Howe had paddled the 1983 Dusi with Simon Mkhize and was passionate about fostering enthusiasm for canoeing amongst the valley residents.

Howe took on the portfolio of safety and security on the Dusi race committee in the mid-1980s, and made it his job to identify the "hot-spots" and to take concrete steps to identify the perpetrators and, where possible, bring them to book. Howe was also tough on inconsiderate paddlers and their seconds who ignored the appeals for drivers to stay off the crops and private farmlands in the valley.

During the politically charged days of the late 1980s, his job, which required frequent visits to amakhosi in the valley, dragged him into the midst of tensions between the ANC and Inkatha, with tribal allegiances aggravating tensions in the valley.

Howe was part of a group of paddlers that had to be "extracted" by a police task team from Dusi Bridge after being caught in the middle of a running gun battle between ANC and Inkatha cadres.

"It was terrifying," Howe admits. "With bullets flying everyone feared for their lives. Then we saw a priest step onto the bridge in the middle of the battle, begging the youths to stop fighting, which they eventually did. It was the bravest thing I have ever seen in my life," Howe says.

Howe was instrumental in establishing working relationships with a number of community leaders during the troubled times in the eighties, including Inkosis Maphumulo (at Broken Bridge), Mdluli (at Cabbage Tree), Shangasi (at Ibis Point), Gwala (at Mbheje's Store) and Bhengu (at Dip Tank).

But it was the young Inkosi Mlaba, who governed an area from Cato Ridge to Table Mountain, who was to have the biggest impact on the relations between the paddlers and the community.

"Mlaba is a great man, a real massive mountain amongst men," says Howe. "Even when he was young, he commanded the respect of the other amakhosi, and in very little time he became their chosen leader, and

was the primary point of contact between the paddlers and the entire valley."

After the incident-marred Dusies of 1992 and 1993, and the redoubled efforts of the VAF, Moore, and a number of committed club leaders became evident. At the confluence section, that had seen the aggravated robberies in the 1992 Dusi, the local residents set up impromptu seconding tables to douse with cold water the sweating paddlers passing by.

The 1994 Dusi was marred by a tragedy at Thombi rapid, which claimed the life of sweep, Chris Davey. However, in the efforts to rescue the trapped canoeist, more than 35 local youngsters joined the rescue party that struggled in vain to save him.

Despite the efforts of Moore and the renamed KwaZulu-Natal Canoe Union (KNCU), incidents of conflict between paddlers and valley residents continued to flare at various times during the 1990s. "HELL RUN" screamed a front-page headline in the *Sunday Tribune* following the first day of a 50 Miler, where not only stone throwing, but armed robbery of seconds and attempted hijackings had occurred.

Another key catalyst in the relationship between the paddlers and the residents of the valleys was Robert Lembethe. A pioneer in so many ways, Lembethe joined Simon Mkhize as Dusi regulars, and in the process sowed aspirations and dreams in the minds of many youngsters on the banks of the rivers.

Lembethe was a bridge builder, and he saw an opportunity to use canoeing to create opportunities for youngsters in the Nagle Dam area he hailed from. His enthusiasm and persistence resulted in donated craft and equipment, and in no time, a group of eager youngsters was learning to paddle at Nagle Dam.

Lembethe and the VAF saw eye to eye, and together they helped forge bonds and realise dreams in the Nagle Dam area. Soon the Robert Lembethe Canoe Club was formalised at Nagle Dam, and the KNCU established a full-scale sprint course there, ensuring that top-level national competition would be a regular occurrence at the dam.

Lembethe's success as an athlete, combined with his passion to champion the cause of the youngsters in the valley, provided the VAF with a valuable ambassador. National Olympic Committee of South Africa head, Sam Ramsamy, was quick to recognise the efforts ploughed into the remote regions of the Valley of a Thousand Hills, and supported them wherever possible.

Part of the indirect reward for the efforts of then SACF President, Des Park, and the VAF, was a disproportionately large canoeing element to

the South African team that travelled to the Barcelona Olympics in 1992. Robert Lembethe was chosen to be part of that squad, as the top black paddler in South Africa at that time.

It was appropriate that the first Robert Lembethe Canoe Club youngster to achieve national colours, Michael Mbanjwa, travelled abroad to the marathon world championships in Dartmouth, Canada, with the South African team that included Lembethe, who had been selected to race as a veteran in the Master's Cup that preceded the world championships.

Lembethe's work, most of it unseen and unrecognised, yielded massive dividends. In a very short space of time a new generation of stars like Mbanjwa and Loveday Zondi were starring in the Dusi, and turning the prospect of a black paddler winning the Dusi into a very real probability.

Based on the success, and acceptance by the local community of the Robert Lembethe Canoe Club, similar clubs began to spring up and enjoy support from the KNCU's canoeing Development Fund, including the club at Number Nine, on the banks at the Dusi's current first overnight stop just above Dusi Bridge.

As this new generation of black paddlers spearheads the transformation of the sport, and the Dusi in particular, it is helping to repair the relationship between the intrusive paddlers and the militant valley residents that at one time threatened the life and future of the sport in KwaZulu-Natal.

The initial sum of one rand per paddler per race that was levied on every paddler in a Dusi qualifier has remained unchanged since its inception. The major change however is the redirecting of the funds generated by this once contentious "paddle-tax" from the VAF, to the KNCU's canoeing Development Fund. This is to meet the ever-increasing demands placed on the KNCU by the rapid emergence of highly talented, elite athletes from so-called development programmes across the province, and the establishment of new clubs around these projects.

The KNCU-driven Development Fund may be channelling funds to more canoeing-specific upliftment programmes, but the Dusi continues to raise funds directly for community facilities in the valley. In recent years the Dusi has embraced the Starfish programme, which generates funds for facilities desperately needed by AIDS orphans in the valley, by selling off places in an early batch in the Dusi, to the highest bidders. This raised R80 000 in 2003, R120 000 in 2004 and R230 000 in 2005, and led to the construction of an impressive home and clinic on the banks of Inanda Dam, that the paddlers in the Dusi each year pass at the old Dip Tank site.

The Dusi is poised to move into a new era—an era in which the valley residents will soon be able to herald a Dusi winner from their own community, which will be a massive step forward in the quest for a harmonious and mutually beneficial co-existence between the paddlers and valley residents that was started by Des Park and Robbie Stewart during truly dark days for the race.

At this point in the history of the Dusi, it is fair to say that Ian Player's great pioneering efforts as a canoe explorer and adventurer, and founding father of the Dusi, have borne unexpected and rich fruits for the people of the Umsindusi and Umgeni valleys, and have helped instigate a positive contribution to the political development of our country. This is not the least because of the outstanding leadership talents and the openhearted commitment of volunteers, and the wisdom of traditional and other community leaders, that the Dusi has over the years unleashed. These contributions are in keeping with Ian's spirit as a canoeist, and as a writer, and it is most fitting that this short history of the way community engagement has grown out of the Dusi should be included in the new edition of his canoeing classic.

Kloof

September 2006

KEY POINTS IN THE DUSI'S DEVELOPMENT

– ∞ –

TIM CORNISH

1951   8 Starters, 1 finisher. Winner, Ian Player, in six days. The first race took place from 22 to 27 December.

1953   Second race started in January, so there was no race in 1952. All subsequent races started in January. Rules introduced making it compulsory to carry a snakebite kit and to compete in pairs whether in doubles or singles. The race was the first National Pairs Championship.

1954   42 Starters. At a meeting the day before the race it was agreed to form a National Canoe Union.

1956   First fibreglass boats used. The race was the official South African Doubles Championship, and for the first time was raced in stages over three days. The first overnight checkpoints were at Dusi Bridge and Khumalo's store.

1958   First overall doubles victory in the race.

1960   A record 66 starters. At this time the second night stop was moved to Khumalo's Causeway.

1962   Gary Player Trophy for the best combined Comrades Marathon and Dusi results awarded for the first time—winner Ernie Pearce.

1968   A record entry of 150 competitors. Due to lack of space, the second night stop was moved from Khumalo's to the Dip Tank, now beneath the waters of Inanda Dam.

1969 Lowest conditions experienced up to that point in the history of the race. Check point introduced at the Confluence, adding approximately 10 km to the course.

1970 Singles allowed to race individually for the first time. Seconding allowed for the first time, and introducing the Yellow Rock checkpoint extended the course of the first day.

1972 Record entry of 222.

1976 Record entry of over 400. Compulsory portaging was enforced at the Confluence and Marianny-Foley Bridge due to the dangerous river conditions. The river conditions on Day Two and Day Three were probably the fullest experienced in the history of the race.

1981 Race won overall in a single. Ladies participated for the first time in doubles with a male partner.

1982 Canalisation of the Umgeni at Sea Cow Lake in the upper part of Blue Lagoon shortened the last section between the outer ring road and the Connaught Bridge.

1983 Over 1000 entries received.

1984 Burma Road Portage was not permitted for this year only.

1985 New rules introducing more compulsory paddling coincided with the lowest conditions since 1969. Ladies allowed to race in singles for the first time.

1986 Race promoted as a doubles event. Ladies allowed to compete in singles without partners for the first time.

1987 Race promoted as a singles race. The main race thenceforth to alternate between singles and doubles each year, with medals to be awarded to the top 10.

1988 Start moved 2 km upstream to include Camps Drift canal and Ernie Pearce Weir.

1990 Inanda Dam completed and filled to capacity. 2nd night stop moved

to current position, close to the original Khumalo's Causeway overnight stop. A record entry of 1647, with 1430 finishers.

1991 Silver Medals were introduced for positions 11 to 50.

1999 1st overnight stop moved back to just above Dusi Bridge bringing the length of Day One back to a similar length of that before the start was moved to Camps Drift.

2000 Record entry of 2217. A special Player/Pearce medal was introduced for positions 51 to 200.

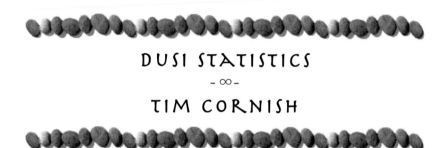

DUSI STATISTICS

– ∞ –

TIM CORNISH

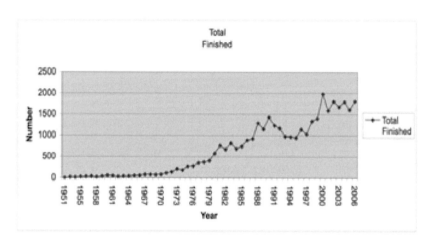

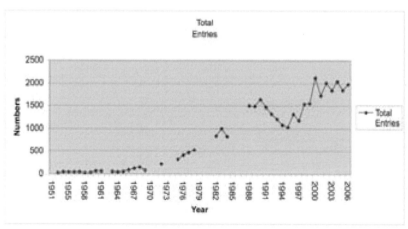

Note: the gaps in the above graph arise from the lack of accurate statistics during these periods.

TABLE OF ENTERED AND FINISHED

YEAR	K1s Entered	K2s Entered	Total Entries	K1s Finished	K2s Finished	Total Finished
1951	8			1	0	1
1953			20	13	0	13
1954			42	10	0	10
1955			38	20	1	22
1956	10	15	40	21	4	29
1957	36	4	44	27	3	33
1958	8	7	22	6	5	16
1959	16	16	32	16	7	30
1960			66	36	9	54
1961	44	9	62	34	5	44
1962				18	5	28
1963			54	32	2	36
1964	30	6	42	26	4	34
1965	38	9	56	32	8	48
1966	54	17	88	34	9	52
1967	52	36	124	24	27	78
1968	50	50	150	22	28	78
1969	32	25	82	8	31	70
1970				17	32	81
1971				18	47	112
1972			222	27	57	141
1973				45	83	211
1974				46	69	184
1975			329	88	92	272
1976	144	138	420	99	92	283
1977			473	121	118	357
1978	251	137	525	174	101	376
1979				182	113	408
1980				226	175	576
1981				276	243	762
1982	376	458	834	277	197	671
1983			1005	318	251	820
1984	343	480	823	285	200	685
1985				294	225	744
1986				252	317	886
1987				499	213	925
1988			1500	237	530	1297
1989			1490	616	268	1152

YEAR	K1s Entered	K2s Entered	Total Entries	K1s Finished	K2s Finished	Total Finished
1990			1647	172	629	1430
1991	740	732	1472	607	314	1235
1992	204	1122	1326	172	498	1168
1993	625	582	1207	485	246	977
1994	193	886	1079	159	405	969
1995	467	564	1031	421	263	947
1996	196	1122	1318	155	493	1141
1997			1177	469	281	1031
1998			1536	157	590	1337
1999			1553	514	443	1400
2000	209	954	2117	173	904	1981
2001	622	553	1728	554	516	1586
2002	184	912	2008	152	824	1800
2003	653	591	1835	577	547	1671
2004	189	926	2041	147	822	1791
2005	668	586	1840	589	510	1609
2006	158	911	1980	132	837	1806

NOTE ON THE LISTS OF DUSI
RESULTS AND FINISHERS

_ ∞ _

TIM CORNISH

Presented in the following pages are the complete results, and the list of all the finishers of the Dusi, for the first fifty-five races from 1951 to 2006.

The results are for all the main races, with each of the divisions as these have evolved over the years. Also included are the results for the Non-stop Dusi races, which began unofficially in 1974 and then became official in 1977.

The list of finishers is for the main races only—more than ten thousand people—and also includes the numbers of races completed. These numbers appear after the names. The record at this time for most races finished is forty-two, shared by Roly Alborough and Graeme Pope-Ellis.

The information supplied, based on thorough research of all known sources, is as accurate as any that is known to exist. If there are any errors, these are regretted.

YEAR	POS	I1	NAME1	I2	NAME2	TIME	REC
Senior Men Singles							
1951	1	I	PLAYER			144,00,0	*
Senior Men Singles							
1953	1		PLAYER	F	SCHMIDT	86,00,0	*
1953	2	E	PEARCE	F	BAKER	102,30 0	
1953	3	D	ELSE	P	OLSEN	102,55,0	
1953	4	S	BAUER		ANDERSON	103,00,0	
1953	5	P	MARRIOT	B	ANDERSON	103,30,0	
1953	6	S	DEAN	D	GREENLAND	127,20,0	
Senior Men Singles							
1954	1	R	PLAYER	R	SCHMIDT	36:41:00	*
1954	1	E	PEARCE	P	TEMPLETON	36:41:00	*
1954	3	P	DUTTON	P	VAN ROOYEN	52:25:00	
1954	4	S	DEAN	M	HILLIER	55:25:00	
1954	5	C	DONLY	H	FISHER	76:00:00	
Senior Men Doubles							
1955	3	E	VORSTER	H	GRANT	32:06:00	*
Senior Men Singles							
1955	1	E	PEARCE	R	TEMPLETON	27:28:00	*
1955	2	P	MARRIOT	P	OLSEN	29:31:00	
1955	4	J	STROOBACH	E	JORDAN	32:55:00	
1955	5	P	DUTTON	B	DUTTON	35:00:00	
1955	6	J	CALENBORNE	A	HAYNES	38:00:00	
Senior Men Doubles							
1956	3	A	HILLIER	T	PINCHEN	22:48:00	*
1956	4	L	HOUGH	H	GRANT	23:39:00	
1956	5	F	DEAN	F	HULLEY	24:38:00	
1956	9	E	VORSTER	A	RUDLING	32:42:00	
Senior Men Singles							
1956	1	E	PEARCE	R	TEMPLETON	19:44:30	*
1956	2	P	MARRIOT	D	VORSTER	21:21:00	
1956	6	H	FISHER	G	ROWE	24:05:00	
1956	7	A	HAYNES	J	CALENBORNE	27:03:30	
1956	10	C	BEUKES	E	HUDSON	31:56:30	
Senior Men Doubles							
1957	3	L	HOUGH	H	GRANT	16:19:00	
1957	6	P	GLADWIN	G	SMITH	18:24:00	
1957	7	S	DEAN	F	HULLEY	19:58:30	
Senior Men Singles							
1957	1	E	PEARCE	R	TEMPLETON	14:55:00	*
1957	2	D	VORSTER	H	MARRIOT	16:12:00	
1957	4	D	HILLIER	H	FISHER	17:12:30	
1957	5	G	ROWE	G	DONLY	17:35:00	
1957	8	D	STIRLING	D	LOADER	20:41:00	
Senior Men Doubles							
1958	1	R	GOULDIE	D	ANTROBUS	17:20:20	
1958	2	S	DEAN	G	HALL	17:58:20	
1958	3	D	VORSTER	C	HOWELL	19:06:20	*
1958	5	E	VORSTER	F	SMITH	22:00:34	
1958	7	N	KELLERMANN	N	OOSTHUIZEN	26:52:05	
Senior Men Singles							
1958	4	R	COOK	D	MCNIVEN	21:13:20	
1958	6	C	DU PLESSIS	D	SHAW	23:14:35	
Senior Men Doubles							
1959	3	P	GLADWIN	D	STIRLING	13:42:33	
1959	4	R	GOULDIE	D	ANTROBUS	14:17:51	*
1959	7	S	DEAN	D	SHUTTE	17:29:30	
1959	9	F	SMITH	G	WALSH	18:22:17	
1959	12	R	SALMONSEN	M	FRY	19:14:34	
Senior Men Singles							
1959	1	H	FISHER	G	ROWE	12:32:14	
1959	2	E	PEARCE	R	TEMPLETON	13:41:34	
1959	6	F	HULLEY	P	MARRIOT	14:46:31	
1959	7	P	DUTTON	N	STEELE	16:24:12	
1959	8	A	HILLIER	M	HILLIER	17:53:18	
Senior Men Doubles							
1960	10	R	GOULDIE	D	ANTROBUS	17:39:49	
1960	12	D	STERLING	P	GLADWIN	18:50:52	
1960	18	D	LOADER	M	BROUGHTON	20:27:10	
1960	19	T	BARTLETT	X	TEDDER	21:27:43	
1960	20	F	SMITH	R	PALFRAMAN	21:53:37	
Senior Men Singles							
1960	1	G	ROWE	H	FISHER	15:45:17	
1960	2	E	PEARCE	R	TEMPLETON	16:29:57	
1960	3	J	STROOBACH	B	JACKSON	16:43:32	
1960	4	L	HOUGH	A	HILLIER	16:48:00	
1960	5	P	DUTTON	N	STEELE	17:01:44	
Senior Men Doubles							
1961	6	D	ANTROBUS	D	STERLING	14:05:21	
1961	8	G	HALL	S	DEAN	14:36:42	
1961	18	F	SMITH	R	PALFRAMAN	19:23:11	
1961	19	D	HENRY	F	MADEL	19:51:58	
1961	22	M	FLINT	P	STEPHENSON	24:51:37	
Senior Men Singles							
1961	1	G	ROWE	H	FISHER	12:18:00	*
1961	2	L	HOUGH	F	SCHMIDT	12:51:24	
1961	3	F	CHALUPSKY	P	CHALUPSKY	13:06:24	
1961	4	J	STROOBACH	B	JACKSON	13:34:44	
1961	5	R	TEMPLETON	J	POTGIETER	13:54:58	

RESULTS OF THE DUSI CANOE MARATHON—1951 TO 2006

YEAR	POS	I1	NAME1	I2	NAME2	TIME	REC
Junior Men Singles							
1961	16	K	TRUNDELL	J	MASSEY	17:33:49	*
Senior Men Doubles							
1962	1	D	ANTROBUS	P	GLADWIN	11:24:36	*
1962	4	C	CAIRNS	R	TEMPLETON	12:35:47	
1962	5	D	COBBLEDICK	N	DYER	13:01:05	
1962	7	S	DEAN	G	HALL	13:06:05	
1962	14	G	MILLS	B	WADLEY	19:22:21	
Senior Men Singles							
1962	2	J	POTGIETER	C	VAN DER MERWE	11:48:07	*
1962	3	A	HILLIER	E	PEARCE	12:29:55	
1962	6	P	CHALUPSKY	K	TRUNDELL	13:05:07	
1962	8	T	HOWECROFT	J	TINLEY	13:06:33	
1962	9	J	BRUTON	I	MCLACHLAN	13:49:14	
Senior Men Doubles							
1963	5	P	GLADWIN	D	ANTROBUS	13:52:35	
1963	6	D	COBBLEDICK	C	CAIRNS	14:25:38	
Senior Men Singles							
1963	1	G	ROWE	H	FISHER	11:30:19	
1963	2	P	CHALUPSKY	R	KNUDSEN	11:32:06	
1963	3	J	POTGIETER	L	HOUGH	11:40:49	
1963	4	J	BASS	B	CARTER-BROWN	13:29:50	
1963	7	A	TAYLOR	W	BRUMMER	14:49:51	
Senior Men Doubles							
1964	3	P	GLADWIN	D	ANTROBUS	12:37:47	
1964	4	A	OSHRY	N	DYER	12:50:46	
1964	7	R	ALING	A	BROCKMAN	13:47:36	
1964	12	J	BARTHOLOMEW	D	HENRY	15:22:19	
Senior Men Singles							
1964	1	H	FISHER	G	ROWE	11:10:05	*
1964	2	C	CAIRNS	J	POTGIETER	12:25:31	
1964	5	D	COBBLEDICK	K	WILLAN	12:51:46	
1964	6	B	WILLAN	C	WILSON	13:28:30	
1964	8	J	ALBOROUGH	K	WRIGHT	14:02:44	
Senior Men Doubles							
1965	1	D	COBBLEDICK	C	MASON	13:33:47	*
1965	4	B	POTGIETER	B	BUTLER	14:35:51	
1965	5	C	CAIRNS	A	HARPER	16:00:31	
1965	9	G	POPE-ELLIS	R	HACKLAND	17:14:02	
1965	10	N	DYER	T	OSHRY	17:21:23	
Senior Men Singles							
1965	2	B	WILLAN	K	WILLAN	13:37:21	
1965	3	H	FISHER	E	PEARCE	13:43:06	
1965	6	K	WRIGHT	J	ALBOROUGH	16:03:21	
1965	7	R	TEMPLETON	D	PALFRAMAN	16:28:40	
1965	8	C	WILSON	A	BROCKMAN	16:55:39	
Junior Men Doubles							
1965	9	G	POPE-ELLIS	R	HACKLAND	17:14:02	*
Senior Men Doubles							
1966	1	J	POTGIETER	C	CRAWLEY	13:20:00	
1966	2	K	WILLAN	C	WILSON	14:05:10	
1966	5	C	MASON	K	RODGERS	16:00:55	
1966	7	A	OSHRY	N	DYER	16:34:13	
1966	9	G	POPE-ELLIS	R	HACKLAND	17:37:03	
Senior Men Singles							
1966	3	L	LEDEBOER	B	GREIG	15:36:59	
1966	4	R	PALFRAMAN	D	PALFRAMAN	15:48:05	
1966	6	B	WILLAN	P	HAMMOND	16:23:15	
1966	8	D	COBBLEDICK	T	HOWECROFT	17:07:34	
1966	10	P	AYLING	M	AYLING	17:44:54	
Junior Men Singles							
1966	16	D	HAYTER	R	COLLINSON	19:36:20	*
Senior Men Doubles							
1967	1	C	MASON	K	RODGERS	10:30:35	
1967	2	W	VAN RIET	R	VAN RIET	10:58:03	
1967	4	E	SCHOEMAN	B	JARDINE	11:44:40	
1967	8	G	POPE-ELLIS	R	HACKLAND	13:15:54	
1967	9	R	GODDARD	A	HARPER	13:42:49	
Senior Men Singles							
1967	3	J	ALBOROUGH	K	WRIGHT	11:43:38	
1967	5	M	AYLING	P	AYLING	12:38:57	
1967	6	M	VAN WIERINGEN	J	KEARNEY	12:41:01	
1967	7	R	STEWART	C	HAYTER	13:11:08	
1967	12	K	CULVERWELL	D	HAYTER	13:56:46	
Junior Men Doubles							
1967	28	D	POPE-ELLIS	H	FLETCHER-CAMPBELL	18:35:13	*
1967	38	R	BINNS	J	GRAY	25:08:37	
Junior Men Singles							
1967	6	M	VAN WIERINGEN	J	KEARNEY	12:41:01	*
1967	12	K	CULVERWELL	D	HAYTER	13:56:46	
Senior Men Doubles							
1968	1	J	POTGIETER	C	HOUGH	10:02:32	
1968	2	K	WRIGHT	B	GODDARD	10:28:02	
1968	4	R	HACKLAND	R	POPE-ELLIS	10:35:07	
1968	5	G	NEBE	H	GREEFF	11:04:12	
1968	6	C	WILSON	T	DEANE	11:07:24	
Senior Men Singles							
1968	3	P	CHALUPSKY	G	HORTON	10:32:11	
1968	7	L	LEDEBOER	R	JONES	11:43:39	
1968	9	J	KEAREY	M	VON WIERINGEN	11:57:59	*

YEAR	POS	I1	NAME1	I2	NAME2	TIME	REC
1968	14	C	MASON	H	GERRARD	13:11:22	
1968	16	J	ALBOROUGH	A	HARPER	13:27:12	
Senior Men Doubles							
1969	1	W	VAN RIET	R	VAN RIET	15:36:03	
1969	2	R	HACKLAND	G	POPE-ELLIS	17:01:01	
1969	3	C	WILSON	E	CLARKE	17:06:53	
1969	4	K	ROGERS	C	CRAWLEY	17:18:55	
1969	5	J	ALBOROUGH	A	HAWARDEN	18:09:45	
Senior Men Singles							
1969	10	R	PREEN	G	CHENNELLS	20:29:12	
1969	26	O	VORSTER	J	ENGELBRECHT	25:00:44	
1969	28	I	VICKERS	M	STEWART	26:29:25	
Junior Men Doubles							
1969	13	R	RUDGE	R	TODD	21:40:39	
Senior Men K2							
1970	1	W	VAN RIET	R	VAN RIET	11:11:26	
1970	3	T	OETIE	G	NEBE	12:24:52	
1970	4	K	WRIGHT	B	GODDARD	12:25:59	
1970	5	R	STEWART	R	RASMUSSEN	12:29:34	
1970	7	G	DELPORT	J	DELPORT	12:49:24	
Senior Men K1							
1970	2	J	POTGIETER			11:53:43	
1970	6	P	PEACOCK			12:47:61	
1970	12	M	VAN WIERINGEN			13:40:17	
1970	13	J	KEAREY			13:40:17	
1970	14	G	WEX			13:54:20	
Junior men K2							
1970	17	D	CULVERWELL	B	BERRIMAN	14:17:44	*
Senior Men K2							
1971	1	W	VAN RIET	R	VAN RIET	11:06:08	
1971	2	J	POTGIETER	A	COLLINS	11:41:41	
1971	3	G	POPE-ELLIS	E	CLARKE	11:44:45	
1971	4	P	HENRY	RA	MAYNARD	12:02:18	
1971	5	K	WRIGHT	L	JENKINS	12:10:23	
Senior Men K1							
1971	6	P	PEACOCK			12:26:00	
1971	8	E	VAN RIET			12:44:00	
1971	14	R	RASMUSSEN			13:31:20	
1971	16	D	WOODWARD			14:07:58	
1971	19	D	FOURIE			15:20:52	
Junior men K2							
1971	10	M	TOCKNELL	H	SANDBERG	13:15:39	*

YEAR	POS	I1	NAME1	I2	NAME2	TIME	REC
Senior Men K2							
1972	1	E	CLARKE	G	POPE-ELLIS	09:28:48	*
1972	2	P	PEACOCK	A	COLLINS	09:33:54	
1972	3	R	STEWART	R	RASMUSSEN	09:43:55	
1972	7	L	JENKINS	G	KEIT	10:07:04	
1972	4	P	HENRY	RA	MAYNARD	10:14:07	
Senior Men K1							
1972	12	R	TODD			12:14:16	
1972	13	P	NOBLE			12:26:37	
1972	15	A	ALBERTYN			12:42:03	
1972	17	D	PAUL			13:03:34	
1972	19	R	WADE			13:30:16	
Junior Men K1							
1972	15	A	ALBERTYN			12:42:03	
Senior Men K2							
1973	1	E	CLARKE	G	POPE-ELLIS	10:56:03	
1973	2	A	COLLINS	S	UYS	11:24:07	
1973	3	R	STEWART	R	RASMUSSEN	12:06:52	
1973	6	B	BOURNE-LANGE	B	HOOGEWERF	13:07:16	
1973	8	B	TAYLOR	B	GODDARD	13:24:56	
Senior Men K1							
1973	4	A	HAWARDEN	A		12:28:49	
1973	5	P	PEACOCK	P		12:56:19	
1973	7	C	CURSON			13:20:03	
1973	9	T	BIGGS			13:48:33	
1973	15	A	FOURIE			14:51:15	
Junior Men K1							
1973	25	R	PENNEFATHER			15:35:39	
Senior Men K2							
1974	1	G	POPE-ELLIS	E	CLARKE	10:55:30	
1974	2	R	STEWART	C	CURSON	11:32:20	
1974	3	T	FOX	T	MCWADE	11:44:17	
1974	5	B	TAYLOR	J	TAYLOR	12:43:04	
1974	7	R	BOURNE-LANGE	B	HOOGEWERF	12:57:37	
Senior Men K1							
1974	4	A	HAWARDEN	A		12:09:40	
1974	6	T	BIGGS	T		12:47:26	
1974	11	B	GODDARD	B		14:07:06	
1974	16	A	FOURIE	A		15:10:06	
1974	18	E	TANNER	E		15:15:13	
Junior men K2							
1974	39	C	ST LEGER	RT	WIMBUSH	17:41:36	

RESULTS OF THE DUSI CANOE MARATHON—1951 TO 2006

YEAR	POS	I1	NAME1	I2	NAME2	TIME	REC
Senior Men K2							
1975	1	P	PEACOCK	G	POPE-ELLIS	10:12:25	
1975	2	R	STEWART	C	CURSON	10:28:21	
1975	4	T	FOX	T	MCWADE	10:47:08	
1975	6	H	PENNEFATHER	H	SANDBERG	11:32:39	
1975	7	W	VAN RIET	A	COLLINS	12:14:12	
Senior Men K1							
1975	3	T	BIGGS			10:46:18	
1975	5	A	HAWARDEN			10:58:02	
1975	10	L	WHEELER			12:29:48	
1975	11	M	TOCKNELL			12:44:32	
1975	12	M	BAM			12:52:53	
Junior Men K1							
Senior Men K2							
1975	24	C	ST LEGER			14:14:12	
Senior Men K2							
1976	1	P	PEACOCK	G	POPE-ELLIS	08:23:12	*
1976	2	T	FOX	T	MCWADE	08:58:14	
1976	3	W	VAN RIET	A	COLLINS	09:06:34	
1976	5	H	SANDBERG	J	TRURAN	09:27:49	
1976	10	J	PARTON	I	GORDON	10:30:02	
Senior Men K1							
1976	4	A	HAWARDEN			09:08:19	
1976	6	A	PENNEFATHER			09:36:11	
1976	7	M	TOCKNELL			09:49:34	
1976	8	L	WHEELER			10:01:54	
1976	9	A	LIGHTBODY			10:17:33	
Junior men K2							
1976	19	J	TAYLOR	A	RENNIE	11:29:38	*
Junior Men K1							
Senior Men K2							
1976	23	K	ELLERKER			11:33:52	*
Senior Men K2							
1977	1	G	POPE-ELLIS	P	PEACOCK	09:15:00	
1977	3	T	FOX	T	MCWADE	10:45:13	
1977	6	B	BOURNE-LANGE	B	HOOGEWERF	11:07:09	
1977	7	A	LIGHTBODY	Q	VORSTER	11:23:12	
1977	8	H	SANDBERG	J	TRURAN	11:24:29	
Senior Men K1							
1977	2	T	BIGGS			09:56:03	
1977	4	R	STEWART			10:50:16	
1977	5	M	TOCKNELL			10:58:55	
1977	9	L	WHEELER			11:34:15	
1977	11	R	GANDY			11:44:14	
Junior men K2							
1977	34	G	DIXON	S	DIXON	13:27:46	

YEAR	POS	I1	NAME1	I2	NAME2	TIME	REC
Junior Men K1							
1977							
Senior Men K2							
1977	13	L	PARK			12:07:00	
Junior Men K1							
Senior Men K2							
1978	1	P	PEACOCK	G	POPE-ELLIS	08:33:59	
1978	2	T	BIGGS	R	STEWART	08:45:39	
1978	4	B	WARLOCK	A	SCOTT	09:28:25	
1978	7	K	DE KLERK	B	DE KLERK	10:04:54	
1978	12	B	FOWLES	G	FOWLES	10:27:06	
Senior Men K1							
1978	3	R	PENNEFATHER			09:13:41	
1978	5	L	PARK			09:59:22	
1978	6	M	TOCKNELL			10:02:28	
1978	8	R	WHITTON			10:16:45	
1978	9	C	ST LEGER			10:17:48	
Junior men K2							
1978	15	S	DIXON	C	JAMIESON	10:34:07	*
Junior Men K1							
1978	5	L	PARK			09:59:22	*
Senior Men K2							
1979	1	T	BIGGS	R	STEWART	08:43:16	
1979	3	R	PENNEFATHER	M	TOCKNELL	09:05:09	
1979	6	CG	VERKERK	B	JOHNSON	09:34:09	
1979	7	L	WHEELER	L	JENKINS	09:44:18	
1979	8	L	LEDEBOER	P	VORSTER	09:47:57	
Senior Men K1							
1979	2	A	HAWARDEN			09:03:43	
1979	4	D	BIGGS			09:24:09	
1979	5	G	POPE-ELLIS			09:33:37	*
1979	10	D	CULVERWELL			10:13:54	
1979	11	C	ST LEGER			10:14:25	
Junior men K2							
1979	14	C	JAMIESON	S	DIXON	10:25:58	
Senior Men K2							
1980	1	P	PEACOCK	G	POPE-ELLIS	09:05:07	
1980	3	DR	BIGGS	PF	VORSTER	09:39:33	
1980	5	CE	ST LEGER	L	WHEELER	10:03:14	
1980	6	TJ	MCWADE	TJ	FOX	10:17:01	
1980	8	LA	PARK	RE	GEORGE	10:26:05	
Senior Men K1							
1980	2	A	HAWARDEN			09:29:03	
1980	4	RE	STEWART			09:48:19	
1980	7	BK	FOWLES			10:22:29	
1980	9	RJ	GANDY			10:29:17	
1980	10	JRT	ARTHUR			10:29:24	

RESULTS OF THE DUSI CANOE MARATHON—1951 TO 2006

YEAR	POS	I1	NAME1	I2	NAME2	TIME	REC
Junior men K2							
1980	23	LP	HOUGH	CG	CULLINGWORTH	11:31:11	
Veteran Men							
1980	28	HL	DE RAUVILLE			11:50:00	*
1980	40	EL	DYKES			12:18:40	
1980	82	W	DEYZEL			13:32:21	
Senior Men K2							
1981	3	M	TOCKNELL	L	PARK	10:23:02	
1981	5	CE	ST LEGER	L	WHEELER	10:50:13	
1981	9	PT	SHAW	JN	MURRAY	11:19:34	
1981	12	J	FOWLER	H	SANDBERG	11:42:32	
1981	14	JR	EDMONDS	MP	EDMONDS	11:45:47	
Senior Men K1							
1981	1	GF	POPE-ELLIS			09:47:19	
1981	2	D	BIGGS			09:55:10	
1981	4	RE	STEWART			10:36:01	
1981	6	BK	JOHNSON			11:08:45	
1981	10	PA	DE KLERK			11:13:14	
Junior men K2							
1981	14	JR	EDMONDS	MP	EDMONDS	11:45:47	
Junior Men K1							
1981	11	RAD	STARR			11:34:39	
Mixed Doubles							
1981	17	A	HAWARDEN	DE	HAWARDEN	12:06:42	
1981	49	CL	GREEFF	C	BOTES	13:23:55	
1981	104	GF	HAINES	WE	COLLINSON	15:13:00	
Veteran Men							
1981	37	HL	DE RAUVILLE			12:54:22	*
1981	73	CD	WADE			14:17:58	
1981	75	WW	DEYZEL			14:21:00	
Senior Men K2							
1982	1	D	BIGGS	T	BIGGS	08:43:22	
1982	2	G	POPE-ELLIS	TJ	CORNISH	08:52:56	
1982	5	R	STARR	P	STARR	09:23:30	
1982	6	C	GREEFF	M	CARLISLE	09:26:54	
1982	11	P	VAN DER MERWE	C	VERKERK	09:52:17	
Senior Men K1							
1982	3	B	JOHNSON			09:16:37	
1982	4	R	STEWART			09:17:24	
1982	7	C	ST LEGER			09:39:22	
1982	8	L	PARK			09:46:52	
1982	9	B	FOWLES			09:49:48	

YEAR	POS	I1	NAME1	I2	NAME2	TIME	REC
Junior Men K1							
1982	25	B	YELLAND			10:46:44	
Mixed Doubles							
1982	13	A	HAWARDEN	DE	HAWARDEN	10:09:15	*
1982	28	R	WHITTON	C	WHITTON	10:53:21	
1982	65	M	LOEWENSTEIN	M	LOEWENSTEIN	11:40:13	
Veteran Men							
1982	31	H	DE RAUVILLE			10:54:36	*
Senior Men K2							
1983	1	GF	POPE-ELLIS	TJ	CORNISH	09:32:39	
1983	2	DR	BIGGS	T	BIGGS	09:53:54	
1983	3	CE	ST LEGER	JR	EDMONDS	10:03:46	
1983	4	BK	FOWLES	BC	WENKE	10:10:34	
1983	6	KJ	REYNOLDS	RI	DYER	10:41:21	
Senior Men K1							
1983	5	M	TOCKNELL			10:20:49	
1983	7	RE	STEWART			10:48:09	
1983	9	MPD	CONWAY			11:06:26	
1983	10	RA	STARR			11:09:48	
1983	14	LA	PARK			11:34:46	
Junior men K2							
1983	8	BR	YELLAND	CD	HACKLAND	11:01:34	
Mixed Doubles							
1983	21	A	HAWARDEN	DE	HAWARDEN	11:51:24	
1983	42	JB	ANDERSON	P	ANDERSON	12:52:10	
1983	60	MB	LOEWENSTEIN	M	LOEWENSTEIN	13:16:38	
Veteran Men							
1983	29	KC	HARRIS	WW	DEYZEL	12:24:56	
Senior Men K2							
1984	3	MPD	CONWAY	KJ	REYNOLDS	10:20:22	
1984	4	BC	WENKE	BK	FOWLES	10:22:27	
1984	8	JN	TRURAN	RE	GEORGE	10:53:52	
1984	11	KJ	MORAN	RS	HEAD	11:13:16	
1984	13	RG	HILLIAR	LJ	KEAY	11:29:23	
Senior Men K1							
1984	1	GF	POPE-ELLIS			09:56:44	
1984	2	DR	BIGGS			10:01:40	
1984	5	JR	EDMONDS			10:22:29	
1984	6	RC	WHITTON			10:39:52	
1984	7	M	TOCKNELL			10:45:13	
Junior Men K1							
1984	20	GA	ROCKETT			12:12:28	
1984	38	MG	MCLEOD			13:02:33	
1984	51	AG	EDMONDS			13:18:03	

189

YEAR	POS	I1	NAME1	I2	NAME2	TIME	REC
Mixed Doubles							
1984	19	A	HAWARDEN	DE	HAWARDEN	12:09:35	
1984	30	MB	LOEWENSTEIN	M	LOEWENSTEIN	12:47:40	
1984	46	DP	RETIEF	J	BENTEL	13:13:08	
Veteran Men							
1984	35	WA	PETTERSON			12:50:50	
1984	40	CJ	VAN DEN BERG			13:05:08	
1984	59	MRB	COOK			13:28:26	
Senior Men							
1985	1	JR	EDMONDS			10:26:38	
1985	2	GF	POPE-ELLIS			10:35:23	*
1985	3	DR	BIGGS			10:50:42	
1985	5	TJ	CORNISH			11:27:50	
1985	7	A	MC KENZIE			11:43:20	
1985	8	CE	ST LEGER			11:47:01	
1985	9	SJ	BLACK			11:47:23	
1985	10	MS	JAMIESON			11:48:27	
1985	13	JN	DEVONPORT			12:03:25	
1985	14	LJ	KEAY			12:09:29	
Senior Women							
1985	113	M	LOEWENSTEIN			15:35:18	
1985	169	J	BENTEL			16:36:36	
1985	459	G	KING			19:50:52	
Junior men							
1985	28	MCG	ELLIS			12:59:09	
Mixed Doubles							
1985	25	A	HAWARDEN	DE	HAWARDEN	12:48:13	
1985	29	RC	WHITTON	CS	WHITTON	13:00:44	
1985	98	RC	BERRY	C	BOTES	15:18:16	
Senior Men							
1986	1	G	POPE-ELLIS	TJ	CORNISH	08:18:02	
1986	2	RF	PENNEFATHER	JR	EDMONDS	08:31:47	
1986	3	M	TOCKNELL	O	CHALUPSKY	08:42:40	
1986	4	B	WENKE	BK	FOWLES	08:43:10	
1986	5	R	STARR	KO	ELLERKER	09:02:45	
1986	6	MS	JAMIESON	GD	SIMMONS	09:04:44	
1986	7	P	SCHOFIELD	K	REYNOLDS	09:06:35	
1986	8	RG	HILLIAR	LK	KEAY	09:06:38	
1986	9	CE	ST LEGER	NI	REYNOLDS	09:08:34	
1986	10	JT	CLAASSEN	RE	STEWART	09:09:16	
Senior Women							
1986	127	M	LOEWENSTEIN	J	BENTEL	12:03:08	*
Junior men							
1986	26	KJ	WHITE	GW	TARR	09:57:16	*
1986	33	CB	MENTZ	S	EXSTEEN	10:21:59	*
1986	49	JA	PITMAN	LRL	EDWARDS	10:43:28	
Mixed Doubles							
1986	23	RC	WHITTON	CS	WHITTON	09:54:24	*
1986	62	HL	DE RAUVILLE	N	KRIGE	11:02:55	
1986	82	DF	LOWE	MF	LOWE	11:25:00	
Veteran Men							
1986	10	JT	CLAASSEN	RE	STEWART	09:09:16	*
1986	38	LH	DU PLESSIS	M	BOTHA	10:29:00	
1986	112	HW	FRIZELLE	A	FALKSON	11:52:26	
Master Men							
1986	190	W	BARRON	M	DRISCOLL	12:45:38	
1986	273	PL	MANN	MB	WATCHORN	13:26:14	
Senior Men							
1987	1	G	POPE-ELLIS			08:48:23	
1987	2	J	EDMONDS			08:48:34	
1987	3	A	HAWARDEN			09:12:14	
1987	4	B	WENKE			09:12:15	
1987	5	M	TOCKNELL			09:18:47	
1987	6	R	PENNEFATHER			09:22:44	
1987	7	S	BLACK			09:24:45	
1987	8	M	CONWAY			09:27:45	
1987	9	L	KEAY			09:29:10	
1987	10	C	ST LEGER			09:33:56	
Senior Women							
1987	121	M	LOEWENSTEIN			11:51:50	*
1987	220	J	BENTEL			12:42:25	
1987	250	J	PENNEFATHER			12:59:10	
1987	282	D	JUNOR			13:15:56	
1987	324	N	RENNIE			13:33:41	
1987	353	C	STYLES			13:46:14	
1987	576	G	KING			15:29:46	
1987	679	J	BIRKETT			17:35:55	
Junior men							
1987	48	A	HACKLAND			10:45:55	
1987	60	G	STARR			11:03:10	
1987	71	D	RAW			11:11:32	
Mixed Doubles							
1987	29	R	WHITTON	C	WHITTON	10:22:43	*
1987	99	DF	LOWE	M	LOWE	11:33:13	
1987	114	B	GARCIN	L	GREWAR	11:47:50	
Veteran Men							
1987	12	J	CLAASSEN			09:42:42	
1987	14	WA	PETTERSON			09:46:18	
1987	20	B	FOWLES			10:01:08	

190

RESULTS OF THE DUSI CANOE MARATHON—1951 TO 2006

YEAR	POS	I1	NAME1	I2	NAME2	TIME	REC
Master Men							
1987	118	M	BOTHA	TJ	CORNISH	11:49:56	
1987	227	W	BARRON	LJ	KEAY	12:44:50	*
1987	316	A	THERON			13:28:36	
Senior Men							
1988	1	G	POPE-ELLIS	TJ	CORNISH	08:07:08	
1988	2	BC	WENKE	LJ	KEAY	08:09:21	
1988	3	MPD	CONWAY	K	REYNOLDS	08:17:40	*
1988	4	R	WHITTON	PR	ZIETSMAN	08:25:54	
1988	5	A	HAWARDEN	J	CLAASSEN	08:26:41	
1988	6	MS	JAMIESON	M	PERROW	08:27:02	
1988	7	B	THATCHER	J	SCHMIDT	08:30:12	
1988	8	SJ	BLACK	J	DEVENPORT	08:32:25	
1988	9	N	BRIGGS	F	SOLL	08:39:16	
1988	10	SJ	STAMP	G	HAW	08:40:19	
Senior Women							
1988	242	M	LOEWENSTEIN	J	BENTEL	12:32:03	
1988	437	C	WHITTON	EJ	RODWELL	14:03:09	
1988	556	P	ARMSTRONG	S	PENALUNA	15:01:45	
1988	584	FM	DAWSON	L	WAKEFORD	15:20:19	
Junior men							
1988	42	DH	RAW	CR	CARLYLE	09:51:09	
1988	46	W	VOLEK	NJB	GOBLE	10:02:43	*
1988	54	GI	DELVAUX	BH	ALLWOOD	10:16:36	
Mixed Doubles							
1988	40	KJ	MORAN	D	JUNOR	09:49:26	
1988	44	BJ	GARCIN	LA	GREWAR	09:52:12	
1988	115	P	PEACOCK	BL	OGILVIE	11:24:08	*
Veteran Men							
1988	5	A	HAWARDEN	J	CLAASSEN	08:26:41	
1988	14	J	MURRAY	WA	PETTERSON	09:00:33	
1988	55	DG	BOTHMA	J	MARAIS	10:17:45	
Master Men							
1988	267	JR	ALBOROUGH	C	VEALE	12:46:39	
1988	419	E	DYKES	DW	SYMINGTON	13:57:34	
1988	492	A	KING	T	LIGHTFOOT	14:29:44	
Senior Men							
1989	1	JR	EDMONDS			08:34:51	
1989	2	G	POPE-ELLIS			08:34:56	
1989	3	LJ	KEAY			08:41:30	
1989	4	BC	WENKE			08:52:28	
1989	5	GW	TARR			09:05:24	
1989	6	TJ	CORNISH			09:07:36	
1989	7	D	BIGGS			09:08:04	
1989	8	RC	WHITTON	JE	DE SYLVA	09:09:41	
1989	9	NW	EVANS			09:17:00	
1989	10	G	MONTEITH			09:18:54	
Senior Women							
1989	154	M	LOEWENSTEIN			11:46:38	*
1989	305	M	ALFORD			13:02:45	
1989	535	EJ	RODWELL			14:41:51	
1989	723	LA	GREWAR			16:00:47	
1989	854	F	DAWSON			17:26:00	
Junior men							
1989	25	WJ	VOLEK			09:49:36	*
1989	42	WS	VALENTINE			10:16:21	
1989	56	GW	RAMSAY			10:38:13	
Mixed Doubles							
1989	119	GJ	DE SYLVA	JE	DE SYLVA	11:28:19	
1989	157	GG	PENNINGTON	L	PENNINGTON	11:47:33	
1989	178	DF	LOWE	MF	LOWE	11:59:55	
Veteran Men							
1989	2	G	POPE-ELLIS			08:34:56	*
1989	23	WA	PETTERSON			09:47:14	
1989	31	BK	FOWLES			09:59:05	
Master Men							
1989	72	MD	WILMOT			10:54:10	*
1989	109	M	BOTHA			11:18:53	
1989	128	CD	WADE			11:33:08	
Senior Men							
1990	1	G	POPE-ELLIS	TJ	CORNISH	08:43:39.64	
1990	2	BC	WENKE	LJ	KEAY	08:48:03.	
1990	3	KJ	WHITE	GW	TARR	08:56:53.26	
1990	4	B	CLARK	H	WATERMEYER	09:10:54.22	
1990	5	MP	CONWAY	K	REYNOLDS	09:17:30.	
1990	6	B	THATCHER	A	VENTER	09:18:41.	
1990	7	RC	WHITTON	PR	ZIETSMAN	09:18:42.19	
1990	8	SJ	STAMP	G	HAW	09:29:48.	
1990	9	MJ	PERROW	MS	JAMIESON	09:30:39.51	
1990	10	GA	HILLIAR	I	O BYRNE	09:36:21.64	
Senior Women							
1990	96	M	LOEWENSTEIN	J	BENTEL	12:20:31.84	
1990	592	F	COWARD	E	BRASH	16:42:56	
Junior men							
1990	32	GM	REDMAN	DR	BRAUTESETH	10:37:53	
1990	35	WS	VALENTINE	AJ	ROWAN	10:42:50.97	
1990	42	PA	HATFIELD	AR	BINNENDYK	11:04:00	

RESULTS OF THE DUSI CANOE MARATHON—1951 TO 2006

YEAR	POS	I1	NAME1	I2	NAME2	TIME	REC
Mixed Doubles							
1990	44	RF	PENNEFATHER	JA	PENNEFATHER	11:07:31	
1990	57	G	WOOLLASTON	S	BANTOCK	11:28:09.22	
1990	88	D	BOHM	B	BLAESER	12:12:48	
Veteran Men							
1990	15	J	CLAASSEN	AG	MC KENZIE	09:49:01.15	
1990	82	T	SMITH	CS	EVERSON	12:09:54.83	
1990	97	SP	BRITTEN	DG	KNOTT	12:22:34	
Master Men							
1990	40	LH	DU PLESSIS	WW	DEYZEL	11:02:02.93	*
1990	55	MD	WILMOT	AB	KING	11:27:26.88	
1990	177	CM	HOWARD	FG	RADLOFF	13:12:55.7	
Senior Men							
1991	1	JR	EDMONDS			08:17:54.65	*
1991	2	G	POPE-ELLIS			08:21:32.65	
1991	3	N	EVANS			08:26:23.65	
1991	4	MR	HUTSON			08:30:16.65	
1991	5	K	REYNOLDS			08:35:13.65	
1991	6	GW	TARR			08:37:41.91	
1991	7	BC	WENKE			08:38:15.36	
1991	8	GA	HILLIAR			08:39:47.91	
1991	9	MS	JAMIESON			08:46:30.51	
1991	10	KJ	WHITE			08:46:57.09	
Senior Women							
1991	118	M	LOEWENSTEIN			10:34:44.79	*
Junior men							
1991	202	M	ALFORD			11:22:11.13	
1991	520	B	LIBBY			13:38:50.82	
1991	810	D	GELDARD			16:32:32.77	
1991	828	L	CARSTENS			16:53:00.11	
1991	848	AJ	BOHM			17:21:04.15	
1991	899	LK	OLIVER			18:45:22.58	*
1991	907	CM	HENDERSON			19:08:11.38	
1991	911	RA	BAAS			19:36:45.93	
Junior men							
1991	20	GM	REDMAN			09:05:48.50	*
1991	52	BA	WATTS			09:45:30.65	
1991	68	AR	MC INTOSH			10:03:21.88	
Junior women							
1991	899	LK	OLIVER			18:45:22.58	*
Mixed Doubles							
1991	50	DP	RETIEF	J	BENTEL	09:39:13.52	
1991	98	FD	MORALEE	D	MORALEE	10:24:16.93	
1991	128	DL	CLARK	S	CLARK	10:44:31.06	
Veteran Men							
1991	2	G	POPE-ELLIS			08:21:32.65	*
1991	36	P	VAN NIEKERK			09:22:20.62	*
1991	57	RJ	FINLAY			09:50:09.98	
Master Men							
1991	94	WW	DEYZEL			10:22:09.83	
1991	134	LH	DU PLESSIS			10:46:09.76	
1991	192	MD	WILMOT			11:18:09.24	
Senior Men							
1992	1	N	EVANS	M	PERROW	08:01:33.27	*
1992	2	TJ	CORNISH	GW	TARR	08:01:41.51	
1992	3	G	POPE-ELLIS	KJ	WHITE	08:03:06.10	
1992	4	JR	EDMONDS	AG	EDMONDS	08:04:38.54	
1992	5	BC	WENKE	LJ	KEAY	08:16:23.01	
1992	6	WJ	VOLEK	MR	HUTSON	08:18:49.28	
1992	7	CH	NORRIS	KO	ELLERKER	08:31:48.94	
1992	8	GA	HILLIAR	E	HILDEBRAND	08:39:13.13	
1992	9	C	SIMPKINS	MS	JAMIESON	08:40:44.74	
1992	10	MR	MC DONALD	D	HAMILTON-BROWN	08:40:47.65	
Senior Women							
1992	72	M	LOEWENSTEIN	J	BENTEL	10:27:07.18	*
1992	239	CS	WHITTON	DJ	GERMIQUET	12:16:37.39	
1992	246	D	FRANKLIN	LK	OLIVER	12:20:26.23	
1992	534	D	GELDARD	KL	WHYTE	14:45:43.69	
Junior men							
1992	23	DT	BRUSS	EP	NEL	09:14:53.79	*
1992	29	CA	VAN AARDENNE	KB	GODDARD	09:32:26.81	
1992	32	TB	MC LAREN	PG	STROMSOE	09:36:42.98	
Mixed Doubles							
1992	41	RG	SWINGEWOOD	N	BARENDSE	09:48:42.89	
1992	108	NS	EVANS	WJ	WHITE	10:59:10.07	
1992	114	DF	LOWE	MF	LOWE	11:02:41.04	
Veteran Men							
1992	30	AG	MC KENZIE	CJ	VAN DEN BERG	09:33:12.02	*
1992	40	NE	BLUE	D	GRANT	09:46:14.38	
1992	52	ME	BORLAND	RJ	FINLAY	10:06:26.75	
Master Men							
1992	55	LH	DU PLESSIS	MD	WILMOT	10:07:14.14	*
1992	131	M	BOTHA	ME	THOMAS	11:09:05.56	
1992	193	CM	HOWARD	I	KOVACIK	11:49:17.18	

RESULTS OF THE DUSI CANOE MARATHON—1951 TO 2006

1994

YEAR	POS	I1	NAME1	I2	NAME2	TIME	REC
Senior Men							
1994	1	JR	EDMONDS	KJ	WHITE	08:47:09.71	
1994	2	MR	HUTSON	LJ	KEAY	08:58:33.26	
1994	3	BC	WENKE	PJ	STRICKLAND	09:02:38.55	*
1994	4	G	STARR	CH	NORRIS	09:06:42.70	
1994	5	RC	WHITTON	K	HOLDEN	09:12:44.00	
1994	6	WJ	VOLEK	JC	ROOS	09:15:52.17	
1994	7	GJ	WAUD	I	O BYRNE	09:15:53.71	
1994	8	SJ	BLACK	E	HILDEBRAND	09:17:56.52	
1994	9	M	PERROW	N	EVANS	09:24:23.59	
1994	10	B	CLARK	RG	MONTGOMERY	09:29:33.75	
Senior Women							
1994	72	NL	RENNIE	WJ	WHITE	11:27:31.21	
1994	73	DJ	GERMIQUET	K	EXSTEEN	11:29:06.56	
1994	135	S	BOHNSACK	A	MANFRONI	12:44:24.91	
1994	206	HJ	PONS	GI	HAMILTON-BROWN	13:31:52.72	
1994	304	TA	CATTERALL	MS	KING	14:41:04.00	
1994	486	EC	PRETORIUS	L	ZOUTENDYK	17:04:39.08	
1994	504	CF	LOUW	DM	EB	17:21:39.43	
1994	558	KL	OLIVER	T	OETTLE	20:35:29.28	
Junior men							
1994	18	S	FISHER	GJ	BEHN	09:48:28.35	
1994	66	AG	STOTT	SR	STOTT	11:22:16.54	
1994	68	JP	HUGHES	KD	OSCROFT	11:24:08.76	
Junior women							
1994	558	KL	OLIVER	T	OETTLE	20:35:29.28	
Mixed Doubles							
1994	37	DT	BRUSS	LK	OLIVER	10:45:52.38	
1994	38	RG	SWINGEWOOD	HM	SKINNER	10:48:11.17	
1994	100	S	EARDLEY	KC	DUNCAN	12:08:09.44	
Veteran Men							
1994	11	G	POPE-ELLIS	TJ	CORNISH	09:31:43.04	
1994	36	NE	BLUE	DG	GRANT	10:43:45.00	
1994	79	A	GILBERT	D	PRICE	11:34:52.10	
Master Men							
1994	78	LH	DU PLESSIS	MD	WILMOT	11:34:25.17	
1994	88	CM	HOWARD	WW	DEYZEL	11:50:43.19	
1994	327	CJ	ROETS	JO	THOMPSON	14:51:04.31	

1993

YEAR	POS	I1	NAME1	I2	NAME2	TIME	REC
Senior Men							
1993	1	KJ	WHITE			09:40:07.05	
1993	2	JR	EDMONDS			09:45:05.74	
1993	3	GW	TARR			09:55:43.15	
1993	4	G	POPE-ELLIS			09:58:51.27	
1993	5	SG	WILSON			10:11:16.39	
1993	6	MS	JAMIESON			10:13:44.41	
1993	7	LJ	KEAY			10:16:10.95	
1993	8	JR	LESLIE			10:16:14.85	
1993	9	TJ	CORNISH			10:19:47.63	
1993	10	MR	HUTSON			10:22:12.20	
Senior Women							
1993	63	M	LOEWENSTEIN			12:25:40.66	
1993	310	D	GELDARD			16:18:01.27	
1993	550	LK	OLIVER			18:40:43.84	
1993	708	CS	ROBINSON			21:11:46.28	
1993	721	S	ARNOLD			22:08:26.11	
Junior men							
1993	42	TB	MC LAREN			11:45:31.48	
1993	45	SD	STANTON			11:50:37.30	
1993	51	BP	LEISEGANG			12:04:07.29	
Junior women							
1993	550	LK	OLIVER			18:40:43.84	*
1993	708	CS	ROBINSON			21:11:46.28	
Mixed Doubles							
1993	38	DP	RETIEF	J	BENTEL	11:37:57.31	
1993	53	DM	KNIGHT	D	TERRABLANCHE	12:10:39.25	
1993	142	C	NATALI	TA	CATTERALL	14:05:13.80	
Veteran Men							
1993	4	G	POPE-ELLIS			09:58:51.27	
1993	26	R	LEMBETHE			10:56:50.30	
1993	56	SP	BRITTEN			12:18:10.78	
Master Men							
1993	68	MD	WILMOT			12:30:18.43	
1993	96	WW	DEYZEL			13:19:36.83	
1993	132	M	BOTHA			13:59:28.33	

YEAR	POS	I1	NAME1	I2	NAME2	TIME	REC
	40	A	HAWARDEN			10:06:17.52	
Master Men							
1995	52	RG	SWINGEWOOD			10:19:28.65	*
1995	112	CM	HOWARD			11:24:22.11	
1995	127	WW	DEYZEL			11:32:05.67	
Master Women							
1995	502	LL	JENKINS			15:06:50.11	*
Senior Men							
1996	1	N	EVANS	M	PERROW	08:15:33.12	
1996	2	BC	WENKE	P	STRICKLAND	08:18:58.10	
1996	3	KJE	WHITE	GW	TARR	08:21:45.67	
1996	4	B	CLARK	H	WATERMEYER	08:27:14.00	
1996	5	JR	EDMONDS	AG	EDMONDS	08:29:23.21	
1996	6	SG	FISHER	KB	GODDARD	08:32:00.90	
1996	7	G	STARR	KO	ELLERKER	08:33:38.06	
1996	8	WJ	VOLEK	K	HOLDEN	08:34:39.64	
1996	9	GA	HILLIAR	F	DEYZEL	08:38:00.99	
1996	10	JR	LESLIE	KJ	MURRAY	08:40:54.39	
Senior Women							
1996	47	DJ	GERMIQUET	WJ	WHITE	10:02:13.21	*
1996	112	AJ	BOHM	S	EARDLEY	11:52:53.47	
1996	190	SL	JOYCE	EK	OETTLE	12:57:25.20	
1996	406	J	JONKER	J	WILSON	15:25:03.69	
1996	421	L	HESTER	AL	MARAIS	15:34:05.99	
1996	509	RA	WIGGETT	D	AGAR	16:39:18.94	
1996	608	N	TURNBULL	C	GRAY	18:41:36.28	
1996	612	M	REYNOLDS	R	DU TOIT	18:50:59.86	
1996	626	T	OETTLE	CH	HORNBY	20:10:33.60	
1996	646	DM	BYRES	JS	JUDAIS	25:25:34.67	
Junior men							
1996	21	AG	STOTT	JC	CALLISTER	09:07:09.35	*
1996	87	HR	MUNDY	GP	POTTER	11:15:29.31	
1996	88	RR	SAINT	NM	DAKERS	11:16:12.33	
Junior women							
1996	190	SL	JOYCE	EK	OETTLE	12:57:25.20	*
Mixed Doubles							
1996	50	G	POPE-ELLIS	WE	POPE-ELLIS	10:02:43.06	
1996	53	NL	RENNIE	CJ	MORCK	10:05:04.34	
1996	67	RG	SWINGEWOOD	D	WINTER	10:40:09.54	
Sub Veteran Men							
1996	50	G	POPE-ELLIS	WE	POPE-ELLIS	10:02:43.06	*
1996	57	NJ	ROCKEY	AT	CHAPLIN	10:24:36.60	
1996	62	J	VLANTIS	GB	BOAST	10:35:50.68	
Sub Veteran Women							
1996	646	DM	BYRES	JS	JUDAIS	25:25:34.67	*

YEAR	POS	I1	NAME1	I2	NAME2	TIME	REC
Senior Men							
1995	1	KJ	WHITE			08:43:28.25	
1995	2	GW	TARR			08:55:27.44	
1995	3	N	EVANS			08:56:46.81	
1995	4	JR	EDMONDS			08:56:47.69	
1995	5	KO	ELLERKER			09:09:27.86	
1995	6	JR	LESLIE			09:09:29.51	
1995	7	AG	EDMONDS			09:09:36.37	
1995	8	KJ	MURRAY			09:12:01.54	
1995	9	G	POPE-ELLIS			09:15:55.08	
1995	10	CH	NORRIS			09:20:59.59	
Senior Women							
1995	159	A	MANFRONI			11:47:20.47	
1995	161	WJ	WHITE			11:49:52.44	
1995	183	AJ	BOHM			12:02:55.14	
1995	219	DJ	GERMIQUET			12:21:01.02	
1995	327	JA	PENNEFATHER			13:17:35.21	
1995	380	J	BARRINGTON			13:47:55.46	
1995	387	S	BOHNSACK			13:50:01.58	
1995	502	LL	JENKINS			15:06:50.11	
1995	587	AJ	COCKSEDGE			16:23:41.84	
1995	646	SM	ORPWOOD			18:20:24.25	
Junior men							
1995	42	AG	STOTT			10:10:07.26	
1995	180	E	VAN RIET			12:02:40.09	
1995	209	JC	CALLISTER			12:14:11.66	
Junior women							
1995	672	T	OETTLE			20:18:16.26	
Mixed Doubles							
1995	35	C	SIMPKINS	DD	YOUDS	10:07:08	
1995	58	LJ	KEAY	LS	JANSSENS	10:25:41.01	
1995	138	TJ	PLATT	SC	ZUIDEWIND	11:35:49.02	
Sub Veteran Men							
1995	4	JR	EDMONDS			08:56:47.69	*
1995	5	KO	ELLERKER			09:09:27.86	
1995	10	CH	NORRIS			09:20:59.59	
Sub Veteran Women							
1995	327	JA	PENNEFATHER			13:17:35.21	*
Veteran Men							
1995	29	I	O BYRNE			09:50:17.10	
1995	33	K	REYNOLDS			09:58:32.80	
1995	36	SJ	BLACK			10:01:10.93	
Sub Master Men							
1995	9	G	POPE-ELLIS			09:15:55.08	*
1995	37	RE	LEMBETHE			10:01:51.50	

194

RESULTS OF THE DUSI CANOE MARATHON—1951 TO 2006

YEAR	POS	I1	NAME1	I2	NAME2	TIME	REC
Veteran Men							
1996	16	SJ	BLACK	T	BIGGS	09:01:19.21	
1996	19	TJ	CORNISH	K	REYNOLDS	09:03:09.32	
1996	44	NE	BLUE	DG	GRANT	10:01:23.64	
Sub Master Men							
1996	161	GH	WILSON	MR	PENGELLY	12:32:58.21	*
1996	272	AL	BARRINGTON	PJ	KEYWORTH	13:58:11.59	
1996	300	BA	BAXTER	MJ	BAXTER	14:09:21.01	
Master Men							
1996	65	RA	SWINGEWOOD	WW	DEYZEL	10:37:42.95	
1996	121	M	JONKER	MD	WILMOT	12:02:02.14	
1996	318	CM	HOWARD	LW	JENKINS	14:23:21.11	
Senior Men							
1997	1	M	PERROW			08:26:30.94	
1997	2	JR	EDMONDS			08:32:30.53	
1997	3	AJA	ROWAN			08:34:07.09	
1997	4	JR	LESLIE			08:39:15.94	
1997	5	L	KEAY			08:43:27.83	
1997	6	WJ	VOLEK			08:43:38.65	
1997	7	KJ	MURRAY			08:47:03.08	
1997	8	KJE	WHITE			08:47:03.24	
1997	9	KB	GODDARD			08:47:03.46	
1997	10	GG	WILSON			08:49:08.25	
Senior Women							
1997	82	WJ	WHITE			10:32:49.86	*
1997	83	DJ	GERMIQUET			10:33:02.27	
1997	158	D	GELDARD			11:23:31.22	
1997	205	AJ	BOHM			11:43:01.93	
Junior men							
1997	305	EK	OETTLE			12:25:41.80	
1997	436	LK	OLIVER			13:24:43.63	
1997	438	E	JAMES			13:25:48.32	
1997	541	EJ	LANG			14:19:55.89	
1997	609	EM	NEL			14:48:41.13	
1997	677	V	STRAUSS			15:41:19.23	
Junior women							
1997	22	B	IRVINE			09:12:14.52	
1997	24	JC	CALLISTER			09:14:54.41	
1997	96	CG	WHITTON			10:44:22.83	
Mixed Doubles							
1997	305	EK	OETTLE	H	SKINNER	12:25:41.80	*
1997	42	RG	SWINGEWOOD	MP	FOUCHE	09:54:56.16	
1997	120	GJ	WAUD	LB	SCHMIDT	10:57:21.93	
1997	123	GM	BIRD			10:59:43.10	

YEAR	POS	I1	NAME1	I2	NAME2	TIME	REC
Sub Veteran Men							
1997	2	JR	EDMONDS	KJ	MURRAY	08:32:30.53	*
1997	16	B	CLARK	N	EVANS	09:01:18.82	
1997	17	KO	ELLERKER	AG	EDMONDS	09:01:24.64	
Veteran Men							
1997	21	KJ	REYNOLDS	H	WATERMEYER	09:10:59.71	
1997	80	AR	HOLD	RF	HERREVELD	10:29:15.68	
1997	87	P	VAN NIEKERK	F	DEYZEL	10:36:40.19	
Sub Master Men							
1997	19	G	POPE-ELLIS	M	WILSON	09:08:44.54	*
1997	47	RE	LEMBETHE	M	HUTSON	09:59:30.10	
1997	109	A	HAWARDEN	KJ	REYNOLDS	10:51:22.63	
Master Men							
1997	74	NE	BLUE	PJ	STRICKLAND	10:25:18.62	
1997	111	HL	DE RAUVILLE			10:53:33.18	
1997	138	MD	WILMOT			11:10:19.69	
Senior Men							
1998	1	AG	STOTT			08:03:09.00	*
1998	2	M	PERROW			08:08:38.50	
1998	3	JR	EDMONDS			08:13:23.29	
1998	4	GW	TARR			08:17:37.16	
1998	5	B	CLARK			08:18:31.64	
1998	6	GA	HILLIAR			08:18:37.74	
1998	7	KJE	WHITE			08:20:58.29	
1998	8	WJ	VOLEK			08:21:00.60	
1998	9	GJ	WAUD			08:24:25.47	
1998	10	BC	WENKE			08:31:21.37	
Senior Women							
1998	51	DJ	GERMIQUET	WJ	WHITE	09:52:11.45	
1998	100	D	GELDARD	H	WENKE	10:47:09.52	
1998	140	SL	JOYCE	S	EARDLEY	11:17:07.72	
1998	165	CT	CLARKE	AL	MARAIS	11:34:12.19	
1998	220	LA	SYMONS	J	COHEN	12:13:05.78	
1998	236	S	BOHNSACK	L	SCHMIDT	12:21:10.51	
1998	316	LK	OLIVER	S	BARRON	13:09:22.54	
1998	357	TA	CATTERALL	MSI	KING	13:32:54.44	
1998	360	D	FRANKLIN	GS	TARR	13:33:58.33	
1998	401	CD	JOYCE	JL	BAXTER	13:55:04.33	
Junior men							
1998	27	SR	BRUSS	SS	BIGGS	09:13:56.94	
1998	60	LW	JENKINS JNR	GP	POTTER	10:01:03.16	
1998	67	JP	ABRAMS	RF	DOMLEO	10:05:23.85	

195

YEAR	POS	I1	NAME1	I2	NAME2	TIME	REC
Mixed Doubles							
1998	58	D	CONRADIE	J	WALDER	09:58:42.45	*
1998	76	JM	SANDERS	SM	HOLMES	10:22:38.43	
1998	94	RAD	STARR	RSM	PETERS	10:42:41.02	
Sub Veteran Men							
1998	10	BC	WENKE	PJ	STRICKLAND	08:31:21.37	*
1998	17	KO	ELLERKER	CH	NORRIS	08:41:15.17	
1998	21	C	SIMPKINS	C	WILSON	09:07:05.71	
Veteran Men							
1998	29	TJ	CORNISH	RE	LEMBETHE	09:15:23.83	
1998	41	NJ	BRIGGS	M	STEYN	09:38:59.30	
1998	79	RC	TREMEARNE	RER	LANGFORD	10:25:23.31	
Sub Master Men							
1998	141	RF	PENNEFATHER	JAS	PENNEFATHER	11:17:15.40	*
1998	179	GH	WILSON	MR	PENGELLY	11:45:52.81	
1998	284	BA	BAXTER	MJ	BAXTER	12:52:35.82	
Master Men							
1998	106	RA	SWINGEWOOD	WW	DEYZEL	10:53:21.17	
1998	119	NE	BLUE	HL	DE RAUVILLE	11:02:26.09	
1998	279	AL	BARRINGTON	PJ	KEYWORTH	12:50:55.71	
Senior Men							
1999	1	M	DREYER			08:49:46.95	
1999	2	KJE	WHITE			08:53:22.53	
1999	3	JR	EDMONDS			08:54:41.24	
1999	4	LW	JENKINS JNR			09:03:41.10	
1999	5	BC	WENKE			09:03:55.60	
1999	6	KJ	MURRAY			09:05:17.77	
1999	7	K	HOLDEN			09:06:14.12	
1999	8	GG	WILSON			09:06:54.55	
1999	9	PA	HATFIELD			09:06:55.04	
1999	10	AG	EDMONDS			09:08:45.83	
Senior Women							
1999	82	DJ	GERMIQUET			10:44:42.64	
1999	104	WJ	WHITE			11:00:54.28	
1999	139	A	MALHERBE			11:27:14.37	
1999	160	J	WALDER			11:39:31.82	
1999	236	LK	OLIVER			12:08:47.75	
1999	263	AL	MARAIS			12:18:41.50	
1999	283	CD	JOYCE			12:27:37.18	
1999	307	D	GELDARD			12:40:05.22	
1999	314	LA	SYMONS			12:41:41.45	
1999	324	SL	JOYCE			12:48:29.10	

YEAR	POS	I1	NAME1	I2	NAME2	TIME	REC
Junior men							
1999	4	LW	JENKINS JNR			09:03:41.10	*
1999	12	SS	BIGGS			09:11:51.81	
1999	32	DS	BIRD			09:54:31.06	
Junior women							
1999	283	CD	JOYCE			12:27:37.18	
1999	314	LA	SYMONS			12:41:41.45	
1999	531	JL	BAXTER			14:06:09.94	
Mixed Doubles							
1999	55	LS	RICHARDSON	JCC	CALLISTER	10:25:42.93	
1999	61	GJ	WAUD	D	HOLTE-SMITH	10:30:02.79	
1999	75	R	WILLIS	J	COHEN	10:40:35.96	
Sub Veteran Men							
1999	3	JR	EDMONDS			08:54:41.24	
1999	5	BC	WENKE			09:03:55.60	
1999	17	E	HILDEBRAND			09:25:20.14	
Sub Veteran Women							
1999	381	PR	MEAKIN			13:13:24.07	*
Veteran Men							
1999	25	G	MONTEITH			09:37:42.68	
1999	39	KJ	REYNOLDS			10:04:38.59	
1999	43	RF	PENNEFATHER			10:11:33.33	
Sub Master Men							
1999	45	RE	LEMBETHE			10:12:42.03	
1999	76	B	THATCHER			10:43:19.72	
1999	116	P	VAN NIEKERK			11:10:59.69	
Master Men							
1999	19	G	POPE-ELLIS			09:30:20.20	*
1999	83	A	HAWARDEN			10:44:50.84	
1999	93	R	VAN RIET			10:53:16.82	
Senior Men							
2000	1	M	PERROW	M	DREYER	07:56:35.77	*
2000	2	GW	TARR	DT	BRUSS	08:07:29.49	
2000	3	AG	STOTT	KJ	MURRAY	08:08:30.79	
2000	4	GG	WILSON	P	CRUICKSHANKS	08:08:31.50	
2000	5	KJE	WHITE	JR	LESLIE	08:08:43.09	
2000	6	JR	EDMONDS	AG	EDMONDS	08:08:52.81	
2000	7	LW	JENKINS JNR	B	IRVINE	08:14:06.00	
2000	8	RA	PEPPER	B	COLLYER	08:16:30.34	
2000	9	WB	PRICE	KV	RICHARDSON	08:18:54.69	
2000	10	GA	HILLIAR	F	DEYZEL	08:21:46.77	

196

RESULTS OF THE DUSI CANOE MARATHON—1951 TO 2006

YEAR	POS	I1	NAME1	I2	NAME2	TIME	REC
Senior Women							
2000	59	DJ	GERMIQUET	WJ	WHITE	09:42:05.15	*
2000	95	J	WALDER	A	MALHERBE	10:20:42.52	
2000	102	D	GELDARD	D	WINTER	10:32:34.07	
2000	135	RA	WIGGETT	D	HOLTE-SMITH	10:52:58.16	
2000	162	LA	SYMONS	J	COHEN	11:08:35.74	
2000	187	CD	JOYCE	SL	JOYCE	11:23:01.14	
2000	210	A	DUNNE	F	COWARD	11:33:17.48	
2000	211	JL	BAXTER	AE	LAUGHOR-CLARKE	11:33:25.00	
2000	253	AJ	BOHM	S	EARDLEY	11:52:42.15	
2000	292	LK	OLIVER	KL	OLIVER	12:14:05.47	
Junior men							
2000	19	P	TERREBLANCHE	MA	RASMUSSEN	08:50:04.41	*
2000	36	GMG	BURDEN	ML	ESSERY	09:25:04.14	
2000	39	SM	RUBENSTEIN	KJ	SMITH	09:25:59.78	
Junior women							
2000	162	LA	SYMONS	J	COHEN	11:08:35.74	*
2000	356	N	IRVINE	AJ	RAWLINSON	12:40:57.77	
2000	1013	NAW	WOODS	KL	MANN	18:56:23.29	
Mixed Doubles							
2000	67	RF	HEREVELD	TA	CATTERALL	09:49:43.39	
2000	68	JM	SANDERS	L	WEBSTER	09:51:40.44	
2000	82	MD	GERMIQUET	K	PAHL	10:11:09.27	
Sub Veteran Men							
2000	11	BC	WENKE	PJ	STRICKLAND	08:23:49.58	*
2000	23	AN	BLACK	G	HAW	09:00:20.12	
2000	24	C	SIMPKINS	C	WILSON	09:02:13.05	
Veteran Men							
2000	22	RC	WHITTON	RA	OSTLER	08:56:01.04	*
2000	30	AG	RENNIE	KO	ELLERKER	09:14:54.47	
2000	76	DC	BURSCOUGH	C	MURRAY	10:03:35.57	
Sub Master Men							
2000	35	TJ	CORNISH	R	BELCHER	09:24:03.28	*
2000	143	G	GREEN	GH	THOMPSON	10:59:09.26	
2000	194	DJ	GILLMER	MP	FRIZELLE	11:28:16.88	
Master Men							
2000	17	G	POPE-ELLIS	DJ	RAWLINSON	08:47:52.15	*
2000	154	RA	SWINGEWOOD	WW	DEYZEL	11:05:07.89	
2000	280	K	LASKEY	MD	WILMOT	12:09:12.49	
Grand Master Men							
2000	1026	L	BENHAM	M	CALLENDAR	19:15:04.88	*

YEAR	POS	I1	NAME1	I2	NAME2	TIME	REC
Senior Men							
2001	1	LW	JENKINS JNR			08:09:09.65	*
2001	2	M	DREYER			08:12:12.08	
2001	3	AG	STOTT			08:17:32.13	
2001	4	DT	BRUSS			08:36:06.83	
2001	5	P	CRUICKSHANKS			08:38:13.29	
2001	6	H	MC GREGOR			08:39:59.42	
2001	7	GG	WILSON			08:42:05.57	
2001	8	WB	PRICE			08:43:51.06	
2001	9	SR	MAYNARD			08:45:06.02	
2001	10	WJ	VOLEK			08:48:46.82	
Senior Women							
2001	91	A	MANFRONI			10:18:09.60	*
2001	103	A	MIEDEMA			10:27:46.20	
2001	142	LK	OLIVER			10:46:38.25	
2001	155	CD	JOYCE			10:53:13.41	
2001	180	J	WALDER			11:06:31.29	
2001	186	LA	SYMONS			11:09:47.79	
2001	247	SM	WHITEAR			11:38:49.45	
2001	348	S	BOHNSACK			12:12:47.82	
2001	383	KL	OLIVER			12:23:38.16	
2001	515	E	JAMES			12:59:23.88	
Junior men							
2001	11	SM	RUBENSTEIN			08:52:47.63	*
2001	45	AT	BUTTON			09:44:21.71	
2001	47	M	MBANJWA			09:45:20.22	
Junior women							
2001	647	NA	WOODS			13:36:02.76	
2001	916	LM	MIDGLEY			15:36:18.69	
2001	957	CG	HUNT			16:19:12.07	
U21 men							
2001	1	LW	JENKINS JNR			08:09:09.65	*
2001	21	DS	BIRD			09:09:22.17	
2001	32	DJ	HOWE			09:31:44.95	
U21 women							
2001	155	CD	JOYCE			10:53:13.41	
2001	186	LA	SYMONS			11:09:47.79	
2001	628	LMJ	OETTLE			13:29:16.54	
Mixed Doubles							
2001	70	GM	BIRD	AJ	STEPHENS	10:07:36.94	
2001	82	B	IRVINE	N	IRVINE	10:12:42.52	
2001	108	AL	FOUCHE	SM	HOLMES	10:30:54.51	

197

RESULTS OF THE DUSI CANOE MARATHON—1951 TO 2006

YEAR	POS	I1	NAME1	I2	NAME2	TIME	REC
Sub Veteran Men							
2001	14	GA	HILLIAR			08:54:27.74	
2001	18	E	HILDEBRANDT			09:00:12.87	
2001	34	GJ	WAUD			09:33:40.23	
Sub Veteran Women							
2001	348	S	BOHNSACK			12:12:47.82	*
0	0		Veteran Men				
2001	17	JR	EDMONDS			09:00:11.78	
2001	22	BC	WENKE			09:09:22.64	
2001	33	RC	WHITTON			09:33:25.32	
Sub Master Men							
2001	30	SJ	BLACK			09:25:44.52	
2001	64	P	VAN NIEKERK			10:00:38.84	
2001	144	AR	HOLD			10:47:03.10	
Master Men							
2001	36	G	POPE-ELLIS			09:34:34.22	
2001	55	RE	LEMBETHE			09:52:20.34	
2001	150	T	SMITH			10:50:35.09	
Grand Master Men							
2001	159	HL	DE RAUVILLE			10:56:08.68	*
Senior Men							
2002	1	DT	BRUSS	MJ	DREYER	07:44:56.3	*
2002	2	AG	STOTT	LW	JENKINS JNR	07:51:26.6	
2002	3	SS	BIGGS	SR	BRUSS	08:09:15.2	
2002	4	KJE	WHITE	JR	LESLIE	08:12:25.7	
2002	5	JP	THERON	SJ	RAWLINSON	08:12:30.8	
2002	6	GG	WILSON	B	COLLYER	08:12:34.9	
2002	7	SM	RUBENSTEIN	P	CRUICKSHANKS	08:20:23.9	
2002	8	WB	PRICE	PA	HATFIELD	08:21:53.4	
2002	9	BC	WENKE	WJ	VOLEK	08:23:57.4	
2002	10	S	MILLWARD	TM	DU PISANIE	08:27:05.3	
Senior Women							
2002	44	J	WALDER	A	MANFRONI	09:31:06.5	*
2002	48	AS	MIEDEMA	AJ	RAWLINSON	09:36:09.7	
2002	89	WJ	WHITE	SM	CHAPMAN	10:08:54.2	
2002	95	D	GELDARD	AL	LOMBARD	10:16:37.6	
2002	99	DJ	GERMIQUET	SL	JOYCE	10:20:39.3	
2002	114	CD	JOYCE	LL	THOMPSON	10:30:50.5	
2002	119	LK	OLIVER	NA	WOODS	10:39:33.2	
2002	128	LA	SYMONS	N	IRVINE	10:46:57.3	
2002	191	NJ	MORPHEW	KD	MARCH	11:22:53.3	
2002	194	E	JAMES	AL	TAYLOR	11:23:29.9	

YEAR	POS	I1	NAME1	I2	NAME2	TIME	REC
Junior men							
2002	16	DL	WOODHEAD	JS	BIGGS	08:52:02.6	
2002	22	GD	CHAPLIN	MO	NORTON	09:12:49.3	
2002	29	LM	ZONDI	TK	NGIDI	09:18:36.7	
Junior women							
2002	191	NJ	MORPHEW	KD	MARCH	11:22:53.3	
2002	332	LM	MIDGLEY	E	LEIBBRANDT	12:21:14.9	
2002	905	LM	MENNIE	CL	MENNIE	17:03:29.2	
U21 men							
2002	3	SS	BIGGS	SR	BRUSS	08:09:15.2	*
2002	21	R	ARMDORF	M	AFRIKA	09:11:20.8	
2002	25	JB	SMITH	MJ	ARTHUR	09:14:25.0	
U21 women							
2002	114	CD	JOYCE	LL	THOMPSON	10:30:50.5	*
2002	128	LA	SYMONS	N	IRVINE	10:46:57.3	
2002	746	GB	MASON	KL	MANN	15:01:08.4	
Mixed Doubles							
2002	36	R	HERREVELD	DM	LEWIS	09:25:46.4	
2002	38	RA	PEPPER	SN	EARDLEY	09:26:41.9	
2002	40	JR	EDMONDS	SM	HOLMES	09:28:15.1	
Sub Veteran Men							
2002	13	M	PERROW	C	WILSON	08:44:43.8	*
2002	15	GJ	WAUD	MJ	BELL	08:52:02.2	
2002	40	JR	EDMONDS	SM	HOLMES	09:28:15.1	
Sub Veteran Women							
2002	444	OA	MORFORD	J	OLIVER	13:00:26.7	
2002	739	CL	VERMAAK	TS	TRODD	14:57:06.4	
Veteran Men							
2002	38	RA	PEPPER	SN	EARDLEY	09:26:41.9	
2002	42	RB	STRICKLAND	GJW	MANN	09:29:46.4	
2002	45	AG	RENNIE	KO	ELLERKER	09:31:21.0	
Sub Master Men							
2002	52	ND	TAYLOR	PG	MORPHEW	09:38:29.0	
2002	74	RA	OSTLER	KA	DAVIDSON	10:00:15.7	
2002	136	N	BESSLER	FR	CLARK	10:52:31.9	
Master Men							
2002	18	G	POPE-ELLIS	DJR	RAWLINSON	08:55:47.1	
2002	87	WH	KUNZ	P	VAN NIEKERK	10:07:14.1	
2002	174	HL	DE RAUVILLE	J	DE RAUVILLE	11:14:40.5	
Master Women							
2002	932	LS	VAN AARDENNE	LG	ATTWELL	18:01:08.9	*
Grand Master Men							
2002	912	AM	LIGHTFOOT	M	CALLENDER	17:16:20.1	*

RESULTS OF THE DUSI CANOE MARATHON—1951 TO 2006

YEAR	POS	I1	NAME1	I2	NAME2	TIME	REC
Senior Men							
2003	1	MJ	DREYER			08:31:31.9	*
2003	2	LW	JENKINS JNR			08:47:57.5	
2003	3	JP	THERON			08:51:00.3	
2003	4	JA	GRAHAM			09:00:56.7	
2003	5	H	MC GREGOR			09:02:53.5	
2003	6	DT	BRUSS			09:04:01.4	
2003	7	SR	MAYNARD			09:07:42.5	
2003	8	SS	BIGGS			09:10:35.3	
2003	9	JS	BIGGS			09:10:38.4	
2003	10	RJ	WILLIS			09:11:58.3	
Senior Women							
2003	50	A	MIEDEMA			10:12:06.6	*
2003	73	AL	LOMBARD			10:36:00.2	
2003	97	LA	SYMONS			10:54:23.7	
2003	120	AJ	RAWLINSON			11:08:02.4	
2003	129	CD	JOYCE			11:14:46.9	
2003	171	SM	CHAPMAN			11:32:26.6	
2003	200	LL	THOMPSON			11:43:25.2	
2003	230	KD	MARCH			11:58:18.3	
2003	236	LK	OLIVER			12:02:15.7	
2003	260	MA	AUSTEN-SMITH			12:11:31.4	
Junior men							
2003	9	JS	BIGGS			09:10:38.4	
2003	17	CG	TURTON			09:24:45.4	
2003	26	MD	TRAUTMAN			09:41:13.4	*
Junior women							
2003	230	KD	MARCH			11:58:18.3	
2003	306	NJ	MORPHEW			12:27:08.0	
2003	577	KG	VOLBRECHT			13:50:26.9	
U21 men							
2003	16	LM	ZONDI			09:24:40.5	
2003	21	M	MBANJWA			09:28:00.1	
2003	37	TP	LAMBLE			10:01:39.7	
U21 women							
2003	97	LA	SYMONS			10:54:23.7	
2003	120	AJ	RAWLINSON			11:08:02.4	
2003	200	LL	THOMPSON			11:43:25.2	
Mixed Doubles							
2003	75	GG	WILSON	SN	EARDLEY	10:36:33.1	
2003	79	GM	BURDEN	C	COLLINS	10:39:10.3	
2003	116	DA	BOSHOFF	SD	HOUGH	11:06:28.7	

YEAR	POS	I1	NAME1	I2	NAME2	TIME	REC
Sub Veteran Men							
2003	13	MJ	DREYER			08:31:31.9	*
2003	13	JR	LESLIE			09:17:36.0	
2003	14	GA	HILLIAR			09:21:10.8	
Sub Veteran Women							
2003	348	DM	LEWIS			12:42:16.9	
2003	523	R	HENDERSON			13:34:56.5	
2003	769	AM	SIMPSON			14:56:15.8	
Veteran Men							
2003	24	E	HILDEBRANDT			09:39:13.8	
2003	33	BC	WENKE			09:50:52.6	
2003	34	AN	BLACK			09:50:53.7	
Veteran Women							
2003	468	CH	GIBBINGS			13:16:55.2	*
2003	771	E	MAREE			14:56:20.1	
Sub Master Men							
2003	35	RC	WHITTON			09:57:00.5	
2003	142	RA	OSTLER			11:20:34.8	
2003	161	BI	WHITEFORD			11:27:08.3	
Sub Master Women							
2003	1033	AM	WITTY			17:41:50.4	*
Master Men							
2003	52	RE	LEMBETHE			10:13:49.3	
2003	54	P	VAN NIEKERK			10:15:40.6	
2003	99	PH	SYMONS			10:55:23.8	
Grand Master Men							
2003	304	WW	DEYZEL			12:26:29.1	
2003	317	HL	DE RAUVILLE			12:31:40.1	
2003	339	CM	HOWARD			12:39:37.1	
Senior Men							
2004	1	A	STOTT	MJ	DREYER	07:45:50.3	
2004	2	DT	BRUSS	SR	BRUSS	08:08:01.4	
2004	3	JP	THERON	LW	JENKINS JNR	08:15:05.8	
2004	4	MA	STEWART	M	MBANJWA	08:15:07.2	
2004	5	WJ	VOLEK	WB	PRICE	08:15:37.1	
2004	6	GM	BIRD	SJ	RAWLINSON	08:18:05.2	
2004	7	SS	BIGGS	JS	BIGGS	08:22:36.0	
2004	8	H	MC GREGOR	B	IRVINE	08:25:01.2	
2004	9	CR	HAYNES	JS	GOLDING	08:25:44.0	
2004	10	P	CRUICKSHANKS	RJ	WILLIS	08:27:08.4	

199

YEAR	POS	I1	NAME1	I2	NAME2	TIME	REC
Senior Women							
2004	51	AL	LOMBARD	D	KAMSTRA	09:27:52.9	*
2004	54	J	WALDER	A	MIEDEMA	09:32:23.6	
2004	83	LL	THOMPSON	KD	MARCH	09:58:54.0	
2004	90	LA	SYMONS	K	SCHOOMBEE	10:08:58.7	
2004	106	SM	CHAPMAN	DM	LEWIS	10:22:43.7	
2004	123	CD	JOYCE	AL	TAYLOR	10:30:12.2	
2004	147	DJ	GERMIQUET	SL	HOLDEN	10:50:40.2	
2004	229	KL	CORNISH	C	LANGENHOVEN	11:32:38.2	
2004	243	D	GELDARD	BK	REW	11:40:41.7	
2004	374	KG	VOLBRECHT	D	VORSTER	12:29:06.9	
Junior men							
2004	29	DB	CHAPLIN	ME	WORRALL	09:05:02.8	
2004	38	G	ADIE	SLJ	JARDINE	09:14:31.9	
2004	58	RM	MC GEARY	JJ	BENNETT	09:35:03.5	
Junior women							
2004	229	KL	CORNISH	C	LANGENHOVEN	11:32:38.2	
2004	374	KG	VOLBRECHT	D	VORSTER	12:29:06.9	
2004	473	KJ	WOOD	T	BROWN	12:56:14.5	
U21 men							
2004	11	CG	TURTON	LM	ZONDI	08:36:24.8	
2004	26	TP	LAMBLE	P	BIRKETT	09:01:46.6	
2004	30	M	MARCH	D	WOOD	09:05:33.2	
U21 women							
2004	83	LL	THOMPSON	KD	MARCH	09:58:54.0	
2004	490	BE	HARTLEY	R	WALSH	13:02:04.2	
2004	832	EA	GILLMER	AJ	KIDD	15:43:23.1	
Mixed Doubles							
2004	53	TM	DU PISANIE	MA	AUSTEN-SMITH	09:30:35.2	
2004	68	BC	WENKE	HM	WENKE	09:46:34.0	
2004	69	GG	WILSON	SN	EARDLEY	09:47:26.7	
Sub Veteran Men							
2004	28	KJE	WHITE	JR	LESLIE	09:04:48.4	
2004	36	MJA	DE VILLIERS	SC	BOTHA	09:13:31.9	
2004	46	A	BOOYSEN	C	DIMOPOULOS	09:22:53.7	
Sub Veteran Women							
2004	381	OA	MORFORD	J	OLIVER	12:30:26.0	
2004	581	DRJ	VAN BART	EM	NEL	13:36:23.9	
2004	705	CL	NEL	LJ	WOLHUTER	14:35:25.4	
Veteran Men							
2004	15	GA	HILLIAR	GJ	WAUD	08:47:59.1	
2004	42	MS	JAMIESON	AG	RENNIE	09:17:51.3	
2004	56	NW	EVANS	C	EVANS	09:33:12.3	

YEAR	POS	I1	NAME1	I2	NAME2	TIME	REC
Veteran Women							
2004	651	JLR	MANNING	L	VAN EEDEN	14:11:44.5	*
2004	841	L	LODGE	DJ	PARKER	15:52:42.2	*
Sub Master Men							
2004	39	RC	WHITTON	RA	OSTLER	09:15:05.0	
2004	64	PG	MORPHEW	ND	TAYLOR	09:43:53.5	
2004	113	R	VAN RIET	C	LOGAN	10:26:44.8	
Master Men							
2004	52	P	VAN NIEKERK	NJ	BRIGGS	09:30:04.1	
2004	84	G	POPE-ELLIS	DJR	RAWLINSON	09:58:57.7	
2004	153	WH	KUNZ	FHI	CARTER	10:53:24.0	
Master Women							
2004	900	LS	VAN AARDENNE	LG	ATTWELL	16:59:53.4	*
SubGrand Master M							
2004	290	NE	BLUE	PG	ELEY	11:59:18.5	*
2004	370	CH	WATTS	R	BOURNE-LANGE	12:27:38.7	
2004	440	GH	WILSON	MR	PENGELLY	12:47:15.0	
Grand Master Men							
2004	408	R	BOWEN	LW	JENKINS SNR	12:37:59.6	*
2004	833	MD	WILMOT	K	LASKEY	15:44:08.5	
Senior Men							
2005	1	H	MC GREGOR			08:16:58.1	
2005	2	A	STOTT			08:18:00.8	
2005	3	L	ZONDI			08:30:17.5	
2005	4	LW	JENKINS JNR			08:34:43.1	
2005	5	JA	GRAHAM			08:35:20.2	
2005	6	M	MBANJWA			08:35:21.3	
2005	7	SR	MAYNARD			08:39:59.1	
2005	8	DT	BRUSS			08:40:51.7	
2005	9	JP	THERON			08:43:38.9	
2005	10	SS	BIGGS			08:43:41.0	
Senior Women							
2005	30	A	MIEDEMA			09:36:02.9	*
2005	58	AL	LOMBARD			10:04:14.4	
2005	121	CD	JOYCE			10:52:41.5	
2005	140	J	WALDER			11:05:37.1	
2005	150	SM	CHAPMAN			11:09:05.3	
2005	197	MA	AUSTEN-SMITH			11:27:18.0	
2005	201	SL	HOLDEN			11:29:33.2	
2005	270	HJ	PITCHFORD			11:53:44.2	
2005	280	KD	MARCH			11:56:19.0	
2005	288	KA	FROST			11:59:42.0	

RESULTS OF THE DUSI CANOE MARATHON—1951 TO 2006

YEAR	POS	I1	NAME1	I2	NAME2	TIME	REC
Junior men							
2005	23	NJ	STUBBS			09:30:47.9	
2005	27	S	BIRD			09:32:36.4	
2005	47	W	GREEN			09:50:54.6	
Junior women							
2005	619	KA	HOWE			13:38:23.7	
2005	767	R	WALSH			14:32:24.6	
2005	1026	CP	OLWAGEN			17:11:39.3	
U21 men							
2005	3	L	ZONDI			08:30:17.5	
2005	33	P	BIRKETT			09:39:30.1	
2005	34	MD	WILLMENT			09:39:31.3	
U21 women							
2005	270	HJ	PITCHFORD			11:53:44.2	
2005	280	KD	MARCH			11:56:19.0	
2005	374	K	VAN DER MERWE			12:26:43.4	
Mixed Doubles							
2005	70	M	HARRIS	SN	EARDLEY	10:13:49.5	
2005	77	LL	THOMPSON	SR	BRUSS	10:18:10.7	
2005	89	JR	LESLIE	RL	LESLIE	10:24:17.8	
Sub Veteran Men							
2005	12	MA	STEWART			09:04:35.0	
2005	13	KJE	WHITE			09:05:21.4	
2005	29	AG	EDMONDS			09:35:45.7	
Sub Veteran Women							
2005	197	MA	AUSTEN-SMITH			11:27:18.0	*
2005	376	R	HENDERSON			12:27:29.1	
2005	934	TS	TRODD			15:54:47.5	
Veteran Men							
2005	17	GA	HILLIAR			09:19:30.3	
2005	20	E	HILDEBRANDT			09:26:18.5	
2005	22	RA	PEPPER			09:29:21.9	
Veteran Women							
2005	404	DM	LEWIS			12:37:11.3	*
2005	484	S	BOHNSACK			12:57:54.0	
2005	721	CH	GIBBINGS			14:13:46.5	
Sub Master Men							
2005	28	JR	EDMONDS			09:35:44.8	
2005	36	BC	WENKE			09:40:54.0	
2005	49	RC	WHITTON			09:54:06.5	
Sub Master Women							
2005	581	CM	HENDERSON			13:24:45.7	*
2005	938	JLR	MANNING			15:57:53.2	
2005	958	L	VAN EEDEN			16:12:43.2	

YEAR	POS	I1	NAME1	I2	NAME2	TIME	REC
Master Men							
2005	61	SJ	BLACK			10:08:13.2	
2005	65	P	VAN NIEKERK			10:10:37.0	
2005	83	B	THATCHER			10:20:22.4	
Master Women							
2005	893	A	PRIOR			15:28:22.6	
2005	1005	JP	DRING			16:51:32.6	
2005	1068	L	LODGE			18:55:28.4	
Sub Grand Master Men							
2005	48	G	POPE-ELLIS			09:52:20.6	*
2005	446	D	COETZER			12:45:15.9	
2005	604	CH	WATTS			13:32:49.5	
Grand Master Men							
2005	300	HL	DE RAUVILLE			12:02:12.9	
2005	389	RA	SWINGEWOOD			12:34:10.0	
2005	445	WW	DEYZEL			12:45:10.0	
Senior Men							
2005	1	H	MC GREGOR	MJ	DREYER	07:40:25.15	*
2006	2	A	STOTT	WG	THOMPSON	07:46:02.84	
2006	3	GM	BIRD	SJ	RAWLINSON	07:49:55.12	
2006	4	CG	TURTON	S	VAN GYSEN	07:56:07.04	
2006	5	SS	BIGGS	L	ZONDI	08:00:10.71	
2006	6	KJ	MURRAY	JA	GRAHAM	08:00:12.03	
2006	7	SR	MAYNARD	KJE	WHITE	08:11:14.68	
2006	8	S	BIRD	CM	SCHOEMAN	08:12:20.48	
2006	9	WJ	VOLEK	WB	PRICE	08:12:22.04	
2006	10	C	PRETORIUS	B	BARTHO	08:14:44.81	
Senior Women							
2006	48	AL	LOMBARD	A	MIEDEMA	09:02:12.17	*
2006	66	C	JOYCE	LL	THOMPSON	09:28:33.65	
2006	72	LK	OLIVER	R	VON MALTZAHN	09:33:41.03	
2006	74	J	WALDER	M	ERAY	09:35:05.93	
2006	82	SM	CHAPMAN	DM	LEWIS	09:40:13.56	
2006	120	KA	FROST	HJ	PITCHFORD	10:08:40.42	
2006	225	A	MULDER	K	VAN DER MERWE	11:09:38.68	
2006	244	D	GELDARD	CH	GIBBINGS	11:17:04.29	
2006	255	S	BOHNSACK	MSI	KING	11:24:01.64	
2006	315	KA	HOWE	VA	CHIAZZARI	11:48:01.93	
Junior men							
2006	8	S	BIRD	CM	SCHOEMAN	08:12:20.48	*
2006	36	B	BINNEKADE	WBA	MAC NICOL	08:51:11.14	
2006	45	CK	BIRKETT	MD	PATRICK	09:01:00.03	

RESULTS OF THE DUSI CANOE MARATHON—1951 TO 2006

YEAR	POS	I1	NAME1	I2	NAME2	TIME	REC
Junior women							
2006	315	KA	HOWE	VA	CHIAZZARI	11:48:01.93	
2006	328	AB	ADIE	R	KIME	11:54:22.92	
U21 men							
2006	4	CG	TURTON	S	VAN GYSEN	07:56:07.04	*
2006	27	BD	PARSONAGE	SP	GRIFFIN	08:42:03.42	
2006	37	GJ	EDMONDS	DA	OELLERMANN	08:53:23.40	
U21 women							
2006	225	A	MULDER	K	VAN DER MERWE	11:09:38.68	
Mixed Doubles							
2006	50	DJ	GERMIQUET	MD	GERMIQUET	09:07:03.67	*
2006	52	MA	STOTHARD	AJ	RAWLINSON	09:09:47.76	
2006	75	RC	WHITTON	CS	WHITTON	09:35:07.53	
Sub Veteran Men							
2006	11	MA	STEWART	B	COLLYER	08:14:51.96	*
2006	31	MJA	DE VILLIERS	SC	BOTHA	08:45:31.43	
2006	33	MIJ	BELL	F	DEYZEL	08:48:34.23	
Sub Veteran Women							
2006	244	D	GELDARD	CH	GIBBINGS	11:17:04.29	*
2006	965	AL	CAMP	E	BUYS	19:16:50.21	
Veteran Men							
2006	24	GA	HILLIAR	GJ	WAUD	08:38:20.32	
2006	29	E	HILDEBRANDT	B	FOKKENS	08:42:05.90	*
2006	41	RA	PEPPER	JD	TUTTON	08:56:54.85	
Veteran Women							
2006	255	S	BOHNSACK	MSI	KING	11:24:01.64	*
2006	370	OA	MORFORD	J	OLIVER	12:08:23.76	
2006	468	EM	NEL	DRJ	VAN BART	12:43:46.35	
Sub Master Men							
2006	22	BC	WENKE	PJ	STRICKLAND	08:35:00.29	*
2006	51	D	BIGGS	M	PREEN	09:09:34.06	
2006	75	RC	WHITTON	CS	WHITTON	09:35:07.53	
Sub Master Women							
2006	808	E	MAREE	K	LAPACZ	15:03:35.37	
2006	874	JLR	MANNING	L	VAN EEDEN	15:50:45.87	
Master Men							
2006	30	G	POPE-ELLIS	DIR	RAWLINSON	08:45:29.45	*
2006	98	WH	KUNZ	RF	DELHOVE	09:49:15.45	
2006	106	PH	SYMONS	SF	SEGAL	09:57:34.09	
Sub Grand Master Men							
2006	282	AC	JONES	BA	BAXTER	11:35:41.93	
2006	424	JA	ROWAN	DC	COOPER	12:25:29.81	
2006	495	CH	WATTS	R	BOURNE-LANGE	12:52:14.45	

YEAR	POS	I1	NAME1	I2	NAME2	TIME	REC
Sub Grand Master Women							
2006	733	J	BAIN	LG	ATTWELL	14:25:56.18	*
Grand Master Men							
2006	222	NE	BLUE	WW	DEYZEL	11:09:13.87	*
2006	547	AJ	VISSER	MD	WILMOT	13:06:29.17	
2006	788	PA	COOKE	J	NEL	14:49:54.00	

Non Stop Dusi

Early Non Stop Dusi Times Prior to Official Race

Year		Name 1	Surname 1	Name 2	Surname 2	Time	Record
1974	K1	JOHN	FOX		LEDEBOER	15:50:00.00	* K1
1974	K1	PHILLIP	NOBLE			15:50:00.00	* K1
1982	K1	RICHARD	STARR			12:20:00.00	*
1985	K2	STEVE	BLACK	CHRIS	GREEF	10:36:00.00	
1985	K1	STEVE	BLACK	JOHN	MURRAY	11:37:00.00	* K1
1987	K2	RICHARD	STARR	KEVIN	MCLELLAND	11:22:00.00	
1996	K2	KEVIN	WHITE	MIKE	MCDONALD	09:53:00.00	*

Non Stop Dusi Race Results

Year	POS	Name 1	Surname 1	Name 2	Surname 2	Time	Record
Senior Men							
1997	1	JOHN	EDMONDS	ANDREW	EDMONDS	08:42:46.00	
1997	2	WAYNE	VOLEK	GARY	CLARKE	08:45:15.00	
1997	3	GLENN	HILLIAR	KENNY	REYNOLDS	08:59:14.00	
Senior Women							
1997	11	DEBBY	WHITTON	WENDY	WHITE	10:36:29.00	*
Senior Men							
1998	1	KEVIN	WHITE	JAMES	LESLIE	07:53:06.16	
1998	2	MARK	PERROW	NEAL	EVANS	08:02:27.06	
1998	3	GARY	CLARKE	WAYNE	VOLEK	08:04:40.75	
Senior Women							
1998	21	WENDY	WHITE	DEBBY	WHITTON	09:34:01.53	*
Mixed Double							
1998	14	BRUCE	WENKE	HEATHER	WENKE	09:19:32.50	*
Senior Men							
1999	1	GAVIN	TARR	MARTIN	DREYER	08:21:24.30	
1999	2	JOHN	EDMONDS	ANDREW	EDMONDS	08:21:24.52	
1999	3	GRANT	WILSON	PIERS	CRUICKSHANKS	09:06:05.16	
Senior Women							
1999	13	DEBBY	WHITTON	WENDY	WHITE	10:36:32.18	
Mixed Double							
1999	18	TERSUS	VILJOEN	SUE	WHITEAR	11:14:11.98	

Senior Men

Year	Pos	Paddler 1	Paddler 2	Time
2000	1	JOHN EDMONDS	ANDREW EDMONDS	07:47:47.31 *
2000	2	KEVIN WHITE	JAMES VAUGHN	07:48:16.15
2000	3	WARREN PRICE	RICHARDSON	08:07:42.12

Mixed Double

Year	Pos	Paddler 1	Paddler 2	Time
2000	8	GARY WAUD	DEBBIE HOLTE-SMITH	09:37:51.10

Senior Men

Year	Pos	Paddler 1	Paddler 2	Time
2001	1	MARTIN DREYER	RORY COLE	07:58:05.50
2001	2	WARREN PRICE	SCOTT MAYNARD	08:06:45.97
2001	3	GLENN HILLIAR	RICHARD STRICKLAND	08:47:41.67

Mixed Double

Year	Pos	Paddler 1	Paddler 2	Time
2001	15	GARY WAUD	SUSAN WHITEAR	09:53:13.47

Senior Women

Year	Pos	Paddler 1	Paddler 2	Time
2002	17	DEBBIE GERMIQUET	JEANNETTE WALDER	09:57:31.48
2002	44	LORNA OLIVER	ELLE DE LA PORT	11:20:23.72

Mixed Double

Year	Pos	Paddler 1	Paddler 2	Time
2002	5	KEVIN WHITE	WENDY WHITE	09:04:57.74

Senior Men

Year	Pos	Paddler 1	Paddler 2	Time
2003	1	DEON BRUSS	SCOTT MAYNARD	08:46:33.34
2003	2	MARTIN DREYER	JASON GRAHAM	08:56:51.09
2003	3	CRAIG NORRIS	LANCE CHAPMAN	09:48:44.12

Mixed Double

Year	Pos	Paddler 1	Paddler 2	Time
2003	4	KEVIN WHITE	WENDY WHITE	09:56:28.30

Senior Men

Year	Pos	Paddler 1	Paddler 2	Time
2004	1	MARTIN DREYER	RORY COLE	08:18:22.19
2004	2	PIERS CRUICKSHANK	JACQUES THERON	08:44:27.98
2004	3	WAYNE VOLEK	WARREN PRICE	08:45:51.60

Senior Women

Year	Pos	Paddler 1	Paddler 2	Time
2004	51	CAROL JOYCE	SANDRA EARDLEY	12:18:46.75

Mixed Double

Year	Pos	Paddler 1	Paddler 2	Time
2004	6	DEON BRUSS	LAURA THOMPSON	08:48:54.46

Senior Men

Year	Pos	Paddler 1	Paddler 2	Time
2005	1	MARTIN DREYER	CRAIG TURTON	08:20:22.52
2005	2	LOVEDAY ZONDI	MICHAEL STEWART	08:47:20.63
2005	3	THOMAS NGIDI	BRANDON COLLYER	08:50:45.53

Senior Women

Year	Pos	Paddler 1	Paddler 2	Time
2005	56	LORNA OLIVER	ELLE JAMES	12:43:25.00

Mixed Double

Year	Pos	Paddler 1	Paddler 2	Time
2005	12	MANDY RAWLINS	RHYS FOSTER	10:20:36.56

Senior Men

Year	Pos	Paddler 1	Paddler 2	Time
2006	1	HANK MC GREGOR	STU RAWLINSON	07:58:39.71
2006	2	GRAHAM BIRD	MICHAEL STEWART	08:07:01.82
2006	3	MICHAEL MBANJWA		08:16:06.31

Senior Women

Year	Pos	Paddler 1	Paddler 2	Time
2006	17	DEBBIE GERMIQUET	ALICE RAWLINSON	09:50:24.45
2006	23	LORNA OLIVER	MANDY AUSTEN-SMITH	10:19:51.50

Mixed Double

Year	Pos	Paddler 1	Paddler 2	Time
2006	32	JULIA NORTON	CRAIG REES	10:35:16.25

* K1

LIST OF ALL FINISHERS IN THE DUSI CANOE MARATHON—1951 TO 2006

AAB,CJ-1
AAB,G-3
AARON,GN-4
ABBOT,B-1
ABBOTT,N-1
ABENDANON,M-3
ABKIN,MN-1
ABOUD,MM-2
ABRAHAM,G-2
ABRAMS,JP-4
ABRAMS,JA-1
ABSALOM,RA-1
ACKER,R-3
ACKERMAN,GJ-4
ACKERMAN,JS-2
ACKERMAN,R-1
ACKERMANN,JB-1
ACRES,JF-1
ACUTT,B-12
ACUTT,DH-2
ACUTT,MC-4
ACUTT,RN-2
ACUTT,SC-3
ADAM,J-1
ADAM,C-1
ADAMS,B-1
ADAMS,KC-6
ADAMS,WM-21
ADAMS,C-5
ADAMS,K-1
ADDICOTT,JR-2
ADDIS,PT-1
ADDIS,CJ-1
ADDISON,RJ-1
ADDY,C-1
ADENDORFF,NB-5
ADENDORFF,B-1
ADENDORFF,CM-2
ADENDORFF,C-2
ADEY,CC-3
ADIE,AB-3
ADIE,C-2
ADIE,G-2
ADIE,PM-2
ADKIN,A-4

ADKIN,K-6
ADKIN,H-3
ADRAIN,J-1
ADRIAN,JW-4
AFRICA,GD-1
AFRIKA,M-2
AGAR,D-7
AIKEN,RP-13
AINGE,W-2
AINSWORTH,RA-1
AITCHISON,KC-1
AITKEN,AP-1
AITKEN,J-2
AITKEN,D-1
ALBERS,GB-8
ALBERTS,LA-1
ALBERTYN,A-2
ALBERTYN,J-1
ALBERTYN,TJ-1
ALBERTYN,W-2
ALBOROUGH,DL-5
ALBOROUGH,J-42
ALBOROUGH,TA-11
ALBOROUGH,BJ-1
ALBOROUGH,C-1
ALBOROUGH,DL-2
ALBRIGHTSON,J-1
ALBRIGHTSON,N-1
ALDERSON,GD-3
ALDWORTH,BM-3
ALDWORTH,D-1
ALDWORTH,MD-22
ALEXANDER,A-3
ALEXANDER,RG-2
ALEXANDER,BR-1
ALEXANDER,DR-2
ALFONSO,MF-1
ALFORD,M-2
ALGIE,PJ-1
ALING,R-3
ALISON,AW-1

ALLAN,BC-3
ALLAN,BD-4
ALLAN,D-1
ALLAN,MD-6
ALLAN,R-3
ALLAN,JG-4
ALLAN,E-1
ALLAN,J-7
ALLCHIN,RJ-10
ALLEN,BD-1
ALLEN,J-1
ALLEN,M-1
ALLEN,MW-24
ALLEN,PM-1
ALLEN,RJ-2
ALLEN,CA-1
ALLEN,DM-1
ALLENBERG,R-1
ALLETSON,J-2
ALLISON,A-1
ALLISON,E-1
ALLISON,JM-1
ALLKINS,RP-1
ALLKINS,JR-15
ALLMAN,LD-1
ALLNATT,RM-1
ALLWOOD,BH-12
ALTERN,MK-1
ALTMANN,J-2
ALVIN,M-16
AMBLER,M-3
AMBLER-SMITH,RC-2
AMOS,PG-7
AMOS,SA-2
ANAGNOSTU,AD-2
ANDERS,PT-4
ANDERS,R-1
ANDERSON,CR-2
ANDERSON,CJ-11
ANDERSON,DS-6
ANDERSON,G-8
ANDERSON,GM-5
ANDERSON,JP-2
ANDERSON,J-7
ANDERSON,JL-3

ANDERSON,K-2
ANDERSON,R-1
ANDERSON,SJ-10
ANDERSON,SI-4
ANDERSON,SA-2
ANDERSON,B-1
ANDERSON,C-1
ANDERSON,G-1
ANDERSON,LW-1
ANDERSON,BD-1
ANDERSON,P-2
ANDERSON,W-2
ANDERSON-READE,MD-2
ANDERTON,A-3
ANDREW,BC-1
ANDREW,CM-5
ANDREW,KG-2
ANDREW,?-1
ANDREWS,CG-7
ANDREWS,D-8
ANDREWS,H-5
ANDREWS,TD-1
ANGEL,M-2
ANGEL,RL-2
ANGELOS,GJ-1
ANGUS,C-2
ANGUS,J-2
ANNANDALE,SE-5
ANTILL,GM-1
ANTROBUS,D-10
ANTROBUS,B-1
APPEL,D-2
APOSTILIDES,PA-1
APOSTOLIDES,PA-2
APPELGRYN,M-5
APPELT,RE-1
APPLETON,A-1
APPLETON,K-4
APPLETON,MD-5
APPLEWHITE,M-2
ARBUTHNOT,G-15
ARBUTHNOT,MM-16
ARBUTHNOT,RM-3
ARBUTHNOT,AJ-1
ARCHIBALD,JG-1

ARDAIN,MM-3
ARDE,BA-2
ARDE,LA-2
AREND,OP-2
ARMDORF,R-8
ARMITAGE,J-10
ARMITAGE,S-1
ARMOUR,C-2
ARMOUR,D-19
ARMOUR,RB-5
ARMOUR,SI-1
ARMSTRONG,AC-21
ARMSTRONG,AJ-3
ARMSTRONG,A-1
ARMSTRONG,BL-6
ARMSTRONG,DW-5
ARMSTRONG,G-8
ARMSTRONG,G-3
ARMSTRONG,JA-2
ARMSTRONG,KC-5
ARMSTRONG,NB-5
ARMSTRONG,P-4
ARMSTRONG,T-1
ARMSTRONG,V-25
ARMSTRONG,KS-4
ARMSTRONG,MF-1
ARNDT,D-2
ARNDT,E-3
ARNOLD,JP-10
ARNOLD,KS-11
ARNOLD,RB-4
ARNOLD,S-1
ARNOLDS,J-1
ARNOT,D-6
ARNOT,RF-4
ARNOTT,JW-2
ARNOTT,TR-1
ARNOTT,P-5
ARPIN,J-20
ARPIN,MH-4
ARPIN,N-5
ARPIN,D-2
ARTHUR,J-7
ARTHUR,J-7
ARTHUR,MJ-1
ARTHUR,MJ-2

ARTHUR,M-4
ARTHUR,SJ-2
ARTHUR,MJ-1
ARTHUR,RE-1
ASCANI,GJ-2
ASH,RG-5
ASHER,BJ-4
ASHER,J-1
ASHER,SN-1
ASKEW,PS-7
ATHERSTONE,N-2
ATHERSTONE,R-1
ATKIN,D-1
ATKINS,TM-3
ATKINS,SA-2
ATKINSON,AR-1
ATKINSON,CJ-2
ATKINSON,G-9
ATKINSON,MM-3
ATLAS,D-1
ATTRIDGE,RJ-4
ATTRIDGE,MG-1
ATTWELL,G-5
ATTWELL,LG-5
ATTWOOD-SMITH,DJ-3
ATWOOD-SMITH,N-1
AUGUST,WM-2
AULSEBROOK,JF-1
AUSTEN,NW-2
AUSTEN-SMITH,B-11
AUSTEN-SMITH,MA-4
AUSTIN,BM-7
AUSTIN,G-5
AUSTIN,GW-5
AUSTIN,MG-2
AUSTIN,QM-2
AUSTIN,RG-3
AUSTIN,R-12
AUSTIN,SM-2
AUSTIN,A-2
AVENONT,N-1
AVIS,L-1
AYLIFFE,AM-7
AYLIFFE,MC-6
AYLIFFE,R-4

AYLING,M-4
AYLING,P-3
AYLING,R-1
AYLWARD,D-1
AYRES,D-3
AYRES,K-4
BOWMAN,RS-1
BAARD,B-1
BAARS,GC-1
BAARS,B-1
BAAS,RA-1
BABICH,GP-3
BACKE-HANSEN,SR-1
BACKHOUSE,CA-5
BACK-WELL,R-1
BADENHORST,DB-1
BADENHORST,LL-8
BADENHORST,A-1
BADENHORST,DB-1
BADENHORST,MM-3
BADENHORST,J-1
BADER,B-4
BADHAM,P-3
BADISH,DR-3
BADSTUBNER,UC-1
BAGLEY,WR-2
BAGNALL,SR-1
BAILEY,DW-2
BAILEY,FW-1
BAILEY,JW-9
BAILEY,NJ-3
BAILEY,PD-2
BAILEY,A-1
BAILEY,B-1
BAILEY,RM-1
BAILING,B-1
BAILLIE,DA-1
BAIN,J-8
BAIN,TT-13
BAINS,SS-1
BAINES,G-1
BAINES,JR-1
BAIRD,AG-4
BAIRD,GA-2
BAIRD,SD-1
BAISE,SD-1

BAKER,AK-2
BAKER,G-5
BAKER,G-3
BAKER,JF-9
BAKER,R-3
BAKER,SM-4
BAKER,SC-2
BAKER,TE-3
BAKER,W-14
BAKER,D-1
BAKER,F-1
BAKER,KD-1
BALDERSON,C-5
BALDWIN,PW-1
BALL,KT-1
BALL,MB-3
BALLADON,M-7
BALLANCE,DC-8
BALLANCE,JT-2
BALLARD,BA-1
BALLENDEN,M-7
BALLOT,CC-1
BALME,AH-18
BALME,GA-7
BALSDON,G-2
BALSDON,BJ-1
BAM,AJ-2
BAM,M-1
BAMBUS,C-4
BAN,A-2
BANDS,PM-5
BANEY,D-1
BANFIELD,BD-3
BANFIELD,P-1
BANKS,B-1
BANKS,D-5
BANKS,M-4
BANKS,WR-1
BANNOCK,PG-2
BANTJES,M-5
BANTIES,M-1
BANTOCK,S-4
BARACHEVY,KC-1
BARAGWANATH,BO-1
BARBEAU,JR-1

LIST OF ALL FINISHERS IN THE DUSI CANOE MARATHON—1951 TO 2006

BARBEAU,R - 1
BARBER,MG - 3
BARBER,GD - 1
BARBER,TJ - 1
BARCLAY,CF - 3
BARCLAY,J - 2
BARDSLEY,D - 3
BARENDSE,M - 3
BARENDSE,CM - 1
BARENDSE,N - 3
BARGATE,G - 11
BARGATE,K - 2
BARICHIEVY,N - 4
BARK,D - 9
BARK,J - 10
BARK,M - 17
BARKER,H - 3
BARKER,K - 3
BARKER,C - 2
BARLOW,KJ - 5
BARLOW,MA - 3
BARLOW,WE - 8
BARNARD,E - 1
BARNARD,GE - 2
BARNARD,JH - 7
BARNARD,R - 1
BARNARD,SE - 4
BARNARD,M - 1
BARNARDO,MP - 7
BARNARDO,P - 2
BARNES,AB - 6
BARNES,AB - 4
BARNES,G - 1
BARNES,AC - 1
BARNES,PR - 1
BARNETT,AJ - 1
BARNITT,N - 1
BARNS,AB - 1
BARR,WG - 1
BARRACLOUGH,HA - 5
BARRACLOUGH,J - 1
BARRACLOUGH,N - 3
BARRACLOUGH,CJ - 3
BARRACLOUGH,I - 1

BARRACLOUGH,YR - 1
BARRAS,T - 1
BARRATT,MR - 1
BARRETT,OJ - 19
BARRETT,BE - 11
BARRETT,L - 1
BARRINGTON,AL - 13
BARRINGTON,JM - 2
BARRON,MJ - 8
BARRON,W - 7
BARRON,K - 1
BARROW,CJ - 2
BARROW,JR - 4
BARROW,RR - 1
BARRY,AC - 1
BARRY,CL - 12
BARRY,E - 5
BARRY,M - 12
BARRY,S - 1
BARRY,T - 2
BARTER,A - 1
BARTHO,B - 2
BARTHO,DL - 5
BARTHO,WG - 1
BARTHOLOMEW,J - 1
BARTLET,PW - 5
BARTLETT,JF - 3
BARTLETT,CR - 4
BARTLETT,G - 1
BARTLETT,LW - 3
BARTLETT,PW - 1
BARTLETT,R - 3
BARTLETT,T - 6
BARTLETT,SW - 1
BARTLETT,WM - 1
BARTON,JR - 6
BARTON,NC - 6
BARTON,G - 1
BARWICK,DW - 1
BASHFORD,G - 1
BASKIN,B - 1
BASS,J - 2
BASSETT,D - 1
BASSETT,P - 2

BASSINGTHWAITE,F - 1
BASSINGTHWAITE,P - 1
BASSON,J - 3
BASSON,JM - 1
BASSON,JT - 3
BASSON,PW - 3
BASTARD,N - 1
BATEMAN,B - 8
BATEMAN,CB - 3
BATEMAN,RG - 21
BATEMAN,HG - 1
BATH,AJ - 8
BATH,GS - 2
BATH,AM - 3
BATH,JM - 1
BATTENH,H - 1
BATTERSHILL,WL - 5
BAUER,JL - 3
BAUER,S - 1
BAUM,C - 2
BAUMAN,P - 1
BAUMANN,MD - 1
BAXENDALE,S - 2
BAXTER,BA - 26
BAXTER,JL - 3
BAXTER,LC - 1
BAXTER,S - 3
BAXTER,W - 1
BAXTER,AC - 1
BAXTER,MG - 3
BAXTER,MJ - 13
BAYES,K - 11
BEADLE,A - 5
BEADLE,G - 1
BEALE,SR - 1
BEARD,GP - 1
BEARPARK,DL - 5
BEARPARK,NI - 6
BEATTIE,DK - 1
BEATTIE,S - 1
BEATTIE,H - 2
BEATTY,JN - 1
BEAUMONT,AC - 3
BEAUMONT,E - 7
BEAUMONT,GI - 1

BEAUMONT,J - 1
BEAUMONT,SN - 6
BEBINGTON,G - 1
BECHET,M - 1
BECK,ML - 4
BECKER,JF - 1
BECKER,MA - 2
BECKER,WF - 1
BECKER,AJ - 1
BECKET,M - 1
BECKETT,G - 1
BECKETT,A - 2
BECKLEY,JM - 16
BEDDOW,R - 1
BEECHING,AJ - 1
BEER,R - 1
BEES,AP - 1
BEESLEY,AD - 1
BEESTON,K - 1
BEEVER,RD - 1
BEGG,K - 2
BEGNI,M - 1
BEHN,G - 14
BEHR,DO - 5
BEHRANS,M - 1
BEHRENS,CB - 7
BEHRENS,M - 1
BEHRMANN,JW - 4
BEITH,AD - 2
BELCHER,R - 1
BELING,D - 3
BELLA,A - 2
BELL,C - 1
BELL,J - 1
BELL,MJ - 18
BELL,RJ - 3
BELL,S - 4
BELLINGAN,PW - 1
BELLINGHAM,P - 1
BENARD,W - 1
BENETTI,T - 1
BENHAM,B - 15
BENHAM,LJ - 8

BENJAMIN,B - 1
BENN,LC - 1
BENNET,AR - 1
BENNET,G - 1
BENNETT,GE - 1
BENNETT,G - 19
BENNETT,GI - 1
BENNETT,JF - 5
BENNETT,MA - 5
BENNETT,MS - 3
BENNETT,MA - 1
BENNETT,NR - 5
BENNETT,P - 2
BENNETT,K - 3
BENNETT,WA - 1
BENSE,RE - 5
BENSE,KP - 2
BENSON,J - 8
BENSON-ARMER,R - 2
BENTLEY,J - 10
BENTLEY,DG - 5
BENTLEY,PJ - 6
BENTLEY,RB - 1
BENTLY,G - 1
BERANGE,PD - 1
BERESFORD,JH - 3
BERESFORD,M - 1
BERESFORD,P - 1
BERG,G - 13
BERGH,G - 2
BERGSET,PJ - 2
BERKS,AN - 5
BERLYN,T - 1
BERMAN,MH - 1
BERMAN,J - 1
BERNHARD,DE - 8
BERNHARD,KD - 8
BERNHARD,OL - 1
BERNING,J - 5
BERRIDGE,E - 7
BERRIDGE,IT - 1
BERRIMAN,AC - 5
BERRIMAN,B - 2
BERRY,BN - 1
BERRY,DM - 5

BERRY,RC - 8
BERRY,R - 2
BERRY,RJ - 2
BERRY,SR - 2
BERRY,WD - 1
BERVOETS,AA - 1
BESNARD,LM - 2
BESSLER,N - 29
BESTEL,A - 1
BESTEL,CA - 12
BESTEL,TC - 3
BESTER,C - 2
BESTER,L - 1
BESTER,AJ - 1
BESTER,G - 1
BESTER,MJ - 1
BESTER,N - 4
BESTER,P - 1
BESTER,R - 1
BESWETHERICK,C - 10
BESWETHERICK,S - 1
BESWICK,AB - 3
BETTY,C - 2
BEUKES,C - 1
BEUKES,J - 3
BEUKES,K - 2
BEUKES,S - 2
BEULES,B - 1
BEVELO,G - 1
BEVERIDGE,AJ - 1
BEVOLO,GG - 1
BEYTHIEN,R - 1
BEZUIDENHOUT,A - 4
BEZUIDENHOUT,A - 1
BEZUIDENHOUT,D - 5
BEZUIDENHOUT,G - 1
BEZUIDENHOUT,K - 1
BEZUIDENHOUT,ME - 1
BEZUIDENHOUT,RM - 5
BEZUIDENHOUT,JJ - 1
BHENGU,HS - 2
BIANCOTTI,MJ - 1
BICCARD,BM - 7
BICCARD,PA - 4
BIDDULPH,SJ - 2

BIEBUYCK,AM - 2
BIELA,R - 1
BIELDT,L - 2
BIEN,AM - 1
BIETJE,J - 3
BIGGS,D - 12
BIGGS,JS - 7
BIGGS,M - 1
BIGGS,PF - 1
BIGGS,SS - 11
BIGGS,T - 11
BIGGS,AM - 1
BIGGS,B - 1
BIGGS,H - 1
BIGGS,S - 1
BILJOEN,W - 2
BINDLEY,D - 1
BINEDELL,SJ - 13
BINEDELL,ML - 2
BINGHAM,C - 3
BINGHAM,G - 1
BINIKOS,Z - 2
BINNEKADE,B - 4
BINNENDYK,AR - 6
BINNENDYK,SE - 2
BINNS,R - 2
BIRCH,G - 2
BIRCH,M - 3
BIRCH,RA - 2
BIRCHALL,B - 2
BIRCHAM,JB - 1
BIRD,B - 4
BIRD,DS - 7
BIRD,GM - 9
BIRD,MS - 5
BIRD,S - 3
BIRKETT,AJ - 2
BIRKETT,CK - 3
BIRKETT,DC - 7
BIRKETT,J - 4
BIRKETT,PD - 4
BIRKETT,AM - 1
BIRTHWISTLE,M - 1
BIRTWHISTLE,MK - 1
BISCHOFF,AD - 1

BISHOP,DR - 1
BISHOP,G - 12
BISSCHOFF,JJ - 1
BISSCHOP,M - 1
BISSETT,AJ - 3
BISSETT,RD - 3
BISSETT,PW - 1
BIZZELL,SL - 3
BJORSETH,L - 3
BLACK,AM - 5
BLACK,AN - 17
BLACK,R - 3
BLACK,S - 18
BLACK,C - 1
BLACK,DA - 3
BLACK,GA - 1
BLACKBEARD,L - 13
BLACKBURN,AB - 2
BLACKBURN,PJ - 1
BLACKBURN,J - 2
BLACKLAWS,J - 4
BLACKLAWS,D - 1
BLAESER,B - 5
BLAIR,B - 1
BLAIR,D - 19
BLAKE,E - 3
BLAKE,LP - 3
BLAKE,C - 1
BLAKER,R - 2
BLANCKENBERG,S - 1
BLAND,HG - 10
BLEND,H - 3
BLEWETT,CJ - 1
BLIGHT,D - 5
BLIGHT,L - 2
BLIGNAUT,B - 1
BLIGNAUT,MJ - 4
BLIGNAUT,SJ - 1
BLIGNAUT,TJ - 2
BLITENTHALL,C - 4
BLOEM,C - 5
BLOEMINK,S - 2
BLOFIELD,PC - 3
BLOMFIELD,BG - 2
BLOMFIELD,D - 2

LIST OF ALL FINISHERS IN THE DUSI CANOE MARATHON—1951 TO 2006

BROOKE,D-1
BROOKE,R-1
BROOKES,R-1
BROOKES,SR-1
BROOKS,TP-2
BROOME,A-1
BROOME,W-2
BROOMHEAD,GI-2
BROUGHTONM-14
BROUGHTON,GM-1
BROUWER,PE-2
BROWN,A-4
BROWN,CA-3
BROWN,C-20
BROWN,C-10
BROWN,CF-1
BROWN,DV-2
BROWN,G-8
BROWN,GI-1
BROWN,GD-10
BROWN,H-7
BROWN,JE-2
BROWN,M-3
BROWN,N-1
BROWN,RC-1
BROWN,WM-7
BROWN,RA-1
BROWN,EJ-6
BROWN,HE-1
BROWN,L-1
BROWN,P-1
BROWN,S-2
BROWN,T-1
BROWNE,C-1
BROWNE,HL-2
BROWNE,RA-4
BROWNE,RA-1
BROWNIE,MR-3
BROWSE,TC-7
BROWSE,TJ-1
BRUCE,GI-1
BRUCE,AE-1
BRUCE,ME-2
BRUMMER,J-2

BRINK,E-2
BRINK,W-1
BRINK,J-7
BRINK,M-1
BRINKMAN,J-1
BRISSENDEN,AR-2
BRISTOL,F-4
BRISTOW,VA-1
BRISTOW,DM-7
BRISTOW,PA-2
BRITS,M-2
BRITTEN,SP-9
BRITTON,GE-1
BRITZ,B-5
BRITZ,D-1
BRITZ,MA-8
BRITZ,P-6
BRITZ,W-2
BRITZ,N-1
BRITZ,PI-1
BRITZ,RJ-1
BROADFOOT,DE-1
BROADWAY,J-1
BROADWAY,C-1
BROCKELHURST,E-1
BROCKLEHURST,B-1
BROCKLEHURST,WA-2
BROCKMAN,A-2
BROKENSHA,BS-2
BROKENSHA,PD-5
BROKENSHA,DR-1
BROKENSHA,R-1
BROKENSHA,SV-1
BROKINSHA,R-1
BROMFIELD,KO-2
BROMFIELD,SK-4
BROMFIELD,WR-2
BROMFIELD,G-1
BROMFIELD,LI-2
BROMLEY,CL-1
BROMLEY,NJ-3
BRON,C-2
BROOK,CF-2
BROOK,R-1
BROOKE,CF-1

BRAY,R-4
BRAY,R-2
BRAY,W-3
BRAZIER,DL-4
BRAZIER,G-1
BRAZIER,ML-1
BREBNER,J-3
BREDELL,MA-1
BREDENKAMP,A-3
BREDENKAMP,J-1
BREEDT,M-1
BREEDT,PH-2
BREETZKE,BJ-2
BREMNER,ME-12
BREMNER,B-1
BRENNAN,R-2
BRENNON,R-2
BRENTLEY,MJ-1
BRENTZEY,K-1
BRETT,CA-7
BRETT,M-17
BRETT,JM-6
BREWITT,PR-10
BREWITT,RJ-4
BRIANT,RJ-1
BRICKELL,D-3
BRICKHILL,D-1
BRICKWELL,DA-1
BRIDGEFORD,S-1
BRIDGES,P-4
BRIEDENHANN,JL-3
BRIGGS,CF-2
BRIGGS,DL-1
BRIGGS,D-18
BRIGGS,N-31
BRIGGS,GR-1
BRIGGS,RF-1
BRIGHT,MW-3
BRIGHT,W-1
BRIGHTON,DP-1
BRIGHTWELL,R-1
BRIMACOMBE,CG-1
BRIMACOMBE,GC-5
BRIMACOMBE,NG-14
BRIMACOMBE,S-4

BOWLEY,BA-2
BOWLEY,S-1
BOWMAN,KS-1
BOWMAN,R-4
BOWMAN,M-1
BOYD,GM-7
BOYD,WL-3
BOYES,B-2
BOYES,C-1
BOYES,DN-18
BOYES,JD-7
BOYES,MI-1
BOYLEY,S-1
BOZZONE,R-1
BRACKLEY,GF-5
BRADFIELD,C-3
BRADFIELD,BT-1
BRADFORD,CS-1
BRADFORD,FB-1
BRADFORD,GN-1
BRADING,AS-3
BRADLEY,A-3
BRADLEY,CM-1
BRADSHAW,L-4
BRAID,S-1
BRAITHWAITE,B-4
BRAITHWAITE,G-3
BRAMMAGE,DN-2
BRAMTONJN-1
BRAND,CP-4
BRAND,DG-5
BRAND,F-1
BRAND,NR-2
BRANDON,R-1
BRANDON-KIRBY,K-1
BRANDT,A-1
BRASH,E-2
BRAUM,D-2
BRAUN,QD-2
BRAUTESETH,DR-3
BRAUTESETH,S-1
BRAUTESETH,CA-1
BRAUTESETH,M-2
BRAUTESETH,NL-1
BRAY,MA-7

BOTHA,T-6
BOTHA,V-2
BOTHA,A-1
BOTHA,A-3
BOTHA,D-4
BOTHA,EA-1
BOTHA,F-1
BOTHA,H-3
BOTHA,J-1
BOTHA,J-1
BOTHA,M-2
BOTHA,M-2
BOTHA,N-1
BOTHA,RM-1
BOTHA,SR-1
BOTHA,DG-8
BOTHMA,EC-18
BOUCHER,GG-5
BOUCHET,GI-2
BOUDRENGHIEN,PJ-1
BOUIC,JM-1
BOULLE,GM-1
BOULLE,VI-7
BOURGIN,G-1
BOURNE LANGE,M-1
BOURNE-LANGE,R-33
BOURNE-LANGE,M-2
BOUSTRED,RN-1
BOUWER,J-1
BOUWER,SF-1
BOWDEN,L-1
BOWDEN,DC-1
BOWDEN,E-2
BOWDEN,GS-1
BOWDEN,S-2
BOWEN,R-15
BOWEN,CR-1
BOWES,G-2
BOWES,DK-3
BOWES,RI-8
BOWIE,J-1
BOWLER,MN-4
BOWLES,DC-4
BOWLES,LG-1

BLOMKAMP,L-3
BLOMQUIST,PA-1
BLOUNT,P-13
BLUE,N-29
BLUMRICK,DL-1
BLUNT,G-1
BLYTH,C-2
BLYTH,IJ-1
BOAKE,D-1
BOASE,NE-1
BOAST,GB-18
BOCKMAIER,SP-1
BODDY,IH-6
BODE,KA-1
BODLEY,D-3
BOEHM,E-1
BOHM,AI-7
BOHM,D-14
BOHN,RW-3
BOHNKE,T-1
BOHNSACK,A-7
BOHNSACK,GH-5
BOHNSACK,J-7
BOHNSACK,S-13
BOK,SN-1
BOLKMAIER,S-1
BOLLSTRED,RN-2
BOLT,A-3
BOLTON,AR-5
BOLTON,DA-5
BOLTON,GB-6
BOLTON,JK-6
BOLTON,MC-3
BOLTON,RG-5
BOLTON,WA-6
BOLTON,B-1
BOLTON,G-1
BOLTON,HA-1
BOLTON,PE-1
BOLTON,R-1
BOLTON,RG-1
BOLTON,RG-1
BOLZE,SL-2
BOMPAS,G-6
BOMPAS,J-6

BONAMOUR,AD-6
BOND,CJ-3
BOND,JE-2
BOND,S-1
BOND,W-2
BOND,CE-1
BOND,D-1
BOND,J-1
BONFILS-PERSSON,J-3
BONNER,KR-3
BONNET,GC-1
BONNET,PJ-1
BONNEY,G-1
BOON,P-2
BOOSEY,P-3
BOOTE,RN-1
BOOTH,AG-20
BOOTH,A-6
BOOTH,JW-6
BOOTH,K-9
BOOTH,LR-1
BOOTH,SD-1
BOOTH,WR-2
BOOTHWAY,DP-1
BOOYSEN,GP-2
BOOYSEN,A-3
BOOYSEN,AB-8
BOOYSEN,RN-2
BOOYSEN,AG-17
BOOYSEN,B-4
BOOYSEN,CP-5
BOOYSEN,PF-1
BORAIN,G-1
BORAIN,RH-23
BORCHERS,SG-2
BORGATE,A-1
BORGEN,B-1
BORKETT,BD-1
BORLAND,ME-16
BORLAND,BT-1
BORLAND,KP-2
BORNMAN,PF-2
BORROWDALE,J-1
BORTHWICK,D-1
BORTHWICK,GP-1

BOSCH,CP-1
BOSCH,E-3
BOSCH,H-1
BOSCH,M-1
BOSCH,G-1
BOSCH,R-1
BOSENBERG,AT-6
BOSENBERG,CH-1
BOSHOFF,B-1
BOSHOFF,C-5
BOSHOFF,DA-5
BOSHOFF,JD-3
BOSHOFF,SE-6
BOSMAN,A-4
BOSMAN,J-2
BOSMAN,DL-1
BOSMAN,M-4
BOSSE,J-1
BOSSE,KJ-1
BOSWARVA,J-1
BOTES,FT-1
BOTES,J-2
BOTES,TJ-21
BOTES,B-1
BOTES,C-2
BOTES,DW-1
BOTHA,AJ-21
BOTHA,B-2
BOTHA,G-8
BOTHA,C-20
BOTHA,J-3
BOTHA,JC-3
BOTHA,JP-4
BOTHA,J-5
BOTHA,JW-8
BOTHA,KJ-1
BOTHA,L-4
BOTHA,L-13
BOTHA,M-2
BOTHA,MA-16
BOTHA,M-2
BOTHA,OG-3
BOTHA,P-9
BOTHA,PC-6
BOTHA,SC-12

LIST OF ALL FINISHERS IN THE DUSI CANOE MARATHON—1951 TO 2006

BRUMMER,G- 1
BRUMMER,W- 6
BRUNINGS,RO- 1
BRUNSDEN,CJ- 3
BRUSS,D- 17
BRUSS,H- 5
BRUSS,SR- 11
BRUTON,J- 2
BRUYNS,LI- 5
BRUYNS,SI- 1
BRYANS,R- 2
BRYANT,M- 3
BRYANT,C- 1
BRYCE,B- 1
BRYMER,D- 2
BRYSON,T- 1
BUBB,W- 3
BUBB,MO- 1
BUCHAN,J- 1
BUCHAN,RL- 2
BUCHANAN,KB- 1
BUCHANAN,B- 1
BUCHANAN,WD- 1
BUCHEL,B- 3
BUCHEL,M- 1
BUCKS,S- 4
BUCKE,JD- 2
BUCKINGHAM,RD- 6
BUCKINGHAM,PS- 2
BUCKLEY,GC- 2
BUCKLEY,D- 2
BUDD,L- 4
BUDGER,- 2
BUFFEY,J- 4
BUS,BB- 1
BUTENDAG,JH- 1
BULEY,R- 2
BULLEY,CR- 4
BULLIMORE,SH- 3
BULLOCK,GB- 1
BULLOY,TM- 1
BULWER,J- 2
BUMPSTEAD,A- 1
BUMSTEAD,M- 1
BUMSTEAD,N- 1

BUNDRED,ME- 1
BUNDY,SG- 2
BUNTING,GJ- 1
BURDEN,C- 20
BURDEN,D- 15
BURDEN,GE- 8
BURDEN,JK- 3
BURDEN,NA- 9
BURDEN,PD- 7
BURDEN,RE- 3
BURGEN,SG- 1
BURGER,AD- 4
BURGER,BF- 5
BURGER,D- 4
BURGER,FM- 1
BURGER,GR- 4
BURGER,J- 5
BURGER,PF- 3
BURGER,R- 1
BURGER,RJ- 1
BURGER,R- 1
BURGER,W- 2
BURGER,X- 1
BURGESS,A- 3
BURGESS,SC- 3
BURGESS,T- 5
BURKE,ND- 7
BURKE,B- 2
BURKE,GD- 3
BURMAN,PR- 4
BURMAN,R- 1
BURN,M- 3
BURN,RO- 4
BURNARD,FW- 9
BURNE,C- 1
BURNE,R- 1
BURNE,B- 1
BURNE,M- 2
BURNETT,DC- 1
BURNETT,KC- 5
BURNETT,TA- 4
BURNETT,CB- 3
BURNETT,RE- 1
BURNETT,SA- 1

BURNHAM,S.- 3
BURNILL,BP- 2
BURNS,KW- 3
BURNS,SD- 3
BURNS,BE- 1
BURNS,JT- 1
BURNSIDE,GC- 23
BURRASTON,M- 1
BURRI,M- 1
BURROWS,N- 1
BURSCOUGH,D- 16
BURT,MC- 2
BURT,SD- 3
BURTON,A- 1
BURTON,D- 6
BURTON,JW- 3
BURTON,JR- 1
BURTON,M- 1
BURTON-MOORE,P- 2
BUSBY,A- 1
BUSH,HC- 1
BUSH,MS- 2
BUSH,PR- 5
BUSH,CJ- 1
BUSH,K- 1
BUSSENS,H- 1
BUTCHER,SR- 2
BUTLER,C- 11
BUTLER,SP- 16
BUTLER,RS- 1
BUTLER,B- 1
BUTOW,M- 2
BUTT,JM- 3
BUTT,RD- 1
BUTTNER,EA- 1
BUTTON,AT- 5
BUTTON,DT- 8
BUTTON,JS- 3
BUTTON,LD- 1
BUTTON,ND- 1
BUTTON,SC- 1
BUTTRICK,JL- 3
BUWALDA,SJ- 1

BUXBAUM,SI- 1
BUYS,M- 1
BUYS,P- 1
BUYS,BL- 2
BUYS,EC- 2
BYDAWELL,P- 15
BYE,AR- 2
BYRES,DM- 1
BYRES,KJ- 7
BYRES,MJ- 9
BYRNE,PB- 1
BYRNE,SC- 4
BYRNE,JG- 1
BYRON,M- 1
CABLE,H- 2
CACKETT,RL- 1
CACKETT,RL- 6
CADDICK,G- 5
CADDICK,A- 1
CADIZ,RF- 1
CADLE,MC- 3
CAFFYN-PARSONS,RR- 2
CAHI,SI- 1
CAIN,S- 2
CAINE,BM- 5
CAINE,G- 1
CAINE,J- 4
CAIRNS,AW- 7
CAIRNS,C- 6
CAIRNS,R- 6
CAIRNS,SK- 1
CAIRNS,C- 1
CAIRNS,HL- 2
CAIRNS,J- 1
CAIRNS,RA- 2
CAIRNS,T- 1
CALDECOTT,TL- 1
CALDER,G- 6
CALDER,MJ- 5
CALDERWOOD,GJ- 1
CALDERWOOD,JM- 1
CALDWELL,SB- 3
CALDWELL,RB- 5
CALENBORNE,J- 2
CALENBORNE,N- 1

CALITZ,P- 2
CALLANAN,J- 1
CALLAWAY,NP- 2
CALLEBAUT,GL- 1
CALLENDAR,M- 1
CALLENDER,S- 3
CALLICHY,N- 1
CALLISTER,JC- 10
CALOTHI,N- 1
CALVERT,TE- 2
CAME,RB- 1
CAMERON,BH- 2
CAMERON,CS- 1
CAMERON,C- 1
CAMERON,CJ- 13
CAMERON,GR- 9
CAMERON,GJ- 4
CAMERON,GR- 1
CAMERON,GE- 1
CAMERON,RJ- 1
CAMERON,SA- 2
CAMERON-CLARKE,JS- 2
CAMP,AC- 11
CAMP,AL- 2
CAMP,GT- 5
CAMP,J- 8
CAMP,LT- 6
CAMP,MC- 1
CAMP,SC- 13
CAMP,AL- 1
CAMPBELL,A- 7
CAMPBELL,GJ- 10
CAMPBELL,GM- 9
CAMPBELL,J- 1
CAMPBELL,S- 17
CAMPBELL,SR- 1
CAMPBELL,S- 8
CAMPBELL,SA- 1
CAMPBELL,AP- 1
CAMPBELL,BA- 1
CAMPBELL,CL- 2
CAMPBELL,DL- 2
CAMPBELL,G- 1

CAMPBELL,J- 1
CAMPBELL,LM- 2
CAMPBELL,R- 1
CAMPBELL,S- 2
CANDLER,J- 1
CANE,GM- 2
CANE,K- 3
CANNON,Q- 1
CANT,SL- 3
CANTAMESSA,AJ- 1
CAPAZORIO,SP- 1
CAPPER,J- 1
CAPPS,DF- 1
CARBONEL,PR- 7
CARBUTT,BA- 1
CARDIN,B- 2
CARDINAAL,SN- 5
CARDINELLI,J- 1
CARDWELL,IJ- 6
CAREY,GA- 2
CARLISLE,M- 10
CARLISLE,P- 11
CARLISLE,S- 2
CARLISLE,J- 2
CARLISLE,M- 1
CARLISLE,M- 1
CARLISLE,P- 5
CARLISLE,DA- 1
CARLSON,JE- 2
CARLSTEIN,KM- 2
CARLYLE,CR- 3
CARLYLE,J- 2
CARLYON,JF- 13
CARNEGIE,CH- 9
CARNEGIE,I- 6
CARPENTER,A- 1
CARPENTER,RK- 4
CARPENTER,N- 1
CARR,BD- 8
CARR,R- 2
CARR,J- 1
CARRINGTON,N- 1
CARROLL,MJ- 1
CARROTHER,CS- 1
CARSTENS,L- 1

CARSTENS,MD- 4
CARTER,F- 13
CARTER,P- 1
CARTER,RK- 4
CARTER,A- 2
CARTER,GJ- 4
CARTER-BROWN,CA- 4
CARTER-BROWN,GJ- 4
CARTER-BROWN,B- 1
CARTWRIGHT,AP- 1
CARTY,S- 1
CARUTH,AG- 21
CARUTH,AD- 1
CARUTH,L- 1
CARVAN-BROWN,C- 1
CARY,CS- 4
CARY,D- 1
CARY,JB- 5
CARY,B- 2
CARY,X- 1
CASALIS,C- 4
CASALIS,G- 1
CASON,CJ- 12
CASTLE,B- 1
CASTLE,P- 3
CASTLE,RM- 1
CASTLE,DI- 1
CASTLE,M- 1
CASTLE,S- 1
CASTLE,W- 4
CASTLEDEN,A- 1
CASTLE-WARD,GP- 1
CATCHPOLE,C- 2
CATHEY,F- 1
CATTERALL,NT- 11
CATTERALL,TA- 9
CATTERICK,J- 2
CATTERICK,K- 2
CATTO,GO- 1
CAVANAGH,M- 2
CAVANAGH,T- 1
CAVANAGH,SI- 1
CAWDRY,HJ- 3
CAWDRY,FJ- 1
CAWOOD,B- 1

CAWOOD,GN- 2
CAWOOD,RM- 8
CAWOOD,H- 1
CAWSE,ML- 1
CEGLOWSKI,AJ- 1
CEITNER,J- 1
CELE,NS- 2
CELE,S- 2
CELE,R- 1
CELLIERS,JH- 2
CESCUTT,LM- 1
CHADWICK,J- 9
CHALLEN,DR- 2
CHALLENOR,BR- 8
CHALMERS,R- 1
CHALUPSKY,F- 2
CHALUPSKY,HF- 3
CHALUPSKY,O- 11
CHALUPSKY,P- 6
CHALUPSKY,WK- 1
CHAMBERLAIN,BH- 7
CHAMBERLAIN,G- 5
CHAMBERLAIN,S- 6
CHAMBERS,ME- 9
CHAMINGS,OS- 2
CHAMPION,AJ- 5
CHAMPION,GC- 3
CHAMPION,S- 2
CHANCE,MJ- 1
CHANCER,- 5
CHANDLER,PS- 1
CHANDLER,CR- 1
CHANGUION,D- 2
CHANGUION,M- 1
CHANING-PEARCE,AJ- 7
CHANU,A- 2
CHAPLIN,AT- 18
CHAPLIN,DB- 3
CHAPLIN,GN- 7
CHAPLIN,P- 1
CHAPLIN,JF- 14
CHAPMAN,D- 2
CHAPMAN,EG- 1
CHAPMAN,JD- 2
CHAPMAN,L- 7

208

COUBROUGH,M - 1
COUCOM,BM - 7
COUCOM,BA - 1
COUCOM,S - 2
COUGHLAN,DC - 1
COULL,TC - 3
COULSON,RE - 1
COULTER,AJ - 2
COULTER,R - 2
COULTHARD,CI - 1
COUSINS,MG - 5
COUSINS,RG - 4
COUSINS,GF - 1
COUVE,CR - 3
COUVE,R - 2
COUZENS,DA - 2
COVERDALE,BM - 1
COVERLY,CA - 5
COVILLE,C - 4
COVILLE,N - 1
COWAN,G - 1
COWAN,N - 6
COWARD,B - 2
COWARD,F - 3
COWARD,S - 5
COWDEN,B - 1
COWELL,MC - 13
COWIE,A - 1
COWLEY,PJ - 1
COWLING,MG - 1
COWPER,J - 1
COX,A - 5
COX,DD - 3
COX,MD - 3
COX,RT - 1
COX,BC - 1
COX,PJ - 1
COXWELL,HG - 1
CRABTREE,EJ - 2
CRAIB,G - 2
CRAIG,R - 1
CRAIG,BK - 1
CRAMPTON,DP - 1
CRANE,PB - 4
CRANE,NB - 1

CRANMER,RL - 4
CRAWFORD,AR - 2
CRAWFORD,BJ - 1
CRAWFORD,G - 2
CRAWFORD,RC - 1
CRAWLEY,C - 12
CREED,W - 1
CRESSWELL,F - 9
CRESSWELL,HS - 1
CRIBBINS,J - 2
CRICHTON,JD - 3
CRICHTON,JS - 10
CRICHTON,RI - 5
CRICHTON,T - 1
CRICHTON,MS - 1
CRICK,C - 2
CRICKMAY,AG - 1
CRISP,GA - 1
CRISSWELL,GA - 1
CROCKART,BR - 6
CROCKER,R - 5
CROCKET,G - 3
CROESER,MR - 2
CROESER,DA - 1
CROMIE,GL - 5
CROMIE,J - 1
CRONJE,AM - 4
CRONJE,B - 2
CRONJE,P - 1
CRONJE,WC - 2
CRONJE,MN - 1
CRONK,BB - 2
CROOKES,J - 2
CROOKS,VJ - 5
CROOKS,N - 2
CROOKS,M - 1
CROSBY,D - 11
CROSLEY,GA - 1
CROSS,Q - 2
CROSS,K - 1
CROSSEY,G - 1
CROSSLEY,G - 3
CROSSLEY,RM - 2
CROSSLEY,B - 1
CROSSMAN,M - 2

CROSTHWAITE,N - 1
CROUCH,P - 6
CROUCH,BJ - 1
CROUCH,NH - 1
CROUDACE,AH - 2
CROUDACE,DH - 2
CROUDACE,MA - 4
CROUKAMP,J - 1
CROUS,PA - 2
CROUS,PA - 1
CROUSE,D - 1
CROUSE,T - 1
CROW,AG - 2
CROWE,C - 11
CROWE,RJ - 10
CROWTHER,PJ - 4
CROXTON,J - 1
CRUICKSHANK,N - 2
CRUICKSHANK,J - 2
CRUICKSHANKS,P - 7
CRUICKSHANKS,GL - 5
CRUIKSHANK,R - 4
CRUIKSHANK,N - 1
CRUIKSHANKS,P - 1
CRUTCHLEY,A - 1
CULLEN,BR - 22
CULLEN,MR - 1
CULLINGWORTH,C - 11
CULLINGWORTH,GR - 3
CULLIS,RM - 1
CULLUM,R - 1
CULVERWELL,D - 23
CULVERWELL,K - 4
CULVERWELL,SS - 1
CUMINGS,SG - 5
CUMMING,N - 3
CUMMING,R - 1
CUMMING,WJ - 2
CUMMINGS,C - 2
CUMMINGS,S - 2
CUMMINGS,SG - 1
CUNARD,A - 2
CUNDILL,PG - 1
CUNINGHAME,AR - 3
CUNINGHAME,BM - 11

CUNINGHAME,BI - 3
CUNINGHAME,GM - 7
CUNINGHAME,NM - 2
CUNNAMA,EC - 3
CUNNAMA,R - 9
CUNNAMA,TP - 2
CUNNAMA,MA - 1
CUNNINGHAM,J - 2
CUNNINGHAM,P - 4
CUNNINGHAM,RG - 3
CUNNINGHAM,CT - 1
CUNNINGHAM,G - 6
CUNNINGHAM,I - 2
CUNNINGHAME,NM - 3
CUPEL,GI - 1
CURRAN,PJ - 6
CURREY,W - 1
CURRIE,AB - 1
CURRIE,CP - 6
CURRIE,GG - 1
CURRIE,NC - 1
CURRIE,RD - 14
CURRIE,DA - 1
CURRIE,TD - 2
CURRY,SA - 12
CURRY,J - 1
CURRY,NA - 1
CURSON,C - 9
CURSON,N - 3
CURSON,A - 2
CURTIS,HM - 3
CUTHBERT,BL - 2
CUTHBERT,DJ - 2
CUTLER,D - 4
CVITANICH,MA - 2
D AUBREY,AR - 3
D AUBREY,JD - 3
D AUBREY,SC - 4
DA VICE,LC - 4
DA COSTA,CA - 3
DA COSTA,N - 1
DA SILVA,DM - 4
DA SILVA,VAM - 11
DA SILVA,MC - 8
DA SILVA,CA - 1

DACOMB,EK - 10
DAFEL,HA - 1
DAGNALL-QUINN,G - 4
DAHL,J - 1
DAHL,MC - 2
DAHL,AM - 1
DAHLMANN,SG - 7
DAKERS,MJ - 1
DAKERS,NG - 2
DALE,A - 16
DALE,IG - 1
DALES,B - 1
DALES,WN - 5
DALES,J - 1
DALLAS,GR - 1
DALRYMPLE,R - 1
DALTON,LD - 2
DALTON,JD - 2
DALY,KJ - 3
DAMALIS,B - 9
DAMALIS,R - 1
DAMANT,DA - 1
DAMANT,KN - 2
DAMM,U - 1
DAMMERMANN,C - 1
DANCKWERTS,SA - 1
DANEEL,JL - 2
DANIEL,GS - 4
DANIEL,S - 3
DANIELS,A - 1
DANIELS,GP - 1
DANRE,J - 1
DANSIE,G - 1
DANSIE,K - 13
DANSIE,M - 3
DANSIE,MB - 2
DARK,S - 1
DARLEY WADDILOVU,RW - 1
DARLING,JT - 1
DARRAGH,J - 1
DART,G - 1
DATE,B - 1
DATE,G - 5

D'AUBREY,AR - 2
D'AUBREY,SC - 1
D'AUBREY,JJ - 1
DAUGHERTY,R - 1
DAVEY,A - 2
DAVEY,CS - 3
DAVEY,L - 2
DAVEY,R - 8
DAVIDSON,AG - 6
DAVIDSON,AJ - 9
DAVIDSON,G - 3
DAVIDSON,KA - 21
DAVIDSON,MJ - 1
DAVIDSON,RG - 7
DAVIDSON,WA - 5
DAVIDSON,BJ - 1
DAVIDSON,EK - 1
DAVIDSON,J - 1
DAVIDSON,JD - 2
DAVIE,CM - 4
DAVIE,K - 17
DAVIE,D - 1
DAVIE,DS - 15
DAVIE,L - 4
DAVIES,A - 2
DAVIES,D - 3
DAVIES,G - 1
DAVIES,G - 5
DAVIES,G - 4
DAVIES,JD - 4
DAVIES,J - 14
DAVIES,KT - 1
DAVIES,MD - 18
DAVIES,NJ - 10
DAVIES,R - 4
DAVIES,S - 2
DAVIES,TR - 4
DAVIES,WE - 8
DAVIES,CS - 1
DAVIES,HA - 1
DAVIES,J - 4
DAVIES,MJ - 1
DAVIS,C - 8
DAVIS,RH - 1

DAVIS,BG - 1
DAVIS,R - 1
DAVISON,CJ - 1
DAVY,LM - 2
DAWKINS,R - 1
DAWS,RG - 1
DAWSON,AR - 3
DAWSON,FJ - 19
DAWSON,FM - 8
DAWSON,M - 2
DAWSON,LR - 1
DAWSON,R - 1
DAWSON,SF - 2
DAY,A - 2
DAY,B - 23
DAY,M - 1
DAY,RP - 7
DAY,N - 1
DAYMOND,D - 4
DE BEER,L - 9
DE BEER,G - 1
DE BEER,JF - 1
DE BEER,LM - 1
DE BEER,P - 2
DE BEER,R - 1
DE BEER,SK - 1
DE BILLOT,RJ - 4
DE BOD,S - 4
DE BOER,B - 9
DE BOER,SM - 1
DE BOER,GE - 1
DE BRUIN,F - 1
DE BRUIN,PR - 2
DE BRUIN,T - 1
DE BRUIN,W - 3
DE BRUIN,LV - 2
DE BRUYNE,R - 2
DE CHALLAIN,A - 1
DE CHARMOY,RM - 2
DE CLERCQ,A - 3
DE CONING,J - 2
DE DECKER,G - 1
DE GERSIGNY,A - 7
DE GIER,AL - 2
DE GRYSE,P - 1

DE HAAN,P - 2
DE HAAS,LH - 4
DE HAAS,K - 1
DE JAGER,C - 1
DE JAGER,FJ - 4
DE JAGER,HG - 3
DE JAGER,JH - 10
DE JAGER,M - 8
DE JAGER,R - 2
DE JAGER,S - 1
DE JAGER,WI - 4
DE JAGER,G - 1
DE JAGER,P - 2
DE KLERK,B - 2
DE KLERK,B - 16
DE KLERK,B - 3
DE KLERK,CW - 4
DE KLERK,F - 1
DE KLERK,GM - 1
DE KLERK,K - 10
DE KLERK,P - 7
DE KLERK,TA - 5
DE KLERK,S - 4
DE KNOOP,NA - 1
DE KOCK,DG - 2
DE KOCK,C - 1
DE KOCK,N - 2
DE KOCK,PR - 2
DE LA HARPE,WA - 1
DE LA MOTTE,JA - 1
DE LA REY,DA - 1
DE LANGE,J - 6
DE LANGE,P - 2
DE LANGE,AM - 14
DE LANGE,AM - 1
DE LANGEN,H - 1
DE MARIGNY,A - 3
DE MEILLON,TA - 3
DE NEEF,J - 5
DE NEEF,J - 1
DE OLIVEIRA,G - 1
DE RAUVILLE,H - 25
DE RAUVILLE,J - 8
DE RAUVILLE,MJ - 5
DE RAUVILLE,MJ - 10

DU PLESSIS,A - 1	DU PLESSIS,D - 1	DU PLESSIS,OJ - 1	DU PLESSIS,PT - 2	DU PLOOY,RJ - 2	DU PLOOY,AR - 1	DU PLOOY,L - 1	DU PREEZ,JP - 1

DU PREEZ,JG - 3
DU PREEZ,MG - 3
DU PREEZ,P - 1
DU PREEZ,JM - 2
DU PREEZ,J - 1
DU TOIT,AK - 3
DU TOIT,BI - 4
DU TOIT,CJ - 1
DU TOIT,EV - 1
DU TOIT,GA - 5
DU TOIT,H - 2
DU TOIT,JA - 7
DU TOIT,K - 2
DU TOIT,MI - 3
DU TOIT,N - 3
DU TOIT,S - 3
DU TOIT,DF - 3
DU TOIT,JM - 1
DU TOIT,J - 2
DU TOIT,J - 1
DU TOIT,LP - 3
DU TOIT,R - 3
DUANE,GK - 3
DUARTE,PD - 1
DUBBER,SH - 4
DUBE,S - 3
DUBE,V - 1
DUCASSE,P - 1
DUCASSE,GD - 1
DUCKHAM,C - 2
DUCKHAM,MA - 3
DUCKHAM,G - 2
DUCKRAY,N - 4
DUCKRAY,R - 3
DUCLER,GP - 1
DUCRAY,N - 1

DRIMAN,T - 1
DRING,JP - 4
DRING,S - 2
DRINN,GD - 1
DRISCOLL,B - 7
DRISCOLL,MV - 5
DRIVER,SS - 3
DRUMMOND,D - 3
DRUMMOND,DJ - 5
DRUMMOND,TI - 7
DRUMMOND,CV - 1
DRUMMOND,JD - 1
DRUMMOND,R - 2
DRY,Q - 2
DRY,S - 1
DRYDEN,RB - 1
DRYSDALE,SR - 2
DRYSDALE,J - 3
DRYSDALE,RD - 1
DU BOIS,CD - 10
DU CLOU,A - 6
DU CRAY,PG - 1
DU PISANIE,L - 6
DU PISANIE,TM - 8
DU PLESSIS, - 1
DU PLESSIS,A - 1
DU PLESSIS,AJ - 2
DU PLESSIS,B - 1
DU PLESSIS,C - 2
DU PLESSIS,DP - 2
DU PLESSIS,D - 2
DU PLESSIS,D - 6
DU PLESSIS,E - 5
DU PLESSIS,F - 1
DU PLESSIS,F - 6
DU PLESSIS,GW - 13
DU PLESSIS,J - 7
DU PLESSIS,LH - 13
DU PLESSIS,M - 2
DU PLESSIS,N - 3
DU PLESSIS,RC - 6
DU PLESSIS,S - 12
DU PLESSIS,X - 1

DOOLEY,B - 3
DOOLEY,MT - 2
DORKIN,M - 1
DORLING,C - 6
DORLING,WM - 3
DORMEHL,J - 2
DORNING,B - 5
DORNING,N - 1
DOTT,A - 1
DOUBELL,A - 1
DOUGLAS,R - 2
DOUGLAS,M - 1
DOUGLAS,S - 2
DOUGLAS,TA - 1
DOUGLAS,WJ - 1
DOVE,VA - 1
DOVEY,GG - 3
DOVEY,J - 1
DOVEY,M - 1
DOWDALL,HB - 11
DOWDLE,JS - 1
DOWELL,DS - 1
DOWLEY,AJ - 1
DOWNES,G - 6
DOWNES,H - 1
DOWNING,G - 1
DOWNING,WC - 6
DOWNS,JD - 2
DOYLE,JO - 1
DOYLE,MO - 1
DOYLE,R - 1
DRAPER,A - 1
DRAPER,MC - 4
DRAY,ME - 1
DREIJER,M - 1
DRESNER,S - 2
DREW,JD - 2
DREW,KL - 2
DREYER,LG - 1
DREYER,MJ - 10
DRIEMEYER,C - 10
DRIEMEYER,R - 6
DRIEMEYER,Z - 18
DRIEMEYER,ER - 2
DRIEMEYER,J - 1

DIXON,G - 32
DIXON,KP - 6
DIXON,RP - 2
DIXON,S - 29
DIXON,BD - 4
DIXON,D - 3
DIXON,JS - 3
DIXON,M - 1
DIXON-PAVER,CH - 1
DIXON-SMITH,CH - 1
DLADLA,SE - 1
DLAMINI,B - 1
DLAMINI,DS - 1
DLAMINI,JP - 2
DO COUTO,P - 1
DOAK,I - 3
DOAK,R - 1
DOBBINS,R - 1
DOBEYN,LR - 1
DOBEYN,MR - 3
DOBEYN,WR - 20
DOBIE,KG - 2
DOBIE,G - 1
DOBYN,L - 1
DOCTOR KHUMALO, - 1
DODS,M - 1
DOEPEL,GB - 1
DOHNE,CP - 17
DOHNE,NB - 6
DOIDGE,R - 1
DOIGL,L - 21
DOLIVEIRA,CJ - 3
DOMLEO,B - 2
DOMLEO,NC - 10
DOMNICK,C - 1
DONALD,OE - 1
DONALDSON,MT - 2
DONALDSON,NJ - 1
DONKIN,AD - 5
DONKIN,DJ - 2
DONLY,C - 2
DONLY,G - 1
DONNOLL,M - 4
DON-WACHOPE,IS - 1

DICK,J - 2
DICK,RN - 5
DICK,WB - 3
DICKENS,D - 1
DICKENS,MJ - 3
DICKENS,R - 5
DICKENSON,JR - 1
DICKERSON,MB - 1
DICKINSON,JR - 2
DICKINSON,B - 1
DICKS,C - 12
DICKS,DU - 1
DICKS,JL - 3
DICKS,L - 1
DICKS,MW - 9
DICKSON,A - 1
DICKSON,BS - 3
DICKSON,N - 3
DICKSON,SO - 1
DIEDERICHS,F - 5
DIEDERICHS,P - 1
DIEDERICKS,J - 2
DIERS,G - 2
DIESEL,G - 2
DIESEL,T - 2
DIEST,M - 1
DIJKSTRA,AC - 9
DILKS,J - 2
DILLON,JF - 2
DIMMICK,RM - 3
DIMMICK,JG - 1
DIMOPOULOS,C - 3
DINGLE,BG - 21
DINGLEY,GW - 3
DINGLEY,CP - 1
DINKELMAN,V - 1
DIPPENAAR,AF - 5
DIPPENAAR,NL - 2
DIPPENAAR,R - 1
DIPPENAAR,K - 1
DIRKS,M - 1
DIRKSEN,P - 1
DISTIN,TR - 1
DIXIE,B - 1
DIXON,CM - 1

DELPORT,EJ - 1
DELPORT,L - 1
DELVAUX,G - 7
DELVAUX,PV - 3
DELVIN,R - 1
DELY,MI - 1
DENEKAMP,LA - 6
DENEKAMP,KJ - 1
DENISSEN,WJ - 6
DENISSON,RC - 1
DENNISON,R - 6
DENNISON,DP - 2
DENNISON,M - 1
DENNISON,P - 1
DENNY,GL - 3
DENNY,G - 3
DENNY,J - 1
DENT,R - 4
DENT,M - 1
DENTON,MR - 3
DEPPE,EE - 12
DEPPE,SE - 2
DERKSEN,CC - 1
DES FONTAINE,B - 1
DES TOMBE,PA - 6
DES TOMBES,PA - 1
DESCROIZILLES,C - 1
DESFONTAINE,B - 3
DESILE,TS,T - 1
DESILLA,N - 3
DESILLA,JP - 1
DESILLA,JP - 1
DETTMER,HK - 2
DETTMER,M - 1
DEUTSCHMANN,R - 3
DEVENPORT,J - 1
DEVONPORT,JN - 5
DEXTER,J - 8
DEYZEL,F - 17
DEYZEL,T - 6
DEYZEL,W - 27
DEYZEL,N - 1
DHOOGE,AH - 1
DIACK,AE - 1
DIAZ,NI - 7

DE WINNAAR,J - 1
DE WINNAAR,NM - 4
DE WIT,GT - 2
DE WIT,PC - 1
DE WITT,F - 1
DE WITT,GP - 1
DEACON,E - 3
DEACON,SL - 1
DEAN,S - 10
DEAN,B - 1
DEANA,A - 9
DEANA,DD - 4
DEANA,A - 1
DEANA,JD - 2
DEANA,K - 1
DEANE,RA - 1
DEANE,T - 2
DEARLING,P - 1
DECKER,G - 1
DEDEKIND,D - 1
DEE,AC - 1
DEEB,EG - 1
DEEBE,E - 1
DEELEY-SMITH,B - 5
DEERING,AU - 3
DEETLEFS,TG - 1
DEETLETS,TG - 1
DEEVES,K - 2
DEIST,J - 1
DEIST,MC - 3
DEKKER,JG - 1
DEKOK,JR - 1
DEKORT,J - 1
DELANEY,GP - 3
DELANEY,NP - 1
DELHOVE,RF - 13
DELL,D - 1
DELL,MI - 1
DELLIS,SR - 4
DELPORT,D - 3
DELPORT,G - 5
DELPORT,J - 9
DELPORT,PJ - 1
DELPORT,RJ - 2
DELPORT,C - 1

DE RAUVILLE,CJ - 1
DE RAUVILLE,LG - 1
DE RICQUEBOURG,B - 2
DE RICQUEBOURG,JB - 2
DE RIDDER,G - 7
DE RIDDER,RJ - 1
DE RIDGER,G - 1
DE ROSE,R - 1
DE RUYTER,PM - 2
DE SAXE,BD - 1
DE SOUSA,D - 1
DE SOUZA,G - 1
DE SWARDT,AV - 3
DE SYLVA,G - 4
DE SYLVA,JE - 1
DE VILLIERS,A - 3
DE VILLIERS,EH - 2
DE VILLIERS,K - 11
DE VILLIERS,L - 5
DE VILLIERS,MJ - 11
DE VILLIERS,PE - 7
DE VILLIERS,PE - 11
DE VILLIERS,R - 3
DE VILLIERS,SP - 10
DE VILLIERS,CT - 5
DE VILLIERS,JW - 1
DE VILLIERS,M - 1
DE VILLIERS,N - 1
DE VINCENZO,AG - 2
DE VLETTER,LJ - 2
DE VRIES,AP - 1
DE VRIES,R - 1
DE WAAL,J - 1
DE WERGISOSSE,A - 1
DE WET,C - 4
DE WET,DS - 6
DE WET,L - 3
DE WET,PR - 2
DE WET,WA - 8
DE WET,AD - 1
DE WET,SM - 1
DE WET,TH - 1
DE WINNAAR,CB - 1
DE WINNAAR,D - 3

LIST OF ALL FINISHERS IN THE DUSI CANOE MARATHON—1951 TO 2006

DUCRAY,P - 2
DUDGER,R - 1
DUDGEON,EP - 1
DUDLEY,D - 1
DUDLEY,H - 2
DUDLEY,R - 1
DUFF,BP - 1
DUFFUS,MJ - 1
DUFFY,DA - 5
DUFFY,G -10
DUGDALE,G - 1
DUGGAN,SJ - 1
DUGGAN,AS - 2
DUGGAN,L - 1
DUGGAN,T - 1
DUIGAN,AN - 2
DUMBRILL,DP - 1
DUMMER,J - 2
DUNBAR,C - 3
DUNBAR,N - 1
DUNBAR,AJ - 1
DUNCAN,C - 2
DUNCAN,C - 7
DUNCAN,G - 3
DUNCAN,J - 3
DUNCAN,KC-16
DUNCAN,PJ - 6
DUNCAN,R - 5
DUNCAN,NS - 1
DUNFORD,SN - 1
DUNLOP,QB - 1
DUNLOP,JP - 3
DUNLOP,RB - 1
DUNN,J - 1
DUNN,A - 1
DUNN,DM - 1
DUNNE,A - 3
DUNNET,T - 1
DUNNETT,GA - 2
DUNNETT,PJ - 4
DUNNETT,S - 2
DUNSMORE,L - 3
DUNSMORE,MD - 1
DUNSMORE,S - 3
DUNSMORE,SS - 5

DUNT,B - 1
DURAND,A - 1
DURANDT,N - 1
DURDEN,T - 1
DURHAM,DA - 2
DURHAM,L - 1
DURHAM,PF - 4
DUSTAN,AJ- 8
DUTKIEWICZ,MK- 1
DUTOIT,D - 1
DUTTON,CR- 3
DUTTON,L - 1
DUTTON,P - 5
DUTTON,B - 1
DUVENHAGE,J - 1
DVTKIEWICZ,MK- 1
DWYER,J - 1
DYASON,JD- 5
DYASON,VL- 4
DYER,CA- 2
DYER,GJ- 2
DYER,GJ- 4
DYER,GB-13
DYER,N- 5
DYER,RJ- 2
DYKE,A - 1
DYKES,E -10
DYKES,S - 1
DYKMAN,P - 3
DYSON,A - 1
DYSON,D - 2
EADES,DW- 1
EARDLEY,SM-14
EARDLEY,K - 1
EARL,J -18
EARL,JI - 1
EARL,JF- 2
EARL,RF- 1
EARLE,DR- 2
EARLE,PL- 3
EARL-SPURR,JA- 2
EAST,BL- 3
EAST,NG-10
EASTHORPE,D - 1
EASTWOOD,RA- 2

EATON,PW- 2
EATON,R - 2
EAYRS,GR- 2
EBJ,G- 5
EB,JDM- 1
ECCLES,B - 3
EDER,J - 1
EDGEBRINK,C - 1
EDGLEY,BG- 4
EDMONDS,AG-16
EDMONDS,A-23
EDMONDS,CR- 3
EDMONDS,CA- 2
EDMONDS,C -21
EDMONDS,DC-18
EDMONDS,GJ- 6
EDMONDS,J -29
EDMONDS,M- 4
EDMONDS,MD- 3
EDMONDS,PH-26
EDMONDS,T - 3
EDMONDS,K - 1
EDMONDS,P - 1
EDMUNDS,P - 1
EDMUNDS,ST- 4
EDWARD,VE- 1
EDWARDS,CD- 2
EDWARDS,DR- 4
EDWARDS,JS- 2
EDWARDS,J - 9
EDWARDS,LR- 7
EDWARDS,MS- 8
EDWARDS,RJ-13
EDWARDS,V -11
EDWARDS,BA- 1
EDWARDS,MV- 1
EDWARDS,SD- 1
EDY,M - 2
EGAN,GA- 2
EGAN,MA- 6
EGAN,WA- 2
EGBRINK,CS- 1
EGEBRINK,E - 1
EGERTON,A -10
EGGERS,KA- 5
EGLING,M - 1

EGLINGTON,MB-15
EGNER,AJ- 3
EGNER,D - 2
EGNER,RR- 5
EHLERS,DC- 1
EHLERS,K - 2
EIGETER,V - 1
EIGETER,L - 2
EISENBLATER,JE- 3
EITZ,D - 1
EKSTRAND,JI- 1
ELDRIDGE,BM- 6
ELDRIDGE,AJ- 1
ELEY,PG- 1
ELGAR,K - 1
ELGIE,GK- 1
ELKINGTON,JD- 1
ELKINGTON,LA- 3
ELLENBERGER,A- 2
ELLERKER,K -28
ELLIOT,B - 1
ELLIOT,FB- 3
ELLIOT,G - 1
ELLIOT,R - 1
ELLIOTT,GP- 5
ELLIOTT,C - 1
ELLIOTT,DA- 1
ELLIOTT,PC- 2
ELLIOTT,PA- 2
ELLIS,G - 7
ELLIS,J - 2
ELLIS,MC- 2
ELLIS,OA- 1
ELLIS,RG-11
ELLIS,PC- 1
ELLIS,WJ- 1
ELLIS-CLARKE,M - 2
ELLIS-CLARKE,RS- 3
ELLISH,G - 3
ELOFF,MJ- 1
ELOFF,D - 1
ELPHICK,C - 4
ELRICK,AA- 1
ELS,A - 4

ELS,A - 6
ELS,P - 3
ELS,T - 1
ELSE,D - 1
ELSE,L - 1
ELSTON,E - 1
ELVES,JG- 1
ELWORTHY,AM- 2
EMANUEL,CR- 1
EMANUEL,DB- 4
EMBERTON,JB-14
EMBERTON,BJ- 2
EMMETT,F - 6
EMMOTT,G - 4
EMMOTT,M - 3
EMMOTT,P - 8
ENDER,EJ- 1
ENDER,RA- 4
ENDER,GE- 1
ENGEL,CJ-12
ENGEL,AS- 3
ENGELBRECHT,C - 4
ENGELBRECHT,D - 2
ENGELBRECHT,MH- 3
ENGELBRECHT,SI- 3
ENGELBRECHT,F - 1
ENGELBRECHT,GC- 1
ENGELBRECHT,J - 2
ENGELBRECHT,SI- 4
ENGELAND,DA- 1
ENGLAND,M - 2
ENGLISH,D - 3
ENGLISH,DR- 2
ENGLISH,MG- 4
ENGLISH,P - 2
ENGLISH,DM- 2
ENTE,BI- 2
ENTHOVEN,A - 6
ENTWISLE,DP- 2
EPHRAIM,NG- 7
EPPEL,D - 1
ERASMUS,AC- 5
ERASMUS,F - 6
ERASMUS,GW- 2
ERASMUS,JA- 4

ERASMUS,LM - 3
ERASMUS,PJ - 2
ERASMUS,S - 2
ERAY,M - 1
ERERMANS,L - 1
ERIKSEN,AC- 1
ERIKSEN-MILLER,MA- 7
ERIKSEN-MILLER,R - 2
ERIKSON,C - 5
ERMACORA,F - 1
ERSKINE,SS - 2
ESLICK,J - 4
ESLICK,MI - 1
ESPIRITO-SANTO,C - 3
ESPITALIER,T - 1
ESSERY,LV - 5
ESSERY,ML - 7
ESTEHUIZEN,CF - 1
ESTERHUIZEN,CF - 7
ESTERHUIZEN,TS - 7
ESTERHUIZEN,J - 5
ESTERHUIZEN,L - 1
ESTERHUIZEN,PW - 1
ESTERHUIZEN,W - 3
ESTERHUYSEN,F - 1
ETHELSTONE,P - 1
ETHERINGTON,RL - 2
EUSTACE,M - 5
EVANS,A - 4
EVANS,C - 16
EVANS,DA - 2
EVANS,GC - 1
EVANS,GW - 3
EVANS,M - 2
EVANS,MG - 6
EVANS,NS - 3
EVANS,NW-14
EVANS,R - 2
EVANS,S - 23
EVANS,WJ - 6
EVANS,W - 4
EVANS,GF - 6
EVANS,IL - 1
EVANS,JC - 2

EVANS,N - 2
EVANS,S - 3
EVANS,SA - 2
EVAN-SMITH,MA - 1
EVE,JR - 3
EVELEIGH,KA - 3
EVELEIGH,JK - 1
EVENETT,C - 1
EVENNETT,C - 2
EVENNETT,MG - 1
EVENS,AS - 2
EVENS,JC - 1
EVERED-HALL,AE-11
EVERED-HALL,GA - 2
EVERED-HALL,M - 3
EVERED-HALL,ME-13
EVERED-HALL,LW - 1
EVERED-HALL,T - 3
EVERSON,CS - 14
EVERSON,TM - 1
EVESON,TM - 1
EXELBY,SA - 2
EXELBY,RM - 1
EXSTEEN,K - 4
EXSTEEN,S - 5
EYSELE,AL - 1
EYSELE,LA - 1
FABER,BP - 2
FABRIS,AG - 2
FAIR,B - 1
FAIRBANK,H - 2
FAIRBROTHER,BM - 4
FAIRFAX,P - 1
FAIRHEAD,AB - 1
FAIRHURST,P - 3
FAIRLIE,B - 1
FAIRLIE,LA - 1
FALCONER,MS - 2
FALCONER,P - 3
FALKSON,MB - 5
FALKSON,T - 3
FALKSON,A - 1
FALLER,JN - 4
FALLET,BE - 2
FANNIN,TG - 1
FARINHA,NP - 4
FARLAND,D - 2

FARLAND,EI-11
FARMER,WD - 1
FARREN,MJ - 2
FARREN,D - 1
FARREN,SF - 1
FARRER,D - 1
FARROW,GA - 1
FARROW,MW - 1
FARROW,DF - 1
FARTHING,R - 2
FAUGHT,JD - 2
FAURE,AP - 4
FAURE,JP - 1
FAWCETT,S - 1
FAWELL,D - 1
FAYERS,TM - 2
FEATHER,M - 2
FEATHERBY,CT - 1
FEATONBY-SMITH,PB - 1
FEEK,DJ - 1
FEEK,JE - 2
FEEK,JS - 7
FEHER,R - 5
FELDON,A - 5
FELDON,GL - 2
FELGATE,GH - 2
FELL,BJ - 1
FELLNER,IK - 3
FENN,AC - 1
FENNELL,OW - 2
FENSHAM,N - 1
FERGUSON,AT- 5
FERGUSON,D - 3
FERGUSON,JA - 5
FERGUSON,MB - 5
FERGUSON,NM - 1
FERGUSON,PA - 1
FERGUSON,RB - 7
FERGUSON,AC - 7
FERGUSON,JR - 1
FERGUSON,S - 1
FERNANDES,MM - 2
FERRANS,GR - 2
FERRAR,JM - 1
FERREIRA,EJ - 1

LIST OF ALL FINISHERS IN THE DUSI CANOE MARATHON—1951 TO 2006

FERREIRA,F - 5
FERREIRA,M - 2
FERREIRA,S - 1
FERREIRA,T - 3
FERREIRO,GB - 2
FERRIER,NE - 1
FERROW,D - 8
FERROW,J - 2
FERROW,J - 13
FICK,KC - 1
FICK,N - 4
FICK,S - 2
FICK,G - 1
FIELD,B - 1
FIELD,CC - 3
FIELD,JJ - 4
FIELD,G - 2
FIELDING,PH - 7
FIELDING,AC - 1
FIGUEIREDO,LM - 1
FILTER,MC - 3
FILTER,OH - 1
FILTER,RA - 1
FINCH,DS - 7
FINCHAM,GR - 2
FINDLAY,AA - 2
FINDLAY,C - 1
FINDLAY,G - 7
FINDLAY,R - 4
FINDLAYSON,R - 1
FINLAY,R - 13
FINLAY,A - 1
FINLAYSON,RP - 2
FINNEMORE,M - 2
FIRMAN,PL - 5
FIRTH,JG - 2
FIRTH,DM - 1
FIRTH,R - 1
FISCHER,N - 4
FISHER,BI - 6
FISHER,C - 3
FISHER,GC - 9
FISHER,H - 10
FISHER,S - 7
FISHER,W - 2

FISHER,JB - 3
FISHER,P - 1
FISHER,TR - 2
FITTON,LC - 3
FITZGERALD,F - 1
FITZ-GERALD,C - 1
FITZPATRICK,ME - 5
FITZSIMONS,GR - 2
FITZSIMONS,MC - 5
FITZSIMONS,R - 4
FLANAGAN,G - 1
FLANAGAN,M - 1
FLANAGAN,PG - 1
FLANAGAN,R - 1
FLANAGAN,SF - 2
FLANAGAN,T - 1
FLANAGEN,LJ - 2
FLANNAGAN,L - 2
FLAVELL,AL - 2
FLEISCHACK,PC - 3
FLEMING,CJ - 1
FLEMING,JH - 2
FLEMMER,K - 2
FLETCHER,G - 8
FLETCHER,KM - 1
FLETCHER-CAMPBELL,H - 1
FLINT,K - 2
FLINT,M - 1
FLORENCE,DW - 20
FLOWERS,GR - 1
FLOYD,KM - 4
FLUSK,NM - 2
FLY,DC - 5
FLY,RD - 5
FOBB,J - 1
FOERG,J - 1
FOKKEMA,LH - 2
FOKKENS,B - 4
FOLKES,PJ - 2
FOLKES,RJ - 6
FOORD,JA - 4
FORBES,BD - 4
FORBES,GB - 5
FORBES,JD - 1

FORBES,MJ - 1
FORBES,SS - 1
FORD,M - 1
FORD,PJ - 1
FORD,R - 1
FORDER,G - 2
FORDYCE,B - 9
FORMBY,DB - 3
FORMBY,RJ - 2
FORREST,JW - 2
FORREST,GL - 2
FORRESTER,DW - 1
FORRESTER,RA - 1
FORRESTER,BS - 1
FORRESTER,EG - 1
FORSHAW,MD - 7
FORSMAN,B - 1
FORSON,A - 3
FORSTER,L - 2
FORSYTH,DD - 2
FORSYTH,W - 1
FORSYTH,G - 1
FORSYTH,K - 1
FOSKER,GJ - 1
FOSKER,GS - 2
FOSS,BJ - 1
FOSSETT,DT - 1
FOSTER,B - 1
FOSTER,CG - 4
FOSTER,CR - 6
FOSTER,DC - 4
FOSTER,LV - 8
FOSTER,RK - 8
FOSTER,A - 3
FOUCHE,AL - 13
FOUCHE,BA - 1
FOUCHE,MP - 4
FOUCHE,PH - 7
FOUCHE,O - 1
FOULIS,G - 2
FOURIE,A - 4
FOURIE,C - 4
FOURIE,D - 6
FOURIE,JC - 2

FOURIE,JL - 3
FOURIE,J - 2
FOURIE,K - 3
FOURIE,L - 1
FOURIE,L - 3
FOURIE,LJ - 12
FOURIE,N - 4
FOURIE,NC - 5
FOURIE,P - 2
FOURIE,S - 2
FOURIE,WA - 10
FOURIE,X - 1
FOURIE,GC - 1
FOURIE,JJ - 5
FOURIE,JE - 2
FOWKES,HP - 3
FOWLER,J - 1
FOWLES,B - 13
FOWLES,C - 6
FOWLES,G - 4
FOWLES,FT - 1
FOX,AJ - 2
FOX,CG - 10
FOX,CW - 6
FOX,D - 3
FOX,N - 2
FOX,T - 11
FOX,TH - 11
FOX,WD - 1
FOX,K - 2
FOX,SP - 1
FRAME,M - 1
FRANCE,AR - 20
FRANCE,A - 3
FRANCIS,D - 3
FRANCIS,J - 4
FRANCIS,KP - 2
FRANCOIS,DG - 9
FRANK,GF - 1
FRANKEN,E - 1
FRANKISH,S - 7
FRANKISH,TM - 1
FRANKISH,D - 4
FRANKLAND,CA - 4
FRANKLIN,A - 11

FRANKLIN,D - 6
FRANZ,DJ - 2
FRANZSEN,JL - 1
FRASER,AD - 18
FRASER,A - 5
FRASER,AF - 3
FRASER,AL - 4
FRASER,C - 5
FRASER,DG - 5
FRASER,GJ - 5
FRASER,HR - 1
FRASER,JK - 3
FRASER,L - 1
FRASER,RJ - 2
FRASER,S - 3
FRASER,SI - 3
FRASER,SD - 1
FRASER,JL - 3
FRASER-JONES,MI - 1
FRASER-SMITH,M - 2
FRAYNE,D - 1
FREDERIC,WS - 1
FREDMAN,J - 3
FREEMAN,D - 2
FREEMAN,J - 2
FREEMAN,M - 1
FREEMAN-SMITH,J - 6
FREEMAN-SMITH,WR - 5
FREEMANTLE,JA - 3
FREEMANTLE,NP - 1
FREER,PE - 4
FREESE,AL - 2
FREESE,C - 1
FREESE,DL - 2
FREIMAN,MA - 19
FREIMAN,SH - 12
FREISLICH,W - 1
FRENCH,MC - 1
FRENCH,PE - 1
FRESTEL,PR - 2
FREW,C - 1
FREY,NG - 2
FREY,R - 1
FREYER,A - 6

FRIDMAN,BI - 1
FRIEND,AJ - 3
FRIEND,PM - 4
FRIEND,S - 3
FRITZ,AJ - 1
FRIZELLE,G - 17
FRIZELLE,H - 17
FRIZELLE,JM - 2
FRIZELLE,M - 17
FRIZELLE,M - 1
FRIZELLE,MK - 4
FRIZELLE,ME - 1
FRIZELLE,M - 4
FROMONBRIL,P - 1
FROST,BL - 15
FROST,C - 9
FROST,KA - 4
FROST,P - 2
FROST,SA - 2
FROST,N - 1
FROST,R - 2
FROSTICK,B - 3
FROUDE,R - 1
FROUNDE,RS - 1
FRY,M - 1
FRYER,B - 6
FRYER,NR - 1
FUCHSLOCH,D - 8
FUCHSLOCH,G - 1
FULCHER,CM - 2
FULCHER,MS - 4
FULFORD,AW - 1
FULLER,CD - 13
FULLER,DJ - 7
FULLER,J - 3
FULLER,JA - 5
FULLER,LA - 8
FULLER,MR - 1
FULLER,J - 2
FULLER,VG - 2
FUNGA,PM - 1
FUNKEY,C - 1
FUNKEY,T - 1
FURNISS,B - 5
FURNISS,G - 1

FURNISS,PW - 2
FURNO,F - 1
FURNO,G - 1
FUSSELL,CI - 1
FUSSELL,MJ - 4
FYNN,R - 2
FYVIE,MJ - 4
FYVIE,W - 1
GABELA,P - 1
GABLE,H - 1
GACE,B - 1
GACE,DC - 14
GACE,GB - 9
GACE,RL - 3
GADDIN,L - 10
GADDIN,B - 2
GADEMAN,E - 1
GAFNEY,DA - 7
GAGIANO,J - 3
GALBRAITH,R - 3
GALE,J - 3
GALE,MD - 2
GALLAGHER,P - 4
GALLAGHER,BI - 1
GALLEID,H - 1
GALLO,CE - 2
GALLOWAY,CA - 3
GALLOWAY,MS - 2
GALLOWAY,RP - 1
GALLOWAY,S - 1
GALLOWAY,TL - 8
GALLOWAY,TP - 16
GALTREY,CA - 1
GAMMIE,K - 7
GAMMIE,M - 15
GANDY,P - 5
GANDY,R - 17
GANDY,T - 5
GARCIN,BJ - 9
GARDEN,A - 2
GARDEN,KJ - 1
GARDENER,DP - 4
GARDNER,AP - 13
GARDNER,DC - 10
GARDNER,MB - 3

GARDNER,R - 4
GARFIELD,P - 1
GARNHAM,MJ - 1
GARNHAM,LH - 1
GARRATT,G - 1
GARREAU,S - 4
GARRETT,GI - 1
GARVIE,CW - 1
GARVIE,G - 1
GASSON,B - 1
GATES,T - 1
GATHERCOLE,A - 1
GATLAND,CA - 8
GATONBY,SP - 5
GAULT,RD - 4
GAUNT,JM - 1
GAUNTLETT,C - 2
GAUNTLETT,LM - 1
GAYER,MJ - 3
GAYLARD,P - 4
GAYLARD,R - 3
GAYLARD,R - 1
GAYNOR,KP - 1
GCABASHE,M - 4
GCABASHE,N - 3
GEACH,PC - 11
GEACH,RA - 5
GEARING,JE - 3
GEARY,R - 1
GEBERS,W - 3
GEBERS,R - 1
GEDDES,G - 1
GEDDIE,L - 1
GEE,GD - 1
GEEL,CF - 4
GEEL,SE - 1
GEERDTS,A - 1
GEERTSEMA,JH - 1
GEILS,A - 4
GEISER,GI - 1
GEITNER,J - 2
GELDARD,D - 15
GELDARD,R - 16
GELDARD,L - 2
GELDART,IC - 3

GELDART,T - 8
GELDENHUYS,BL - 3
GELDENHUYS,E - 3
GELEYN,FJ - 1
GEMMEL,RJ - 2
GEMMELL,R - 7
GEMMELL,AR - 1
GEMMELL,D - 1
GEMMELL,JW - 1
GENZMER,JH - 1
GEORGE,A - 1
GEORGE,QJ - 1
GEORGE,R - 6
GEORGE,WD - 1
GEORGE,D - 1
GERAGHTY,RB - 1
GERBER,A - 3
GERBER,B - 5
GERBER,DC - 5
GERBER,S - 2
GERHARD,M - 9
GERHARD,R - 1
GERMAINE,BV - 1
GERMIQUET,DI - 11
GERMIQUET,MD - 5
GERMISHUIZEN,LE - 1
GERRARD,H - 5
GERRISH,G - 2
GERRITZ,W - 1
GERTENBACH,JA - 2
GETTLIFFE,R - 1
GEVERS,EH - 2
GEVERS,ME - 5
GEYER,M - 5
GEYSER,A - 1
GEYSER,CA - 8
GEYSER,W - 1
GEYSER,J - 1
GEYVE,JA - 4
GIAI-MINIETTI,GM - 3
GIBB,A - 3
GIBBINGS,C - 11
GIBBINGS,CH - 3
GIBBINGS,CH - 2

GIBBON,J - 1
GIBBS,C - 7
GIBBS,KJ - 5
GIBBS-JONES,CG - 1
GIBSON,CA - 2
GIBSON,PH - 8
GIBSON,S - 1
GIBSON,TE - 7
GIBSON,WA - 20
GIBSON,AS - 1
GIBSON,B - 1
GIBSON,H - 7
GIBSON,L - 1
GIBSON,MS - 3
GIBSON,Z - 1
GIDDY,MR - 2
GIELINK,A - 3
GIESE,MA - 2
GIFFORD,WR - 5
GIFFORD,J - 1
GILBERT,A - 26
GILBERT,CS - 1
GILDENHUYS,CJ - 1
GILDENHUYS,D - 1
GILDING,J - 2
GILES,J - 1
GILES,PN - 9
GILES,RA - 7
GILFILLAN,CM - 1
GILFILLAN,E - 1
GILFILLAN,RM - 1
GILKS,MA - 3
GILL,T - 1
GILLATT,CB - 1
GILLESPIE,MD - 2
GILLESPIE,LD - 1
GILLESPIE,PF - 1
GILLHAM,WE - 2
GILLICK,B - 2
GILLITT,CG - 6
GILLMER,BT - 13
GILLMER,DJ - 15
GILLMER,EA - 6
GILLMER,JE - 6
GILLMER,JM - 8

GILLMER,M - 7
GILLMER,J - 1
GILLON,CM - 2
GILSON,AB - 8
GILSON,KJ - 3
GILSON,MD - 1
GILSON,ST - 2
GILSON,F - 1
GINTNER,SK - 1
GIPSON,S - 4
GIRD,M - 1
GIRDLESTONE,SI - 2
GIRLING,BW - 1
GLADWIN,P - 8
GLAISTER,SB - 8
GLASHAM,D - 1
GLASL,E - 6
GLASL,N - 4
GLASS,A - 2
GLASS,I - 6
GLASS,J - 1
GLASSON,E - 1
GLENDAY,B - 2
GLENN,C - 14
GLENN,F - 1
GLENNIE,RP - 1
GLENNIE,HR - 2
GLENNIE,R - 1
GLOVER,MR - 6
GLOVER,AR - 1
GLUTZ,M - 1
GOADSBY,GC - 1
GOATCHER,A - 2
GOBEY,D - 9
GOBLE,BG - 9
GOBLE,BD - 15
GOBLE,CR - 4
GOBLE,JM - 5
GOBLE,NJ - 18
GOBLE,PE - 23
GODDARD,B - 13
GODDARD,KB - 15
GODDARD,R - 4
GODDARD,DG - 6
GODDARD,GD - 1

GODDARD,KL - 1
GODDEN,JR - 1
GODFREY,GD - 1
GODFREY,MR - 1
GODLONTON,J - 1
GODWIN,AK - 1
GOEDEKE,KE - 4
GOEDEKE,R - 1
GOEDHART,H - 1
GOEDHART,P - 1
GOELLER,E - 2
GOELLER,R - 2
GOELLER,JC - 1
GOETZ,R - 1
GOETZSCHE,AP - 2
GOETZSCHE,G - 1
GOLACH,D - 9
GOLACH,CR - 1
GOLD,AR - 1
GOLD,D - 4
GOLD,RE - 2
GOLD,LF - 3
GOLDACRE,JJ - 4
GOLD,ES - 1
GOLDIN,R - 1
GOLDING,JS - 6
GOLDING,P - 1
GOLDIONG,C - 1
GOLDSCHMIDT,MJ - 1
GOLDSTEIN,J - 1
GOLDSTONE,MP - 8
GOLDSTONE,RI - 1
GOLDSWORTHY,B - 7
GOLDSWORTHY,A - 1
GOLDSWORTHY,G - 1
GOMM,CI - 1
GOODJ,W - 1
GOODALL,AI - 1
GOODBRAND,BN - 3
GOODEN,G - 1
GOODES,FW - 1
GOODING,A - 11
GOODLD,MD - 1
GOODMAN,P - 6
GOODMAN,SM - 1
GOODSON,AP - 1

GOODSON,C - 3
GOODWIN,C - 1
GOODWIN,D - 6
GOODWIN,R - 1
GOODWIN,J - 1
GOOSEN,CA - 5
GOOSEN,DN - 4
GOOSEN,MA - 2
GOOSEN,R - 5
GOOSEN,GI - 1
GORDON,AB - 9
GORDON,AW - 2
GORDON,CB - 6
GORDON,D - 4
GORDON,GL - 5
GORDON,J - 2
GORDON,K - 1
GORDON,R - 3
GORDON,GB - 3
GORE,BG - 6
GORE,SR - 4
GORLE,I - 13
GORLI - 3
GORLEI,RA - 7
GORVEN,DG - 9
GORVEN,JC - 3
GORVEN,TR - 5
GORVETT,LC - 2
GOSCHEN,WS - 3
GOSLING,BN - 2
GOSLING,MB - 1
GOSLING,RG - 1
GOSS,NP - 3
GOSSAYN,G - 2
GOSSAYN,JM - 8
GOSSELP - 5
GOTTE,KP - 15
GOTTE,TB - 2
GOULD,A - 1
GOULD,D - 2
GOULD,MD - 1
GOULDIE,R - 5
GOULDIES,A - 4
GOUNDEN,SM - 16

GOVENDER,R - 1
GOVLE,J - 1
GOW,D - 7
GOW,P - 1
GOWER-JACKSON,SK - 2
GRAAF,JP - 21
GRAAF,M - 4
GRABE,PJ - 2
GRACIE,JW - 1
GRADWELL,C - 1
GRAF,RR - 1
GRAHAM,DC - 7
GRAHAM,EJ - 6
GRAHAM,JR - 5
GRAHAM,JA - 10
GRAHAM,MD - 7
GRAHAM,M - 6
GRAHAM,RW - 3
GRAHAM,WE - 1
GRAHAM,KA - 2
GRAHAM,P - 3
GRAHAM,TA - 1
GRAIG,R - 1
GRANGE,LA - 1
GRANGER,R - 2
GRANGER,T - 1
GRANT,A - 3
GRANT,BE - 3
GRANT,D - 4
GRANT,H - 4
GRANT,H - 1
GRANT,MC - 1
GRANT,CL - 1
GRANT,D - 1
GRANTHAM,AC - 5
GRANTHAM,RB - 5
GRASSBY,RP - 1
GRASSET,M - 1
GRAVETT,E - 1
GRAY,A - 1
GRAY,BR - 6
GRAY,HP - 3
GRAY,J - 2
GRAY,M - 3

GRAY,P - 2
GRAY,S - 2
GRAY,C - 3
GRAY,J - 1
GRAY,RN - 2
GREEF,AR - 1
GREEFF,C - 17
GREEFF,W - 2
GREEFF,H - 1
GREEN,A - 2
GREEN,BJ - 7
GREEN,D - 1
GREEN,GR - 2
GREEN,G - 2
GREEN,G - 9
GREEN,JD - 2
GREEN,MP - 8
GREEN,R - 2
GREEN,W - 3
GREEN,GR - 1
GREEN,PA - 2
GREENBERG,RS - 1
GREENE,JS - 3
GREENE,RB - 1
GREENFIELD,J - 1
GREENHALGH,M - 1
GREENHALGH,P - 1
GREENHALGH,RB - 1
GREENHAM,M - 14
GREENHAM,DC - 2
GREENLAND,CG - 19
GREENLAND,D - 1
GREENWAY,AJ - 1
GREENWAY,J - 1
GREGAN,S - 1
GREGG-MACDONALD,MD - 1
GREGG-MACDONALD,MJ - 1
GREGORY,L - 1
GREGORY,SD - 1
GREIG,KM - 4
GREIG,NM - 2
GREIG,B - 2
GREIG,D - 1
GRENFELL,SJ - 1

GREVILLE,R - 8
GREWAR,LA - 5
GREWAR,MS - 2
GREY,NH - 1
GREY,B - 1
GREYLING,JB - 2
GREYLING,M - 5
GREYLING,PM - 1
GREYLING,SJ - 1
GREYLING,TJ - 1
GREYVENSTEIN,L - 5
GRIEG,KM - 1
GRIEVESON,A - 11
GRIFFIN,B - 1
GRIFFIN,CE - 1
GRIFFIN,D - 4
GRIFFIN,M - 1
GRIFFIN,SP - 6
GRIFFIN,PR - 1
GRIFFITHS,A - 4
GRIFFITHS,T - 2
GRIFFITHS,HW - 1
GRIFFITHS,SG - 1
GRIM,C - 1
GRIM,G - 1
GRIMBEEK,AA - 1
GRINDLEY,DM - 1
GRINVER,CI - 4
GRIX,GF - 1
GROBBELAAR,C - 1
GROBBELAAR,P - 1
GROBLER,BR - 14
GROBLER,VA - 2
GROBBLER,BA - 4
GROBBLER,CM - 1
GROBICKI,AG - 3
GROBICKI,MS - 1
GROBLER,AJ - 1
GROBLER,E - 5
GROBLER,GP - 3
GROBLER,MA - 6
GROBLER,PC - 5
GROBLER,RT - 8
GROENEWALD,HJ - 1
GROENEWEG,DM - 1

LIST OF ALL FINISHERS IN THE DUSI CANOE MARATHON—1951 TO 2006

GROENEWOUD,PJ-1
GROESBEEK,C-1
GRONBECK,PJ-1
GROOM,S-1
GROOM,BA-1
GROSE,KJ-1
GROSSKOPF,M-1
GROTEPASS,M-6
GROUND,PG-2
GROVE,J-1
GROVES,CK-1
GRUAR,TM-1
GRUNOW,NC-3
GUEST,SP-8
GUINLEN,D-1
GUMEDE,M-1
GUMEDE,J-1
GUNN,AD-1
GUNNING,D-1
GUNNING,NC-2
GUNNING,R-1
GUNTER,BL-7
GUNTER,LW-2
GURNELL,G-1
GURNEY,BD-11
GURNEY,D-4
GURNEY,RJ-1
GUSH,RW-2
GUTHRIE,G-3
GUY,R-1
GWALA,NP-1
H00K,BA-1
HAARHOF,G-2
HAARHOFF,G-1
HAARHOFF,V-3
HAAS,P-1
HACKLAND,AJ-6
HACKLAND,B-5
HACKLAND,C-5
HACKLAND,CE-4
HACKLAND,CE-1
HACKLAND,JJ-12
HACKLAND,JJ-1
HACKLAND,SG-6
HACKLAND,D-1

HACKLAND,JH-1
HADDEN,MP-1
HADFIELD,RD-2
HADFIELD,M-1
HADARIS,BH-1
HADLEY-GRAVE,AS-3
HADLEY-GRAVE,CJ-1
HADLOW,MJ-3
HAESTIER,R-2
HAGEMANN,BK-5
HAGEMANN,GJ-1
HAGEN,R-4
HAGERTY,RC-1
HAINES,GE-26
HAINES,JA-4
HAINES,LJ-1
HAINES,RA-1
HAINES,SM-14
HAINES,VM-1
HAINES,Y-1
HAINS,MI-2
HAKEN,P-2
HALADA,-1
HALES,LE-2
HALL,AI-3
HALL,D-1
HALL,G-8
HALL,GL-2
HALL,GB-1
HALL,J-7
HALL,MR-7
HALL,MJ-4
HALL,RM-2
HALL,J-1
HALL,JB-2
HALL,SE-2
HALLATT,C-1
HALLATT,F-2
HALLIDAY,AM-5
HALLIDAY,MB-1
HALLIER,RC-2
HALLOWES,A-5
HALLOWES,C-1
HALLOWES,P-2
HALSE,HR-3
HALSE,R-1
HALSTEAD,KR-1
HAMANA,I-1
HAMANN,J-1
HAMANN,A-4
HAMILTON,DR-1
HAMILTON,RJ-3
HAMILTON,J-4
HAMILTON,MC-1
HAMILTON-BROWN,GD-3
HAMILTON-BROWN,GI-3
HAMILTON-BROWN,DJ-3
HAMMAN,R-1
HAMMILL,DE-3
HAMMOND,DA-3
HAMMOND,P-2
HAMMOND,A-1
HAMMOND,E-1
HAMPSON,CA-8
HAMPSON,RG-21
HAMPTON,PL-3
HAMPTON,SD-5
HANBURY,RM-4
HANBURY,PJ-2
HANCOCK,MJ-1
HANDLEY,M-3
HANE,D-3
HANEKOM,P-1
HANKINSON,RG-1
HANLON,ST-1
HANLY,GH-1
HANNATH,S-1
HANNWEG,NH-5
HANSEN,MR-3
HANSEN,L-10
HANSEN,P-2
HANSEN,TC-1
HANSON,GL-3
HANSON,P-1
HANSON,AM-2
HANSON,L-1
HANSON,R-1
HANSSON,GB-5
HARBORTH,G-8

HARBORTH,J-1
HARBORTH,N-1
HARBURN,CR-10
HARCOURT,JB-1
HARCUS,TJ-1
HARDIE,AG-4
HARDIE,GS-3
HARDIE,WJ-6
HARDIE,C-2
HARDING,DS-16
HARDING,WJ-2
HARDING,WS-17
HARDING,AJ-1
HARDMAN,PA-3
HARDMAN,R-1
HARDWICK,AG-3
HARDWICK,G-1
HARDWICK,L-2
HARDWICK,CL-1
HARDWICK,MJ-2
HARDY,RJ-4
HARDY,JA-1
HARDY,TJ-1
HAREL,DC-6
HARELL,L-1
HARGRAVES,P-1
HARKER,DE-5
HARKER,WR-2
HARLEY,JC-4
HARLEY,KL-14
HARLEY,RJ-7
HARLEY,HJ-1
HARLEY,VC-1
HARMESE,G-1
HARMSE,L-10
HARPER,A-6
HARPER,AM-7
HARPER,DA-8
HARPER,A-2
HARPER,PM-2
HARRIES,LJ-2
HARRINGTON,RA-1
HARRIOTT,BG-1
HARRIS,AJ-7

HARRIS,B-7
HARRIS,BW-1
HARRIS,BD-1
HARRIS,HV-7
HARRIS,J-3
HARRIS,KC-10
HARRIS,M-1
HARRIS,PM-3
HARRIS,RJ-2
HARRIS,SG-1
HARRIS,CA-1
HARRISON,GW-1
HARRISON,GN-1
HARRISON,HM-1
HARRISON,M-3
HARRISON,TC-2
HARRISON,N-1
HARRISON,R-3
HART,BR-4
HART,JG-2
HART,NE-10
HART,A-1
HART,PA-3
HARTLEY,BE-1
HARTLEY,HT-4
HARTLEY,NW-2
HARTLEY,JL-1
HARTLEY,MJ-1
HARTMAN,G-2
HARTMAN,A-1
HARTMAN,CB-2
HARTMAN,C-1
HARTO,TF-1
HARTZENBERG,M-1
HARVEY,DE-1
HARVEY,GC-3
HARVEY,P-5
HARVEY,PJ-3
HARVEY,P-2
HARVEY,RD-3
HARVEY,NW-1
HARVEY,T-1
HASENBROEK,G-1

HASSALL,BO-7
HASSALL,RM-2
HASSALL,S-1
HASSELBACH,K-2
HASSELBACH,TL-4
HASTIE,RJ-3
HATCH,GP-1
HATCHETT,D-1
HATFIELD,BE-1
HATFIELD,PA-14
HATFIELD,JB-1
HATFIELD,P-1
HATTINGH,A-5
HATTINGH,AK-6
HATTINGH,EJ-2
HATTINGH,NM-1
HATTON,BL-7
HATTON,JM-1
HAUFF,PM-5
HAUMANN,J-2
HAUPT,C-1
HAUPTFLEISCH,D-4
HAVEMAN,PQ-1
HAVEMANN,NP-3
HAVEMANN,RS-6
HAVENGA,S-1
HAW,G-18
HAW,L-18
HAW,SC-1
HAWARDEN,A-34
HAWARDEN,HW-1
HAWARDEN,DE-5
HAWKINS,TG-1
HAWKSWORTH,LA-1
HAWLEY,AJ-1
HAWLEY,NM-1
HAWORTH,RJ-1
HAWTHORN,SA-1
HAY,JW-4
HAY,P-21
HAY,A-1
HAY,RL-2
HAYCOCK,CA-2
HAYES,DP-1
HAYES,GW-2

HAYES,J-6
HAYES,SD-2
HAYES,H-1
HAYES-HILL,JR-4
HAYETT,PR-3
HAYETT,S-1
HAYLLE-DICK,F-1
HAYMAN,A-1
HAYMAN,DD-2
HAYNES,A-2
HAYNES,CS-8
HAYSOM,N-1
HAYTER,D-2
HAYTER,KM-2
HAYTER,MP-1
HAYTER,P-2
HAYWARD,A-13
HAYWARD,B-4
HAYWARD,PE-3
HAZELL,CR-2
HEAD,R-7
HEALEY,CB-5
HEALEY,I-1
HEAN,HE-17
HEAN,SJ-4
HEAN,C-2
HEARD,CC-1
HEARD,R-1
HEASMAN,GR-4
HEATH,B-1
HEATH,M-1
HEATH,R-1
HEATLIE,C-1
HEATON-NICHOLLS,M-1
HEAVER,SD-6
HEDGCOCK,DG-2
HEDGES,BC-1
HEENAN,GB-1
HEENAN,R-1
HEENOP,L-1
HEERMAN,RJ-1
HEERMANN,T-9
HEESAKKERS,MM-1

HEFER,CJ-2
HEGTER,KT-1
HEIJNIS,CE-2
HEINE,KG-3
HEINER,JS-1
HELBERG,MC-2
HELFRICH,LC-1
HELLENS,TC-3
HELLYER,BN-1
HELYAR,B-22
HELYAR,D-4
HEMINGWAY,B-1
HEMINGWAY,O-18
HEMINGWAY,G-1
HEMMINGS,M-1
HENDERSON,BE-5
HENDERSON,CB-4
HENDERSON,CM-10
HENDERSON,DV-2
HENDERSON,GS-8
HENDERSON,JW-1
HENDERSON,JD-5
HENDERSON,MS-10
HENDERSON,R-4
HENDERSON,B-1
HENDERSON,MN-1
HENDRICKS,SG-2
HENDRIE,WV-6
HENDRIKSE,C-3
HENDRIKSEN,G-2
HENDRIKZ,M-1
HENDRIKZ,N-2
HENDRY,B-1
HENDRY,N-1
HENDRY,R-13
HENDRY,VL-5
HENEBREY,TP-4
HEBBELMANN,JN-7
HENNETT,DA-1
HENNING,P-1
HENRY,A-4
HENRY,BO-1
HENRY,D-5
HENRY,J-3
HENRY,P-5
HENRY,RA-3

LIST OF ALL FINISHERS IN THE DUSI CANOE MARATHON—1951 TO 2006

HENSMAN,SM - 2
HENWOOD,GC - 2
HENWOOD,R - 1
HERBERT,B - 6
HERBERT,C - 2
HERBERT,RM - 1
HERBERT,S - 1
HDE,C - 2
HESTERMANN,H - 3
HERMAN,N - 3
HERMAN,R - 13
HERMAN,AK - 1
HERMON,RB - 5
HERMON,DD - 2
HILDEBRAND,ES - 12
HERON,AS - 2
HERON,G - 1
HERREVELD,RF - 5
HERRIDGE,S - 1
HERTZBERGER,KA - 13
HESKETH,A - 1
HESP,T - 1
HESTER,L - 3
HESTERMANN,CM - 1
HEUGH,A - 1
HEUNIS,J - 1

HIBELL,DR - 1
HICKEY,DJ - 1
HICKMAN,BJ - 1
HICKMAN,MJ - 4
HICKS,L - 10
HICKS,RM - 1
HICKSON,RM - 2
HDE,C - 2
HIESTERMANN,H - 3
HINGLE,GC - 3
HINTON,MA - 1
HIPKINS,DP - 1
HIRSCH,CA - 2
HIRST,BS - 23
HIRST,B - 3
HISCOCK,GL - 6
HISCOE,R - 1
HISLOP,MH - 1
HITCHCOCK,J - 3
HITCHINS,CD - 9
HITCHINS,DM - 3
HITCHINS,GP - 4
HITCHINS,MP - 3
HITCHINS,RM - 4
HITCHINS,PC - 1
HLENGWA,JZ - 3
HLONGWANE,A - 3
HLONGWANE,SE - 1
HLONGWANE,ZH - 4

HILARY,GD - 5
HILLARY,MA - 1
HILLEBRANDT,S - 2
HILLIAR,DS - 4
HILLIAR,GA - 23
HILLIAR,JW - 6
HILLIAR,JD - 12
HILLIAR,RG - 9
HILLIAR,SD - 6
HILLIAR,WH - 7
HILLIAR,TA - 2
HILLIER,A - 9
HILLIER,R - 2
HILLIER,M - 3
HILLOCK,A - 1
HILLS,P - 2
HILLS,JT - 1

HEUSTON,P - 1
HEUSTON,L - 1
HEWAT,IM - 3
HEWITT,R - 3
HEWITT,PN - 1
HEYDENREICHL - 1
HEYNE,D - 2
HEYNES,K - 3
HEYNES,S - 1
HEYNS,CH - 2
HEYNS,HE - 2
HEYNS,RD - 1
HEYWOOD,M - 1
HIBBERT,RN - 6
HIBBERT,E - 1
HIBBERT,GD - 1
HIBBS,JA - 1

HINCHLEY,S - 2
HIND,AD - 10
HIND,CA - 6
HIND,EF - 28
HIND,N - 8
HIND,MR - 1
HINDLE,G - 2
HINDSHAW,B - 1

HODGES,KR - 2
HODGINSON,BA - 1
HODGKINSON,A - 2
HODGKINSON,GB - 1
HODGSKISS,D - 28
HODGSKISS,CA - 1
HODGSKISS,D - 2
HODGSKISS,TP - 2
HODGSON,A - 2
HODKINSON,SG - 1
HODKINSON,TJ - 2
HODSON,D - 6
HODSON,G - 11
HODSON,JL - 2
HODSON,J - 1
HODSON,P - 1
HODSON,WA - 4
HODSON,LC - 4
HOEKSTRA,RG - 1
HOEPNER,UA - 1
HOETS,AA - 3
HOETS,DC - 8
HOETS,G - 6
HOETS,GC - 4
HOETS,H - 1
HOETS(JNR),GC - 1
HOFER,P - 1
HOFFMAN,DP - 1
HOFFMANN,M - 2
HOFFMANN,IA - 3
HOFFMANN,JS - 1
HOFMEYER,DA - 5
HOFMEYER,PG - 1
HOFSAJER,IF - 2
HOGAN,M - 2
HOGG,GA - 4
HOGG,RC - 2
HOGG,SG - 3
HOGGS,SR - 1
HOHLS,GE - 14
HOCKLY,L - 1
HODGES,A - 6
HODGES,BJ - 1
HODGES,CR - 2

HOLMES,ME - 2
HOLMES,N - 3
HOLMES,S - 6
HOLMES,SM - 4
HOLMES,GB - 2
HOLMES,SH - 1
HOLMWOOD,AG - 2
HOLT,GS - 1
HOLTE-SMITH,D - 2
HOLTSHAUSEN,WL - 2
HOLDSWORTH,MA - 17
HOLTZHAUSEN,WL - 5
HOLZBACH,M - 1
HOMANN,BL - 4
HOMPES,D - 4
HONETH,R - 3

HOLD,LM - 2
HOLD,S - 2
HOLDCROFT,P - 6
HOLDEN,K - 14
HOLDEN,SL - 2
HOLDER,CJ - 4
HOLDER,HR - 2
HOLDING,C - 1
HOLDING,BL - 1
HOLDSWORTH,DP - 19
HOLDSWORTH,MA - 17
HOLDSWORTH,TJ - 2
HOLDSWORTH,WL - 5
HOLDSWORTH,CW - 1
HOLGATE,S - 1
HOLIDAY,PJ - 1
HOLING,DP - 2
HOLLAGAN,M - 1
HOLLAND,OC - 4
HOLLAND,BE - 1
HOLLAND,C - 1
HOLLEY,CG - 3
HOLLEY,MN - 11
HOLLEY,N - 1
HOLLEY,OH - 2
HOLLEY,AL - 1
HOLLICK,PG - 2
HOLLIGAN,M - 2
HOLLINGSWORTH,WH - 2
HOLLINGTON,R - 1
HOLLINSHEAD,JM - 9
HOLLIS-GRAY,KM - 3
HOLLOWAY,FJ - 1
HOLLOWAY,L - 3
HOLLOWAY,TM - 1
HOLM,GK - 6
HOLM,LD - 3
HOLMAN,S - 1
HOLMES,A - 2
HOLMES,BC - 7
HOLMES,D - 4
HOLMES,GD - 10
HOLMES,K - 5
HOLMES,MJ - 1
HOLMES,MG - 8
HOLMES,MR - 10

HONEYBORN,R - 2
HONEYSETT,CJ - 1
HONIBALL,HW - 1
HONNEYSETT,R - 3
HOOD,GW - 1
HOOGEWERF,B - 10
HOOK,JR - 2
HOOK,K - 1
HOOK,R - 1
HOOKER,RT - 4
HOOKER,B - 2
HOOKER,MR - 2
HOOPER,GA - 3
HOOPER,IV - 9
HOOPER,WJ - 13
HOOPER,RA - 2
HOPE,CA - 1
HOPE,E - 1
HOPE,L - 1
HOPE-BAILLIE,A - 1
HOPE-JOHNSTONE,N - 1
HOPKINS,GC - 1
HOPPE,PJ - 1
HORACEK,J - 1
HORN,C - 4
HORN,D - 2
HORN,G - 1
HORN,ND - 4

HORN,EM - 1
HORN,F - 1
HORN,LH - 6
HORN,WL - 1
HORNBY,GC - 1
HORNBY,JD - 4
HORNBY,N - 3
HORNBY,CH - 1
HORNE,KD - 2
HORNE,MK - 6
HORNE,SA - 1
HORNSVELD,R - 1
HORSLER,FU - 4
HORTON,G - 2
HORWOOD,CE - 3
HORWOOD,FJ - 1
HOSE,MR - 1
HOSKEN,TA - 1
HOSKIN,RC - 2
HOSKIN,S - 1
HOSKING,B - 2
HOSKING,D - 2
HOSKING,MA - 1
HOSKING,S - 2
HOSKING,TL - 1
HOUGH,C - 2
HOUGH,GR - 6
HOUGH,L - 9
HOUGH,SD - 5
HOUGHTING,R - 9
HOUGHTING,SI - 7
HOUGHTING,M - 1
HOUGHTON,DA - 1
HOUNSON,K - 1
HOURQUEBIE,F - 1
HOUSE,G - 1
HOUSEMAN,BR - 3
HOUSEMAN,MG - 1
HOWARD,AG - 1
HOWARD,CM - 25
HOWARD,G - 5
HOWARD,JG - 5
HOWARD,M - 1
HOWARD,R - 2
HOWARD,SD - 4

HOWARD,HI - 1
HOWARD,J - 1
HOWARD,L - 2
HOWARD,WB - 4
HOWARD,X - 1
HOWARTH,BE - 3
HOWARTH,LR - 6
HOWARTH,LA - 1
HOWAT,RF - 1
HOWCROFT,KD - 5
HOWE,DJ - 12
HOWE,DI - 2
HOWE,KA - 2
HOWE,R - 6
HOWE,H - 3
HOWE,H - 1
HOWECROFT,T - 6
HOWELL,AD - 2
HOWELL,C - 2
HOWELL,E - 5
HOWES,CE - 4
HOWES,DM - 1
HOWES,SR - 2
HOWES,TS - 5
HOWES,F - 1
HOWES,R - 1
HOY,BR - 1
HUBBARD,GM - 2
HUBBARD,F - 1
HUBBLE,IH - 3
HUBERT,EJ - 3
HUDSON,GP - 5
HUDSON,R - 1
HUDSON,SP - 1
HUDSON,E - 1
HUDSON,MI - 1
HUGHES,AD - 1
HUGHES,BI - 7
HUGHES,CD - 4
HUGHES,GC - 2
HUGHES,JP - 2
HUGHES,JR - 1
HUGHES,J - 6
HUGHES,JP - 4
HUGHES,JC - 4

HUGHES,MA - 1
HUGHES,NA - 1
HUGHES,ST - 3
HUGHES,KA - 1
HULETT,BN - 3
HULETT,GI - 2
HULETT,CN - 1
HULL,GA - 1
HULL,PJ - 2
HULLEY,DM - 9
HULLEY,F - 3
HULLEY,SC - 8
HULLEY,TR - 3
HULLEY,A - 1
HULLEY,CF - 2
HUMAN,N - 1
HUMAN,C - 1
HUMAN,D - 1
HUME,JB - 1
HUME,D - 5
HUMM,LA - 1
HUMPHREY,M - 5
HUMPHREYS,KA - 3
HUMPHREYS,L - 3
HUMPHREYS,X - 1
HUMPHREYS,GR - 1
HUMPHREYS,SN - 3
HUMPHRY,RN-21
HUMPHRY,SR - 6
HUNDT,P - 2
HUNKIN,MA - 6
HUNT,CG - 2
HUNT,M - 1
HUNTER,DC - 2
HUNTER,J - 1
HUNTER,J - 9
HUNTER,M - 3
HUNTER,P - 1
HUNTER,TJ - 3
HUNTER,B - 1
HUNTER,JM - 1
HUNTER,RN - 2
HUNTER-SMITH,M - 1
HUNTLEY,RB - 3
HURLVAIT,AJ - 1

HURNDALL,K - 1
HURST,G - 1
HUTCHEON,KJ - 3
HUTCHEON,RE - 1
HUTCHINSON,TJ - 3
HUTCHINSON,B - 1
HUTCHINSON,LT - 1
HUTCHISON,R - 1
HUTSON,MR-12
HUTTON,HD - 1
HUTTON,K - 6
HUTTON,MB - 2
HUTTON,VM - 1
HUXTABLE,MP - 1
HUYSAMEN,M - 1
HYATT,R - 4
HYDE,RP - 1
HYDE,J - 1
HYDE,S - 1
HYNES,S - 2
HYSLOP,RC - 2
IEVERS,G - 2
IGGULDEN,RJ - 1
ILSLEY,JP - 1
ILSLEY,B - 1
IMMELMAN,A - 1
INGHAM,P - 7
INGHAM-BROWN,D - 1
INGLE,J - 2
INGLE,RP - 1
INGLIS,A - 7
INGLIS,A - 4
INGLIS,JR - 4
INGLIS,R - 5
INGLIS,S - 2
INGLIS,PA - 1
INGRAM,BR - 7
INGRAM,T - 9
INOCCO,DJ - 1
INOCCO,RA - 2
IRELAND,BK - 4
IRELAND,PA - 1
IRELAND,T - 6
IRONS,RB - 3

IRVINE,BR - 1
IRVINE,B - 7
IRVINE,DJ - 3
IRVINE,MR - 2
IRVINE,N - 6
IRVINE,BR - 3
IRVINE,CW - 1
IRVINE-SMITH,B - 2
IRVING,AG - 1
IRVING,G-13
IRVING,MA - 2
ISAAC,MI - 1
ISBISTER,A - 1
ISHERWOOD,TR - 1
ISRAELSOHN,C - 2
IVAN,J - 1
IVE,BD-25
IVE,RB - 1
IVINS,CI - 1
IVINS,GA - 1
IVINS,JM - 4
IVINS,J - 1
IVY,AJ - 3
IVY,RG - 1
IZZETT,MD - 1
J V RENSBURG,B - 1
J V RENSBURG,ET - 1
J VAN RENSBURG,LW - 1
JACOBS,GC - 1
JACKA,CP - 1
JACKA,P - 1
JACKLIN,JM - 3
JACKSON,B - 4
JACKSON,B - 6
JACKSON,C - 2
JACKSON,GW - 6
JACKSON,JF - 4
JACKSON,LT - 7
JACKSON,M - 5
JACKSON,NP - 9
JACKSON,PG - 2
JACKSON,RD - 8
JACKSON,RS - 3
JACKSON,E - 1
JACKSON,KN - 1

JACKSON,YG - 1
JACKSON,WF - 2
JACOBS,B - 11
JACOBS,GC - 5
JACOBS,G - 9
JACOBS,KC - 3
JACOBS,W - 8
JACOBS,W - 2
JACOBS,DF - 2
JACOBS,L - 2
JACOBSEN,MD - 1
JACOBSOHN,FG - 1
JACOBSON,E - 3
JACOBY,SB - 1
JACOBY,M - 1
JACQUELINE,P - 1
JACQUES,. - 1
JAGER,GT - 4
JAMIESON,G - 1
JAMES,BJ - 2
JAMES,BM - 2
JAMES,D - 3
JAMES,E - 11
JAMES,H - 1
JAMES,J - 6
JAMES,M - 7
JAMES,M - 7
JAMES,MW - 8
JAMES,NP - 2
JAMES,RD - 4
JAMES,C - 2
JAMES,LA - 1
JAMES,NJ - 5
JAMES,X - 1
JAMESON,RD - 1
JAMESON,MA - 1
JAMESON,NA - 1
JAMIESON,C - 8
JAMIESON,AD - 6
JAMIESON,C - 4
JAMIESON,DB - 2
JAMIESON,GA - 6
JAMIESON,M -17
JAMIESON,W -10
JAMIESON,NA - 1
JANKIELSOHN,LE - 2

JANNEKER,MW-18
JANNEKER,AL - 1
JANOS,C - 1
JANSCHEK,P - 2
JANSE V RENSBURG,E - 4
JANSE V RENSBURG,LW - 1
JANSE V RENSBURG,MJ - 8
JANSE V RENSBURG,TJ - 1
JANSE VAN RENSBURG,JJ - 2
JANSE VAN RENSBURG,LW - 1
JANSE VAN RENSBUR,R - 1
JANSE VAN RENSBUR,S - 1
JANSE VAN VUUREN,GC - 2
JANSEN,MC - 2
JANSEN,SF - 2
JANSEN,WJ-11
JANSEN,BC - 1
JANSEN,ED - 1
JANSEN,G - 1
JANSEN,JW - 2
JANSEN V RENSBERG,L - 1
JANSEN V RENSBURG,L - 3
JANSEN VAN RENSBU,P - 2
JANSEN VAN VUUREN,B - 1
JANSEN VAN VUUREN,P - 1
JANSSENS,A -10
JANSSENS,LS - 1
JANSSENS,P - 2
JARDIN,AP - 7
JARDINE,C - 4
JARDINE,DB - 2
JARDINE,SL - 3
JARDINE,B - 1
JARMAN,K - 1
JARVEL,LC - 1
JARVIE,AD - 5
JARVIE,GI-10
JARVIE,JA - 9
JARVIE,EM - 3
JARVIE,PA - 4
JAYES,G - 1
JEARY,R - 1

JEFFERYS,SB - 4
JEFFREY,MI - 1
JEFFREYS,G - 1
JELF,C - 1
JELINSKI,T - 9
JELLIS,A - 7
JENKINS,JT - 5
JENKINS,L-12
JENKINS,LL - 1
JENKINS,S - 8
JENKINS,S - 1
JENKINS,TT - 1
JENKINS JNR,LW-12
JENKINS SNR,LW - 1
JENNINGS,AG - 8
JENNINGS,C-11
JENNINGS,PG - 5
JENNINGS,D - 1
JENSEN,SF - 2
JENSEN,AJ - 5
JENSEN,WJ-11
JENSEN,W - 3
JENZEN,A - 1
JENSEN,G - 1
JENSEN,JW - 2
JEROME,JC - 1
JESSOP,C - 7
JEVON,D - 1
JEWELL,GD - 4
JEWETT,G - 1
JEWITT,GP-14
JEWITT,MS - 8
JEWITT,JA - 1
JOFFE,A - 1
JOHNS,G - 1
JOHNS,MN - 5
JOHNSON,A - 4
JOHNSON,B - 8
JOHNSON,BC - 5
JOHNSON,C - 2
JOHNSON,DN - 3
JOHNSON,J-15
JOHNSON,J - 6
JOHNSON,MR-23
JOHNSON,MK-16
JOHNSON,N - 3
JOHNSON,P - 3
JOHNSON,S - 1
JOHNSON,TW - 4
JOHNSON,E - 2
JOHNSON,KA - 1

JOHNSON,L - 2
JOHNSTON,C - 6
JOHNSTON,DM - 2
JOHNSTON,EH - 4
JOHNSTON,GK - 6
JOHNSTON,L - 6
JOHNSTON,M - 3
JOHNSTON,O - 1
JOHNSTON,S - 8
JOHNSTON,S - 1
JOHNSTON,S - 5
JOHNSTON,S - 6
JOHNSTON,DF - 1
JOHNSTON,I - 1
JOHNSTONE,B - 4
JOHNSTONE,D - 2
JOHNSTONE,GH - 8
JOHNSTONE,GI-11
JOHNSTONE,JP - 1
JOHNSTONE,SM - 1
JOHNSTONE,LH - 1
JOHNSTONE,T - 1
JOINER,AJ - 3
JOLLIFFE,S - 1
JOLLY,ND - 4
JONES,AC - 5
JONES,AR-21
JONES,BA - 6
JONES,B - 1
JONES,BK - 2
JONES,BR - 6
JONES,CA - 7
JONES,D - 8
JONES,D - 1
JONES,J - 1
JONES,M - 8
JONES,RD - 3
JONES,R - 1
JONES,R - 6
JONES,RR - 5
JONES,S -14
JONES,SD - 3
JONES,T - 9
JONES,WR - 2
JONES,ZM - 1
JONES,AD - 3

JONES,G - 1
JONES,JB - 1
JONES,KG - 1
JONES,S - 2
JONES,S - 1
JONES,SG - 1
JONES,SE - 1
JONKER,D - 3
JONKER,J - 6
JONKER,M - 20
JONSSON,C - 1
JONSSON,S - 2
JOOSTE,E - 3
JOOSTE,T - 3
JORDAAN,EA-12
JORDAAN,JP - 1
JORDAAN,JL - 9
JORDAAN,JL-16
JORDAAN,SN - 4
JORDAAN,D - 1
JORDAAN,J - 1
JORDAAN,BP - 3
JORDAN,BP-26
JORDAN,M - 2
JORDAN,T - 1
JORDAN,BV - 1
JORDAN,E - 1
JORDAN,KG - 1
JORDAN,R - 1
JORGENSEN,DG-11
JORGENSEN,WH - 1
JOSEPH,L - 1
JOSS,AR - 5
JOUBERT,A - 5
JOUBERT,CS - 7
JOUBERT,DI - 1
JOUBERT,D - 9
JOUBERT,DD - 8
JOUBERT,FV - 3
JOUBERT,G - 6
JOUBERT,L-13
JOUBERT,LD - 6
JOUBERT,MG - 5
JOUBERT,TT - 2

LIST OF ALL FINISHERS IN THE DUSI CANOE MARATHON—1951 TO 2006

LAATZ,GA-2
LABASCHAGNE,W-1
LABURN,R-2
LABUSCHAGNE,EJ-2
LABUSCHAGNE,NG-1
LABUSCHAGNE,DI-1
LABUSCHAGNE,DL-1
LABUSCHAGNE,M-1
LABUSCHAGNE,T-1
LABUSCHAGNE,W-2
LACHENICHT,DC-1
LACOCK,RA-8
LACOCK,LG-1
LADBROOKE,GR-6
LAESECKE,SC-3
LAGGAR,RW-4
LAIL VAUX,DP-1
LAING,AT-3
LAING,GL-5
LAING,BC-1
LAING,C-3
LAKE,GA-6
LAKE,WT-5
LAKER,P-1
LALONDE,J-1
LALOR,K-1
LAMB,JW-1
LAMBE,GM-7
LAMBERT,BC-5
LAMBERT,DF-12
LAMBERT,JH-3
LAMBERT,M-3
LAMBERT,JR-1
LAMBERT,GA-3
LAMBIE,JS-1
LAMBLE,NP-5
LAMBLE,T-7
LAMBOOY,C-2
LAMBSON,W-5
LAMING,SJ-4
LAMONT,SE-4
LAMPRECHT,C-2
LANCASTER,PM-10
LANCASTER,WM-6
LANCASTER,BA-3
LANDAU,R-12

LANDER,PA-1
LANDMAN,M-2
LANDMAN,WA-3
LANDY,D-1
LANE,WJ-1
LANG,EJ-3
LANG,PM-9
LANGAAS,OC-1
LANGE,D-1
LANGE,PD-3
LANGENHOVEN,JH-7
LANGENHOVEN,C-1
LANGENHOVEN,HP-1
LANGFORD,RE-4
LANGLEY,MC-7
LANGLEY,GI-1
LANGLOIS,V-4
LANGSHOW,G-1
LANGSLOW,S-1
LANGTON,BA-4
LANGTON,G-1
LAPACZ,K-1
LAPONDER,PH-1
LAQUA,C-1
LARCOMBE,PJ-2
LARSAN,E-1
LARSEN,DA-4
LARSEN,PT-1
LARSEN,A-1
LARSON,E-2
LARSSEN,E-1
LASKEY,K-11
LASKEY,RA-1
LAST,RD-2
LAST,WJ-16
LATIMER,LP-3
LATTER,K-4
LAUBSCHER,CB-5
LAUBSCHER,GL-1
LAUBSCHER,RH-2
LAUBSCHER,KB-1
LAUE,A-3
LAUEL,LH-1
LAUER,GB-2
LAUER,TG-1

LAUF,T-2
LAUGHOR-CLARKE,AE-3
LAUGHOR-CLARKE,J-2
LAVARACK,J-12
LAVERY,SW-3
LAVERY,LC-3
LAVETT,P-1
LAVOIPIERRE,SR-2
LAW,MD-1
LAWLER,IA-2
LAWLOR,MR-2
LAWRENCE,AJ-3
LAWRENCE,CR-1
LAWRENCE,K-2
LAWRENCE,MP-2
LAWRENCE,B-2
LAWRENCE,PE-2
LAWRENCE,RC-1
LAWRENCE,SH-1
LAWRIE,AJ-9
LAWRY,B-2
LAWS,S-1
LAWSON,CJ-3
LAWSON,J-2
LAWSON,AC-1
LAWSON,BA-1
LAWSON,SB-1
LAX,A-10
LAX,MH-2
LAY,RD-1
LE CONDEUR,MJ-1
LE CORDEUR,JD-5
LE CORDEUR,MJ-1
LE FEVRE,GJ-1
LE GRANGE,GM-1
LE GRANGE,S-6
LE GROS,L-1
LE MEME,GC-1
LE ROUX,A-1
LE ROUX,B-2
LE ROUX,CL-1
LE ROUX,D-9
LE ROUX,E-6
LE ROUX,E-1
LE ROUX,HP-1

LE ROUX,JG-2
LE ROUX,JE-5
LE ROUX,E-2
LE ROUX,G-2
LE ROUX,M-1
LE ROUX,PA-1
LE SEUR,C-1
LE SMEUR,D-1
LE SUEUR,CR-2
LE SUEUR,D-2
LE SUR,BJ-1
LE TOURNEUR,B-1
LEA,RA-2
LEACH,CP-2
LEACH,DB-3
LEACH,E-2
LEASK,F-1
LEASK,T-1
LEATHEM,LM-3
LEATHER,DT-1
LEATHERBARROW,S-3
LEATHERBARROW,D-2
LEATHERN,EW-1
LEAVER,C-2
LECK,HJ-2
LECLER,NL-1
LECLEZIO,P-1
LECLEZIO,VF-3
LECLEZIO,Y-7
LEDEBOER,L-12
LEDERLE,MI-1
LEE,C-4
LEE,J-2
LEE,TH-2
LEE,RB-1
LEEB,JL-7
LEEB,S-1
LEEMHUIS,J-1
LEFEVRE,DF-1
LEFEVRE,G-1
LEFEVRE,R-4
LEGGE,C-1
LEGH,JA-1

LEHMACHER,A-3
LEHMAN,BJ-1
LEHMAN,PB-8
LEHMAN,RA-4
LEIBBRANDT,CL-1
LEIBBRANDT,JN-1
LEIBBRANDT,N-4
LEIBBRANDT,E-1
LEIBBRANDT,C-5
LEIBBRANDT,JN-1
LEIGH,DP-5
LEIGH,R-1
LEISEGANG,BP-7
LEISEGANG,KC-2
LEISEGANG,HK-1
LEITH,WA-1
LEITH,A-5
LEITNER,W-1
LELLO,AD-5
LEMBETHE,R-17
LEMKE,G-2
LEMMER,D-3
LEMMER,WM-12
LEMMER,PJ-2
LEMMON WARDE,JM-1
LEMOS,AP-1
LENNON,BM-15
LENNOX,GS-3
LENNOX,MH-1
LENNOX,NA-1
LENTELL,RA-1
LENTZ,G-1
LEONARD,D-5
LEONARD,J-3
LEONARDA,A-1
LESLIE,J-3
LESLIE,JR-16
LESLIE,P-1
LESLIE,RL-3
LESLIE,B-2
LESLIE,MD-1
LESSING,Q-1
LESUR,JB-2
LETCHER,WC-2
LETINIC,J-5

LETOURNEUR,BJ-1
LEVELL,M-2
LEVERTON,G-4
LEVICK,MR-1
LEVICK,PG-1
LEVIEUX,CA-2
LEVIN,D-2
LEVINSOHN,L-2
LEVINSON,L-14
LEVINSON,RG-5
LEVINSON,DA-1
LEVINSON,ER-1
LEWIN,BA-5
LEWIN,MA-1
LEWIN,RC-1
LEWIS,DM-8
LEWIS,GV-3
LEWIS,G-1
LEWIS,AJ-1
LEWIS,CG-1
LEWIS,P-3
LEWIS,RL-1
LEWIS,TE-3
LIBBY,B-1
LICHFIELD,NB-1
LIDDLE,AN-2
LIDDLE,BM-2
LIEBENBERG,JG-1
LIEBENBERG,R-1
LIEBENBERG,J-3
LIEBENBERG,J-1
LIEBENBERG,J-2
LIEBETRAU,ZL-2
LIEBRANDT,N-1
LIEVESLEY,D-13
LIEVESLEY,JB-1
LIGHTBODY,A-8
LIGHTBODY,CM-4
LIGHTFOOT,A-3
LIGHTFOOT,AI-1
LIGHTFOOT,T-5
LIGHTFOOT,QC-1
LILFORD,F-1
LINCOLN,DW-2
LIND HOLMES,AG-1

LIND HOLMES,CJ-20
LINDE,JU-5
LINDEN,TA-1
LINDHEIM,MS-1
LIND-HOLMES,AG-2
LINDSAY,AI-7
LINDSAY,CK-3
LINDSAY,R-3
LINDSAY,B-1
LINDSAY,E-1
LINDSAY,G-1
LINDSAY,K-1
LINDSAY,NI-1
LINLEY,M-1
LINTS,JH-5
LINTVELT,EA-4
LION-CACHET,B-15
LION-CACHET,L-4
LION-CACHET,J-1
LIPCHICK,G-3
LIPCHICK,R-1
LIQUORICE,PS-6
LIQUORISH,GP-2
LISHMAN,PB-1
LISHMAN,S-5
LISTER,BD-2
LISTER,HG-1
LITCHFIELD,N-2
LITTLE,B-1
LITTLE,JE-5
LITTLE,DP-1
LITTLE,LB-1
LITTLEWOOD,JM-3
LIVERSAGE,JP-2
LIVINGSTONE,G-4
LIVINGSTONE,MG-6
LIVINGSTONE,P-2
LLOYD,PH-3
LLOYD,RN-8
LLOYD,JT-1
LLOYD,LK-1
LLOYD,MA-1
LLOYD-ELLIS,T-2
LOADER,D-3
LOCHNER,JP-2

LOCHNER,L-2
LOCK,M-1
LOCKETT,AM-1
LOCKETT,RN-2
LOCKHART,R-7
LOCKHART,FM-2
LOCKHART,L-1
LODER,SR-1
LODGE,L-7
LOEDOLFF,FC-1
LOEDOLFF,A-1
LOEWENSTEIN,M-13
LOEWENSTEIN,MB-18
LOGAN,CP-4
LOGAN,PJ-1
LOGAN,RR-3
LOGIE,M-4
LOMBAARD,MJ-2
LOMBARD,A-6
LOMBARD,RA-9
LOMBARD,CG-1
LOMBARD,J-3
LOMBARD,P-1
LOMBRINK,D-1
LONG,JC-2
LONG,RB-4
LONG,TJ-17
LONG,G-1
LONG,H-1
LONG,MK-3
LONG,R-2
LONGHURST,G-1
LONGLEY,?-1
LONGLEY,BE-2
LONGSHAW,T-1
LONGSTON,AW-1
LOOCK,M-1
LOOSE,AD-1
LOOTS,F-6
LOOTS,LH-3
LOOTS,H-2
LOOTS,RJ-2
LORAM,S-3
LORENZ,CH-4
LOSER,DT-2

LIST OF ALL FINISHERS IN THE DUSI CANOE MARATHON—1951 TO 2006

LOSER,TG-3
LOTT,SA-2
LOTTER,D-3
LOTTERING,AG-4
LOTTERING,F-3
LOTZ,LE-3
LOTZ,RS-3
LOTZE,GM-1
LOUBSCHER,M-1
LOUBSER,C-1
LOUBSER,MR-1
LOUGHOR-CLARKE,S-1
LOUMEAU,MJ-1
LOUMEAU,R-1
LOURENS,MG-1
LOURENS,D-1
LOUW,CF-2
LOUW,GC-2
LOUW,G-2
LOUW,JG-2
LOUW,LO-1
LOUW,RA-4
LOUW,TJ-5
LOUW,A-3
LOUWRENS,PA-4
LOVE,GA-4
LOVE,DJ-2
LOVEMORE,BB-5
LOVEMORE,SL-3
LOWE,D-1
LOWE,DF-12
LOWE,J-2
LOWE,MW-11
LOWE,R-7
LOWE,R-4
LOWE,S-2
LOWES,K-1
LOWMAN,AM-1
LOXTON,DG-1
LOXTON,GM-1
LUBBE,CL-2
LUBBE,DR-2

LUBBE,L-2
LUBBE,JS-1
LUBOUT,K-9
LUCAS,GW-1
LUCK,D-10
LUCK,R-2
LUCKEN,K-2
LUDEWIG,G-1
LUDICK,C-1
LUDWICK,KG-1
LUFFINGHAM,L-6
LUTINGH,M-1
LUIZ,DA-2
LUMGAIR,D-6
LUND,A-6
LUND,R-2
LUNDIE,MA-6
LUPKE,A-1
LUPTON,D-3
LUPTON SMITH,SP-5
LUPTON-SMITH,S-2
LUSCOMBE,M-4
LUSIGNEA,E-10
LUSTED,M-6
LUTZ,SA-2
LUTZKIE,FW-1
LUYCKX,C-1
LUYT,CJ-2
LUYT,D-2
LYALL,CW-2
LYLE,MG-2
LYLE,B-1
LYNCH,BJ-1
LYNCH,GP-1
LYNE,C-4
LYNN,MW-5
LYNSKY,R-6
LYONS,J-3
LYONS,K-10
LYSTER,M-3
MORRIS-JONES,G-1
MAARSCHALK,TR-9
MAARTENS,WF-4
MAC DONALD,G-1
MAC DONALD,N-2

MAC DUFF,AL-2
MAC DUFF,D-1
MAC GREGOR,FG-3
MAC GREGOR,SD-2
MAC INTOSH,D-1
MAC KAY,GJ-2
MAC KAY,SM-2
MAC KAY,JC-1
MAC KENZIE,AG-1
MAC KENZIE,BO-3
MAC KENZIE,CA-7
MAC KENZIE,DB-2
MAC KENZIE,G-4
MAC KENZIE,HL-2
MAC KENZIE,JB-3
MAC KENZIE,M-2
MAC KENZIE,PC-1
MAC KENZIE,JA-3
MAC KENZIE,TS-1
MAC KINLAY,AJ-6
MAC KINNON,AC-5
MAC LACHLAN,JR-2
MAC LAINE,R-1
MAC LEAN,D-8
MAC LEOD,HD-4
MAC LEOD,S-1
MAC NICOL,JC-12
MAC NICOL,DI-3
MAC PHERSON,DN-2
MAC PHERSON,W-1
MACASKILL,D-2
MACDONALD,GR-3
MACDONALD,R-1
MACDONALD,DB-1
MACDUFF,A-1
MACFARLANE,C-1
MACFARLANE,RJ-10
MACFIE,O-2
MACFIE,SC-2
MACGILLICUDDY,D-1
MACGILLIVRAY,RH-2
MACGREGOR,A-10

MACGREGOR,RS-1
MACGREGOR,AI-2
MACGREGOR,JL-1
MACGREGOR,S-2
MACHELL-COX,MF-2
MACK,A-4
MACK,X-1
MACKAY,PD-1
MACKAY,SR-1
MACKAY,DJ-1
MACKELLAR,CD-1
MACKENZIE,LC-2
MACKENZIE,K-1
MACKENZIE,R-1
MACKENZIE,T-2
MACKINNON,AC-2
MACKINTOSH,G-1
MACKINTOSH,J-1
MACKINTOSH,C-1
MACKINTOSH,E-1
MACKINTOSH,IM-3
MACKINTOSH,TD-1
MACLACHLAN,SA-1
MACLACHLAN,AC-2
MACLEAN,TG-1
MACLENNAN,A-3
MACLENNAN,H-1
MACLENNAN,SH-1
MACLEOD,DJ-13
MACLEOD,P-1
MACLEOD,SB-2
MACLEOD,AJ-1
MACMILLAN,G-4
MACNAB,AS-1
MACNAB,MU-1
MACNEILLIE,D-1
MACPHERSON,DF-2
MACQUET,GJ-6
MACQUET,JD-1
MADDEN,JG-2
MADDEN,G-1
MADDEN,R-5
MADEL,F-1
MADIMA,L-1
MADONDO,DM-2

MAEHLER,DR-6
MAEHLER,JG-7
MAGER,PK-1
MAGETE,KS-1
MAGNI,A-5
MAGNI,MA-4
MAGUBANE,BN-3
MAHER,AT-11
MAHER,AL-3
MAHER,CL-3
MAHER,TM-5
MAHONEY,AA-2
MAHOOD,B-2
MAHOOD,K-2
MAIER,B-1
MAIER,RA-1
MAIER,TG-1
MAINGARD,B-2
MAIN,S-8
MAITRE,PA-1
MAJOLA,CK-3
MAKEIN,M-1
MAKHUDU,MS-4
MALAN,D-1
MALAN,H-1
MALAN,JH-6
MALAN,P-1
MALAN,C-1
MALCOLM,JG-3
MALENGRET,M-3
MALHERBE,A-2
MALHERBE,GJ-1
MALHERBE,L-2
MALHERBE,F-1
MALLEN,L-1
MALLEN,CL-1
MALLINSON,J-4
MALLON,AP-5
MALONE,AG-2
MALTBY,J-1
MALTBY,MA-5
MANANA,M-1
MANDY,D-6
MANDY,GL-2

MANFRON,C-7
MANFRON,R-4
MANFRONI,A-4
MANGOLD,TI-2
MANGOLD,JC-1
MANLEY,DR-6
MANN,GL-9
MANN,KL-7
MANN,PL-10
MANN,RL-10
MANN,SL-12
MANN,B-1
MANN,LC-1
MANNHEIM,C-1
MANNHEIM,R-1
MANNING,GF-6
MANNING,JL-4
MANNING,PJ-20
MANNING,RP-3
MANNING,SC-3
MANNING,SP-4
MANNING,A-1
MANNING,P-1
MANNING,SP-1
MANOCK,K-1
MANOS,D-1
MANSER,AJ-1
MANSON,B-2
MANSON,D-1
MANSOUR,GA-1
MANTON,CG-3
MANTON,G-3
MANYATHI,T-10
MANZIE,SA-1
MAPHAM,TR-5
MARAIS,AG-2
MARAIS,AJ-1
MARAIS,AL-7
MARAIS,AL-1
MARAIS,B-6
MARAIS,JC-8
MARAIS,P-4
MARAIS,R-2
MARAIS,SJ-1
MARAIS,D-1
MARAIS,H-1

MARAIS,JI-2
MARAIS,LJ-1
MARAIS,M-4
MARCH,KD-5
MARCH,MG-7
MARCH,NP-2
MARE,J-7
MARE,LA-3
MARE,P-2
MARE,W-1
MAREE,E-4
MAREE,EJ-4
MAREE,M-6
MAREE,J-1
MAREE,P-1
MARFORD,R-1
MARITZ,EA-4
MARITZ,M-2
MARITZ,NA-1
MARITZ,J-2
MARKHAM,GE-7
MARLAND,C-6
MARLAND,P-1
MARLIN,M-1
MARLIN,SR-14
MARLIN,B-1
MARLIN,PC-1
MARLTON,GH-2
MAROSEK,P-1
MARQUIS-JONES,GA-1
MARRIOT,P-7
MARRIOTT,BG-1
MARRIOTT,B-13
MARRIOTT,RD-2
MARRIOTT,Y-1
MARRIOTT,IC-1
MARS,M-13
MARSHALL,AJ-1
MARSHALL,CM-1
MARSHALL,J-4
MARSHALL,J-3
MARSHALL,J-1
MARSHALL,RJ-2

MARTEGOUTTE,SL-1
MARTELL,CE-10
MARTENS,JE-4
MARTENS,B-1
MARTENS,UA-1
MARTHINUSSEN,J-1
MARTIN,E-6
MARTIN,GA-2
MARTIN,J-7
MARTIN,PR-1
MARTIN,RJ-2
MARTIN,S-5
MARTIN,T-1
MARTIN,AC-1
MARTIN,M-2
MARTIN,V-1
MARTINS,GP-5
MARTINS,J-5
MARWICK,KA-4
MARX,G-4
MASEFIELD,J-3
MASKELL,PC-1
MASOJADA,MA-4
MASON,C-11
MASON,GH-7
MASON,SR-1
MASON,WA-3
MASON,AE-2
MASON,J-2
MASON,J-1
MASSEY,KG-2
MASSEY,AI-2
MASSEY,WT-1
MASSEY,GF-1
MASSEY,J-1
MASSEY,NJ-1
MASTERS,B-2
MASTERS,PB-1
MASTERSON,G-4
MATCHETT,PJ-1
MATHEBULA,M-1
MATHER,CI-1
MATHEWS,CB-9
MATHEWS,T-3
MATHIE,JJ-1

LIST OF ALL FINISHERS IN THE DUSI CANOE MARATHON—1951 TO 2006

MATHIOT,E.-1
MATLALA,BI-1
MATTER,JR.-2
MATTERSON,A.-1
MATTHEW,S.-2
MATTHEWS,D.-4
MATTHEWS,GK.-4
MATTHEWS,G.-2
MATTHEWS,G.-14
MATTHEWS,LG.-6
MATTHEWS,R.-18
MATTHEWS,E.-1
MATTHEWS,KL.-1
MATTHEWS,VJ.-1
MATTHEYS,HH.-1
MATTUSHEK,VR.-5
MAU,CR.-1
MAUD,CR.-1
MAUD,GK.-1
MAURER,R.-9
MAVUNDLA,ZE-2
MAXWELL,F.-4
MAXWELL,K.-1
MAY,DA-8
MAY,WH.-2
MAY,RW.-1
MAYALL,JW.-10
MAYALL,TI-1
MAYBERY,PA.-3
MAYBERY,DE.-1
MAYERS,AR.-8
MAYNARD,M.-4
MAYNARD,RA-16
MAYNARD,SR.-8
MAYNE,B.-4
MAYNE,M.-2
MAZOUE,NJ.-6
MAZOUE,PA.-7
MAZOUE,JP.-1
MAZOUE,WA.-1
MBANJWA,M.-8
MC ALLISTER,SJ.-5
MC ALPINE,S.-1
MC ARAVEY,RN.-1
MC ARTHUR,A.-1

MC ARTHUR,N.-3
MC BEY,GW.-2
MC CALGAN,TM.-2
MC CALLUM,SC.-2
MC CALLUM,R.-7
MC CANN,B.-2
MC CARTAN,SA.-1
MC CARTHY,JP.-4
MC CARTHY,MJ.-2
MC CARTHY,RB.-1
MC CATHIE,A.-5
MC CAUL,LJ.-2
MC CONNACHIE,JC.-1
MC CONNELL,A.-1
MC CORMACK,JD.-1
MC CORMICK,B.-2
MC CORMICK,CJ.-5
MC CREADIE,B.-1
MC CREE,AW.-3
MC CREE,T.-4
MC CULLACH,G.-1
MC CULLOCH,G.-2
MC CULLOCH,KJ.-1
MC DERMID,ME.-4
MC DERMID,RE.-1
MC DERMID,WR.-1
MC DONALD,BD.-7
MC DONALD,BC.-2
MC DONALD,DI.-1
MC DONALD,BD.-5
MC DONALD,JC.-9
MC DONALD,M.-22
MC DONALD,RJ.-2
MC DONALD,WD.-3
MC DONALD,BD.-5
MC EWAN,GB.-1
MC FARLAND,AD.-2
MC GAGHEY,G.-4
MC GARRY,BL.-1
MC GARRY,TJ.-2
MC GEARY,RM.-3
MC GHEE,D.-1
MC GIBBON,WA.-1
MC GIDDY,MS.-8
MC GILLIVRAY,H.-2

MC GLASHEN,MJ.-1
MC GLEW,B.-1
MC GLINCHEY,MG.-1
MC GLOUGHLIN,R.-1
MC GREGOR,H.-5
MC GREGOR,JA-23
MC GREGOR,R.-2
MC GREGOR,TS.-2
MC GUIGAN,S.-3
MC HARDY,JL.-1
MC HUGH,B.-1
MC ILRATH,MJ.-9
MC INERNEY,RJ.-4
MC INTOSH,AR.-6
MC INTOSH,CN.-4
MC INTOSH,E.-2
MC INTOSH,G.-4
MC INTOSH,LK.-2
MC INTOSH,H.-1
MC INTYRE,A.-2
MC INTYRE,P.-1
MC KAY,G.-1
MC KEAN,SG.-2
MC KENNA,PD.-2
MC KENZIE,AG.-9
MC KENZIE,BJ.-1
MC KENZIE,C.-12
MC KENZIE,DJ-12
MC KENZIE,RG.-7
MC KIE,CJ.-3
MC KIE,J.-5
MC KIE,R.-2
MC LAREN,JR.-1
MC LAREN,R.-5
MC LAREN,TB.-8
MC LAVERTY,LA.-3
MC LAVERTY,PG.-3
MC LEAN,RJ.-10
MC LEAN,J.-1
MC LELLAN,KA.-2
MC LENNAN,K.-3
MC LEOD,G.-1
MC LOUGHLIN,MK.-4
MC LOUGHLIN,P.-2

MC LUCKIE,DP.-1
MC LUCKIE,RK.-1
MC LUCKIE,VK.-1
MC MARTIN,BR.-3
MC MARTIN,RJ.-5
MC MASTER,KD.-6
MC MASTER,N.-3
MC MILLAN,GD.-1
MC MURCHIE,J.-1
MC MURRAY,PM.-2
MC NABB,AJ.-1
MC NABB,BJ.-1
MC NALLY,K.-13
MC NALLY,JR.-4
MC NAUGHTON,AR.-1
MC NEIL,DH.-1
MC NEIL,PD.-8
MC NEIL,DR.-1
MC NEIL,SR.-1
MC PHERSON,GI.-1
MC QUADE,SM.-1
MC QUADE,J.-1
MC QUEEN,JR.-3
MC QUEEN,KL.-1
MC TAVISH,DA.-3
MCAFEE,M.-2
MCALEXANDER,E.-1
MCALPINE,T.-13
MCBAIN,CS.-2
MCBRIDE,P.-3
MCCALGAN,T.-1
MCCALLUM,AJ.-1
MCCALLUM,JW.-1
MCCALLUM,RS.-1
MCCANN,J.-1
MCCARTHY,C.-2
MCCARTHY,J.-3
MCCARTHY,NJ.-1
MCCAULEY,JF.-1
MCCLURE,J.-1
MCCLURE,I.-1
MCCONNACHIE,J.-1
MCCORMACK,M.-1
MCCORMICK,RG.-1
MCCRINDLE,B.-1

MCCULLACH,G.-1
MCCULLOUGH,M.-1
MCCUTCHEON,KR.-1
MCDONALD,D.-2
MCDONALD,R.-1
MCDOUGALL,B.-5
MCDOUGALL,G.-1
MCDULLING,H.-2
MCEWEN,D.-2
MCGARRY,BL.-1
MCGARRY,H.-1
MCGAVIN,JG.-3
MCGIBBON,C.-3
MCGIBBON,WA.-1
MCGILLVRAY,H.-3
MCGLOUGHLIN,J.-1
MCGREGOR,C.-2
MCGREGOR,R.-2
MCGURK,K.-1
MCINTOSH,VK.-2
MCINTOSH,R.-1
MCINTOSH,TD.-1
MCINTYRE,R.-6
MCINTYRE,A.-1
MCINTYRE,J.-1
MCINTYRE,P.-3
MCISAAC,C.-3
MCISAAC,DC.-1
MCIVER,K.-2
MCIVOR,DM.-3
MCKEAN,D.-1
MCKENZIE,CB.-1
MCKENZIE,D.-1
MCKENZIE,J.-2
MCKENZIE,L.-2
MCKENZIE,M.-1
MCKENZIE,CM.-1
MCKENZIE,G.-1
MCKEON,SK.-1
MCKERROW,MJ.-2
MCKIE,RS.-3
MCKIE-THOMPSON,C.-1
MCKILLOP,NJ.-1
MCKINLAY,BW.-5
MCKINNELL,R.-1

MCLACHLAN,J.-1
MCLACHLAN,PM-1
MCLAREN,PF-2
MCLAREN,TB-1
MCLAREN,B.-1
MCLENNAN,KA-2
MCLEOD,MJ-4
MCLOUGHLIN,P.-1
MCLURE,JC-2
MCMANON,M.-1
MCMARTIN,RJ-4
MCMAWUS,A.-1
MCMEEKAN,MA-1
MCMILLAN,GC-2
MCMILLAN,J.-1
MCNAMARA,RG-1
MCNAMARA,GP-2
MCNAUGHT,B.-1
MCNIVEN,D.-2
MCPHERSON,JN.-2
MCQUADE,B.-1
MCQUADE,S.-1
MCQUOID-MASON,MP.-1
MCQUOID-MASON,T.-1
MCROBERT,C.-2
MCWADE,T.-13
MCWADE,AJ-1
MEAD,DI-1
MEAD,P.-1
MEADOWS,S.-1
MEAKER,J.-1
MEAKIN,PR-12
MEARNS,G.-11
MEARNS,JD.-7
MEASROCH,J.-1
MEENEHAN,AP.-2
MEGAN,D.-1
MEGANNETY,CE-3
MEIER,KB-10
MEIKLEJOHN,SA-2
MEINTJIES,RR.-2
MEINTJIES,FJ-1
MEINTJIES,I.-1
MEINTJIES,JI-1

MEIRING,F.-2
MEIRING,GF-7
MEIRING,JP.-4
MEIRING,A.-1
MELLOR,G.-7
MELLOR,K.-2
MELLOR,A.-3
MELLOR,D.-1
MELLOR,LE-1
MELLORS,ER.-5
MELLOW,JB.-2
MELLOW,WL.-5
MELOUNEY,CR.-1
MELVILLE,GL.-2
MELVILLE,BC.-1
MENDES,AR.-2
MENDES,FG.-1
MENDIES,FG.-3
MENDZIES,P.-1
MENEZES,L.-3
MENGER,R.-1
MENNIE,BR.-7
MENNIE,LM.-5
MENNIE,CL.-1
MENTZ,B.-4
MENTZ,C.-10
MENTZ,JH.-1
MERCER,GI.-1
MERCER,C.-1
MEREDITH,S.-5
MERRETT,GI-11
MERRETT,JN-22
MERRILL,B.-1
MERRILL,K.-4
MESTER,SW.-3
METCALF,B.-2
METCALF,T.-1
METCALFE,B.-3
METER,C.-3
METER,M.-1
METER,R.-2
METHERELL,T.-1
MEYER,CM-1
MEYER,C.-3
MEYER,CJ-7

MEYER,D.-3
MEYER,GS.-2
MEYER,J.-11
MEYER,J.-7
MEYER,KB.-4
MEYER,TJ.-7
MEYER,F.-2
MEYER,S.-2
MEYER,S.-1
MEYER,WP.-7
MHLONGO,M.-1
MHLOPHE,AT.-3
MICHAU,R.-1
MICHELL,MA.-2
MICKEYREILLY,JW.-1
MICKLEBURGH,R.-4
MIDDLETON,KB.-4
MIDDLETON,T.-6
MIDDLETON,H.-1
MIDDUP,GW.-1
MIDGLEY,LM.-4
MIDGLEY,TJ.-2
MIEDEMA,A.-6
MILES,B.-2
MILES,GB-17
MILES,P.-1
MILES,SB.-1
MILFORD,.-1
MILFORD,J.-1
MILLAR,BJ-11
MILLAR,GD-4
MILLAR,R.-3
MILLAR,W.-1
MILLARD,LA-4
MILLER,AM.-1
MILLER,A.-8
MILLER,J.-2
MILLER,Q.-1
MILLER,R.-11
MILLER,RG-11
MILLER,AH-4
MILLER,A.-1
MILLER,A.-1
MILLER,BH-1
MILLER,DI-1

221

NEL,DD- 6
NEL,EM-10
NEL,EP- 8
NEL,FC- 3
NEL,G - 9
NEL,G -11
NEL,J - 5
NEL,J - 7
NEL,JB-16
NEL,J - 1
NEL,KP-16
NEL,MJ- 2
NEL,N - 2
NEL,RL- 6
NEL,SA- 2
NEL,TK-14
NEL,WU- 6
NEL,AR- 2
NEL,E - 1
NEL,J - 1
NEL,JA- 1
NEL,PD- 1
NELL,JC- 1
NELSON,A - 1
NELSON,CJ- 2
NELSON,GS- 1
NEPGEN,L - 1
NESS,DC- 1
NEUBERT,PK- 2
NEUHOFF,E - 2
NEUHOFF,GE- 3
NEUMANN,P - 4
NEVE,NM- 1
NEVILLE,JD- 8
NEVIN,B - 1
NEW,CM- 1
NEW,JN-12
NEWLANDS,CS-10
NEWLANDS,G - 7
NEWMAN,BK- 1
NGCOBO,DT- 5
NGCOBO,J - 3
NGCOBO,T - 1

NGCOBO,TA- 2
NGCOBO,B - 1
NGCOBO,TB- 1
NGIBA,M - 1
NGIDI,B - 4
NGIDI,C - 2
NGIDI,CK- 2
NGIDI,GL- 2
NGIDI,LM- 4
NGIDI,TK- 7
NGIDI,M - 1
NGOBO,J - 1
NGUBANE,DB- 4
NGUBANE,S - 1
NGWANE,T - 4
NICHOL,RH- 2
NICHOL,MJ- 6
NICHOL,WN- 2
NICHOLAS,PB- 1
NICHOLAS,MC- 2
NICHOLLS,D - 1
NICHOLLS,M - 1
NICHOLLS,GR- 1
NICHOLSON,A - 9
NICHOLSON,B -10
NICHOLSON,D - 1
NICHOLSON,J - 3
NICHOLSON,KH- 1
NICHOLSON,PJ- 3
NICHOLSON,SP- 5
NICHOLSON,LB- 3
NICHOLSON,S - 2
NICHOLSON,S - 2
NICOLAS,M -16
NICOLAS,G - 1
NICOLAS,L - 1
NICOLAY,S - 1
NICOLL,AR- 3
NICOLL,WJ- 1
NICOLSON,H - 1
NIEDIENGER,H - 3
NIEDINGER,H - 4
NIEHAUS,J - 1
NIELSAN,T - 1
NIELSEN,AT-13

NIELSEN,LL- 2
NIELSEN,SJ- 1
NIEMAND,E - 1
NIEMANDT,AD- 1
NIEMANDT,S - 1
NIEMANN,DP- 4
NIEMANN,JP- 2
NIEMANN,RS- 2
NIENABER,JH- 2
NIENABER,LP- 6
NIENABER,PJ- 4
NIENABER,T - 1
NIENABER,J - 1
NIENABER,JH- 1
NIENABER,L - 3
NIENHUSER,A - 8
NIEUWENHUIZEN,A - 4
NIEUWHOUT,J - 1
NIEWOUDT,A - 1
NIGHTINGALE,DM- 1
NIJHOUT,P - 1
NIKSCH,T - 2
NIKSCH,JA- 1
NILAND,M - 2
NISBET, - 1
NISBET,D - 7
NISBET,JA- 1
NISBETT,GM- 2
NISH,C - 6
NIVEN,R - 1
NIXON,TL- 8
NOBLE,P - 6
NOCTON-SMITH,AJ- 1
NOCTON-SMITH,JM- 1
NODDEBOE,P - 1
NOLTE,M - 2
NORMAN,E - 2
NORMAN,H - 8
NORMAND,G - 2
NORRIS,CH-18
NORRIS,R - 2
NORRIS,GA- 2
NORRIS,JC- 1
NORRIS-JONES,AS- 1

NORTH,AD- 1
NORTH,MS- 5
NORTH,MR- 5
NORTH,KE- 1
NORTHEND,BA- 1
NORTHWOOD,N - 1
NORTHWOOD,? - 1
NORTHWOOD,J - 1
NORTJE,CA- 6
NORTJE,FJ- 2
NORTJE,MB- 2
NORTJE,A - 1
NORTON, - 1
NORTON,DO- 7
NORTON,E - 1
NORTON,G -14
NORTON,H - 4
NORTON,JI- 4
NORTON,MH- 3
NORTON,MO- 7
NORTON,P - 4
NORTON,JS- 4
NORTON,KM- 1
NORTON,SW- 1
NORTON-SMITH,T - 1
NORVALL,GR- 1
NOTELOVITZ,M - 1
NOTHLING,P - 4
NOTHNAGEL,HB- 2
NOTHNAGEL,M - 1
NOTT,RJ- 4
NOTTEN,DH- 3
NOYCE,R - 1
NTSIZA,L - 1
NUNES,J - 1
NUNN,AA- 1
NURDEN,OW- 4
NUSS,RR- 1
NYAWASE,M - 1
NYDAHL,J - 2
NZUZA,LA- 2
NZUZA,Z - 2
O BRIEN,M -15
O BRIEN,P - 3
O BRIEN,ST- 2

O BYRNE,I -14
O BYRNE,G - 1
O CONNOR,CG- 4
O CONNOR,GS-10
O CONNOR,G - 1
O CONNOR,P - 4
O CONNOR,RP- 2
O CONNOR,T - 1
O DONAGHUE,RB- 3
O FARRELL,KS- 1
O GORMAN,M - 2
O HARA,SG- 1
O LEARY,GJ-10
O NEILL,BA- 5
O NEILL,RD- 6
O NEILL,T - 5
O REGAN,BP- 1
O REILLY,CJ- 4
O REILLY,GP-10
O REILLY-BARGATE,K - 1
O SPRADBURY,P - 1
O SULLIVAN,PP-10
O SULLIVAN,SF- 5
OAKLEY,MD- 2
OATES,GJ- 3
OATES,TI- 2
OATES,B - 3
OATS,G - 2
OBERHOLZER,GJ- 2
O'BRIEN,PA- 2
OCONNER,T - 1
O'CONNOR,CG- 2
O'CONNOR,BL- 1
ODELL,G - 1
ODEMAERE,J - 1
ODENDAAL,DC- 3
ODENDAAL,E - 1
ODONOGHUE,A - 1
OELLERMANN,CD- 1
OELLERMANN,DA- 4
OELLERMANN,H - 1
OELLERMANN,RJ- 5
OELLERMANN,LA- 1
OETIE,T - 1

OETS,HL- 1
OETTLE,EK- 3
OETTLE,LM- 4
OETTLE,N - 6
OETTLE,PM- 1
OETTLE,T - 4
OFFEBRO,GB- 3
OGG,D - 4
OGG,MC- 1
OGGEL,S - 1
OGGLE,S - 1
OGILVIE,A - 1
OGILVIE,NE- 1
OGILVIE,BL- 2
OGRAM,MN- 1
OGRAM,A - 1
OHLSON DE FINE,MJ- 3
OLCKERS,P - 5
OLDACRE,DA- 1
OLDEN,AJ- 9
OLDEN,BY- 2
OLDEN,MJ- 1
OLDERT,N - 1
OLDS,D - 2
OLDS,EA- 1
OLIARO,PG- 6
OLIARO,R -14
OLIPHANT,D - 7
OLIVER,DK- 1
OLIVER,JB- 5
OLIVER,JL-11
OLIVER,JF-13
OLIVER,KL- 8
OLIVER,LK-18
OLIVER,P - 1
OLIVER,VM- 1
OLIVER,J - 5
OLIVER,MM- 2
OLIVER,SJ- 2
OLIVIER,C - 1
OLIVIER,HW- 1
OLIVIER,L - 4
OLIVIER,SC- 1
OLIVIER,A - 1
OLIVIER,D - 1

OLIVER,R - 2
OLMESDAHL,A - 1
OLSEN,P - 2
OLWAGEN,CP- 1
O'NEILL,N - 1
OOSTHING,MB- 1
OOSTHUIZEN,DI- 1
OOSTHUIZEN,AC- 2
OOSTHUIZEN,CD- 3
OOSTHUIZEN,DN- 8
OOSTHUIZEN,DI- 1
OOSTHUIZEN,D - 1
OOSTHUIZEN,FJ- 1
OOSTHUIZEN,H - 5
OOSTHUIZEN,L - 7
OOSTHUIZEN,SE- 2
OOSTHUIZEN,WJ- 5
OOSTHUIZEN,JH- 2
OOSTHUIZEN,N - 1
OOSTHUYSE,GC- 1
OPENSHAW,NK- 1
OPPENHEIM,C - 1
OPPERMAN,2 - 1
OPPERMAN,K - 3
OPPERMAN,D - 3
OPPERMAN,EC- 1
OPPERMAN,PJ- 1
ORBE,JM- 1
ORCHARD,R - 4
ORCHARD,SP- 1
O'REILLY,J - 1
ORMEROD,SJ- 1
ORMSHAW,J - 3
ORMSHAW,E - 1
ORPWOOD,DO- 1
ORPWOOD,JM- 6
ORPWOOD,SM- 2
ORSMOND,GR- 2
ORZECHOWSKI,J - 1
OSBORN,RP- 1
OSBORNE,CB- 1
OSBORNE,E - 1
OSBORNE,PG- 3
OSCROFT,KD- 5
OSCROFT,RD- 6

OSHRY,A - 2
OSHRY,T - 1
OSTLER,RA-15
OSTLER,MR- 1
OTTER,TW- 1
OTTO,AL- 4
OTTO,D - 1
OTTO,HV- 5
OTTO,J - 2
OVENSTONE,H - 2
OVENSTONE,SO- 1
OVERY,MP- 2
OWEN,D - 1
OWEN,JW- 1
OWEN,K - 1
OWEN,SB- 1
OXENHAM,CJ- 8
OXENHAM,NP- 8
OXENHAM,DL- 2
PACE,KM- 1
PACHONICK,JA- 3
PACKHAM,MJ- 2
PAGE,C - 2
PAGE,K -21
PAGE,B - 2
PAGE,E - 1
PAGEL,A - 1
PAHL,K - 2
PAINTING,A - 5
PAINTING,BJ- 6
PAINTING,M - 1
PAIZES,J - 1
PALFRAMAN,KP-17
PALFRAMAN,MB- 3
PALFRAMAN,R - 3
PALFRAMAN,A - 2
PALFRAMAN,D - 2
PALLET,MW- 1
PALLET,BC- 1
PALMER,GR- 1
PALMER,KJ-10
PALMER,TL- 5
PALMER,B - 1
PALMER,DT- 2
PALMER,P - 2

PORRILL,J - 1
PORT,G - 6
PORT,W - 3
PORTER,CJ - 1
PORTON,CF - 1
POSNER,CM - 1
POSNETT,SJ - 2
POSTHUMA,B - 1
POTGIETER,C - 5
POTGIETER,HJ - 1
POTGIETER,JM - 1
POTGIETER,J - 11
POTGIETER,KA - 1
POTGIETER,M - 7
POTGIETER,M - 18
POTGIETER,M - 16
POTGIETER,W - 1
POTGIETER,A - 1
POTGIETER,BM - 2
POTGIETER,DL - 2
POTGIETER,JT - 1
POTGIETER,JF - 3
POTGIETER,JH - 1
POTGIETER,SA - 1
POTT,AJ - 1
POTTER,CM - 8
POTTER,DJ - 9
POTTER,GP - 5
POTTER,GM - 8
POTTER,PR - 1
POULTNEY,PH - 1
POUSSON,MF - 7
POUSTIE,WJ - 1
POVALL,G - 7
POWELL,A - 3
POWELL,C - 2
POWELL,M - 8
POWELL,RJ - 1
POWELL,JB - 4
POWELL,LA - 1
POWELL,SM - 1
POWERS,AM - 1
PRATT,J - 3
PRATT,RD - 3
PRATT,TW - 2
PRAZESKY,A - 1

PRECE,R - 6
PRECE,MA - 1
PREEN,E - 1
PREEN,MV - 3
PREEN,R - 2
PRENTICE,PJ - 3
PRENTICE,M - 1
PRESBURY,PD - 1
PRESCOTT,MG - 5
PRESCOTT,M - 1
PRESTON,GW - 5
PRESTON,P - 1
PRESTON,RG - 1
PRESTON,L - 2
PRESTON,P - 1
PRETORIUS,A - 4
PRETORIUS,A - 16
PRETORIUS,AJ - 8
PRETORIUS,A - 1
PRETORIUS,C - 7
PRETORIUS,D - 6
PRETORIUS,EC - 2
PRETORIUS,H - 9
PRETORIUS,JS - 6
PRETORIUS,SA - 1
PRETORIUS,PB - 1
PRETORIUS,TG - 5
PRETORIUS,VR - 2
PRETORIUS,A - 1
PRETORIUS,NF - 2
PRICE,BB - 2
PRICE,CW - 1
PRICE,D - 3
PRICE,D - 8
PRICE,G - 26
PRICE,K - 31
PRICE,M - 1
PRICE,R - 5
PRICE,ST - 13
PRICE,WJ - 2
PRICE,WB - 14
PRICE,E - 4
PRICE,ST - 1
PRICE,SG - 1
PRICE,T - 6
PRICEMOOR,DP - 1

PRIDE,SQ - 2
PRIDGEON,AL - 1
PRINCE,M - 5
PRINGLE,DF - 14
PRINGLE,G - 13
PRINGLE,RG - 11
PRINGLE,T - 19
PRINGLE,BR - 1
PRINGLE,M - 1
PRINS,RJ - 1
PRINSLOO,JJ - 2
PRINSLOO,W - 4
PRINSLOO,LW - 1
PRINSLOO,MC - 2
PRIOR,A - 4
PRISLEY,MD - 7
PRIVETT,S - 1
PROBERT,M - 4
PROCTOR,A - 12
PROCTOR,G - 2
PROCTOR,P - 3
PROCTOR,PD - 5
PRONK,R - 4
PRONK,N - 1
PROST,SJ - 3
PROTHEROE,MB - 1
PROUDFOOT,A - 1
PROWSE,C - 7
PROWSE,A - 1
PROWSE,RJ - 1
PROZESKY,A - 2
PRYBA,W - 1
PUCKRIN,J - 1
PULLEN,M - 2
PULLOCK,MS - 4
PULVENIS,WM - 1
PULVIRENTI,SM - 2
PURCHASE,A - 6
PURCHASE,C - 2
PURCHASE,T - 1
PURDON,BA - 3
PURVES,G - 1
QUABECK,A - 1
QUIBELL,G - 4
QUIBELL,P - 7

QUIN,RB - 4
QUINLAN,PD - 1
QUINN,PI - 1
QUINN,WP - 1
QUINTON,AM - 1
QUINTON,RT - 1
QUIRK,I - 4
QUIST,JA - 10
RAATGEVER,R - 1
RAATH,AA - 5
RAATH,RJ - 4
RAATH,J - 1
RABE,MA - 3
RABE,T - 1
RABIE,A - 1
RABIE,F - 1
RABIE,SJ - 1
RADCLIFFE,SJ - 1
RADFORD,SA - 3
RADLEY,LB - 1
RADLOFF,G - 1
RADLOFF,FG - 1
RADLOFF,G - 1
RAFINETTI,M - 1
RAGG,J - 2
RAINIER-POPE,M - 7
RAINNIE,A - 6
RAKE,JP - 2
RALEY,PA - 1
RALFE,DA - 8
RALFE,ED - 2
RALFE,GA - 1
RALFE,BD - 1
RALFE,MC - 1
RALPH,CA - 1
RALPHS,MC - 3
RAMKE-MEYER,ML - 1
RAMKREPAL,RK - 1
RAMPTON,RW - 1
RAMSAMY,D - 1
RAMSAY,GW - 3
RAMSDEN,G - 1
RAMSDEN,TG - 2
RAMSEY,B - 2
RAMSEY,JA - 1

RAMUTUMBU,MG - 1
RAN,C - 1
RAND,N - 1
RANDAL,N - 2
RANDALL,N - 4
RANDALL,T - 1
RANDALL,W - 1
RANDLES,RT - 1
RANKIN,AG - 1
RANKIN,B - 3
RAPSON,WA - 5
RAS,BD - 6
RAS,KG - 1
RASMUSSEN,LC - 4
RASMUSSEN,MA - 3
RASMUSSEN,R - 7
RATTRAY,JD - 2
RAULT,M - 5
RAUTENBACH,DP - 3
RAUTENBACH,T - 1
RAUTENBACH,ME - 1
RAUTER,DF - 1
RAVENHILL,B - 11
RAVENHILL,P - 1
RAW,D - 9
RAW,HF - 7
RAW,J - 1
RAW,MA - 1
RAW,N - 6
RAW,PJ - 3
RAW,R - 2
RAW,SM - 6
RAWLINS,C - 5
RAWLINS,JM - 1
RAWLINS,M - 1
RAWLINS,M - 7
RAWLINS,P - 3
RAWLINS,W - 1
RAWLINSON,AJ - 7
RAWLINSON,DJ - 17
RAWLINSON,P - 11
RAWLINSON,SJ - 7
RAWSON,GI - 6
RAWSON,L - 1
RAWSON,DJ - 1

RAWSON,P - 1
RAWSON,RI - 2
RAY,GM - 3
RAY,J - 1
READ,R - 1
READ,GI - 1
READ,J - 1
READHEAD,BC - 1
READMAN,JE - 1
REANEY,C - 25
REDDING,MM - 6
REDDING,MP - 2
REDFERN,AM - 9
REDFORD,GL - 2
REDMAN,GM - 3
REDMAN,LM - 1
REDPATH,CA - 1
REECE-EDWARDS,HM - 5
REED,DW - 1
REED,HD - 1
REED,M - 5
REEDERS,BJ - 14
REES,BF - 5
REES,C - 7
REES,MO - 2
REEVE,DJ - 3
REEVE,JB - 4
REEVES,GN - 4
REEVES,K - 1
REEVES,MM - 2
REEVES,N - 1
REEVES,P - 5
REEVES,A - 1
REEVES,MC - 1
REEVES,PL - 2
REGNARD,C - 1
REIJ - 6
REIBELING,E - 1
REICHLING,M - 2
REICHLING,P - 2
REICHLING,R - 1
REID,AS - 2
REID,AW - 3
REID,CF - 4
REID,CW - 10

REID,GM - 5
REID,J - 3
REID,MJ - 2
REID,NA - 9
REID,PJ - 2
REID,R - 3
REID,EM - 1
REID,KJ - 2
REID,L - 1
REILLY,JW - 2
REILLY,RM - 2
REINBACH,KA - 2
REINECKE,NO - 3
REINHARDT,CJ - 2
RENAUD,AE - 1
RENAUD,P - 1
RENCKEN,A - 2
RENCKEN,R - 1
RENISON,CC - 15
RENNIE,A - 12
RENNIE,JT - 1
RENNIE,N - 3
RENNIE,R - 4
RENSHAW,M - 1
RETHMAN,HL - 9
RETHMAN,CW - 1
RETIEF,D - 9
RETIEF,P - 2
RETIEF,FJ - 2
RETIEF,ML - 3
RETZLAFF,RG - 1
RETZLAFF,SH - 1
RETZLAFF,T - 1
REUSCH,WH - 1
REUTER,DB - 10
REVENHILL,B - 1
REW,BK - 1
REYNDERS,BF - 15
REYNDERS,F - 1
REYNDERS,N - 1
REYNEKE,D - 1
REYNEKE,RP - 1
REYNOLDS,AI - 3
REYNOLDS,BA - 3
REYNOLDS,GR - 5

REYNOLDS,JC - 2
REYNOLDS,KJ - 23
REYNOLDS,M - 3
REYNOLDS,NI - 2
REYNOLDS,PT - 9
REYNOLDS,RN - 4
RHEEDER,D - 3
RHEEDER,N - 2
RHEEDER,RP - 3
RHEEDER,K - 1
RHEEDERS,BW - 1
RHIND,CA - 6
RHODES,CJ - 10
RHODES,GE - 1
RHODES,P - 1
RHYNES,J - 1
RHYNES,M - 3
RICE,B - 8
RICE,J - 1
RICE,S - 5
RICEMAN,M - 1
RICH,JM - 1
RICH,BI - 1
RIC-HANSEN,J - 5
RIC-HANSEN,WJ - 2
RICHARDS,DP - 1
RICHARDS,C - 1
RICHARDSON,B - 1
RICHARDSON,G - 17
RICHARDSON,KA - 7
RICHARDSON,LS - 2
RICHARDSON,PN - 6
RICHARDSON,R - 2
RICHARDSON,TJ - 2
RICHARDSON,C - 2
RICHARDSON,GB - 2
RICHARDSON,WL - 1
RICH-BOWLES,HJ - 10
RICHMOND,JL - 15
RICHMOND,MG - 15
RICHTER,MW - 1
RIDDERHOF,SA - 2
RIDDERHOF,PC - 1
RIDDIN,WA - 18
RIDDIN,VJ - 2

RIDDLE,GM-3
RIDE,C-1
RIDGEWAY,MW-2
RIDGWAY,K-2
RIDING,P-1
RIDL,CW-2
RIDL,MN-1
RIDL,FW-1
RIDL,L-4
RIDL,TJ-1
RIDLEY,A-1
RIDLEY,IB-1
RIES,J-1
RIETZ,DN-4
RIGGEN,G-2
RIGOTTI,G-2
RILEY,JA-2
RILEY,T-3
RINKE,A-1
RINKE,B-1
RISSIK,J-1
RIST,BA-2
RITCHIE,JW-1
RITCHIE,M-3
RITSON,RP-7
RITSON,H-3
RITSON,ME-1
RIVETT,K-2
RIX,L-1
ROBB,A-3
ROBB,T-1
ROBBERTSE,JH-9
ROBERT,DF-3
ROBERTS,A-4
ROBERTS,AF-5
ROBERTS,AJ-6
ROBERTS,B-2
ROBERTS,BD-8
ROBERTS,C-3
ROBERTS,C-1
ROBERTS,CJ-8
ROBERTS,GD-5
ROBERTS,K-1
ROBERTS,MI-2
ROBERTS,MR-2

ROBERTS,N-1
ROBERTS,SG-18
ROBERTS,T-2
ROBERTS,M-1
ROBERTSE,AB-3
ROBERTSE,T-1
ROBERTSON,BM-7
ROBERTSON,CS-2
ROBERTSON,PL-1
ROBERTSON,D-1
ROBERTSON,G-1
ROBERTSON,JG-2
ROBERTSON,J-1
ROBERTSON,JS-1
ROBERTSON,SW-2
ROBERTSON,BM-1
ROBERTSON,IL-1
ROBERTSON,NJ-1
ROBERTSON,S-1
ROBINS,JS-5
ROBINS,KE-1
ROBINS,SE-1
ROBINSON,AS-1
ROBINSON,AG-4
ROBINSON,AD-4
ROBINSON,AD-4
ROBINSON,B-2
ROBINSON,C-7
ROBINSON,DP-5
ROBINSON,J-3
ROBINSON,J-3
ROBINSON,PA-4
ROBINSON,RB-5
ROBINSON,S-8
ROBINSON,WC-3
ROBSON,CB-4
ROBSON,N-1
ROBSON,F-1
ROBSON,SS-2
ROCHAT,BJ-1
ROCHE,GJ-1
ROCHE,SJ-1
ROCHE,J-1
ROCHE,PW-1

ROCKETT,G-4
ROCKEY,NJ-10
ROCKEY,MJ-2
RODD,KR-1
RODE,DL-1
RODEL,A-1
RODGERS,G-1
RODGERS,K-3
RODGERS,PL-1
RODRIGUES,N-2
RODSETH,ND-2
RODSETH,PG-1
RODSETH,RN-1
RODWELL,CP-11
RODWELL,EJ-2
ROE,DK-3
ROE-SCOTT,MG-2
ROETS,CJ-2
ROETS,C-23
ROETS,SI-16
ROETS,CW-1
ROETS,E-1
ROGERS,DS-5
ROGERS,K-6
ROGERS,PL-2
ROGERS,MH-1
ROGERS,SD-5
ROGERS-BROWN,S-1
ROGERSON,SL-1
ROHRS,AE-11
ROHRS,MB-3
ROLAND,P-1
ROLLASON,JD-1
ROLLER,GE-1
RONALD,P-2
RONDEL,C-2
RONQUEST,LC-2
ROODT,FD-1
ROODT,NJ-1
ROOS,D-1
ROOS,JJ-4
ROOS,JC-9
ROOS,W-1
ROOT,G-1
ROOTMAN,G-3

ROOTMAN,GP-3
ROOYEN,ML-1
RORICH,LC-2
RORICH,WJ-1
ROSE,DA-2
ROSE,MI-2
ROSE,NC-6
ROSE,RG-4
ROSE,V-1
ROSE,L-1
ROSE-INNES,A-2
ROSE-INNES,M-1
ROSE-INNES,NC-3
ROSENBERG,AT-1
ROSENBERG,B-2
ROSHOLT,AH-1
ROSS,FB-2
ROSS,J-17
ROSS,C-23
ROSS,K-2
ROSS,T-1
ROSS,A-2
ROSS,CM-2
ROSS,DE-2
ROSS,G-1
ROSS,M-3
ROSS,SB-4
ROSSEAU,MJ-10
ROSSER,CA-1
ROSSER,CA-1
ROSSER,CJ-1
ROSSOUW,PJ-12
ROSSOUW,WH-2
ROSSOUW,SR-5
ROSTRON,P-1
ROSWELL,K-1
ROTH,WD-1
ROTHENBURG,B-1
ROTHMALL,J-1
ROTHWELL,C-2
ROUILLARD,AJ-1
ROUILLARD,MI-2
ROUX,G-3
ROUX,NJ-1

ROUX,P-1
ROUX,T-1
ROUX,B-1
ROUX,GT-1
ROUX,J-1
ROUX,S-1
ROWAN,AJ-7
ROWAN,GE-1
ROWAN,JM-3
ROWAN,J-24
ROWAN,KJ-2
ROWAN,PA-6
ROWAN,AC-1
ROWAN,AJ-3
ROWAN,DJ-2
ROWAN,S-1
ROWBOTHAM,DR-3
ROWE,C-5
ROWE,CS-6
ROWE,DA-5
ROWE,E-2
ROWE,F-4
ROWE,G-8
ROWE,G-6
ROWE,G-3
ROWE,G-5
ROWE,P-3
ROWE,X-1
ROWE,BP-1
ROWLAND,C-1
ROWLEY,GC-5
ROWLEY,J-1
ROWNEY,A-3
ROWNEY,B-4
ROWNEY,K-18
ROWSELL,JP-2
ROWSELL,KA-16
ROY,MA-6
ROY,IR-2
ROYAL,PH-6
ROYDEN-TURNER,SH-1
ROYSTON,R-1
RUBENSTEIN,SM-4
RUBENSTEIN,TA-21
RUDD,BW-2

RUDGER,R-2
RUDLING,A-1
RUDMAN,RA-1
RUMBOLD,JB-2
RUMSEY,MV-2
RUNCIMAN,J-1
RUSH,G-2
RUSHTON,C-1
RUSHTON,LA-1
RUSHTON,MB-2
RUSHTOW,C-1
RUSHWORTH,RJ-2
RUSSELL,A-1
RUSSELL,AM-7
RUSSELL,G-1
RUSSELL,J-6
RUSSELL,R-5
RUSSELL,RA-6
RUSSELL,SD-5
RUSSELL,BM-1
RUSSELL,DB-1
RUSSELL,RG-1
RUSSELL-WADE,H-1
RUSSILL,AR-1
RUTHERFOORD,SP-2
RUTHERFORD,M-5
RUTHERFORD,Q-9
RUTHERFORD-SMITH,W-9
RUTISHAUSER,AE-2
RUTTER,AP-1
RYAN,AT-5
RYAN,DE-4
RYAN,J-1
RYAN,RD-1
RYCROFT,BR-3
RYDER,H-3
RYDER,T-1
RYDER,PD-2
SOUTHEY,WM-1
SAAYMAN,C-1
SACCO,NM-2
SACHS,B-8
SACKE,K-2
SACKE,CA-1

SACKS,D-2
SADLER,CJ-4
SADLER,PJ-5
SADLER,MP-2
SAINT,CG-1
SAINT,RR-4
SAINT,RC-1
SAINT,D-1
SAINT,RC-1
SALES,D-12
SALMON,S-2
SALMONSEN,M-2
SALVAGE,GD-3
SALVESON,E-1
SAMKIN,G-2
SAMKIN,JG-2
SAMPSON,R-5
SAMPSON,T-5
SAMUELSON,M-2
SANDBERG,H-14
SANDBERG,R-2
SANDELL,PR-1
SANDENBERGH,J-1
SANDER,D-1
SANDER,MA-2
SANDERS,C-3
SANDERS,JM-14
SANDERS,R-11
SANDERS,ME-1
SANDERS,V-3
SANDY,RJ-3
SANFORD,BS-1
SANTORO,F-2
SARA,AM-1
SARTORI,DA-3
SATCHWELL,T-3
SATES,JH-3
SAUNDERS,AJ-5
SAUNDERS,DI-1
SAUNDERS,J-9
SAUNDERS,RJ-3
SAUNDERS,SJ-4
SAUNDERS,S-1
SAUNDERS,SE-3
SAUNDERS,B-1

SAUNDERS,CR-1
SAUNDERS,S-2
SAUNDERS,WM-5
SAUNT,RA-14
SAUVAGE,AB-2
SAUVAGE,B-1
SAUVAGE,CA-4
SAVAGE,A-22
SAVAGE,AL-3
SAVAGE,CH-3
SAVAGE,L-10
SAVAGE,R-1
SAVILLE,CA-6
SAVILLE,JP-2
SAVILLE,PF-1
SAWERS,JR-4
SAWERS,RJ-1
SAWKINS,JF-1
SAWKINS,RJ-2
SAYERS,J-1
SBISI,S-1
SBOROS,G-4
SCAGGIANTE,D-1
SCALLAN,RE-3
SCALLAN,JV-1
SCATES,D-1
SCHAAP,AJ-1
SCHAAP,PA-1
SCHABORT,B-1
SCHABORT,K-1
SCHABORT,J-1
SCHAFER,MG-1
SCHAFER,RE-9
SCHAFER,M-3
SCHAFER,TE-1
SCHAFFER,G-1
SCHAFFER,JM-2
SCHECH,BJ-1
SCHEEPERS,E-3
SCHEEPERS,GF-4
SCHEEPERS,P-2
SCHEEPERS,TM-3
SCHEFFER,EW-5
SCHENKER,A-1
SCHERZER,PJ-2

LIST OF ALL FINISHERS IN THE DUSI CANOE MARATHON—1951 TO 2006

SCHEUER,DJ- 1	SCHREINER,WG- 2	SEGAR,CE- 1	SHAW,J- 1	SIM,W- 1	SKINSTAD,AD- 1	SMIT,P- 1
SCHILLER,MG- 1	SCHREUDER,H- 2	SEGAR,SJ- 1	SHEARAR,KA- 1	SIMKISS,BJ- 1	SKINSTAD,B- 1	SMIT,P-15
SCHIPOLT,R- 2	SCHRODER,JH-10	SEIDLER,G- 1	SHEDLOCK,MP- 3	SIMMONDS,F- 1	SKOWNO,A- 2	SMIT,RE- 1
SCHIPPER,E- 1	SCHRODER,R- 7	SEIGE,SF- 1	SHEDLOCK,P- 7	SIMMONS,GD- 7	SKUSE,J- 5	SMIT,WP- 3
SCHIPPER,JN- 2	SCHRODER,D- 2	SEILER,RJ- 2	SHELLEY,NP- 6	SIMMS,RP- 5	SLABBERT,EB- 1	SMIT,ZS- 1
SCHIRGE,MM- 3	SCHROEDER,ME- 3	SELBY,P- 4	SHELWELL,RJ- 3	SIMON,J- 1	SLABBERT,JA- 3	SMIT,DT- 1
SCHLEBUSCH,LA- 2	SCHROEDER,DW- 1	SELKIRK,C- 5	SHENTON,G- 1	SIMON,ER- 1	SLABBERT,C- 1	SMIT,P- 1
SCHLEBUSCH,NP- 2	SCHROENN,MR- 8	SELLSCHOP,RM- 4	SHEPHERD,BH- 7	SIMONATO,RD- 1	SLABBERT,G- 3	SMITH,AP- 9
SCHLEMMER,J- 2	SCHROENN,NH- 2	SENEKAL,P- 1	SHEPHERD,DF-14	SIMONETTI,C- 2	SLACK,G- 1	SMITH,BH- 6
SCHLOMS,H- 1	SCHRUDER,B- 1	SENEQUE,S- 3	SHEPHERD,RG- 6	SIMONI,NF- 1	SLADE,N- 4	SMITH,B- 5
SCHLUTER,W- 1	SCHRUEUR,MR- 1	SEPHTON,S- 2	SHEPHERD,A- 1	SIMONS,JW- 1	SLATER,BJ- 2	SMITH,B- 4
SCHMIDT,AC- 1	SCHUBACH,J- 2	SEPPINGS,N- 6	SHEPPARD,CJ- 4	SIMONS,JC- 1	SLATER,CR- 6	SMITH,CJ- 6
SCHMIDT,F- 5	SCHUBERT,AC- 1	SERDYN,JD- 1	SHEPPARD,DW- 4	SIMPKINS,C-15	SLATER,GM- 4	SMITH,CD-12
SCHMIDT,JE-15	SCHUCK,C- 4	SERUTI,M- 1	SHEPPARD,E- 1	SIMPKINS,D- 1	SLATTERY,PJ- 1	SMITH,D- 4
SCHMIDT,KG- 6	SCHUERMANS,JH- 3	SETAR,E- 1	SHEPSTONE,GW- 2	SIMPSON,AM- 3	SLATTERY,MD- 2	SMITH,D- 1
SCHMIDT,LE-15	SCHULTZ,C- 2	SETARO,EM- 2	SHEPSTONE,NM- 1	SIMPSON,A- 1	SLAUGHTER,MN- 1	SMITH,EJ- 8
SCHMIDT,ME- 1	SCHULTZ,SW- 1	SEVERN-ELLIS,A- 2	SHER,W- 2	SIMPSON,CC- 6	SLEED,M- 5	SMITH,F- 5
SCHMIDT,U- 2	SCHULTZ,NA- 1	SEYMOUR,T- 1	SHERRARD,DL- 2	SIMPSON,E- 1	SLEED,?- 1	SMITH,G- 4
SCHMIDT,HL- 2	SCHULZ,F- 1	SEYMOUR,R- 1	SHERRIFFS,PG- 1	SIMPSON,G- 5	SLEVIN,CN- 2	SMITH,GS-10
SCHMIDT,LB- 2	SCHULZE,AD- 1	SHAFTO,A- 1	SHERWEN,P- 7	SIMPSON,J- 1	SLEVIN,M- 3	SMITH,GS- 9
SCHMIDT,S- 1	SCHUSS,TJ- 9	SHAND,K- 1	SHIELDS,B- 6	SIMPSON,KM- 1	SLEVIN,AJ- 2	SMITH,GF- 2
SCHMIDTHAUS,UR-15	SCHUTTE,AI- 1	SHANLEY,D- 1	SHILLER,S- 3	SIMPSON,S- 1	SLEVIN,G- 1	SMITH,G- 7
SCHMIDTHAUS,C- 2	SCHUTTE,CE- 6	SHAPLAND,M- 1	SHIRLEY,FM- 1	SIMPSON,A- 2	SLIER,HA- 1	SMITH,JT- 5
SCHNELL,R- 2	SCHUTTE,M- 1	SHARLAND,R- 1	SHIRRAN,MJ- 2	SIMPSON,L- 1	SLOLEY,LG-13	SMITH,J- 5
SCHNELL,RS- 3	SCHUTTE,WE- 1	SHARP,A- 3	SHOOTER,ID- 2	SIMPSON,M- 1	SLOLEY,SR- 2	SMITH,JT- 1
SCHNELL,SG- 4	SCHWARZ,J- 6	SHARP,GH- 5	SHORE,PE- 1	SIMPSON,N- 3	SLOLEY,BS- 2	SMITH,JB- 3
SCHOEMAN,CG- 8	SCHWARZER,G- 1	SHARP,JA- 1	SHORT,BR- 1	SIMPSON,RM- 1	SLOLEY,JR- 1	SMITH,K- 1
SCHOEMAN,E- 1	SCHWEGMAN,CL- 4	SHARPE,DI- 3	SHORT,M- 2	SINCLAIR,A-20	SLOLEY,L- 1	SMITH,K- 2
SCHOEMAN,F- 4	SCHWEGMAN,G- 2	SHATTOCK,M-10	SHORTER,AA- 5	SINCLAIR,DG- 1	SMAIL,B- 2	SMITH,KD- 1
SCHOEMAN,JT- 6	SCHWEGMAN,M- 1	SHATTOCK,DG- 2	SHOZI,MC- 1	SINCLAIR,G- 8	SMAIL,D- 1	SMITH,K- 2
SCHOEMAN,NM- 1	SCHWEGMAN,NA- 4	SHAVE,A-14	SHRIVES,RH- 1	SINCLAIR,SD- 2	SMALL,CJ- 6	SMITH,KJ- 8
SCHOEMAN,JB- 2	SCHWEYER,P- 3	SHAVE,G- 1	SHRIVES,AA- 2	SINCLAIR,JA- 2	SMALL,FI- 4	SMITH,LR- 2
SCHOEMAN,PA- 4	SCHWIKKARD,GC- 3	SHAVE,J- 4	SHUNN,PD- 1	SINGERY,CV- 1	SMALL,L- 1	SMITH,M- 7
SCHOEMAN,SJ- 5	SCHWIKKARD,M- 2	SHAVE,N- 3	SHUTER,MG- 9	SINGERY,DD- 1	SMART,C- 1	SMITH,MD- 2
SCHOEMAN,T- 1	SCHWIKKARD,GW- 1	SHAVE,TP- 2	SHUTER,R- 8	SINGH,A- 8	SMART,W- 4	SMITH,M- 1
SCHOFIELD,P- 2	SCLANDERS,CC- 1	SHAVE,D- 1	SHUTER,B- 1	SINGH,H- 1	SMART,B- 1	SMITH,N- 3
SCHOLES,JH- 2	SCLANDERS,IJ- 2	SHAVE,M- 1	SHUTTE,D- 1	SINGH,MS- 1	SMETHERHAM,D- 1	SMITH,P- 2
SCHOLTZ,F- 1	SCOTNEY,C-10	SHAW,A- 4	SHUTTLEWORTH,BG- 7	SINNETT,MI- 4	SMIDT,HR- 1	SMITH,P- 1
SCHOLTZ,F- 1	SCOTNEY,DM- 2	SHAW,GM-14	SHUTTLEWORTH,GE- 1	SINNETT,G- 2	SMIT,A- 3	SMITH,PR- 2
SCHOOMBEE,K- 2	SCOTNEY,D- 8	SHAW,P- 7	SHUTTLEWORTH,RR- 1	SIVRIGHT,GW- 2	SMIT,B- 4	SMITH,P- 7
SCHOU,D- 1	SCOTT,AC- 8	SHAW,RD- 5	SIEDLE,JB- 5	SKEA,N- 1	SMIT,C- 1	SMITH,P- 2
SCHOU,RK- 3	SCOTT,B- 8	SHAW,RD- 2	SIEGFRIED,D- 2	SKELTON,RP- 1	SMIT,H- 5	SMITH,R- 4
SCHRAM,PE- 1	SCOTT,BA- 2	SHAW,RD- 2	SILCOCK,S- 2	SKEWS,GC- 2	SMIT,JH- 4	SMITH,RE- 6
SCHRAVESANDE,C- 2	SCOTT,DI- 7	SHAW,D- 1	SILVERSTON,B- 1	SKINNER,RE- 4	SMIT,M- 4	SMITH,RM- 4
SCHREIBER,M- 2	SCOTT,G- 2	SHAW,GR- 1	SILVERSTONE,L- 2	SKINNER,H- 3	SMIT,NR- 2	
SCHREINER,GD- 2						

LIST OF ALL FINISHERS IN THE DUSI CANOE MARATHON—1951 TO 2006

THRING,DW-4
THRING,T-2
THRING,W-1
THURMAN,GD-2
THURTELL,SE-5
THURTELL,BC-1
THURTELL,GP-1
TIEDT,VC-1
TELEMAN,L-2
TILEY,MJ-1
TILL,WC-3
TILLETT,RG-1
TIMCKE,C-2
TIMM,SG-1
TIMMERMAN,AW-1
TIMMERMAN,D-2
TIMMERMAN,H-3
TIMMERMAN,P-1
TIMSON,RC-1
TINDALL,MT-2
TINDALL,MA-1
TINDALL,RJ-1
TINDALL,WJ-1
TINGLE,M-4
TINGLE,A-2
TINLEY,J-1
TIPPETT,G-6
TISSIMAN,P-1
TITLESTAD,S-1
TITMUSS,BM-2
TOCKNELL,DE-10
TOCKNELL,M-23
TOCKNELL,R-1
TOCKNELL,VE-3
TOD,CJ-4
TOD,D-2
TOD,MG-1
TODD,BS-1
TODD,E-1
TODD,G-9
TODD,R-9
TODD,MD-1
TODD,WT-2
TOERIEN,CL-1
TOMASZEWSKI,T-1

TOMICH,WB-2
TOMLIN,NR-5
TOMLIN,RD-1
TOMLINSON,AD-4
TOMLINSON,D-20
TOMLINSON,G-9
TONGE,AL-3
TONKIN,K-3
TONKINSON,A-1
TOPHAM,R-1
TOPKA,U-2
TOPMAN,AJ-7
TOPP,GA-4
TOPP,RS-2
TORDOFF,MR-1
TOREIN,CL-1
TORLAGE,BJ-2
TORRINGTON,MR-2
TOSE,RW-1
TOUCHER,KM-3
TOUNTAS,VM-2
TOWNLEY,S-2
TOWNSEND,CT-1
TOWNSEND,TH-1
TRATTLES,D-1
TRAUTMAN,C-10
TRAUTMAN,KB-3
TRAUTMAN,MD-4
TRAUTMAN,D-2
TREBBLE,BG-2
TREDGOLD,HR-2
TRELEAVAN,N-1
TRELEAVEN,GM-1
TRELEAVEN,RT-2
TREMEARNE,B-3
TREMEARNE,RC-15
TREMEARNE,DC-1
TREMLETT,PJ-1
TRENT,HK-2
TRIPP,A-1
TRIPP,G-22
TRODD,DC-3
TRODD,KD-9
TRODD,WT-2
TRODD,TS-6
TURNER,AR-3

TRODD,C-2
TROIS,JK-3
TROLLIP,PJ-2
TROMP,W-2
TROSKOLANSKIJ-1
TROTT,GS-1
TROTTER,LW-1
TROTTER,W-2
TROTTER,DH-1
TROTTER,R-3
TROXLER,GI-1
TRUBY,SP-10
TRUBY,J-2
TRUNDELL,K-2
TRURAN,J-5
TRUTER,MA-1
TRYBUS,B-1
TRZEBIATOUSKY,PD-2
TRZEBIATOWSKY,P-1
TSHAMANO,M-1
TUBERVILLE-SMITH,R-1
TUCK,B-2
TUCKER,BJ-3
TUCKER,JF-4
TUCKER,P-7
TUCKER,RF-3
TUCKER,SM-1
TUCKER,JK-1
TUDOR-JONES,DR-5
TUDOR-JONES,GV-4
TUMNER,GL-1
TUMNER,GL-5
TUNSTALL,AP-1
TUPPER,N-34
TUPPER,NK-3
TURBERVILLE-SMITH,R-1
TURK,K-1
TURNBULL,B-3
TURNBULL,G-18
TURNBULL,G-7
TURNBULL,G-12
TURNBULL,N-2
TURNBULL,D-3
TURNER,AR-3

TURNER,CR-2
TURNER,MF-3
TURNER,MC-4
TURNER,MA-2
TURNER,MF-1
TURNER,S-1
TURNER,NL-1
TURNER,RJ-1
TURNER,W-1
TURTON,CG-5
TURTON,RA-1
TUTTON,JD-10
TUTTON,GJ-2
TWEEDIE,R-1
TYACK,AP-3
TYACK,CR-1
TYACK,GP-1
TYLER,DB-1
TYRELL,DR-1
TYRER,J-1
TYRER,KA-2
TYRRELL,DR-1
TYRRELL,Z-1
TYSON,B-5
UANNAKAKIS,P-1
UBSDELL,AB-1
UDAL,GN-1
UDAL,M-1
UKEN,R-1
ULANSKY,C-1
ULETT,BD-1
ULLYETT,KP-3
ULLYETT,C-4
ULYATE,JF-1
UNITE,PF-3
UNSWORTH,RJ-6
UNSWORTH,CM-1
UPPINK,E-4
UPPINK,L-5
UPTON,CJ-1
UPTON,W-4
URBAN,BP-2
URBAN,LH-1
URQUHART,HG-3
URQUHART,AJ-6

URQUHART,D-1
URQUHART,AC-2
USHER,A-10
USHER,B-4
USHER,G-5
USSHER,ML-6
UYS,C-1
UYS,D-1
UYS,E-6
UYS,G-1
UYS,MA-2
UYS,PC-4
UYS,P-1
UYS,TW-3
UYS,WS-1
UYS,C-1
UYS,M-5
UYS,S-1
UZZELL,F-1
V D MERWE,H-1
V D WESTHUIZEN,J-1
V D WESTHUIZEN,WM-1
VACY-LYLE,MB-8
VALE,DW-1
VALENTINE,MW-1
VALENTINE,BG-1
VALENTINE,RS-7
VALENTINE,VE-1
VALENTINE,WS-11
VALENTINE,CG-1
VALENTINE,I-1
VAN AARDENNE,CA-7
VAN AARDENNE,H-12
VAN AARDENNE,LS-5
VAN AARDENNE,S-1
VAN AARDT,R-3
VAN AS,DI-1
VAN AS,RK-2
VAN ASWEGAN,S-1
VAN ASWEGEN,J-5
VAN ASWEGEN,DJ-1
VAN BART,DR-3
VAN BILJON,CW-10
VAN BLERK,BD-3
VAN BLERK,P-1

VAN BLERK,D-1
VAN BLOMESTEIN,BI-7
VAN BREDA,MI-1
VAN BREDA,TK-10
VAN BREDA,CV-2
VAN D WESTHUIZEN,H-1
VAN DAM,H-1
VAN DE PUTTE,JA-8
VAN DEN BERG,CJ-13
VAN DEN BERG,D-3
VAN DEN BERG,F-1
VAN DEN BERG,J-7
VAN DEN BERG,CD-1
VAN DEN BERG,GJ-1
VAN DEN BERG,M-1
VAN DEN BERG,SM-1
VAN DEN HEEVER,D-1
VAN DER BERG,C-1
VAN DEN BERG,W-1
VAN DER BOS,RP-6
VAN DER BURGH,CA-1
VAN DER HEEVER,IM-2
VAN DER HEYDEN,P-4
VAN DER HEYDEN,A-1
VAN DER LINDE,PG-2
VAN DER LINDER-1
VAN DER LINDE,W-2
VAN DER LINDE,W-1
VAN DER MEER,NS-1
VAN DER MERWE,A-10
VAN DER MERWE,BH-15
VAN DER MERWE,ED-1
VAN DER MERWE,GB-1
VAN DER MERWE,H-5
VAN DER MERWE,J-4
VAN DER MERWE,JH-1
VAN DER MERWE,J-1
VAN DER MERWE,K-4
VAN DER MERWE,MJ-11
VAN DER MERWE,Q-1
VAN DER MERWE,RM-4
VAN DER MERWE,S-10
VAN DER MERWE,S-12
VAN DER MERWE,T-3

VAN DER MERWE,V-2
VAN DER MERWE,W-3
VAN DER MERWE,W-7
VAN DER MERWE,W-5
VAN DER MERWE,AJ-1
VAN DER MERWE,C-6
VAN DER MERWE,FJ-2
VAN DER MERWE,JA-1
VAN DER MERWE,LC-3
VAN DER MERWE,N-1
VAN DER MERWE,S-2
VAN DER MERWE,S-1
VAN DER MERWE,SB-2
VAN DER MERWE,W-1
VAN DER MESCHT,GS-2
VAN DER PLANK,G-3
VAN DER POLL,R-2
VAN DER REYDEN,ND-1
VAN DER RIET,H-4
VAN DER BERG,W-1
VAN DER RIET,ML-1
VAN DER RYST,R-1
VAN DER SPOEL,DR-4
VAN DER SPOEL,RE-5
VAN DER SPUY,DG-2
VAN DER VELDEN,AM-2
VAN DER WAAL,HP-1
VAN DER WALT,DD-11
VAN DER WALT,DC-3
VAN DER WALT,HJ-1
VAN DER WALT,M-1
VAN DER WALT,N-2
VAN DER WALT,W-4
VAN DER WAT,J-1
VAN DER WAT,HG-5
VAN DER WATH,T-1
VAN DER WATH,D-3
VAN DER WATT,GE-1
VAN DER WEELEN,N-6
VAN DER WESTHUIZE,J-4
VAN DER WESTHUIZE,C-1
VAN DER WESTHUIZE,IP-1
VAN DER WESTHUIZE,L-2

VAN DEVENTER,GJ-2
VAN DEVENTER,JA-2
VAN DEVENTER,BA-1
VAN DEVENTER,CF-2
VAN DEVENTER,F-1
VAN DEVENTER,RA-1
VAN DIJK,R-2
VAN DIJKHORST,L-7
VAN DONGEN,BG-10
VAN DYK,GA-2
VAN ECK,V-1
VAN EDEN,MC-9
VAN EDEN,L-5
VAN EEDEN,BR-1
VAN EEDEN,PJ-1
VAN ELLEWEE,A-1
VAN EYCK,B-1
VAN EYSSEN,MG-2
VAN GEEST,G-3
VAN GOFRVERDEN,RG-1
VAN GREUNEN,G-1
VAN GREUNEN,FC-2
VAN GREUNEN,J-1
VAN GREUNEN,PJ-1
VAN GYSEN,S-2
VAN HASSELT,AR-1
VAN HEERDEN,A-6
VAN HEERDEN,CG-11
VAN HEERDEN,CD-1
VAN HEERDEN,CL-4
VAN HEERDEN,CW-1
VAN HEERDEN,E-2
VAN HEERDEN,GC-1
VAN HEERDEN,JH-1
VAN HEERDEN,JS-2
VAN HEERDEN,J-3
VAN HEERDEN,NL-3
VAN HEERDEN,PW-2
VAN HEERDEN,PJ-9
VAN HEERDEN,AA-1
VAN HEERDEN,B-1
VAN HEERDEN,J-2
VAN HEERDEN,JS-4
VAN HEERDEN,NL-1

LIST OF ALL FINISHERS IN THE DUSI CANOE MARATHON—1951 TO 2006

LIST OF ALL FINISHERS IN THE DUSI CANOE MARATHON—1951 TO 2006

LIST OF ALL FINISHERS IN THE DUSI CANOE MARATHON—1951 TO 2006

WILLSON,MN-1
WILLSON,S-1
WILMANS,C-1
WILMANS,PA-2
WILMOT,M-28
WILMOT,SD-13
WILMOT,M-4
WILSON,AG-7
WILSON,C-17
WILSON,CD-7
WILSON,GR-20
WILSON,GB-8
WILSON,G-5
WILSON,G-14
WILSON,GP-1
WILSON,GH-25
WILSON,JC-5
WILSON,JH-1
WILSON,K-14
WILSON,MB-11
WILSON,M-7
WILSON,M-5
WILSON,M-2
WILSON,P-10
WILSON,P-8
WILSON,RA-6
WILSON,RG-3
WILSON,RL-20
WILSON,SK-1
WILSON,S-1
WILSON,SG-8
WILSON,SR-3
WILSON,TP-5
WILSON,TB-2
WILSON,TP-2
WILSON,WA-9
WILSON,D-3
WILSON,G-4
WILSON,GA-2
WILSON,JD-1
WILSON,JS-7
WILSON,M-1
WILSON,MA-2
WILSON,PR-2

WILSON,PB-2
WILSON,X-1
WIMBUSH,RT-10
WINDISCH,MI-1
WINDSON,GG-1
WINDT,R-2
WINDT,H-1
WINDUST,AR-3
WING,CL-4
WING,GD-2
WINKLER,SJ-1
WINN,G-2
WINSEN,W-1
WINSHIP,B-1
WINTER,A-9
WINTER,A-2
WINTER,R-2
WINTER,R-20
WINTER,SJ-1
WINTER,D-2
WINTER,RN-1
WINTER,R-1
WINTER,WP-5
WINTHROP,B-1
WINZER,DJ-1
WISDOM,AD-13
WISDOM,MS-2
WISE,P-18
WISEMAN,BC-16
WISEMAN,GG-1
WISEMAN,JA-4
WISEMAN,B-1
WISEMAN,PJ-1
WISSEKERKE,CP-3
WISSING,RM-1
WITE,J-1
WITHERDEN,A-3
WITHERS,CI-1
WITHEY,D-4
WITHEY,G-2
WITTEVEEN,R-5
WITTHOFT,TH-12
WITTSTOCK,GH-5
WITTY,AM-2
WOLFF,A-3

WOLFF,MD-2
WOLFF,N-1
WOLHUTER,J-1
WOLHUTER,LJ-2
WOLHUTER,M-1
WOLHUTER,NR-1
WOLKERS,FT-4
WOLKERS,G-1
WOLMERHANS,J-1
WOLPE,C-1
WOLTER,G-4
WOLTER,M-1
WOOD,A-3
WOOD,DD-5
WOOD,GA-5
WOOD,KB-5
WOOD,KJ-3
WOOD,KR-3
WOOD,MR-3
WOOD,RR-5
WOOD,B-1
WOOD,CJ-2
WOOD,GP-2
WOOD,I-1
WOOD,JR-1
WOOD,KL-1
WOODBURN,VJ-1
WOODCOCK,DG-2
WOODGATE,C-4
WOODGATE,E-2
WOODGATE,J-8
WOODHEAD,DL-3
WOODHEAD,GA-11
WOODHEAD,RC-9
WOODHEAD,K-1
WOODHOUSE,D-1
WOODLAND,BG-2
WOODLEY,R-2
WOODLEY,W-1
WOODS,CG-2
WOODS,EL-4
WOODS,NA-6
WOODS,RM-3
WOODS,MG-1
WOODWARD,D-3

WOODWARD,J-1
WOODWARD,LJ-1
WOOLASTON,G-1
WOOLER,V-1
WOOLF,J-2
WOOLLASTON,G-12
WOOLLATT,PN-2
WOOLEY,IM-1
WORLOCK,FB-2
WORMS,A-1
WORRALL,ME-4
WORSLEY,PP-1
WORTHINGTON,C-2
WORTHINGTON,D-1
WORTHINGTON,MG-1
WORTHINGTON,G-1
WORTHINGTON,S-1
WORTMANN,K-1
WRAITH,MR-2
WRATHMALL,J-1
WRAY,E-1
WRIGHT,AH-1
WRIGHT,AD-3
WRIGHT,B-9
WRIGHT,CB-8
WRIGHT,D-2
WRIGHT,DC-12
WRIGHT,JS-2
WRIGHT,JD-8
WRIGHT,K-13
WRIGHT,MV-1
WRIGHT,M-15
WRIGHT,RM-4
WRIGHT,RA-10
WRIGHT,R-4
WRIGHT,S-6
WRIGHT,V-1
WRIGHT,AC-1
WRIGHT,DA-1
WRIGHT,G-3
WRIGHT,M-1
WRIGHT,MT-1
WRIGHT,MJ-1
WRIGHT,RJ-3
WRIGHT,R-7

WULFF,RA-1
WULFF,D-1
WULFSE,G-6
WUST,AD-3
WYER,SD-6
WYLDE,CR-1
WYLIE,CJ-2
WYLIE,D-1
WYLLIE,SM-1
WYLY,L-12
WYNBERG,D-4
WYNN,R-1
YAFFE,G-3
YANNAKAKIS,P-1
YATES,BP-1
YATES,M-1
YATES,S-1
YEATES,S-1
YEATS,M-11
YELLAND,B-2
YELLAND,DM-3
YORK,GE-1
YOUDS,AK-10
YOUDS,DD-2
YOUENS,BM-15
YOUENS,H-2
YOUNG,B-1
YOUNG,D-4
YOUNG,DM-6
YOUNG,G-20
YOUNG,MK-2
YOUNG,N-1
YOUNG,PM-3
YOUNG,RD-8
YOUNG,SG-3
YOUNG,WK-8
YOUNG,KG-1
YULE,M-2
ZAAYMAN,GD-3
ZABOROWSKI,AG-1
ZACA,PN-3
ZACHAROPOULOS,B-5
ZACHAROPOULOS,K-19
ZALOHA,M-1
ZALOUMIS,A-5

ZAMMIT,R-1
ZANDBERG,C-1
ZANDBERG,JH-1
ZEEMAN,H-6
ZEEMAN,D-1
ZETTLER,L-2
ZIADY,NR-3
ZIERVOGEL,M-3
ZIERVOGEL,WG-1
ZIETSMAN,BH-8
ZIETSMAN,P-19
ZIMMERMAN,D-3
ZIMMERMAN,M-4
ZIMMERMAN,P-2
ZINN,AG-5
ZIPP,RM-1
ZIQUBU,SB-1
ZITTLAU,FE-1
ZITTLAU,W-2
ZOGHBY,MS-1
ZONDI,D-1
ZONDI,LM-7
ZONDI,XE-1
ZONDI,E-1
ZOUTENDYK,L-1
ZUGG,JB-1
ZUIDEWIND,C-1
ZUIDEWIND,SC-2
ZULU,PS-2
ZUMPT,M-1
ZUNCKEL,IC-8
ZUNCKEL,LA-1
ZUNCKEL,TL-1
ZWAHLEN,K-1
ZWART,H-1
ZWART,M-4